Wild Food School

ARMAGEDDON
Cookbook
and
Doomsday Kitchen

Marcus Harrison

First published in 2013 by Marcus Harrison
Lostwithiel, Cornwall. PL22 0ER

Copyright © Marcus Harrison, 2013

ISBN-13 978 0 9544158 8 4

All rights reserved. No part of this publication may be reproduced or transmitted in any form or by any means mechanical, electronic, photocopying or otherwise without the prior consent of the publisher.

A Wild Food School development.
Wild Food School is a registered Trademark.

www.wildfoodschool.co.uk

CONTENTS

Introduction	5
Mental Preparedness	9
Doomsday Decision-Making	12
Safety and Food Tolerance	17
Sustainability and Cost of Acquisition	19

Animals

Insects and Worms	21
Snails	28
Rat	31
Guinea Pig	34
Rabbit	38
Deer	44
Goat	48
Squirrel	49
Amphibians	49
Birds	50
Fish	52
Marine Molluscs	75
Crabs and Prawns	88

Plants

Edible Wild Plants	93
Trees with Edible Uses	120
Plants – Ornamental, Essential	125
Seaweeds	127
Wild Beverage Plants	134
Berries	137
Nuts	140

Food and Cooking

Locating the Doomsday Kitchen	145
Keep the Homefire Burning	149
Cooking Designs and Fire Tips	154
Fuel Conservation	165
Hay-Box Cooker	169

Doomsday Kitchen Utensils	174
Cooking with Fire	183
Cooking with Clay	188
Soil Texture and Moisture	191
Water Resources	198
Surface Water Harvesting	200
Capping Springs	210
Filtration	213
Solar Distillation / Bleaching Water	215
Organizing Water Usage	217
Water-borne Disease	218
Botulism	224
Preserving Foods	226
Fats and Oils	238
The Armageddon Menu	
Soups and Broths	243
Meat	254
Fish	278
Poultry and Game Fowl	286
Bread, Biscuits and Baking	292
Cheese and Dairy	305
Vegetables	307
Seaweed	318
Fruit	321
Desserts	327
Beverages, Wines and Beers	329
Brewing and Distilling	331
Root Crop and Fruit Storage	336
Cereal Grains and Milling	338
Salt, Saltpetre & Soap	344
Candlemaking	351
Ice Houses	355
Herbal Medicines	359
Recipe Index	361

INTRODUCTION

What IF? What if a tsunami took out your region of the country and you were left to provide your own food unaided? What if there was a pandemic that took out the infrastructure that feeds your cosy everyday existence which you are comfortable living with? What if supermarket shelves are empty, and there is NO electricity, NO water in the taps, NO fuel at the gas station, NO nothing. What if you were faced with the modern equivalent of the Stone Age?

Imagine that as far as the eye can see your world lies in millions of shattered pieces. How quickly could you adapt to your new food and provisioning environment – without *handouts* that is? Would you know where to start with the construction of a fire to cook on, remembering that two thirds of your day might be spent looking for wood to cook with? Could you construct your stove to burn that fuel efficiently? Would you know which edible plants in the wild could be harnessed to your needs? Would you know how to use all the parts of an animal that you killed – not just the prime steak cuts? Would you have the skills to preserve meat and vegetables to see you through the winter months when there is little or no fresh food available? This book is aimed at filling in the gaps and missing links in your survival knowledge, while at the same time helping you develop the analytical tools for appraising the available resources around you, their acquisition, and their utilization for food production at a time when you are going to need every bit of ingenuity that you can muster. If I were trying to describe it in a nutshell then this book is about giving you the edge – the most comprehensive set of keys to the door between two covers, as it were – to secure food and water in desperate times when the chips are down.

Outline work for this tome began in 2008 but then it got placed on the backburner while several other, and still on-going, projects took over. However, the events in Japan in March 2011 (and, as I was catching up with finalization of the text, *Hurricane Sandy* hit north-east America), brought home the realization of how perilously *unprepared* many western civilian populations are in times of true emergency, particularly in urban areas, and so back to the keyboard it was to get on with this project. In the case of *Sandy* the outcome could have been infinitely worse; just a few more feet of water height (let alone the water levels of the Japanese tsunami which in some areas reached 30 metres in height), higher wind speeds or barometrics, and the flooding could have laid waste to swathes of the United States' eastern industrial heartland with all the woes which would have accompanied that globally.

A key problem for the survival of pampered civilian populations of industrialized Western cultures, as I view it, is that they have come to expect they will be taken care of no matter what happens, and that there is *always* going to be someone to help them in their time of need. If a really major disaster takes place then that help will not be there. Get real, there will be no shiny cavalry appearing on the horizon. You may be isolated on your own, or with family, neighbours or friends. Singly, or collectively, you will need to gain control of the situation that you find yourself in, if you want to survive.

There are folks who are actively preparing for the end of the world, the so-called *preppers*, but in the United States the government agency FEMA (Federal Emergency Management Agency) advises citizens to have at least 3 days water and food supplies for any general disaster emergency, and advises families to create their own 'disaster supplies kit'. Just having that little amount of preparedness for some nasty event is a great idea and buys a few days of time as you come to terms with a newly reorganized world. Personally, I do not *prep* though I carry a small emergency kit for when I go to inhospitable areas where there is a possibility of becoming stranded and there are no nearby human habitations. For me preparedness comes from having knowledge upstate of what to do should things really do turn pear-shaped, rather than living under the cloud of viewing the world as a dark doomladen place and sitting on piles of stored food – though it should be said that small emergency kit of mine contains several methods of easily lighting a fire (no rubbing sticks for me), items for collecting and purifying water, items to string up a quick shelter, and also means of signalling for help.

As a point of reference, I should point out that the contents of this book relate to my direct involvement with teaching about, and using, foods in the wild, whilst I have also been involved in working with Services' SERE instructors for a number of years. Indeed, some of the survival methodology that they employ has rubbed off onto my own world of wild foods and there are influences of SERE in this book which survival professionals will probably recognize. These guys do not have the luxury of having *prepped* supplies. Rather, they need to survive in a truly life-threatening, hostile, environment, living by their wits, and off the resources of whatever environment they find themselves in.

There are many bushcraft and survival books available on shelter building, fire-lighting, trapping, hunting and a myriad of other related topics. In this book I'll stick to those topics which relate to my own specific expertise of finding and using wild foods, and further related arts needed to preserve food and secure water, and leave other subjects such as lighting fires by rubbing sticks, trapping and making shelters from ferns and palms to those skilled practitioners with specific expertise. After all, would you go to a plumber for heart surgery, or ask the surgeon to mend your boiler? Exactly! For my own part my association with plants began more than forty-five years ago; being brought up on a farm where, as a youngster, I knew almost every blade of grass and plant, micro-habitat and micro-climate, and from an early age observed the effects of soil mechanics and hydrology in action, and how the landscape ticked and purred.

The content of this book is not designed as an exhaustive description of edible plants or animals but, rather, to provide you with a general knowledge-base framework from which you can develop your own foraging discipline and food and water provisioning methodology should that need ever arise for whatever reason. My own view (aside from the thought that every individual should have a basic degree of mental preparedness for troubled times) is that you should be able to source enough food, and then cook it up to a degree that gives you a feel-good comfort factor, which is also a bit of a morale-booster to help improve your outlook on life in the new post-disaster Stone Age.

On the recipe side the aim here is to provide you with food ideas above the level of grubbing round for roots and nuts, although this action will be required. The recipes are not sophisticated, nor make too many demands, though it is imagined that you would be able to fashion yourself a rudimentary oven or baking facility such as a mud oven. In a post-disaster world many of the tasty ingredients that we would normally incorporate into our daily food will not be available; though some scavenged items may exist for a short period among the debris of a disaster area, while individuals with access to land (from a backyard or small garden, to the corner of a field) will undoubtedly start to raise crops that will eventually circulate and be bartered for. So you will find ingredients such as potatoes and onions mentioned among the recipes, since scattered legacy pools of these plants will continue to exist somewhere in agricultural land and allotments, and will almost certainly reappear as bartered items. Potatoes would be a relatively easy vegetable species to find places to grow.

Since this book is designed for a situation when your world is in meltdown it covers some highly unconventional (and controversial) food sources as well as those which are known or easily identified, or even quickly reared for human food. There are parts of this book which you should not read if you are easily offended since it contains food items that in normal daily life you may not find acceptable. There are some species mentioned in the text that have 'protected' status, and my view is that status should be fully respected in normal times, but in times of emergency then self-preservation and personal survival becomes the more important issue. General hunting and trapping methods are not covered, and any good survival book will explain the background to creating and setting traps.

I have not made the number of edible and animal species exhaustive, since that would take up vast numbers of pages. Indeed, much has been left out of this work. Rather, I have tried (certainly when it comes to edible plant species) to present a range of easily identified and relatively common species found across a range of different northern temperate habitats – shoreline, fields, and so on – plus short lists of species that may be useful in other parts of the northern hemisphere. You can build on these with time, while the core species covered present you with a starting point that fit a large number of habitats. The other criteria for inclusion is that the species have to provide you with something that is both easy to harvest, does not taste too bitter, or can at least be doctored to render it more palatable.

If you work with the listed species, alongside visits to the countryside or coast, then you will gradually build up a mental picture of the dynamics of different types of terrain and how they 'work', for want of a better word. Should you ever need to put into practice what is included in this book then these terrains will not feel like strangers, at least from a knowledge-base point of view. For someone like myself who has pottered around the countryside and been associated with edible wild plants for around fifty years it is possible to get a 'feel' for what a terrain may provide as food within a matter of seconds of casting eyes upon it. Sometimes you can get caught out, but every landscape has tell-tale signatures that can be read once you are familiar with them.

The other two subject areas covered in relation to my own interest in the wild food side are fire and water, since these obviously go hand in hand with cooking food. In pure human survival terms water is much more important than food. If your body runs out of water and is in a diminished state through dehydration then the body and brain begin to malfunction after a few days. Without water death will occur within about seven to ten days. You can go without food for three to six weeks, up to about eight if water is available.

FEMA advises working on 1 gallon, per person, per day, with half of that used for drinking water. Other medics recommend 3 litres of drinking water a day for males, and 2 litres for women, though this will obviously vary depending on weather and energetic activity. In physical terms, a 2% water deficit will begin to impair your performance and you will start to feel a little discomfort. At a 4% deficit muscle fatigue and apathy set in, and there may be nausea. Tingling limbs, dizziness, headaches and a dry mouth set in at a deficit of around 6%, and there may also be indistinct speech and the inability to walk.

So I tend to follow the general creed of the professional SERE folks that I work with in that water sometimes comes first over the need for protective cover, or food. This, however, belies circumstances that individuals may find themselves in. In high altitudes immediate protective cover would dominate your thinking over water acquisition... in a cold environment keeping warm would be at the forefront of survival activity and actions... food when energy needs expending, and so on.

There are most certainly good and best ways of doing many things in survival, but slavish adherence to a technique just because that is what some survival 'expert' on TV has said could be at detriment to your personal survival. Adaptability and flexibility, as well as knowledge upstate, are key in my view when it comes to your armageddon menu and doomsday kitchen, whether your kitchen is set up in the backyard, municipal garden, a field, or down by the shore, and hopefully the contents of this book will provide you with a framework and methodology for keeping yourself fed and watered in a post-disaster world.

If you are interested in developing a contingency plan for the family in case of emergency, then you could do no better that looking at the FEMA website, and download their free digital publication called *Are You Ready*.

One final thought. Depending on what region or part of the world you live the picking of wild plants, or hunting and trapping wild animals may be restricted by licence or by law, so keep that in mind as you read onwards and are considering experimenting with some of the doomsday options suggested in this book.

> *Economy of Effort, Flexibility of Mind*

MENTAL PREPAREDNESS

To be in a situation that demands the use of *survival skills* inevitably means that something *unexpected* or *extraordinary* has impacted upon your normal, day-to-day, existence and routines of life. That change may have been sudden or immediate, or it could have been expected over time, while the consequences could have been life-threatening, or life-changing. Either way brings a new set of circumstances which you need to adapt to in order to gain control of the situation, or take control so that you are not wrong-footed as you go about your new world.

When the event has been long-term in arriving then you will, in theory, have had time to prepare, and adapt your mind and actions to the expected situation long before it happens. For sudden, unexpected, events such as a plane crash, shipwreck, earthquake, or tsunami, then the human mind can have a difficult time in adjusting, which is where the psychology of survival, and instinctively knowing what to do, becomes important.

Through my SERE work I have been fortunate enough to sit in on two days of talks about survival psychology by Dr John Leach, one of the world's leading specialists in this rather unique field of psychology, and I want to precis a few of his ideas on the subject that could help if you ever find yourself in an unexpected survival situation.

The model that Dr Leach outlined back in the 1990s (the Dynamic Disaster Model) remains one of the best ways of understanding how people react in stressful situations, and is the bedrock for much research since. The DDM breaks the disaster scenario into a number of phases and stages: Pre-Impact, Impact and Post-Impact.

In the *Pre-Impact* phase the individual/s are aware of the threat and warning signs of some imminent danger, although those signs may be ignored or acted upon. The next *Impact* phase is not the physical impact of hitting the ground, being swept off your feet, or ambushed by kidnappers, but the impact upon the individual's senses as they are overwhelmed and stunned, and for awareness of the situation or event to sink in after a number of seconds or minutes, and a new model of the world registered. A moment ago you might have been quietly eating lunch, then the world turns upside down and you find yourself with your nose rubbing against the ground or staring at the sky. The model of the world that you were so intimately connected to and comfortable with has dramatically changed. In fact it no longer exists, and it takes the brain time to re-model the new environment (from a few seconds to minutes, as mentioned). What happens next – the *Post-Impact* phase – is how people cope, react, and so on, and is a quite complex but very interesting subject and I'd suggest you read one of the references listed later, or at least take a look at '*The Won't to Live*' in *Psychologist* magazine. Vol. 24, Jan. 2011.

Among the practical suggestions in the talks that Dr Leach gave was that you prepare yourself in the 'pre-impact' phase if that is at all possible; in other words think about what could happen before the event ever manifests itself. It's one reason why you <u>should</u> read those safety instruction cards in an aircraft or train, or quickly establish the nearest exit points in a crowded cinema or football arena as you find your seat.

For example, my photographic recording work of plants regularly takes me to the edge of a fast-flowing tidal river with steep vertical banks that prevent any possibility of scrambling up them to safety. However, there are four or five bends along the four mile stretch to the sea where the banks give way to shallow pans of mud offering the possibility of scrambling to safety. Should I ever to fall in the river then my hope is that I would have the wherewithal to put my plan into action. Of course I might miss the first planned stopping off point because it arrives within the first re-modelling phase of the brain, but thereafter I have a gameplan should some eventuality ever occur, and not become a casualty. On, the other hand a pre-impact phase may literally be a short public announcement that trouble is imminent, with little time to prepare mentally.

With your world re-modelled mentally, and the realization that things are no longer as they once were, Dr Leach identified three key time phases in the early survival scenario – 3 hours, 3 days and 3 weeks. These time phases work as follows: if you haven't died within three hours of injuries sustained in the disaster then you have a good chance of staying alive; if you can adapt to your new environment in three days then there is a good chance you will physically succeed in that environment; at three weeks the mind begins to doubt that you may ever be rescued or find a way through the situation, which is where ideas of self-harm might arise.

To my mind just understanding that these three phases exist in a survival scenario provides a framework that could give you an edge on taking control of an emergency situation, though that is not to say that states of mental anxiety will not interrupt play. They most certainly do, and that is where you need to read up on the subject more fully to understand things like *perseveration*, *cognitive paralysis*, *hyper* and *hypoactivity*.

On a slightly different, but related and overlapping, psychological tack, there are the longer term psychological stresses on an individual or group; what one might bracket under the banner post-traumatic stress disorder [PTSD]. But then someone who has simply witnessed a violent scene can suffer from PTSD, whereas living through a long-term recovery from a major catastrophe is somewhat different. Indeed, you might have to endure *years* of hardship, discomfort and hunger. This is where those who have the ability to tolerate and cope with loss and disruption are going to be more resilient to the new stresses of life, while folks with pre-existing health and emotional problems are likely to find the additional stresses of a post-disaster event will make them vulnerable.

Inevitably PTSD, in one form or another, goes hand in hand with a disaster situation, and for the majority of people they will go through a transitory phase of mild to moderate symptoms as a natural response to quite extraordinary and abnormal events. Among the sort of symptoms may be sleep disorder due to grief, or anxiety about the future, there may also be intrusive recollections of events, trouble concentrating, but also depression and substance-abuse, often in those who have a pre-existing problem with this. Feelings of frustration may be evident, and also the perception of chaos.

In the group dynamic there are also things to be aware of. Initially there is a honeymoon period where everyone pulls together and helps out. Then, as the situation may or may not improve, disappointment, resentment and disillusion set in, tensions may arise, and a blame culture evolve. If the disaster is of a man-made, artificial, nature then an individual may certainly try to attribute blame. Where the disaster is a freak event of nature then others may question their belief systems. Trying to 'construct the meaning' of an event is another aspect of individual survivors dealing with their disaster experience.

Anyway, the psychology of post-disaster events is not really within the remit of this book, but having a bit of insight may prove advantageous. Just reading through this book will, I hope, provide you with a little preparedness for getting some semblance of normality back should disaster actually happen; the contents being in the back of your mind to be recalled, rather than in the forefront – unless you happened to scan through these words the day before disaster struck. Having overcome the psychological pitfalls of a disaster another thing that will be important in a post-disaster world is your ability to make creative, innovative, problem-solving decisions, and the following section should provide you with a few tips on that.

FURTHER READING

Leach, J. *Survival Psychology*. Basingstoke: Palgrave Macmillan; 1994.

Vorst, Harrie C.M. *Evacuation Models and Disaster Psychology*. Procedia Engineering 3 2010; 15-21.

Leach, J. *Maladaptive Behaviour in Survivors*: *Dysexecutive Survivor Syndrome*. Aviation, Space, and Environmental Medicine 2012; 83:1152-1161.

Porter, H, Leach, J. *Executive Dysfunction in a Survival Environment*. Applied Cognitive Psychology 2010; 24:41-66. [A quite technical article.]

Robinson, S, Bridges, N. *Survival: Mind and Brain*. Psychologist 2011; Vol. 24, January.

DOOMSDAY DECISION-MAKING

If you're used to making decisions as a matter of course, then you may like to skip this section.... In stressful conditions or circumstances making the correct decision can be a difficult task, particularly if you are not used to making key decisions that clearly affect your physical outcome and safety. Where you are establishing a long-stay doomsday kitchen, as opposed to a transitory fire and brief hunt for water for a quick brew, then there will be a myriad of inputs that will need to be considered, and opposite is a schematic of various parameters that will need to be resolved; everything from the season of the year and its impact on available food, to the quality of the soils, to the physical risks involved with harvesting plant or animal resources, to sourcing fuel and water. These parameters are in addition to other general camp requirements such as shelter, security, and so on, while *economy of effort* will need to be factored in.

The other thing about all these parameters is that they are likely to be 'up in the air' for want of a better term; unknowns that will impact upon the efficiency and viability of producing food, and about which you will need to make decisions. Unfortunately, conventional decision-making theory (which is a science in its own right, and leans heavily on mathematics) is largely used for modelling business risks with a limited number of input options, and generally seeks a profit-loss outcome. Such models will not come to the rescue for setting up your doomsday kitchen since there are too many unknowns to factor in. Again, just look at that schematic opposite. The seasonal influence box and six ovals represent the major items, and each of these has layers of other factors that will influence decision, while many items are inter-dependent. This is where personal *experience* comes in.

Someone with *true experience* will be able to size up a situation without the need for lots of fact hunting and time-consuming, evaluative, studies. Through personal experience they can instinctively assess a situation because they have encountered similar situations before, and will have knowledge of what works in some circumstances and what does not; which will also save time and effort, both of which may be important in a survival situation. It should be said, however, that there will be no *absolutely correct* decisional outcome; rather achieving a state of affairs that meets whatever requirements are sought after. That may require compromising over certain things, and an evaluation of whether a bare minimum will be sufficient at the start (and which can then be improved with time). Much of this will need to be tied in with innovating items for use around your doomsday kitchen (see page 174).

Having established that there will be many factors to consider when it comes to setting up a substantial or permanent-ish doomsday kitchen, I want to look at a couple of methods to make life easier (*economy of effort*) when it comes to making decisions about problems or certain tasks; making a water storage tank for example, or perhaps managing your foraging or water harvesting sorties. There's nothing new about the methods, but if you have never encountered them before then they may seem rather novel, and in my view a methodical decision-making process in time of stress could help you assert more control and structure over your new world.

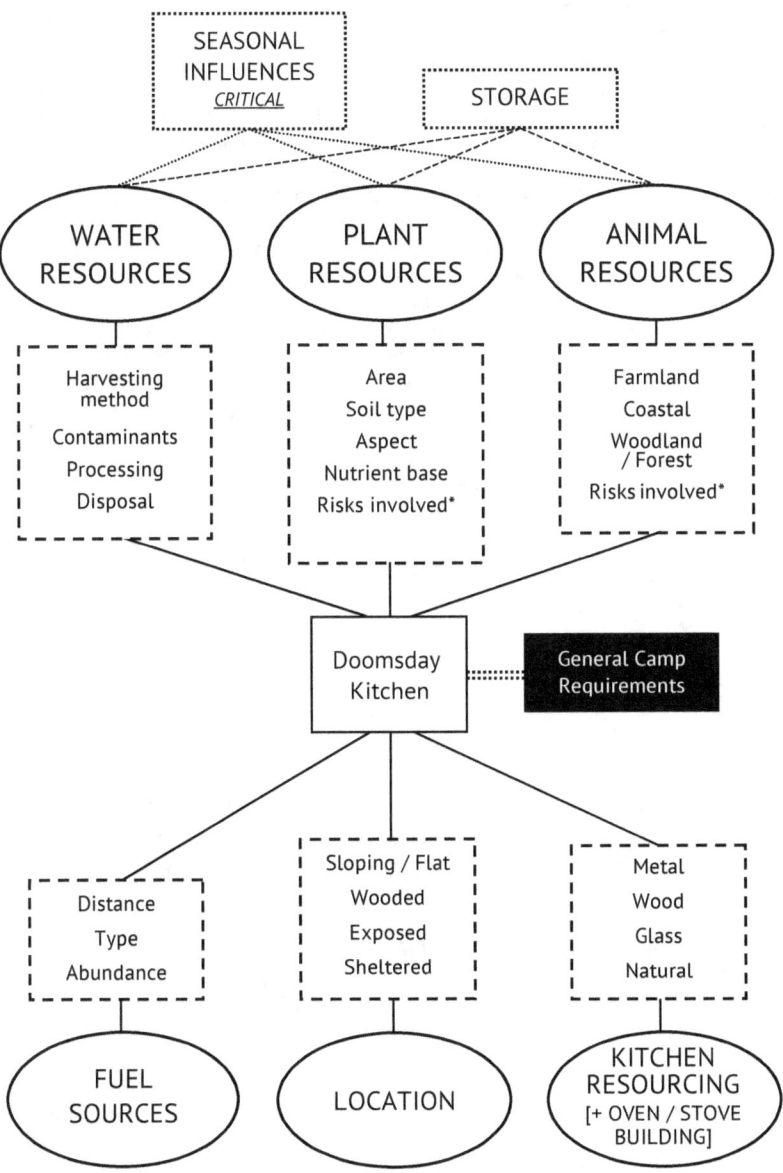

[* This would include an understanding of plant or animal toxicity, required processing techniques, contamination sources, accessibility, and so on.]

The first of the problem solving and decision-making tools is known as the OODA Loop, sometimes referred to as the Boyd Cycle after the American Air Force officer who came up with the original concept in the 1950s. OODA is still used in a modified and enhanced form by USAF today, those enhancements including items such as Root Cause Analysis. At its core OODA describes the active processes of decision-making which, when you stand back from it and think about many tasks, seem rather self-evident and perhaps makes you wonder why defining the Loop is necessary at all. What OODA provides, in my view, is a *structured* methodology that can be *routinely* used to deal with, and solve, problems. When you look at OODA it can also be applied to many general construction or fabrication 'tasks' that you may want to employ around the doomsday kitchen. Once you have made or fabricated your item then you might expect the Loop to cycle through several more iterations as glitches to the original task are identified and then ironed out. The sort of questions you would need to be asking are What is the problem in relation to What *should* be happening, Where is the problem occurring, and When did problem appear?

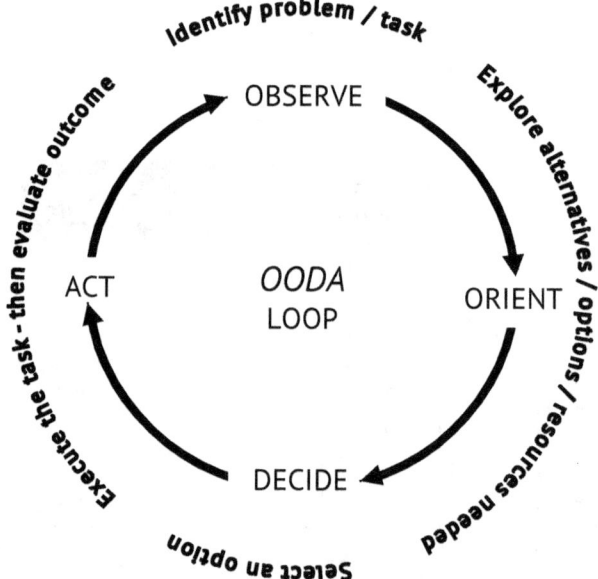

When it comes to looking for options to solve a problem or task think outside the field of the problem or task and see if techniques or solutions used in other unrelated disciplines might be applied to the one at hand (*free association*). Similarly, *observe* how things are in the world around you for insight, and see whether the processes or techniques used can be applied to something useful to you. What you're seeking is that flash of inspiration which can make things happen or resolve problems. If you do a bit of brainstorming don't just accept the first idea that comes to mind, but generate a whole lot of ideas and write them down, however outrageous they may seem (*flexibility of mind* in action). Then work through and reduce the list, eliminating ideas that have implausible aspects and perhaps merging useful bits of some ideas, until you have a final solution. Where you need to *experiment* do it on a small scale first before committing to full-scale execution, remembering that in a survival situation physical resources may be precious while there will be the need to conserve your personal energy.

Another tool that might help you in getting at the *root causes* of problems around the doomsday kitchen also comes from USAF, and is known as the 'Five Whys'. Having identified a problem, and got a basic answer to why some problem has occurred, the problem solver should then inquire 'Why' four more times. It's like a 'Why' did that 'Why?' actually occur; the reasoning behind this being that there might be a chain of interconnected factors leading to the single, visibly manifest, problem itself. A good example of using this technique to drill down and get to the bottom of things is the following one that comes directly from the USAF training manual:

"Why did the aircraft launch late? *Because the fueling team was slow.*

- Why was the refueling team slow? *Because one Airman from the fueling team was in the infirmary with a broken leg.*

- Why did the Airman break his leg? *Because the Airman slipped on an oil spill in the hangar.*

- Why was there an oil spill in the hangar? *Because a machine in the hangar had old washers that were leaking oil.*

- Why didn't the maintenance department change the washers? *Because the maintenance department's budget was cut, and they chose to slide all the preventive maintenance events by six months.*"

Having chosen a course of action it is then down to planning the execution of the main task, and prioritizing various criteria that are regarded as essential to a successful outcome. Usually there will be five or six key criteria to focus on (time, materials, manpower, morale, and so on) and these may need to be weighted; preferably with a numbered rating scale since simple 'yes' or 'no' options might lead to clashes in priority.

A really handy tool for planning and prioritizing all the aspects of executing a task is that of the Fishbone diagram, pictured overleaf. It is the sort of thing best used for a longer term planning, rather than for something immediate or on-the-spot decisions. These diagrams allow each of the factors behind the selected main criteria to be listed and identified, and for sub-factors to be considered. The fishbone diagram should also help you determine if there are any *task dependencies*; whether one action needs to be completed before another can be started. The downside of the diagram is that it requires pen and paper, which may not be available to you.

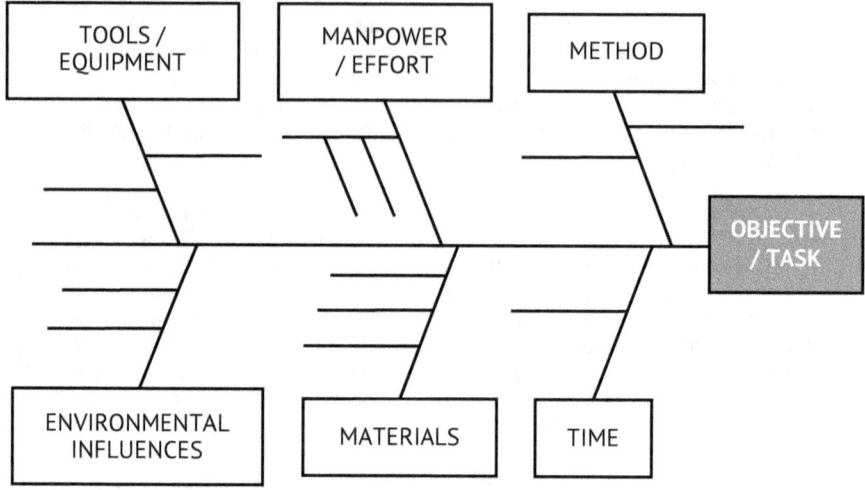

Above is a representation of the Fishbone diagram layout. Horizontal lines associated with each of the Categories represent stages or key points, while the downstrokes under the Manpower / Effort category shown represent a further breakdown of the activities. There could also be more or less key Categories included, whilst their position along the central backbone line can be ranked according to importance; the more important factors being placed closer to the Objective / Task box, lesser items further away. For example, if Materials and Method were crucial then these could be ranked at the front of the queue, and if Tools and Equipment were regarded as important these would slip right behind Method. If you were working in a cold climate then the Environmental category might leap to the front of the queue.

To a certain extent the more that you can acquire knowledge of, and practice, some of the subjects covered in this book the better will be your personal experience to stand you in good decision-making stead in any hour of need.

FOOD SAFETY AND TOLERANCE

From the *safety* standpoint here I am not referring to the health and hygiene issues revolving around food preparation, though that is obviously important, but rather personal reactions to foodstuffs. In my view, this is one of THE *most* important things to check before you launch yourself into eating any edible wild plants in quantity. It is a topic rarely mentioned by many so-called wild food 'teachers' and 'experts' who blithely tell everyone that this and that plant are edible. Many surely are, but there could be long-term downsides with many of them, and some folks do occasionally react to plant species on an individual basis. In emergency situations you most certainly do not want compromise your safety and find that you react badly to something. There will be no ambulances, doctors, or medical drip-feeds to resuscitate you in a post-disaster scenario. And in a long-term survival situation the stresses of living in your new world may compromise your auto-immune system, making your body weaker in its ability to fend off medical problems.

In dealing with many folks over a number of years it is quite clear that wild greens too, may cause reactions in some hyper-sensitive folks so please do be careful. In running my courses I have come across folks who react negatively to common sorrel (*Rumex acetosa*), elderberries (*Sambucus nigra*), and I personally do not tolerate hawthorn berries too well, and can only handle the young leaves in small quantities. I have heard of a case of anaphylactic shock to Hedge Garlic/Garlic Mustard (*Alliaria petiolata*), and a reaction (dermatological) to the popular three-cornered leek (*Allium triquetrum*). So do not go around in the belief that every edible wild plant can be eaten with impunity, despite what is said on television.

However, many edible wild plants have been used for centuries. Nettles have been commonly used as food for a very long time and in survival situations too, and in other parts of Europe nettles are quite commonly used as a vegetable green to this day. So the real question is your own *personal tolerance* to any specific plant species and the substances it contains.

The first time you encounter any known wild plant species as a potential food source my recommendation is to take a small piece of the raw 'part' used (not raw in the case of nettles though), suitably peeled or whatever, bite on it a few times to get a little of the sap on your tongue and inner lip then spit everything out. Do not ingest anything. Wait for 20 to 30 minutes to see if you develop any bad physical reaction (nausea, headache, etc). If you have any physical reaction at this initial stage, then it could be a signal that you will not tolerate the plant as a food.

Assuming your initial tolerance test is fine, you next need to try eating a piece of the plant. If it is one of the mild salad plants, then just consume a small leaf, or part of a larger one. If it is a bitter-tasting plant or needs to be cooked then boil one of the leaves, or specified part of the plant, and consume a very small piece. Again, wait for about 30 minutes to an hour and keep an eye on your reaction. Any physical reaction at this point I would consider as a warning to ditch the plant as a possible foodstuff. If everything is fine then the suggestion is to go ahead with eating a small quantity – a small handful – of the plant cooked, or whatever. Once you've eaten the food just keep an eye on how you feel for 2 to 3 hours. If everything is okay then, I would suggest, you're in business. Whatever you do, never eat large amounts of any edible wild plant the first time round without having tested your tolerance to it. Everyone is different and you might be one of the unlucky ones intolerant to something, just as some of the examples mentioned earlier show. If you were on your own and you reacted badly to something then the results could be life threatening.

My personal view is that if you are intolerant to a type of vegetable in the *real* world of supermarket foods, say onion or mustard, then there is a good possibility that you may be intolerant to edible wild relatives of these. However, this familial connection should NOT be applied to the *Umbellifer* family which includes edible parsley and carrot members, but also includes deadly hemlock, hemlock water-dropwort, and other such similarly highly toxic plant species. In other words, being able to eat carrots, parsley or caraway (*umbellifers*) does not mean that any other *umbellifer* is going to be edible. Far from it! This is where learning about edible wild plants with a seasoned professional forager pays dividends in terms of your personal safety. And, as mentioned before, in a true emergency survival situation where you are isolated and on your own there is going to be no one to help take you to hospital or administer medicines to help you recover if you get it wrong.

A WORD ON ROAD-KILL / DEAD ANIMALS
Despite the sensationalist nonsense on TV and in the media by people trying to become celebrities, cooking up road-kill comes with some caveats which need considering, quite apart from the fact that there may be a dearth of vehicles to do any animal damage in a post-disaster world. The key consideration is the health of the animal killed – although physical decay needs to factored in. Why was it that the animal was able to be struck in the first place, since most wild animals shy away from contact with humans and vehicles? A healthy animal would probably have scurried away, though deer often jump slam into vehicles as they attempt to leap between their feeding grounds on either side of a road, and during the autumn it is not uncommon to see pheasants reared for game shoots stranded in country lanes. These are generally healthy animals in the wrong place at the wrong time and are fair game for your cooking pot.

The other side of the coin are those animals which are diseased (or possibly old), have been poisoned, or are too ill to get out of the way of oncoming traffic, and you need to consider whether the illness, poison or disease could in any way hurt you – either when handling the carcass or through consumption of the muscle tissue or offal. Any animal found dead away from a road-kill environment should be treated with the greatest suspicion.

SUSTAINABILITY and COST OF ACQUISITION

When it comes to procuring food in times of emergency, particularly where the situation looks as if it may become long-term, then sourcing your food *sustainably* is ABSOLUTELY CRUCIAL to your doomsday survival. Without proper management of your foraged food resources they may well dry up, at which point you will need to become nomadic in your quest for food. In that case, however, you might well intrude into someone else's hunting and gathering territory at which point lethal conflict could well occur.

Plants fall into three groups from a *sustainability* point of view, based on their life-cycle:

Annual plants – species which germinate, develop foliage, flower then set seed and die in a single year. Wheat is an example, as are the edible wild species chickweed, shepherd's-purse, fat-hen, and goosegrass.

Biennial plants – are those of two years' duration; producing only leaves in the first year of their growth, then in the second year produce blossom, seeds, and then die. Turnips are a good domesticated example, or burdock in the wild.

Perennial plants – are species which live for three years or more, and do not need manual propagation. Seeds are produced at intervals. Good edible wild examples are the common stinging nettle, common sorrel and sea beet.

So for your own good think sustainably when gathering from the wild... allowing numbers of plants or animals to remain behind so that they can propagate to provide the food resources you may need in the future, or face the prospect of eating yourself out of existence. If necessary you may have to feed and nurture your wild food resources, rather than assume they will always be there. By collecting seeds you may propagate your own wild plant resources. In this case select seeds from the strongest growing (or best tasting) members of each batch and use these to grow on the next generation.

Overall, in a long-term post-disaster world, you will need to *develop a foraging and food gathering strategy specific to the habitat type and resource availability of your local area*, using the data provided in this book as your starting point. My own preference would be to put water at the top of my list of required resources, since this would be needed both for drinking and cooking purposes, though the hygiene side would also need to be factored in.

And while sustainability and developing a foraging strategy are important in the survival mix, shambling aimlessly around hedgerows for food like some zombie tree-hugger is misguided and out of place in the dynamics of a post-disaster world. New sets of food acquisition rules apply and one of these is of crucial importance, *Cost of Acquisition*.

Cost of Acquisition is a somewhat abstract, conceptual, equation in which every aspect of the food acquisition and its processing needs to be assessed and evaluated. Factors such as energy expended [personal and fuel to cook] to *reach* a harvestable resource, time / resources expended on *gathering*, time / resources to *prepare* the food, and weighing up any physical *risks* associated with harvesting the resource come into play. Other factors that must be fed into the *Cost of Acquisition* are the likely *net yield* which can be obtained from any given resource, its *seasonality*, *nutritional* value and, ultimately, your personal *satisfaction* with the resource as a food item and its value of making you want to live another day in the doomsday world.

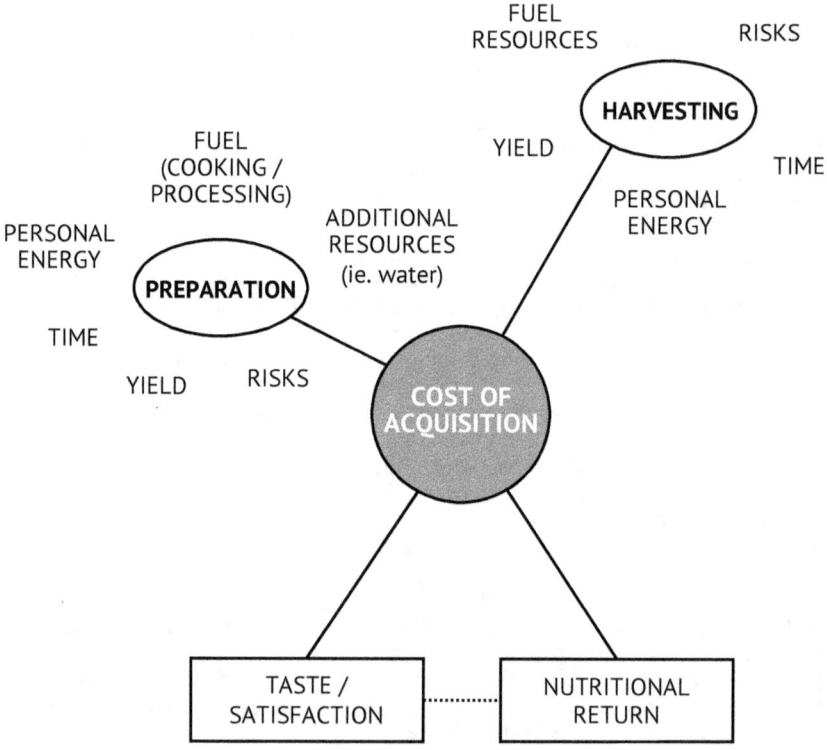

Ultimately the bottom line for *Cost of Acquisition* is whether you get a nutritional return for all the effort put in, and if you are rewarded by something tasty. Personally I find that I gravitate towards a relatively small number of edible wild plant species that I know will give me a quick return on my foraging efforts, are commonly found or reasonably abundant, and also taste good or can be made to do so.

EDIBLE INSECTS & WORMS

Let's begin the food side of things with one of the 'yuk' items – bugs! Many insects are highly nutritious, particularly in their larval and pupal stages of development, and should not be dismissed just because they look gross. Older and mature insects are often less nutritious (because the fats associated with the early larval / pupal stages have been consumed to produce body mass), while insect exo-skeletons will have hardened off and be less than pleasant to eat, let alone digest.

Insects are used as food by more than 2.5 billion people, so you would not be alone in eating insects if you needed to add them to your armageddon menu. For a lot of those people who DO eat insects currently, many species are regarded as delicacies, <u>not</u> as famine or survival food, and are not viewed as poor man's food. In Mexico, for example, various types of *Sphenarium* grasshopper are fried and sold by street vendors as *Chapulines*. One highly regarded, and sometimes very expensive, Mexican insect delicacy are the eggs of ants which are sold as *Escamoles*.

Thailand has a very large usage of edible insects which, again, include ant eggs, various types of large crickets and grasshoppers, numerous beetles including giant water-beetles (*Belostoma* and *Eretes* species), and silkworm pupa. The latter are also eaten in Korea, China, and in parts of India where there is silk manufacturing.

In many parts of Africa and the tropics various species of locust are eaten, and also the caterpillars of some moth species. So, in case of emergency and survival, who are WE to deny insects as food when they are relished by many people around the world. Time to get over your bug eating phobia!

Of course, the insect species which we have in northern temperate Europe are generally very different from those in the tropics. However, the basic principle of eating insects and bugs, and the safety precautions and cooking methods involved, are universal in their approach.

Significantly, insects in Britain and temperate Europe are smaller compared with those in the tropics (presumably because a cooler climate makes metabolism and development slower), so in some respects our bugs are not as useful a source of food as those found elsewhere in the world. However, they <u>are</u> a source of food, and some reproduce prolifically.

Of the types of species here that I would suggest are worthwhile hunting down in times of emergency would be ants (eggs and adults), wasps (grubs), and the grubs of domestic flies. The latter sounds yuck I know, but in parts of provincial China the larvae of these are eaten as food, and have been elsewhere. And while we have our field crickets, grasshoppers, and such like, these are very small when compared to the bite-sized ones in the tropics; although one could perhaps 'farm' our species in captivity as they do in Thailand.

I cannot say that I have tried eating adult ants or their eggs of any UK species as they are really too small, but have eaten weaver ant (*Oecophylla smaragdina*) offerings from Thailand. Ant eggs (which need to be fried) are *really* good, while the adults have a slight acid taste like lemon or rhubarb due to the formic acid found in their sting. Indeed, in some parts of the world ant adults are pounded into a paste and used as a lemon-like condiment to accompany food.

Wasp grubs (leave bees alone as they are needed to pollinate the plants to keep you alive in the future), are really quite good when cooked. If you smoke out a nest by putting burning brushwood, paper, or whatever by the entrance to the nest, this will drive out many active adult wasps while those still remaining inside, and the grubs, will be partly cooked by the fire – if it is hot enough. All you need to do then is dig out the nest, break it open, and winkle out the grubs. Make sure to wear adequate physical protection to prevent adult wasps stinging you.

The grubs should be washed and then cooked in some way – though you will see folks in Japan and China eating wasp and bee larva and pupa raw and unwashed. That may be fine for healthy folks but if your immune system is lowered in a survival situation it is probably wise to wash and cook the grubs – as would be the case with the ant adults and eggs too.

Washing and cooking would most definitely be on the agenda if you are going to consider the larva and pupa of domestic flies (*Musca domestica*) as food since flies are the vectors for some dreadful and incapacitating diseases affecting humans, and botulism (see page 224) would be a major concern in my view. It would be unwise to harvest fly grubs from rotting meat or domestic food, but domestic fly grubs do also breed in the warmth of grass compost heaps which would be a much cleaner source.

And then there are woodlice which are useful in converting inedible cellulose (wood, paper, dried grass) into animal fats and proteins which can be consumed by humans. Or you could use any of these insects to feed small livestock that you have managed to procure. Woodlice can be stir-fried or boiled in water and then consumed. Personally I think they are pretty dreadful compared to some of the tropical bug offerings.

If you really cannot face the prospect of eating bugs whole, then consider drying and pulverizing them and adding to other food items as a meat supplement. Indeed, there is research going on in Africa (as at 2010) to fortify bread with powdered lake flies. Mealworms (*Tenebrio molitor*) could similarly be used, and make a reasonably easily reared insect resource. The downside is that you will need to sacrifice cereal grains or flour to do this, which makes the exercise somewhat self-defeating in times of hunger, and the growth cycle of this particular insect is slower when compared to some other insects.

Generally speaking raising insects as human food in post-disaster northern temperate Europe is not really going to be a very fruitful operation, since the environmental temperatures are on the cool side. Admittedly crickets are raised as food for pet lizards, but then these are raised in heat controlled environments. So it is only in the Mediterranean region and warmer climes that it would make sense to attempt raising insects for food. Cicadas raised for their eggs and larva might be an option, while in the hotter southern parts of the United States the large prolifically breeding mormon cricket (*Anabrus simplex*) – a scourge in some parts – could make a valuable contribution to a post-disaster diet given their size and vast swarms of them. However, they are dependent on vegetation as food so the presence of plant greenery is required.

INSECT ANATOMY

Insects from larva to adult, generally have three distinct body parts – head, thorax and abdomen – six legs, one or two pairs of wings, and go through three or four life stages, from egg to adult. By comparison spiders have eight legs, two body parts, and no wings (and are not 'insects'). As you would expect, an insect head has the mouthparts, brain and eyes, and also the sensory antennae which are used to detect odours and for touch, and vary enormously from species to species. However, there are occasional exceptions to this anatomical generalization of insects.

The middle thorax part of the body is what I like to think of as the 'mobility' section, the part to which the legs and wings, and their necessary muscles, are attached to. The wings are sometimes frail and almost transparent, at others quite leathery. The rear part of insect, the abdomen, is the engine house as it were, containing the heart, digestive system, and also reproductive organs – in other words the gooey bits. For caterpillars it is this tail end which in many cases needs to be evacuated before the insect can be considered as food, while in the case of crickets, locusts and many other edible bugs it is the wings and legs attached to the thorax which must be divested.

Insect bodies have readily discernible body segments, the head [H], thorax [T], and abdomen [A], shown in the schematics overleaf of ants, a grasshopper-like / locust species, and generic caterpillar that would correspond to a butterfly / moth species. The long upright 'worm' is the maggot (larvae) of *Tenebrio molitor* which is actually a beetle, but again the body segments are quite discernible. They are quite easy, but a little slow, to raise, and you might use up cereal grains that would otherwise be used as food.

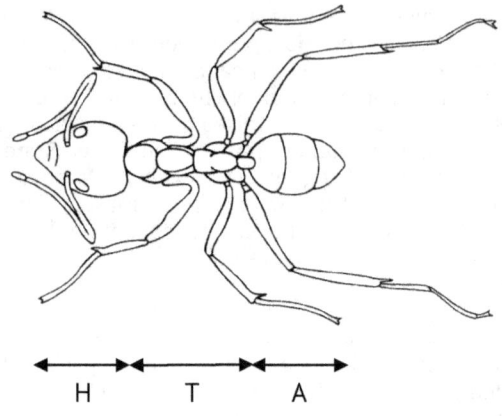

H   T   A

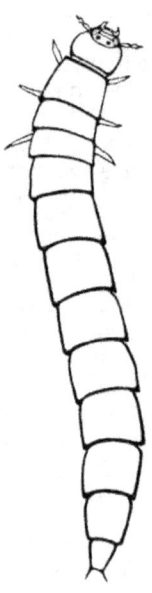

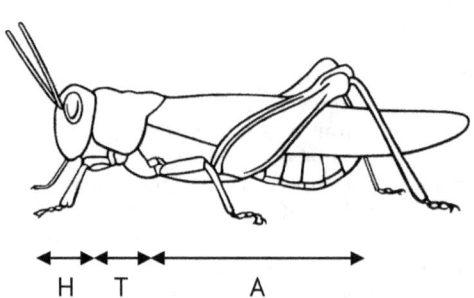

H T   A

Above: larva of *Tenebrio molitor* / Darkling Beetle, which can be raised on oat bran. Often used for fishing ground bait, and feeding pet reptiles and birds, it will be found in stored grains, but also decaying leaves and grasses, and among food 'leftovers'. In which case it would need to be harvested with caution.

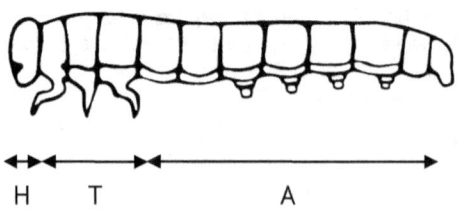

H T   A

EATING INSECTS - KEY SAFETY ISSUES

When harvesting insects from the 'wild' it is essential that they are harvested from habitats where there are no pesticides, agricultural chemicals, pollutants or chemical residues in the soil or, indeed, in the water table where harvesting aquatic insects is concerned.

Insects should be kept alive until the point of cooking. Where they are killed as part of the capture process then they should be consumed as quickly as possible as they deteriorate rapidly (in hot climates dead bugs deteriorate very quickly making them unsafe to eat). In tropical areas it is common to sun-dry insects to extend storage life, after first boiling them.

Starve all live insects for a period before cooking (allowing time for the guts to work through passively). Some insects may need 'active' evacuation of the guts (ie. squeezing) before processing. Earthworms would be a case in point, though they are not 'insects'. Relating to digested gut material, it is a good philosophy not to harvest insects off vegetation which is known to be toxic to humans. And similar to the treatment of mussels when cooking, any insects in a 'live' batch which appear to be dead or inactive (while the bulk of insects remains active) should be discarded.

Refrigeration or cooling slows down insect metabolism (particularly active, jumping, species), making them easier to handle. But you may not have the luxury of refrigeration in your brave new world.

Insects need to be washed before use, particularly those associated with 'dirt' and muck. Dunking in boiling water for a minute or so ensures a degree of cleanliness, but not the absolute assurance of proper cooking through.

The advice is that all fresh insects should be cooked before use – boiled, roasted, fried. It is safer. As with normal foodstuffs they can be frozen for storing after they have been cooked – assuming that facility is available to you. Personally, I do not think the natural drying of insects found in temperate Europe is a particularly safe option given the rapid decaying nature of insects, though I could be wrong. In the tropics there is the natural heat of the sun, day after day to dehydrate collected insects. Drying over a constant heat might be possible, though the freeze-drying employed in the production of insects for human use would be totally out of the question in a post-disaster world.

BREEDING FLIES – BASICS

No one said the new Stone Age was going to be fun. Raising flies is not going to be for everyone, but the larvae (maggots) and pupae of the domestic housefly (*Musca domestica*) could make a useful protein resource *if* they can be safely reared. As mentioned above, the maggots are eaten by one of the indigenous peoples in China, and there is, in fact, a pending patent for an industrial rearing process of *Musca domestica* from China. There also appears to have been human use of *Musca domestica* as food in South America.

Confronting domestic flies as human food is on two levels: one, the sheer disgust at the thought of consuming one of our most prolific pests, and two, overcoming the disease potential that they present. Indeed, this species inhabits the most unsavoury corners or our world: dung and manure heaps, general faecal material, rotting meat and garbage, and putrefying vegetative matter. It does not sound a too hopeful start does it?

Yet, *Musca domestica* is raised for laboratory purposes (often clinical), as is the *Drosophila* fruit fly, so there must be some potential for flies to be bred as a clean food source. I think the answer lies in those words above: *putrefying vegetative matter*. What we are talking about here is piles of old garden refuse such as grass lawn clippings and so on, NOT manure heaps which will contain animal faecal material intermixed with straw, where *M. domestica* also lays its eggs. If one could isolate batches of eggs, or the creamy-white cone-shaped larvae (maggots) or, indeed, the pupae from this vegetative matter, and then raise several successive generations from these, it may be possible to obtain a clean source of *M. domestica*. Someone did it for the laboratory flies at some stage, so why not clean some up for foodstuff breeding?

Right now I will admit to not having personally tried *Musca domestica* either as food or as a raised mini-livestock, since I am not quite sure how hygienically clean you could make them. However, I have been ferreting around trying to piece together data about what the potential of *M. domestica* might be...

To begin with, by all accounts they are a lot harder to breed than nature itself would suggest. It appears they are a bit finicky about the types of vegetable food source they feed off, at least from reading between the lines of available literature on the subject. My own thought was that vegetable or fruit scraps from the doomsday kitchen could be used to feed and raise the isolated colony, but I find the guys that produce lab quality flies use a variety of mixtures of skimmed milk / water, sugar, bran, and in the case of the Chinese patent application, soybean products. Other items which have been used are grass meal (very much akin to the food source found in a garden compost heap), dry malt extract and dried yeast. None of these papers, curiously, have any mention of vegetable or fruit solutions or slurries as the feedstuff.

The other aspect of *M. domestica* is its reproductive capacity, which is enormous. Over several days fertilized females will lay batches of 75 to 150-ish eggs, which hatch in about 12 hours. Over the laying period up to 500 eggs may be laid. The maggots (larvae) that hatch out go through three development stages known as *instars* the third stage of which sees larvae at about the size of 10 mm. This, as far as I am concerned, would be the harvesting point, rather than further along the life-cycle. The last instar stage then gives rise to the pupa, which looks a little bit like a dark brown rice grain. Within a matter of days the young adult emerges from this. Available nutrient levels and ambient temperature in the breeding ground affect speed of growth, but the egg to adult cycle takes about a week. In temperate climates it is possible to have ten to twelve generations in a year.

For more information on fly breeding seek out:
Harrison, R. A. 1949: Laboratory breeding of the housefly (L.).
NZ. J. SCI. TECHNOL. SECT. B: 30:243-247

On general insects as food there's a Wild Food School *Edible Bugs Guide* available as a digital eBook, which breaks down the available edible insect species by world region.

COOKING WITH INSECTS

There are no insect recipes included in this work but here are some general recommendations for using edible insects as food. Where worm-like or maggot-like insects are in play, then these can be dried, ground, and then added to other meats as an 'extender' with high nutritional value. Adding the same ground powder to flour can provide you with nutritious cookies or bread products. Where grasshopper like species are used, then the wings are best removed since they can uncomfortably stick to the back of the throat, while the indigestible hard legs should be removed because they can cause stomach blockages. Grinding up grasshopper type species would overcome these last problems. Deep-frying of bugs is always a way of making them seem palatable. For Western palates whole gooey bug burgers or sausages are not generally appreciated (hence their use as a meat 'extender'), and they really need a binder of bread, gelatine, or similar.

WORMS

The common garden worm can make a useful desperation food but is not an 'insect' so has been left till last. They are not inspired eating in my view but they might see you through tough times. They also, in my view, should not be eaten raw since they may harbour nasty pathogens (see botulin section) depending on where they are gathered from. Once harvested you can either let them starve for a day or so until the gut contents have worked through, then wash and cook them, or my own preferred option is to squeeze them to express all the innards till you get something like a minute sausage skin, then wash thoroughly and stir-fry or deep fry. Where very small worms (6 to 8 cm long) can be obtained then these can be starved overnight to allow passive evacuation of the gut contents – spray or sprinkle with a little water to keep them moist – then wash properly before using. Another way of preparing worms for your armageddon menu, and one which can be used to overcome the squeamish thought of consuming them, is to add prepared worms to an omelette or to scrambled egg. Overall, though, worms cannot be classified as 'gourmet' food even if you have plenty of flavourings on hand. Potentially worms could be farmed as doomsday food, then dried, ground up and used as a meat extender.

One important point about collecting worms: in my view they need to be collected from a source that is free from animal detritus, so dung heaps with animal faeces are out of the question. Much better are piles of grass clippings and leaf mulch. If you were going to 'farm' worms for human consumption then it would no doubt be best to source the initial breeding stock away from farmed areas, heading for woodland or tops of hedge banks and so on.

SNAILS

Snails could form a useful and easy to harvest, occasional, part of your doomsday diet – if you like snails, that is. Even if you don't, many species are still edible, and they are *food*. The reason of the mention 'occasional' is that it takes three to four months-ish for a garden snail (*Helix aspersa*) to mature to a worthwhile fork size. So unless a disaster situation is long-term then snail ranching is not a really valid project or prospect, though long-term that situation could change.

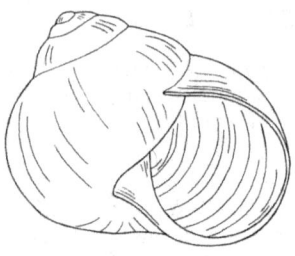

The other potential drawback with farming snails is that if they are not controlled then they could escape into your precious foraged greens area and decimate that food resource to your detriment. So there are good and bad angles to snail ranching, and in this short section I will cover simple processing of casually harvested snails, plus a few basic ideas on rearing snails so that you can research further if you wish.

To begin with, when harvesting snails from the wild for food you need to consider what they have been feeding on (as in terms of plants that are normally toxic to humans) while also considering if there are chemicals at work in the localized environment – either in the topsoil and substrata, or from sprayed insecticides, although in the latter case there is unlikely to be much insecticide floating around in a post-disaster world if there is a collapse of the industrial-agricultural infrastructure.

SNAIL PREPARATION

There are very slightly different ways of preparing snails for the cooking pot, but a pretty robust one is as follows: if the snails are taken straight from the wild then they need to be placed in a 'pen' and starved of food for about 5 or 6 days though at the same time being provided water in both the form of a sprinkling and also a proper drinking water source. If the snails are being harvested from an area where some of the plant species are known to be toxic to humans then I would feed them with a handful of bran or crushed oatmeal for a day or two, or a few green leaves or a piece of carrot, and then starve them. The most important thing is to allow the guts to fully work through. Each day sprinkle or mist the snails with water.

The penning area should be a snail-tight wooden or plastic box that allows the snails to get air. If using a plastic box it is worth piercing a few small holes in the base to allow excess water to run away as snails do not live 'in' water, although they will almost certainly climb up the sides of the box to escape excess moisture if there is space.

Once the guts have been purged put the snails in a colander and wash well with water. And then, if possible, for several minutes in a bowl of water acidulated with a little vinegar – this is useful for helping get rid of the slimy mucous. Then wash again with clean water.

Now comes the cooking part, which is in two stages. First is a boiling stage that kills the snails and permits extraction from the shell, and then follows the recipe stage which cooks them as a 'dish'.

Although it is possible to drop the snails into rapidly boiling water for 5 or 6 minutes I think that a much more humane way is to try and chill them (but this may not be possible in a doomsday scenario) so that they almost go into hibernation, and then drop them into boiling water. Once cooked the meat needs to be removed from the shell. However, some garden snails are small and very fiddly to extract the meat from, in which case a light tap on the shell to crack it prior to extraction will help. It's not an ideal way for meat extraction, and you need to make sure to remove all bits of shell fragments. If possible select the very largest snails in the first place. All that remains then is to cook them up in a recipe (though I have not inlcuded any in the recipe section to save space – just look in any French cookery book).

REARING SNAILS – BASICS
When ranching snails the beasts need to be penned in; either in a small enclosure or box, or penned into areas or tracts of land specifically set round cultivated foliage greens like cabbage, sprouts and kale. The latter is a rearing tactic used by large commercial snail farmers on the Continent. For a small producer a simple wooden crate will do, or even one of those large plastic storage boxes – providing the lid is bored with holes to allow adequate ventilation, or a hole cut and covered over with a fine breathable mesh. Rearing in a plastic box is a quite good option for reasons that will become apparent, and it can also be washed out and sterilized from time to time to keep the snail stock disease-free.

A key aspect of rearing snails is to have decent humidity (which is where that sealed but breathable plastic container comes in), while hot or dry conditions must be avoided. In the case of plastic containment vessels small drainage holes must be bored into the floor as garden snails cannot live in water. Where a dry spell occurs then a snailery will need to be regularly sprinkled with water to keep up the humidity. The other item required is shelter; somewhere where snails can take refuge from light and heat. Shelter may simply be the addition of manmade artefacts like drainpipe or leaning slates, or in the case of commercial growers the snails will hide under the leaf foliage of any greens growing in their pens.

Another major requirement is protection from predators – such as birds, frogs and toads, and insects – and also protection from escape. The latter can be achieved by covering an open containment box with mosquito-like netting, although in very dry conditions netting will absorb any morning dew that might otherwise precipitate around the floor of the snail pen, keeping the snails moist. In these situations manual hydration of the pens will be necessary.

The soil or other ground that the snails trundle across needs to be moist but not wet, and there must be calcium available either in the soil or as an additive. Calcium is required for shell formation and commercial growers sometimes add powdered calcium carbonate to the dry feed, but crushed eggshells are a domestic alternative. Dry feed may contain ground soy and wheat flour which are something unlikely to be donated to snails when times are hard.

If you are going to breed from snails collected in the wild, then select good-sized and healthy ones; and as new broods of snails mature then the biggest can be selected out for breeding the next generation, and so on, until you have developed your own super-snail. Snails are hermaphrodites and the recommendation is for equal numbers of pairs to be placed into the breeding pen.

Which brings us to overcrowding in pens. The fewer snails per metre then obviously the less competition for food resources, which has an influence on the mature size of the snails. Less food equals smaller snails, and potentially weaker and therefore more prone to disease too. For *Helix aspersa* a ratio of 25 to 30 snails per metre is reckoned a good norm for breeding pens, while a fattening pen with plenty of food provided can handle up to 300 individuals. All of which necessitates keeping two or three snail pens, or even more if you go into large-scale production.

In normal conditions garden snails lay clutches of about 80 to 100 eggs (which should hatch in two to four weeks) in the soil, which again needs to be kept moist but not wet. In a totally artificial pen then trays or pots of soil with 5 to 8 cm of earth need to be provided for egg laying. In northern temperate Europe the likely breeding season is around March to October, but in hotter Mediterranean climes the reverse is true, with the summer being too hot and dry, so that the wet and cool period from September to May offers better breeding opportunities. Indeed, you are looking for just the right combination of moisture with warmth. Anything below about 12°c and laying stops, and during cold weather snails hibernate in the topsoil which is not much use to a proper snail rancher. In these cases snails are reared in indoor artificial pens which may well artificially warmed and lit to extend productivity during winter months.

As for their food, snails are strictly vegetarian. Nettles and clover are good vegetative greens that can be gathered from the wild, with cabbage-type and spinach-type domestic greens also useful, as are bits of carrot and left-over salad greens (if available) such as tomato, cucumber or lettuce, or even small amounts of oatmeal softened with water. From experience snails do not seem to be attracted to dandelion or grasses, while younger snails seem to prefer softer green vegetation graduating to more solid greens and chopped fruit as they mature.

RAT

In the absence of rabbits, chickens, or other traditional livestock, then rats can provide protein, while also having the advantage – from a food procurement point of view – of breeding prolifically.

Note, however, that we are talking here of domesticated rats, or those caught in country districts far away from metropolitan habitats and not feeding on refuse. This is simply because of the disease factor (Weil's disease being the best known), and also that those found in urban areas may well have been living in sewers and feeding on just about every piece of junk food or contaminated item that can be gnawed at. Sewer rats should be avoided as food – except in absolute dire desperation.

For rats which can be sourced from a controlled environment (and it wouldn't take much to set up a breeding programme to provide a regular supply of meat from domestic or pet rats), then preparation is not overly complex, but slightly different from the methods of preparing traditional livestock.

The best place to see the preparation of rats for food are in countries like Thailand, Vietnam and Cambodia, where rats caught in fields or paddies are a regular part of the diet, and even regarded as a delicacy. There is also a much larger bamboo rat (*Rhizomys sinensis*) which enters the human food chain in those areas, and is somewhat reminiscent of a large guinea pig in appearance (more of which shortly).

The rat preparation method which follows is tried and tested and used day in, day out, by folks is Asia, and runs as follows:

Kill your rat/s (humanely please) and drop into scalding water for two or three minutes – or until the fur pulls easily away from the skin (tug a clutch every minute or so). Transfer to a second bowl of hand-hot water and remove all the fur.

The next step is to gut each rat. Being careful not to puncture any of the digestive organs make a small incision in the skin on the underside of the rat and then extend the cut towards the anus and throat (keeping the blade edge facing outwards). Reach in with your fingers and pull out all the internal organs, then remove the head and tail. Finally, rinse the cavity thoroughly with water, washing all traces of blood away. Often you'll see folks gutting rats under a constant flow of running water, but this may not be available in a doomsday world. What you end up with is a cleaned rat carcass, complete with the skin which will have a blanched look almost the colour of cooked chicken flesh.

All that remains to do is portion and cook the rat – they are generally roasted or fried, although in one particular instance I have seen the rats were chopped into bite-size pieces which suggests that it may have been destined for a stew or similar (though not necessarily, since this was my pre-conceived notion of what would be cooked with fork-sized pieces of rat meat).

The couple of diagrams below show two examples of rat butchering, one from Vietnam the second from Cambodia. In the Vietnamese example the carcass is divided into 5 pieces: a centre saddle portion, and four leg pieces. You'll typically find these portion configurations deep-fried and served as snacks in local bars in Hanoi. The second example (right) is the one from Cambodia. Here the carcass is split along the backbone, then a second cut made below the legs and start of the rib-cage. The saddle and hind-quarter portions are then chopped into 5 or 6 pieces, and the front part into 3 sections. The pieces should be deep-fried for 5 or 6 minutes or until cooked through, or whole spatchcocked rats will grill in about 30 or 40 minutes.

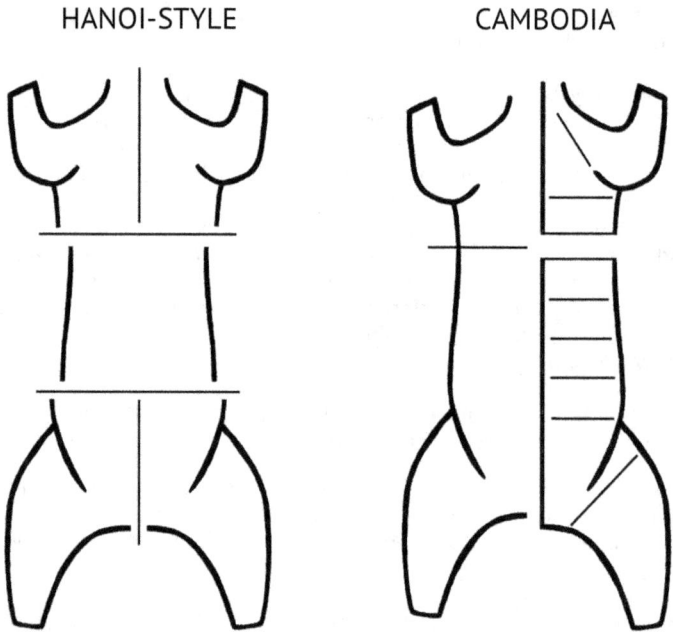

HANOI-STYLE   CAMBODIA

RAISING RATS – BASICS
Raising rats for food! Horror! Well in a meltdown environment it could well be that rats become a source of food, so get used to that idea, and also the possibility of breeding them from domesticated sources only.

As a brief background to rat breeding for your food... Female does come into 'heat' about every 4 to 6 days, gestation is generally about 3 weeks after mating (females becoming noticeably fatter at about 2 weeks), while litters range from 8 to 12 in number, sometimes 15 to 20. In the winter months breeding activity tends to drop.

Age is important, in that females need to be mature enough to breed productively (so a 5 to 7 month old doe is considered a good starting point as that is the time they have gained a good body weight, while 12 to 15 month old doe is regarded as getting past it). The male buck should be between 6 and 12 months old – any younger and they may be rejected by a doe, while older ones may also be past it. Again, by the 6 month age a male should be at a healthy mature weight (choose healthy muscular specimens for breeding, not unhealthy fat ones). Rats are considered coming into the start of their adult phase at around 12 weeks.

Incidentally, one of the problems you may encounter with continually inter-breeding within the same group is that litter size, individual body weight, and general health will decline the longer individuals from within the colony are interbred. I did read somewhere that for 'show rats' it was suggested that 'new blood' should be introduced into the colony after 6 generations. Of course, in a post-disaster world obtaining new rat genes may not be possible, but potentially you could select the biggest individual in each generation to breed your own super-rat, while at the same time avoid breeding from sickly and genetically weak individuals. Perhaps rat bloodstock will become an item of barter in the new world!

Mating is sometimes done on a one-to-one basis in the rat fancier's world, allowing strains within successive generations to be monitored. In this case a buck and doe are matched and allowed to co-habit for 10 days, which should have seen the doe being in 'season' at least once. Once the doe is visibly pregnant the pair are then separated (note that females come into 'season' right after giving birth and an immediate second litter is likely to be weak and sickly). For human food production it would seem that colony breeding would present the best option; a single male buck living among a number of females, with each doe removed from the colony once visibly pregnant and put into her own cage until birthing and the few subsequent litter-nursing weeks.

It's a good idea not to mix does and their respective new litters within the same nursery cage, since the mothers can become antagonistic towards the other's offspring and the other doe itself. So if you are going to breed rats for food then you need to work out the number of cages required for separation and rearing purposes. The cages should have plenty of wood shavings, or shredded paper, as does build nests as they get nearer to giving birth.

Youngsters grow at a rapid pace and require a good amount of food, and by week two their eyes should be open. Male bucks in the new litter are sexually mature as early as 6 or 7 weeks, so they need to be separated out at about 4 to 5 weeks.

Rats have a reputation for not being particularly choosy about what they eat, certainly that's the case with city rats. They will consume everything from grains and porridge-like mixtures, to eggs and the bread tidbits and scraps from your doomsday kitchen. Indeed, perhaps a small rat colony could consume all those awful bits of animals that you find awkward and squeamish to eat.

Conversely, if you have to start sharing valuable survival carbohydrate stores to raise rats for meat then you will have to weigh up the benefits against the disadvantages given the individual circumstances that you find yourself in.

Maintain the normal feeding regime during pregnancy, rather than upping it to a higher octane, fat producing, level. Similarly, overfeeding youngsters can cause health problems further down the line, although they may look visibly healthy because they look large.

WARNING - IF YOU ARE EASILY OFFENDED OR SQUEAMISH PLEASE SKIP THIS NEXT SECTION

GUINEA PIG

In parts of South America such and Peru and Equador the guinea pig is reared for human consumption on a quite large scale, as opposed to the western view that guinea pigs are solely pets. Guinea pig, or 'Cuy' (roughly pronounced *kwee*) as it is called locally, has been on the menu for thousands of years in South America. So, again, why should we Westerners balk at the prospect of eating guinea pig in times of emergency, and take a leaf of out other cultures well-versed with the preparation of guinea pig as food. If you want to stay alive in an emergency you can turn to guinea pig for food, and I think most people would find the prospect of that less daunting than eating rat. Otherwise sit back, twiddle your thumbs, and wait for your inevitable demise.

The cuy that arrive for slaughter in South America are quite large and well fattened up for the table. Indeed, they are sometimes a little fatty when cooked, though the meat has a delicate flavour somewhere between pork and chicken, but there isn't a great deal of it.

The first part of cuy preparation is very similar to that for rats; the animals being slaughtered then placed in hot water to enable the fur to be easily removed, before evisceration. However, it is at this point that the method of gutting changes depending on how the cuy is to be cooked – either *roasted* whole on a stick (or metal spit), or *spatchcocked* and then fried.

Where the cuy is *roasted* on a spit the following procedure is used... An incision is made with a knife at the bottom of the rib cage and then a short-ish cut made towards the anus – not quite to the end. The guts and organs are then removed (and could be used in their own right as food). Next, the knife is used to cut away at the teeth and jaw so that the jaw can be widened to accommodate the insertion of a roasting stick (it's usually about a couple of centimetres in diameter).

The stick or spit is pushed through the widened jaw, then down through the thorax / chest until it reaches the far end of the body cavity (where that shortened knife incision ensures a bit of the stomach skin is left to hold the stick in place). However, some folks push the spit all the way through. I guess it's just down to visual presentation. All that remains to do is oil and season the prepared cuy (some folks will place herbs and spices in the body cavity too) and then roast over coals until the skin is nice and crispy and golden in colour.

The second, *spatchcock*, method is much more time consuming... An incision is made in the belly of the cuy, from the rear end right up to the throat, then the rib cage pulled apart and the innards removed. Note, that in neither preparation process do locals seem to remove the head.

The next stage involves using a cleaver or sharp, heavy, knife to cut through the rib-cage bones, and other vertebra, at their base near the backbone. The rib-cage bones themselves are then cut once more, in the middle of their length this time. And all these cuts are made <u>without</u> cutting completely through the meat or skin.

What you end up with through this process is a carcass that is limp and floppy, almost like a piece of rag. There are now two ways of proceeding before frying... Some folks will hang the limp carcasses on a washing line or similar to allow some moisture to evaporate, while others will dredge the cuy in flour and then fry in a couple of centimetres or so of oil.

After seasoning the cuy is generally fried skin side down first – for about 6 to 8 minutes – then turned over and similarly cooked on the other side. As with cooking fish with the skin in place, cuy also curls, and one of the local tricks to prevent this from happening is to place a non-porous stone on top of the frying cuy to keep it pressed flat.

While we are on the subject of cuddly critters there may come a time in a real doomsday scenario when you have to consider pet animals as a source of food. Yes, dogs and cats, or even a pet snake (or pet rat). In that battle for your personal existence what are *you* going to do? Are you going to step over the line, reluctantly, and eat what is around you, or are you going to become a casualty of circumstance because your psyche remains firmly embedded in the world that previously existed, or are you going to get a grip on reality and take control of your circumstances to live another day?

Only the heartless would relish despatching a pet animal but there is absolutely no reason why pet animal species should not be considered as food, other than the human aspect of losing a family friend. There are cultures that eat cats and dogs around the world, and there's a 16th century recipe in the Catalan language that describes the roasting of cat. If you personally wish to survive you may need to sacrifice a pet animal. Living through survival times is not only physically demanding, but will make demands on mental resources too.

RAISING GUINEA PIGS – BASICS

Guinea pigs are wholly herbivores and can be fed on a mixture of thoroughly dry grasses and hay, grains, and fresh vegetables (veggie and fruit parings from the doomsday kitchen, or foraged greens like clover and dandelion); a rich source of vitamin C being important for their health. Stale, but not mouldy, bread can also be added to the food mix. Meats and fats are not permissible. Once you have established a dietry regime stick closely with it rather than suddenly switching.

From about 4 weeks old the female *sow* can become sexually active, and should produce between 1 to 5 offspring per litter. Sometimes there may be as many as half a dozen. Five litters can be raised in a year (4 is regarded as healthy optimum for the sow), with the gestation period around 60 to 70 days. Males are called *boars* and the offspring *pups*, and longevity ranges from 4 to 7 years. Pups can start eating solids from about 2 days onwards, although weaning takes between 3 and 4 weeks.

There are some potential health risks to breeding, the key point being that guinea pigs give birth to large, furry babies, which start to run around within a few hours. So it is important to start breeding the first litter before a sow is 8 months old. If that doesn't take place then the sow can have difficulty in delivery and both sow and pup can die. Breeding at around 3 or 4 months seems like a sensible starting age.

Similar to rats, females are able to reproduce immediately after they have given birth, and so no male boar should be present, otherwise there's the possibility of another generation quickly on the horizon. Also, you would need to separate new male and female offspring at around 3 to 4 weeks to prevent immature pregnancies. Unlike the rat breeding scenario multiple litters and their mothers can coexist side by side in the same pen without too much bother, although allowing a sow to give birth amongst other litters is not regarded as a good idea.

Make the pens a decent size for these furry critters, at least a couple of feet square. In South America great gaggles of the animals can be seen roaming freely in the houses (in fact guinea pigs do not survive the outdoors and very cold weather, so they are ideal for indoor domestication). While the sides of a pen may be constructed of mesh the base should <u>not</u>. And that is important because guinea pigs do not have a protective covering of fur on their feet so long-term housing upon a mesh floored pen (such as that used for rabbits) can lead to painful foot sores. Despite the fact that these animals are destined for your cooking pot does not mean that they should live in pain or suffer. Thinking about it, in a post-disaster world something like a large plastic laundry basket scavenged from the rubble might make a reasonable guinea pig 'home'.

Bedding in pens should be fine wood shavings (not sawdust), dry plant fibre, torn newspaper, towelling or an old fleece. The advantage of material fabrics is that when the pen starts to whiff of ammonia (via urine), then the fabric can be washed, dried, and then returned to the pen, whereas wood chippings will need to be thrown away. In relation to this, guinea pigs frequently use just one area of their housing as a toilet, so if you can identify this spot then a separate piece of material can be placed in that area and washed regularly. Folks that keep guinea pigs for pets recommend cleaning out the corner loo on a daily basis, so it's perhaps wise to follow that same regime to keep the animals healthy. Doing that routine can also tie-in with changing the drinking water each day.

Planning for breeding is essential in terms of having enough pens available; exactly as with breeding rabbits and rats. At about 4 months old breeding individuals can be moved to new pens, one male to four females being a good mix of the sexes. As with any other animal over-demands on individual sows to breed, and too much inter-breeding will produce weaknesses in the offspring and possible genetic defects.

Guinea pigs are remarkably clean critters and do not suffer from nearly so many diseases as poultry and rabbits, so when you consider a long-term survival situation, guinea pigs make could make a much more viable and reliable meat source for your doomsday kitchen.

RABBIT

Like some other game meats, rabbit is a very lean, low-fat, meat. Although the meat is slightly more pink coloured than chicken, rabbit can have a similar texture when cooked properly, and the rabbit is of a reasonably young age. Older and larger ones can have pretty tough muscle tissue however, and need long slow cooking or roasting over the fire. With rabbit be careful of the fine small bones when both preparing the carcass, and also eating.

Indeed, one basic difference between game meat and that from domesticated animals is that game animals have had a lot more exercise as well as a different diet. Although younger animals tend to be more tender, game animals generally have little fat and tougher muscle tissue. What fat there is often doesn't taste very nice and is removed, and if it turns rancid will make the meat very 'gamey'.

Rabbit is generally 'hung' for 2 or 3 days and has quite dry flesh if in good condition. Increasing the time the meat is hung will increase the gamey flavour. If that's not to your liking then soak the skinned and gutted carcass; covering it in water to which has been added salt [1 tsp. to 1 litre] or vinegar [1 cup to 1 litre], then discard the water.

Real tenderness is achieved through slow cooking, braising, and moist heat. Whole rabbits can be slowly casseroled on a fire for around 4 to 5 hours, while joints can be braised 1½ to 2 hours, or simmered gently for 40 to 60+ minutes. Frequently I simply use rabbit meat stripped from the bone, and where uncertain about the age of a rabbit tend to err towards long, slow, cooking to avoid a disappointing outcome.

Boiled rabbit can be pretty tasteless and looks pretty unappetizing too (boil for 2 hours till the meat falls off the bones otherwise it can have the consistence of a rubber duck). A much better way is to spatchcock the rabbit on a suitable branch and then place this 60 to 90 cm from your fire source to slowly roast. Meat carved from the carcass cooked like this is almost like chicken, although pieces of the outer muscle membrane can be a little tough, though nothing untoward.

The age of a wild rabbit can be difficult to determine if all that you are presented with is a dressed rabbit. Chatting to a friend who supplies me with rabbit livers and meat – and who has seen more rabbits in his time than Santa has delivered presents at Christmas – about a foolproof way of determining a grown rabbit's age... the answer is that there isn't really one. Size is a potential indicator, and where you have a whole rabbit the jaw of young animals is pliable but not in older ones. Where a rabbit is already dressed my friend's suggestion is that you look at the muscle tissue which will be more grainy or fibrous in older animals. If you are uncertain of the age of the rabbit my suggestion is that you extend the cooking time [while cooking gently].

SKINNING & GUTTING A RABBIT

There are many ways of skinning a rabbit, and seasoned hunters have their own preferred way of gutting and skinning them. The more practice you get at skinning, the more easy it becomes. If you have never skinned a rabbit then a good starting point is the process outlined below. This method also allows you to retrieve the pelt in one piece, and which could then be cured and used for its fur.

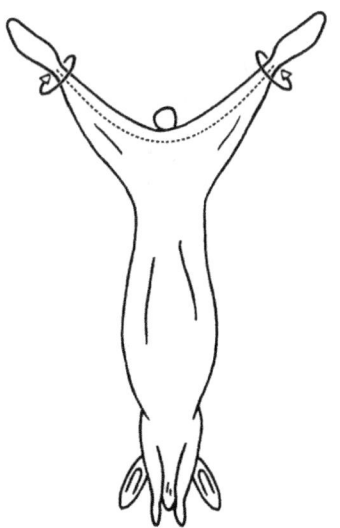

Hang the rabbit up by its rear legs. Take a knife and make an incision and circular cut through the pelt and fur around the lower leg above the ankle joints.

Cut the pelt between the two leg incisions. Pull off the tail / tail fur then cut the skin around the tail and connect it with your previous cut. Using your fingers begin to gently unpeel the pelt from around the legs, and then slowly pull it down over the body as if you were removing a sock, as shown in the next two diagrams.

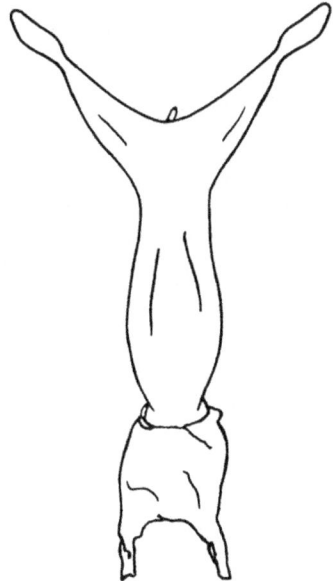

If you tug at the pelt you may tear the flesh and the pelt too, so work it down gradually. Once you have pulled the pelt down as far as you can towards the head, cut off the front legs at the knee joint (this can also be done at the very beginning) and pull the skin over the legs. Ease the pelt around the neck and then cut off the head. You should now have something that looks like the diagram to the right. If you are going to use the brains for food (see recipe section) then pull the pelt right over the head having freed the pelt from the front legs.

Next, make an incision in the skin between the rib-cage and anus. Use just the tip of the knife, with the sharp side of the blade facing outwards to prevent the internal guts being punctured. In this position there is downward and outward pressure on the guts, so beginners might want to start the first cut at the top and work downwards.

Open the cavity (allowing the guts to spill forward) and ease out the guts. Cut round the anal end to detach that exit point of the guts. Cut off where they are attached near the diaphragm. Remove the liver and kidneys and keep these as they can be used for food.

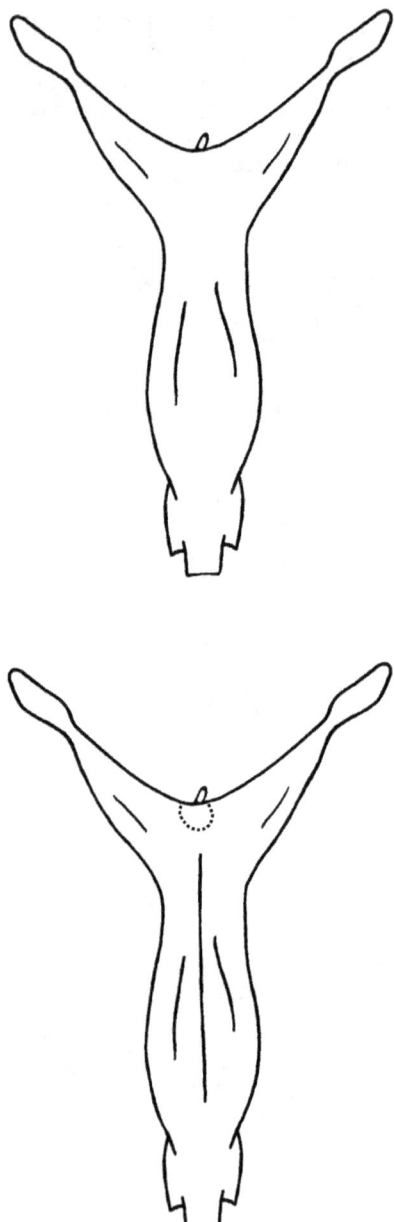

If the chest cavity is not already exposed, work the main incision down towards the neck and through the thorax / rib-cage. Remove the heart (in the centre) and the two lungs. All of which can be used for food.

IMPORTANT NOTE
If there is any sign of a granular yellow-white mottling on the liver this could be a sign of *tularemia* (more on this overleaf). DO NOT use the rabbit if this is the case. In a survival scenario it would be better to avoid rabbits with ANY sign of disease since there will be no medical service to administer pills.

If harvesting rabbit pelts for their fur is not a consideration, then a very quick method of skinning is as follows (diagram below right).

Cut the feet off above each ankle. Remove tail. Then make an incision into the skin and fur around the belly region and cut right round the circumference of the body (some folks make the first incision on the back to minimize the chance of piercing the abdominal cavity). Grasp hold of the rear and front fur and simultaneously pull to the front and rear, pulling the pelt clean off the legs, which can be cut off before. Cut off at the neck again, and then remove the internal organs as previously described.

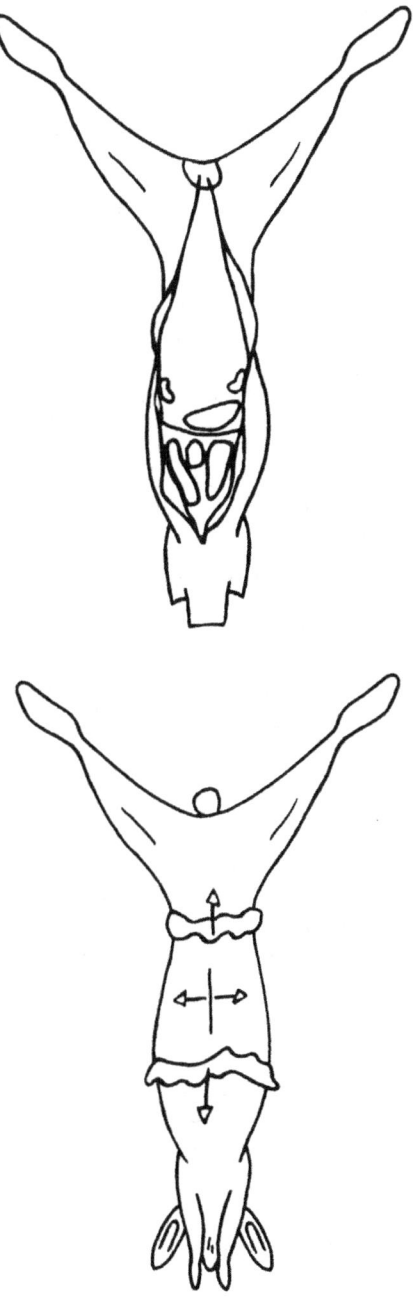

TULAREMIA
Tularemia is a relatively rare disease in humans from what I understand, certainly when compared to flu, although it does exist right across the northern hemisphere in pockets, with there being regular outbreaks of the disease dotted around various regions (the US had over 1,000 cases between 1981 and 1987).

The disease is caused by the *Francisella tularensis* bacterium getting into the human body through broken skin, insect or animal bites and, it would also appear, through airborne transmission. There were 50+ cases of the latter in northern Finland in 1982 resulting from farming activities like hay-making and threshing. There are also reports of a water-borne outbreak too.

Handling animals carrying the disease potentially exposes humans to tularemia too. Rabbits are our main concern here, particularly for anyone gutting them. The key internal sign regarding rabbits is a white spotted liver; on the liver surface it looks a bit like large sand grains dotted all over, rather than fatty blobs.

As for the physiological manifestations in other animals that carry the disease I do not know what those are. However squirrels, cats, and racoons can carry the disease too, as may deer ticks. There is a recorded case of tularemia transmission from a cat bite, and one from a dormouse bite.

Technically, there are about half a dozen clinical manifestations of the disease in humans, though for lay-simplicity these can be broken into glandular forms and pneumonic forms. In the first form the lymph glands become enlarged and sometimes ulcerated, while the pneumonic form tends to manifest itself with severe flu and typhoid-like symptoms such as high fever, headache and muscle pain. With correct and swift antibiotic treatment recovery is very good, but left untreated tularemia can be fatal.

REARING RABBITS – BASICS
Trapping any wild animal is actually a very hit and miss affair, and in a pure end-of-world survival situation where you need to conserve energy (remembering our *economy of effort* motto) then you would, in my opinion, be better off trying to raise caged rabbits as opposed to hunting for them. Obviously you need to source your original stock, so it may be that you have to go and track those down from the wild, but then you might come across domesticated ones in the debris of the post-disaster world around you, though the temptation might be to bundle those into your cooking pot at once. If you can think beyond that initial temptation to eat the bunny from the rubble then you can plan ahead to producing a regular source of meat for your doomsday kitchen.

As with the rat rearing operation previous, you want to plan ahead for the number of cages that will be required to produce a constant supply of rabbit meat. You will need individual cages or hutches for each male buck (you only need one or two of those), a number of cages to house individual pregnant females, and then large nursery cages for the litters once they have been removed from the mothers.

If there is metal mesh available then this is much the best material to make cages from since they are easy to clean out and sterilize, and thereby keep the rabbit colony as free from disease as possible. Wooden hutches tend to absorb urine and spilled water, and really need cleaning out with disinfectants that are unlikely to be available in a post-disaster world. At a push, metal cages can be slung over the camp fire (minus occupants, that is) to be sterilized in the flames.

Suitably thought out, a buck and three does could supply you with rabbit meat once or twice a week if you work on a principle of no more than 5 litters a year (7 is possible), and raising only the healthiest 5 or 6 of each litter. A female doe should be of sufficient size to breed when eight to twelve months old. Rabbits can give birth from 28 to 32 days after mating, and normally a nesting box should be placed in the hutch a few days before the expected birth. After about one or two weeks the small rabbits will start jumping out of the nesting boxes, so tip the box on its' side so mother and offspring can more easily cosey-up. Give new offspring their own cage at eight weeks.

During weaning it is suggested that more solid vegetative materials such as dandelion roots or carrots plus a few oats (if you can spare these items) are among the diet, and then a variety of vegetative greens from dandelion leaves to grasses introduced as they get older.

Where you are introducing new stock rabbits into the colony to increase the genetic bloodline then isolate that rabbit for a month before introducing it into your main breeding group in case it has some infection.

Rabbits as a long-term survival food? Well they do potentially provide a decent amount of meat once fully grown, but they are subject to some diseases and in the initial phases they may require some of the same food resources that could otherwise be feeding you or those around you. Like all matters related to survival, there's a judgement call depending on the unique circumstances that you, individually, confront. What may suit one individual circumstance, may not suit another. One final matter: over-dependence on rabbit meat as food can have health implications for humans – rabbit starvation, as it is called (after some 19th century explorers died after living of rabbits for an extended period of time). In essence what you are looking at here is 'protein poisoning', or the over-consumption of ultra-lean meat without balancing that with additional fat, carbohydrate and vitamin sources. So, make sure to eat some greens and other foods alongside any lean meat intake.

DEER

Venison is one of my favourite meats, being very lean (and therefore presumably good on the health front) and also having a flavour and texture somewhat in between lamb and beef; though it should be said that the texture will largely be influenced by the length of 'hanging' as will the flavour. Although venison may be sourced from the wild, it is quite frequently farm-raised these days which makes venison from these sources little different from meats bought off a supermarket shelf. Raising deer for food is something for folks with large areas of land and not the kind of post-disaster enterprise of rabbit, rat or guinea pig breeding that could be easily undertaken.

As with rabbit, if you find the meat is a bit too gamey in flavour, it may be marinated for a few hours with a mixture of equal parts water and vinegar [cider or wine depending on the recipe you will be using] and a small amount of sugar (indeed this was a typical technique used in old times to tackle spoiled meat in general). Bay leaf and onion may also be added for flavouring, as might some spices if you were intending to use the meat in more exotic recipes.

Venison medallions and steaks can be fried or broiled successfully over a medium-high heat for about 6 to 7 minutes per side; about the same time if you were using the ground meat for burgers. If using minced venison it is wise to use this straight away as exotic carcass-borne bacteria could multiply among the mince if it is not kept suitably chilled. For stews the meat should be cut into fork-sized pieces and simmered for about 2 to 3 hours in a covered casserole. Roasts take from between 25 to 40 minutes per pound in a moderate oven, depending on whether the cuts are on or off the bone. The liver, kidneys, lungs and heart also make good food sources.

Since venison is such a lean meat with virtually no marbling, moisture retaining cooking methods are needed to prevent the meat drying out. So when roasting venison frequent basting may be an essential part of the recipe, as can larding the meat, or adding other fats or bacon.

SKINNING & GUTTING DEER

There appear to be a couple of different methodologies for skinning deer from what I have personally encountered – removing the skin before gutting, or gutting before skin removal. Those guys who sell deer meat have strict sets of butchering rules that require gutting first, with an 8 cm wide piece of the skin removed along the entire length of the belly before any incision is made into the abdominal cavity for gutting purposes. The reasoning behind this is that where gutting proceeds through a tight-fitting hide then hair and bacteria from the hide are transferred to the meat carcass as it is worked on. So that 8 cm gap provides a clean working space where gutting is done with the hide still in place.

The gutting process should be done as soon as possible after the animal has been killed, even more so where the method of killing has punctured the main body cavity that contain the viscera are. In the field it is common for deer to be gutted on the spot, while reared deer are carefully head-shot so the need for immediate gutting is not so critical. However, even these farmed deer need to be gutted within an hour or two otherwise the contents of the stomach will ferment and bloat, making the carcass more difficult to handle and eviscerate. The other advantage of gutting and skinning soon after death is that the hide is very much easier to remove.

While the animal is still on the ground begin by making a circular cut round the knuckles of the back legs and then bend the joint back against itself and twist off the lower leg. Then make an incision just above the knee (where the hock at the end of the tibia bone, and tarsals, join the meta-tarsals). Use the knife to loosen the skin round the area to expose the tendon, then slide the knife in beside the tendon on both legs to widen a space for the rope to be threaded through; but do not cut through the tendon. Although tying ropes round the feet may seem an obvious way of doing things, generally this does not work because the ropes slip off due to the weight of the carcass.

With a strong rope threaded through the tendon spaces hoist the animal over the bow of a tree, or whatever suspension rig you have constructed, and tie it off firmly at a comfortable working height.

Now you can begin processing the carcass. If you have never gone through the following actions before, take your time. Don't try to be a deer skinning whiz straight off, but instead get a 'feel' for the anatomy and how it comes apart, for want of better words. Once you understand the animal, then the easier successive ones will be to process.

The first stage is to remove the hide, which is achieved by cutting the skin along the dotted lines shown in the figure to the right. Work with the sharp edge of the knife facing outwards, away from the animal's body, as this helps prevent cutting into the skin or accidentally piercing the guts inside the abdominal cavity.

Make your first cuts from the existing circular 'knee' cut along the underside of each leg down to the genital area. Then make a circular cut around the lower part of the genital area to connect your first two leg cuts.

From here extend the cut downwards along the line of the belly (remember to keep the knife blade facing outwards), and then down to the throat where it joins the head. Next, go through the same motions of cutting along the underside of the front legs, extending the cut to that of your existing belly-neck cut line. The last important cut to make is another semicircular one – on the other side of the body – round the tail. It should now be possible to remove the hide in one whole piece; beginning by easing the skin round the rear legs and then working it down the body. When you get to the head-neck area, stop. Feel for the 'apex' where the neck vertebra meet the skull and cut through with a heavy-duty knife.

There is a recommended technique to remove the hide so that you do not tear or cut the meat beneath. Beginning at the top simply work one hand between the hide and underlying parts, while pulling the hide with your other hand. If you come to a stubborn part resist the temptation to haul on the hide, as this can tear either the hide or the tissue underneath. Instead, use the *tip* of your knife at a *flat angle* and tease away the hide from the white membrane below. Keeping that membrane intact, and without knife cuts, is to your advantage for reasons that we will come to shortly. Once you've got round the obstacle, keep on using one hand to pull and one to poke, as it were, around the back and the sides; and once you get to the main body mass you can start to use some of your own bodyweight to pull the hide down. Remember – avoid the temptation to hack the skin off with

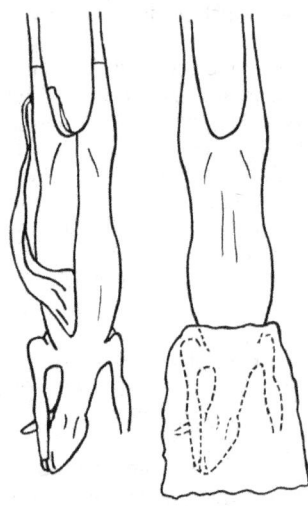

a knife, leaving gashes in the carcass. In fact, if you see a carcass covered in skinning slashes then it's a pretty amateur affair. The same technique outlined above may be used with skinning goats, though sheep are an entirely different story; the tightly attached hide requiring the butcher to punch the skin off with their fist.

The next step is to work on eviscerating the body. And for this you may want to place a tub or wheelbarrow below the body to allow the viscera to fall into. Begin by making an incision around the anus, cutting close to the tail and pelvic bones until the rectum is loose and may be pulled away with a length of the colon attached. Squeeze any contents in the colon back towards the intestines and then tie a piece of string round the tube.

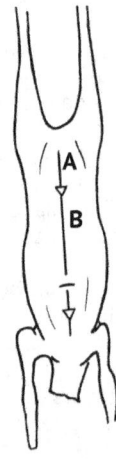

Another way of doing this is to make the first, top, incision in the abdominal cavity (right, at A), and then reach inside for the colon. Reaching as far as you can along the colon towards the anus (still integral with the carcass) squeeze any gubbins backwards towards the stomach, then tie round the emptied section with string, and cut above the string to separate the colon from the attached anus; the tied end of the colon falling back into the cavity.

In my view that second way is perhaps preferable in terms of hygiene since only the tied-off colon end returns to the body cavity. In the case of the anus with colon attached, if this is left hanging outside the first abdominal incision it gets somewhat in the way of cutting further down the abdominal cavity (B on previous diagram), while at worst the whole lot, fur and everything, falls back into the cavity potentially contaminating it. However, it does have the advantage that once the body cavity is open a gentle pull of the complete tied anal end will bring all the intestinal innards with it, followed by the bladder and kidneys once the ureter is cut.

Gravity does most of the work for you (right). Sometimes the bladder is removed as a deliberate second step after the colon has been tied off and cut. Look for a yellowy-white balloon-like structure near the hind legs (it will probably be inflated with urine) and, once located, squeeze the exit tube tightly to hold back the urine, and then cut away and discard the bladder.

Separate and remove the kidneys and liver from the rest of the entrails, in readiness for taking out the heart and lungs. There are slightly different methods of doing the latter and you can take your pick. In the previous diagram I have marked two underside cuts A and B – the main abdominal one and then a second through the chest cavity. This is because some folks gutting deer in the suspended position will saw through the sternum, or chest bone, while the deer is on the ground, and also make the first incisions into the body cavity, though leave the guts in place. Others simply cut through the thin chest diaphragm that separates the heart and lung cavity from the intestinal cavity, to get at those organs when the animal in the suspended position. To a certain extent in a post-disaster world you might not have access to a saw, so reaching internally for the heart / lungs makes more sense. The drawback is that sometimes the oesophagus is a bit difficult to pull out, but if this is the case cut down along the neck underside, work the windpipe and oesophagus loose, and then pull them out from inside the body cavity.

ABDOMINAL CUTTING TECHNIQUE
To open the abdominal cavity, pinch together a piece of skin between the two hind legs and gently make a horizontal cut – until you can visibly see darkness beneath. Extend the incision till it is just big enough to insert your index and second fingers plus a little bit extra. Insert those fingers of your free hand into the cut, facing towards you and pushed apart. Place the tip of the knife between your fingers with the blade facing outwards towards you, and then gradually make the abdominal cut by working your fingers under the skin to keep it away from the intestines then lengthening the cut, and so on. Take your time, there's no rush. In fact cutting into the intestines with all the gloop they contain is probably an infinitely worse crime than slashing into the carcass while removing the hide.

All that remains to do is butcher the carcass along the lines that you would expect from other supermarket meat products – chops, shank, ribs, and so on. You already have the heart, lungs, liver, kidney and spleen, not forgetting the blood (nothing goes to waste in the doomsday kitchen). That said, in an emergency situation it would be better to leave the eviscerated carcass as untouched as possible, with the tough white membrane that covers the muscle left intact. It acts as a very good barrier against flies laying their eggs in the meat, and the more the membrane dries off after skinning the tougher that barrier becomes. If the carcass is also hung near the smoke and warmth of a fire (but not hot enough to cook it!) then this also helps with fly deterrence. This is why not slashing the outer membrane when removing the hide becomes important. Exposed, moist, meat is inviting to flies. What's more, if you portion the meat along Continental lines where individual muscles are separated into 'cuts', then the use of that protective 'membrane barrier' concept can be continued for some time.

GOAT

In a long-term survival situation you might consider rearing a goat or two, or maybe you will need to barter for goat milk or meat should it materialize. Goats seem to be pretty rugged animals, amiable and friendly, and can be pets too, while they also provide milk for a large period of the year and good tasting meat (why do you think people in many other corners of the world have goats as their chief livestock?).

Many readers, like myself, have probably come across some goaty-smelling cheese which doesn't appeal to the senses, and the milk *can* be like that if not treated properly. When goat's milk is very fresh it doesn't smell 'goaty' at all, although when still warm it may smell a little. It is a bit thicker and sweeter than cow's milk but does not keep as long, and when used in cooking seems to curdle more readily if not absolutely fresh. Once cooled in an airy place it loses any animal smell, though if left for a couple of days and it begins to decompose the milk will begin to get that 'goaty' smell. You also have the option of boiling the fresh milk to pasteurize it and extend its keeping life.

Goat's milk cheese and butter (rather pale looking and not keeping very well) can be made from the milk too, and the recipes for making cheese elsewhere can be used for goat's milk too. As with the milk itself, if, when making the butter, any of buttermilk remains within the fat solids then it will turn the butter goaty smelling after few days.

Goat meat is rather more dark than mutton, has a grain closer to that of venison, and tastes great, particularly young kid meat. If you have never tried goat meat before, see if you can find a Caribbean restaurant near to you and try the goat curry. Thinking about it, some supermarkets now stock fresh goat's milk, so you can give that a try too. Personally, I am not too keen on goat's milk as a drink on its own, but in tea, coffee, or cooking you would be hard-pressed to tell the difference from cow's milk. Like venison, goat's meat is also very lean (although the kidneys are generally fatty), so like venison and pheasant the meat needs regular basting or a form of 'moist' cooking to keep the meat from becoming too dry. As with any other four-legged animal, almost every part of the goat carcass can be utilized as food; from the traditional meat cuts, to brains, offal and other bits, and the meat may be similarly cured and pickled to preserve it.

To butcher a goat follow exactly the same procedure as for deer on the previous pages.

SQUIRREL

The grey squirrel (*Sciurus carolinensis*) is a major pest well known to gardeners and foresters, and makes a useful food resource. Since it has a decided weakness for stealing food and tidbits left for birds, and is not shy of being seen, squirrel is capable of being easily hunted / trapped.

Skinning grey squirrels is tricky; the pelt being quite hard to remove while the scrawny body doesn't really give you very much to hold on to when skinning and gutting. Essentially, for dressing squirrel, follow the basics as for rabbit, though I wouldn't bother going to the effort of hanging the animal up by its rear legs. Another alternative is to make an incision in the pelt at the centre of back, widen to a couple of fingers width, and then pull off the skin towards the front and rear.

Squirrels obtained from deciduous woodland are preferable in taste to those from pure pine forest regions. On the occasions when I have eaten squirrel they have mostly been roasted over the fire, or parts broiled or fried, and are not much shakes in the gourmet stakes in either in terms of taste or amount of food provided. But it is food nevertheless. Something I must put on my 'to do' list is simply jointing the carcass and then very slowly stewing it so that the meat flakes away from the bones, while at the same time perhaps extracting some of the goodness from those bones for soup or gravy. The brains can be roasted over a fire inside the skull and then eaten.

AMPHIBIANS

Given that the frog population in this country is somewhat fragile, I would not consider eating the legs as a foodstuff even if times were hard. Frogs have a role to play in the environment so I think it is worth conserving them. Maybe, if there *really* was *nothing* else around, I would eat the legs.

The other thing is that the frogs here tend to be rather small for the food reward offered. That said, I think there might be a case for experimenting with breeding a captive frog population if there was long-term meltdown of society... The process would need to begin with a small clutch of eggs taken from a larger batch, and then reared over several years to produce a viable colony. For their feed they could be raised on home-raised insect or snail populations (see page 28), so creating an almost closed-loop production method.

BIRDS

Small birds are such an integral part of the landscape that most Outdoors' people love that it would perhaps somehow feel inappropriate to use them as food. In normal life most wild birds have some sort of 'protection', but if there is no food, then where do you draw the line? Most small birds really do not have a body weight sizeable enough to make them useful. However, that is not to say that they have not been used as food in the past. Larks, thrushes and ortolans have all been kitchen fare at some time or other.

Larks and wheatear, for example, were not drawn nor feet cut off, but simply larded or wrapped with bacon then roasted on wooden skewers. Ortolans were plucked, singed, the beak and feet cut off and then wrapped in paper and baked or roasted. Even humble sparrows (now becoming rather rare) were regarded as potential food as the following early 20th century snippet shows:

'To kill mercifully a sparrow that has been trapped, place the thumbnail at the base of its skull and dislocate its neck by hard and quick pressure. To dress it, cut off the legs, the wings at the outer joint, and the neck close to the body; strip off the skin, beginning at the neck; make a cut through the body wall extending from the neck along the backbone till the ribs are severed, then around between the legs to the tail, and remove the viscera. If sparrows are to be broiled, save only the breasts, as this method of cooking so shrivels and parches the lesser parts as to render them worthless. In this case tear off a strip of skin from wing to wing across the back; grasp the wings, in front of the body, in one hand and the neck in the other, and by a quick pull separate the breast from the ribs; turn the breast out of the skin that covers it, and sever the wings at the second joint. The whole operation requires but a fraction of a minute and it can be done by the fingers alone. Sparrows may be cooked by any of the methods employed for reedbirds or quail. When boned, broiled, buttered, and served on toast they are particularly good and compare favorably with the best kinds of small game.'

An early 19th century gardening book gave the trap design pictured right for catching small birds. Something similar could be used for catching birds of various sizes, and the design principle be transferred to a below ground-level bird trap.

PHEASANT & PIGEON

Plucking a fresh pheasant can be a bit of a messy affair, with the skin sometimes looking a bit torn. I often skin them (although in a survival situation you may not wish to throw away this potential edible morsel) and then remove the breast and leg meat – the latter becoming a source of pheasant 'mince' once the sinews are removed. Areas of meat that look bruised or are shot-damaged should be cut away, and make sure to check for any stray shot within the meat. Pheasants are usually 'hung', unplucked, for about two or three days before using.

Young birds are best, but if uncertain of the age this can be roughly determined by flexing the beak which is flexible in younger birds, while the breastbone is also softer. Old cock birds are best suited to recipes that involve stewing, casseroles and braising – in other words 'moist heats' suitable for dealing with the tougher, drier meat. Smaller hen pheasants, and younger ones, can be roasted or broiled. Roasting can take from 60 to 90 minutes.

The same sort of cautions apply to cooking game fowl as when cooking chicken – cook to the bone, as the saying goes. When baking or roasting a game bird if you insert the tip of a knife into the thigh or breast the juices that run out should be clear. A pinkish or bloody tinge demands extra time. And if you do ever come across raw meat on a cooked bird then it isn't 100% safe. If the meat has just come from the cooking process then it's fine to carry on cooking, but otherwise the same rules apply to the re-heating any meat that has cooled or chilled.

Pigeons (doves too), although tasty, are also pretty tedious to pluck, in return for what they deliver to the pot. If you have time on your hands then by all means pluck pigeons, then gut and roast them. For a simpler life (*economy of effort*), strip the skin and feathers off in one go, then gut, and stew the whole thing. Alternatively, remove the breast meat and fry, while putting the remaining carcass into your soup pot.

Pigeons, ducks and similar birds should be dressed as soon as possible after being killed, particularly pigeons where the crops need to be emptied of corn. The birds do not have to be plucked until they are about to be used.

In coastal areas seagulls, cormorants and guillemots have their uses, mostly for their eggs rather than being eaten for their meat which can have a fishy taste. Crow breast meat is very much like pigeon breast. Ornamental species like peacock make sizeable birds for food, and are usually killed two or three days before use. On the domestic front it might be worth considering raising canary birds, although they are very small, and might consume useful food while you fatten them.

FISH

The fish species covered below are almost all freshwater species, with the exception of mackerel, since it is imagined that the reader will be land-based rather than at sea. Apart from that, there would be inherent dangers in going 'out to sea' to catch fish if you are not experienced, while there may also be no fuel to propel a launch through choppy waters. The species have been selected for their widespread distribution across Europe, though some are not always found in the British Isles.

Mackerel, however, can be line caught from the shoreline so is included, while coastal rock pools would provide prawns and shrimps for your doomsday kitchen. Wrasse would also be another potential sea-fish line-caught over rocky areas.

If you are not a fisherman yet then it might be worth investing a little time in either practice – perhaps buying a few angling bits and bobs – or doing some background reading.

BARBEL – *Barbus barbus*
The barbel derives its name from the four fleshy appendages, called barbels, which protrude from around the small mouth and nose region of its head. In colour the barbel is a greenish-olive-brown above, and yellowish green on the sides; sometimes spotted with brown on the back and sides, and all the scales have a metallic lustre. The abdomen is white. The shape of the fish is quite long, generally reaching from 25 to 75 cm, and a good specimen weighs in at around 5 or 6 kilos.

Avoiding sluggish waters barbel is often found in shoals, instead preferring medium-temperature, pebbly and sandy rivers with good fast-flowing water, and dips and hollows in the bed. However, when it comes to feeding barbel roots around in the mud for insect larvae, worms and other small crustacea. More of a deep water species, particularly in winter, barbel avoids bright light and feeds during the twilight hours. While the flesh is not regarded as much of a foodstuff the roe is poisonous and should not be consumed. March to November are good times for fishing.

BLEAK, COMMON – *Alburnus alburnus*
Bleak is a delicate, slim, elongated species that rarely grows beyond 12 to 15 cm (maximum about 25 cm), with a slightly protruding bottom jaw. It prefers still water, lakes, slow-moving rivers and streams.

However, it is known to swarm in huge shoals where there is sufficient water. The soft scaled fish has an overall silvery look, with the sides, belly (scaleless), cheeks, and gill-covers all of a shining silvery white. The eyes too, are silvery, though tinged with yellow in older specimens. The back of the fish is a light greenish ash-brown tinged with blue. Bleak will rise to almost any small fly dibbed by an angler on the water surface on a fine day. Its normal food are insects and their larvae, caddis flies, small crustaceans and worms, and paste. In warm weather bait often taken higher in the water, lower when colder. Bleak has never had much of a reputation as food, but still it's food.

BREAM, COMMON – *Abramis brama*
The bream is mostly found in rather large lakes or slow running rivers, but also in brackish waters, often hiding in deep parts and feeding in the mud, although it is a gregarious, shoal-forming species in the summer. Bream has rather a deep, chunky, body appearance, being coloured a yellowish-white, with the exception of the cheeks and gill-covers, which have a silvery lustre without any tinge of yellow, while the fins have a somewhat bluish-grey tinge.

Sometimes the bream attains a considerable size, reaching 30 to 50 cm in length (maximum 80 cm), feeding in the evening on bottom-dwelling insect larvae, crustacea, wasp grubs, grasshoppers, caddis, worms and other organic bits, even paste. The boundary between deep and shallow water can be a good place to cast a line.

Once regarded as quite a delicacy there is not, in fact, very much flesh on the fish and it is rather bony. A specimen of 5 to 6 kilos is good, with the best bream caught during spring and autumn. One reference that I came across mentioned that the flesh could be dried like cod.

Other widespread related European species are the very common Silver Bream (*Abramis bjoerkna* syn. *Blicca bjo.*) which will be found in shallow waters of lakes and slow-running rivers, and the Blue Bream (*Abramis ballerus*). The latter is a gregarious, shoal-forming, bottom-fish feeding upon insect larvae, crustacea, mollusca, and worms.

CARP, COMMON – *Cyprinus carpio*
There are many forms of carp but this species is the one which is most widely distributed throughout Europe. Averaging 25 to 75 cm in length (the largest specimens can reach one metre), this particular carp species is distinguishable from all others from its long dorsal fin and four barbels by the mouth. A reasonable fish would weigh around 3 kilos.

Carp is a shy fish and in the wild will be found in slow-flowing rivers, lowland lakes, gravel pits and ponds, often with muddy bottoms; older specimens gravitate to deeper water, and immature ones closer to the banks (often collecting near trees that have collapsed into the water). Mostly bottom-feeders the main dietry items are plant materials, small invertebrates, insects and their larvae, wasp grubs, maggots, mollusca, and worms. Like the perch, carp can survive out of water for some considerable time, so could be caught and then transported to an environment where it can be raised or 'cultivated' as food. Good fishing times February to April, July and August.

Other carp species are the Crucian Carp (*Carassius carrasius*) and the Goldfish (*Carassius auratus*). Yes, goldfish!

CHUB – *Leuciscus cephalus*

A widespread species around much of Europe the chub's characteristics change with age; being a gregarious shoal-forming species when young, then becoming more solitary and recluse as it ages; seeking out quiet, deep, bottom water in winter though rising near the surface in summer. It is often found lurking beneath tree foliage overhanging the water, overhanging banks, or under blankets of surface debris. Ranging from 30 to 50 cm long (maximum about 60+ cm) chub tolerates a variety of habitats from rapid-running streams, to slow-moving rivers, gravel pits and lakes. In colour the whole of the upper part of the back is bluish-black, with a blackish-brown streak running from the top of the head towards the tail; the belly is silvery-white; ventral and anal fins are orange-white, the pectorals more red-brown; eyes are golden yellow, and the large silvery scales are dark at the base and edges.

I read somewhere that in the winter months chub prefers an animal diet, and also becomes more predaceous with age. Being large mouthed its prey can be everything from small fish to frogs, but also worms, slugs, snails, insects and their larvae, even paste. In its vegetarian and younger phase chub will eat roots, seeds and freshwater plant buds. Most anglers try to catch chub with a large fly or other bait at the surface of the water, moving the bait on the water surface with motions of the rod (a technique known as dibbing). November-March is a good fishing time, good specimens reaching 3.5 to 4.5 kilos in weight, though the flesh is regarded as rather coarse and bony, being best suited to broiling with the scales attached.

DACE – *Leuciscus leuciscus*

Dace is a small species (15 to 25 cm, maximum 30 cm), that prefers the deep, clear, quite rapid, running water of streams and rivulets, also rivers, often being found in trout streams in association with chub. Just occasionally it is found in brackish freshwater estuarine locales. It is also a gregarious, shoal-forming species. The upper part of the head and back are an olive-green to dusky blue colour, becoming paler on the sides and silvery-white on the underside. The eyes are straw yellow, the lower fins tinged a pale yellow-red, and scales quite large.

Tending to err on the side of being carnivorous dace feeds on worms, crustacea, soft water-insect larvae, maggots, grasshoppers, winged insects, paste, and it rarely achieves more than about 500 gm in weight. Tactically, try dry flies on the surface, or worms in deeper water.

GOLDFISH – *Carassius auratus*

Also known as the Gold Carp, it is doubtful that this species needs any introduction since it forms the basis of fish stock in many garden ponds. It can be eaten, and if the temperature of a pond can be raised with artificial warmth, then young fish can attain quite rapid growth to about 12 cm in length during the first twelve months. Apparently in the days of 19th century industrial expansion, excess heat from mill boilers was channelled through goldfish ponds, though there is no mention of whether the goldfish fish output was for human consumption, breeding purposes, or stocking garden ponds.

GUDGEON, COMMON – *Gobio gobio*
A somewhat variable species, gudgeon is a slim fish reaching 10 to 20 cm in length, prefers sandy or gravelly rivers and streams, particularly where shallow scours increase the water current, but is also found in canals and flooded gravel pits. Gregarious and shoal-forming, in colour gudgeon has sort of olive-brown upper parts, blotched with black spots, the throat is scaleless, and it has a flat belly. Indeed, gudgeon is more of a bottom-feeder, feeding on worms, aquatic insects and their larvae, and small mollusca. Easily caught (best time in hot summer months) with rod and line, an old angling trick of the past was to rake up or disturb the gravel bed in a stream which would entice the gudgeon to go hunting for newly exposed food. They can be semi-farmed also, in that young fry about 2 cm long can be kept in freshwater-fed tanks and fattened till large enough to eat – about 2 to 3 years.

LOACH, STONE – *Barbatula barbatula*
Not only is the stone loach a small fish but it can also be a hard fish species to spot since it tends to lurk under stones and hide among the weeds of clear, shallow, fast-running streams and rivers. It is also found in some lakes and occasionally in brackish waters. Growing to about 8 to 12 cm (maximum 18 cm), the loach is found across much of Europe though not in the northern and southern extremes. It has an elongated, smooth, body covered with a mucous secretion that makes it slippery to handle. The head is rounded with a flattened top, the eyes and mouth small, nose downward pointing, and six barbels – four above the upper lip and two to the sides of the mouth. In colour the stone loach is a spotted or blotchy brown with the belly tending to a yellowish white, while the fins are spotted dark brown that give the impression of banded rays. It is a night feeder, and also a bottom-feeder, the diet being a mixture of worms, maggots, and aquatic insects, particularly the larvae. Despite their small size loach meat tastes good.

There is also a Spined Loach (C*obitis taenia*) which can be usefully fished.

ORFE – *Leuciscus idus*
Orfe, once known as the Ide, is a species mainly of rivers, but finds its way into rivers to spawn in the spring period. It is sometimes found in brackish waters. The range is limited in the British Isles, but orfe is widely found through northern continental Europe, being an important fish stock towards Russia.

Growing to about 35 to 50 cm (maximum 100 cm) the forehead and back are a dark bluish-black, the belly silvery white, fins of an orange-red colour, scales large, and the eyes straw yellow with black pupils. The mouth is relatively small, and the diet omnivorous tending towards being more carnivorous with age. When young the diet will include some plant material, while the meat intake includes small invertebrates, crustaceous larvae, and mollusca which are a favourite food.

PERCH – *Perca fluviatilis*

Perch is found in rivers, ponds and lowland lakes across most temperate parts of Europe, and has a firm, white, flesh. The perch is not a large fish [20 to 35 cm, sometimes to 50 cm], specimens of 1 to 1.5 kilos being considered rather heavy. The colour is a greenish brown above, gradually becoming golden-white below. A row of 5 to 7 dark transverse bands mark the sides. The first dorsal fin is brown, with a little black; the second dorsal and pectoral fins are pale brown; all other fins are bright red. Perch does not like too rapid a current so it is not often seen mid-stream, preferring to haunt the banks and similar retreats where there is bottom weed cover, or root and tree debris. When the water is clear, and on a fine day, perch will resort to deep holes by the bank.

It feeds upon all kinds of aquatic worms, insects, maggots, and small fishes (such as minnow, young roach, dace, and gudgeon), preferring the latter diet as it becomes older and larger. A bait formed of these fish, or in imitation of them, will often work well. Although generally inhabiting mid or deep water (particularly older specimens), perch will sometimes come to the surface to snap up a casual fly that has fallen into the water, so fishing with a fly for trout may work too. By all accounts this is a good species to fish for during the winter months. One particular aspect of the perch that might prove useful for long-term farming of the species is that it can live for a long time out of water, and be transported over considerable distances with only occasional watering. This could be an advantage if you wanted to set up fish-ponds to farm perch.

PIKE – *Esox lucius*

The pike is represented in most of northern Europe, preferring standing and slow-flowing waters. The pike is a long-lived fish, attaining sizes up to 150 cm, though generally in the range of 30 to 120 cm. Weights of 4.5 to 5.5 kilos are considered good, but specimens of up to 34 kilos have been caught. In colour the pike is olive-brown along its' back, lighter-hued on the sides, and variegated bands of greenish-yellow. The abdomen is silvery white. Dorsal fin often spotted or striped. It has a reputation of being the shark of freshwater such is its voracious appetite, eating almost anything that comes within reach including small fish. A young perch with the dorsal fin removed is said to be a good pike bait, and anglers can use lures and deadbait (the latter particularly above areas of bottom weed cover).

Pike often make their home in secluded holes or hollows sheltered by overhanging soil or roots, from which they can pounce on passing prey, as they also do in weed bed areas. Between February and May, older pikes move from larger rivers and ascend creeks and narrow ditches to spawn, providing an opportunity for capturing by penning between nets rather than using rod and line.

ROACH, COMMON – *Rutilus rutilus*
Roach is a common freshwater fish somewhat variable in appearance (often hybridizing with the Rudd – *Scardinius erythrophthalmus*), and lives in both slow- flowing and still waters though, by all accounts, can tolerate some salinity in the water. Where there is faster running water then roach may be found retreating in the eddies and calmer areas. Overhung areas of canals can be good too. Reaching 20 to 35 cm, with a top end of around 50 cm, the roach has upper parts of a silvery to greyish-green tinged with blue coloration, with the purest forms of the species being almost black in colour. The abdomen is frequently silvery white, with the pectoral, ventral, and anal fins of a bright orange-red-brown colour, and the scales large. Although the flesh is firm and white, it is regarded as having a somewhat muddy flavour.

Although a gregarious, shoal-forming, omnivorous species it can be somewhat picky in its feeding habits; warm weather seeing roach rise to pick off flies, while often bottom feeding, particularly in winter, when it prefers deeper waters. In these areas worms and maggots can be used as bait, worms particularly in spring. Paste can also work. Autumn to spring is a good time to fish for this species.

RUDD – *Scardinius erythrophthalmus*
A very common fish in Europe the rudd, unfortunately, does not have a good reputation as food, nor does it get much bigger than about 1 kilo in weight; ranging from about 15 to 30 cm in length, maximum 45 cm. Still, it's food for the doomsday cook. It is a species of sluggish rivers, lakes and sometimes brackish waters, loving spots where there are weeds to lurk among.

The body is somewhat deep, with a slight concave dip behind the head, and there is a steep, upward-slanting mouth. In colour, the upper part of the back is brown, tinged green-blue; the sides more pale with the belly a light golden yellow. Indeed, with the large shiny scales, the body surface has a brilliant orange-red golden hue, the angle of view giving different specular coloration. The eyes too have a yellow-orange-gold coloration. The lower fins are a bright red, while the tail and upper dorsal fin more reddish-brown. Its diet includes some vegetable matter, but also worms, mollusca and insects (which it sucks from the water surface – a good place to start casting baited hooks).

RUFFE – *Gymnocephalus cernuus*
Related to the perch, the ruffe is a freshwater species that likes slow to moderately-flowing rivers, also canals and lakes, where there is deep, shady water, but it is also known to exist in areas of brackish water in the Baltics. Growing roughly 10 to 15 cm in length, rarely to 30 cm, the flesh is considered good. The summer months from May to August are a good time to fish.

The name derives from the rough nature of the scales, while the colour of the upper part of the body and head is a light olive brown, passing to a yellow-brown on the sides, and nearly silver-white on the belly. Eye irises are brown and the pupil blue, while another distinguishing feature are the two joined dorsal fins. Ruffe feeds on the fry of other fish, and various aquatic mollusca, invertebrates, crustacea and also insect larvae, so a morsel of red worm is a good starting point for bait.

TENCH – *Tinca tinca*
Tench is a light-avoiding, mud loving, bottom-dweller of still water lakes and ponds, pits, sometimes of slow-flowing rivers. With an average size of 20 to 40 cm, reaching a maximum of about 60 cm, tench is of a greenish-olive colour, darker above than below, and with a fine yellow sheen. Other distinguishing features are golden-reddish eyes, the two short barbels by the mouth, quite rounded fins, and the scales are covered in slime. The flesh is white and firm, and much valued as food.

Tench is a night feeder, with a fondness for freshwater snails, but also eats worms, insect larvae, wasp grubs, maggots, crustacea and plant material. Paste with a little honey is an old bait used. April to August is a good time for taking tench.

TROUT, BROWN – *Salmo trutta*
Probably a very familiar fish, even to those who do not consider themselves to be anglers, the trout is found in rivers and suitable lakes right across Europe; from the northern Mediterranean to tip of Scandinavia. Ranging in size from 15 to 50 cm (70 cm maximum), the trout is variable in coloration; from greenish-dark reddish brown (in freshwater) to more silvery (sea run form), but always with dark spots – varying in number – on the body and gills.

Trout is found in rapid and clear-running streams and rivers, preferring the shelter of a hole in the bank or stone to open and shallow areas of water. As with the pike, the hiding-hole is a lair from which it can predate, taking minnows, worms, or flies as food.

VIMBA – *Vimba vimba*
Vimba is not a species encountered in British waters – as far as I know – but is another of the continental European species thrown into the freshwater mix since it is found pretty widespread, although its ecology means that it is a species more of brackish (even marine) waters but migrates into rivers to spawn in summer. It grows to a maximum of about 50 cm in length, but more generally from 25 to 35 cm. Vimba is still called Silver Bream in some parts of Europe where it is commercially exploited; in some areas to a point that there are now worries about over-exploitation. The body has a dark bluish-grey back coloration with the sides silvery, though during spawning season that becomes tinged with yellow. The eyes are yellow. In freshwater areas it prefers fast-

flowing gravelly waters, breeding in shallows, with a diet of mollusca and insect larvae.

ZANDER – *Sander lucioperca* (syn. *Stizostedion lucioperca*)
Common mainly across northern and central continental Europe, but introduced into the UK, zander is sometimes referred to as the pike-perch. And while this species is regarded as good eating by anglers, conservationists despair at its voracious, predatory, ways. Growing some 30 to 70 cm on average (sometimes 1 metre) zander has a grey-green or brown back, pales below, plus two large dorsal fins, one quite spiny.

The sort of habitat that zander likes is a little similar to pike – slow-flowing water, shallow lakes, fens, and canals. However, they do not tolerate eutrophic, oxygen deficient, waters well. Unlike pike, which likes clear water for hunting its prey, zander can tolerate murky waters. When young the zander's diet is mainly small invertebrates, gradually migrating to larger fish as it matures, and hence the conservationists' worries.

EEL – *Anguilla anguilla*
Eels need little descriptive introduction. They like a quite still water with a muddy bottom, and are found in canals, ponds, mill dams / ponds, under weirs, bridge piles, reservoirs and rivers where a quieter hollow of water provides a more calm habitat, often where there are weeds, tree roots and large stones. They are somewhat averse to cold weather.

If line rod / line fishing then a dark and gloomy, or rainy, day is a good time, and they can often be caught on multi-hooked nightlines pegged to a stake. A traditional osier eel 'trap' can be made for catching them, or a sealed wooden box with a hole cut in it used, or a weighted bag full of offal and suchlike bits. These traps are sunk into those places where eels are known, or expected, to lurk. Two other old 'trap' tricks were a loosely bound bundle of hay inside which offal was placed, and also bundles of brushwood similarly baited, which were lowered into the water and tied off to the bank. When hauled out of the water the eels find it difficult to escape from the mass of straw or twigs. Bottom cast baits are a good tactic; eel taking worms, small fishes like gudgeon and minnows, while fish entrails, and also raw meat, foul meat, and poultry guts are good for baiting those eel 'traps' mentioned.

To skin an eel hold the head in your hand with a piece of cloth round the head to stop the eel slipping. Cut through the skin round the neck and peel it down a couple of centimetres to give you something to grasp with your free hand. Take hold of the skin and then pull in one direction while pulling the head in the opposite direction. Then carefully open along the belly with a knife and removed the guts without breaking any internal organs.

SANDEEL, Greater & Lesser – *Hyperoplus* and *Ammodytes*
Although they share the name 'eel' with the previous species above, the sandeels are actually unrelated. Normally sandeels do not appear on the food radar, except as angling bait, and indeed local fishermen near me are sometimes seen prodding round a sandspit in the river (it's estuarine) for sandeels as bait.

These two species have long, slender, silvery bodies, a slender pointed snout, and a shallow dorsal fin running almost all along the back. A similarly shallow anal fin runs along about one third of the underside. A key identification difference between the two species is that the greater sandeel (*Hyperoplus lanceolatus*) develops a dark smudge on the snout in front of the eyes, while this smudge is absent in the lesser sandeel (*Ammodytes tobianus*). They respectively grow to about 20 cm and 15 cm in size. That may sound small, but they are often found in shoals, particularly the lesser sandeel which has a quite gregarious nature. Industrially, they have been harvested for fertilizer and fishmeal – such a terrible waste. They are generally found 15 cm under shallow gravelly and sand substrates, often in estuarine areas, where they can rapidly (like lightning) burrow to hide from predators, and also shelter against the tides. The greater sandeel will inhabit water depths to 100 / 150 m and the lesser down to 30 to 50 metres.

To harvest sandeels you will need to head for wet sand and dig them out with a spade which helps prevent them slithering away and hiding again. As a precaution wear gloves when scrabbling for them if they fall back since there may be weaver fish inhabiting the same sand beds. To prepare as food, hold them for a few hours in a bucket of the same local water to allow the guts to work through, and / or massage the belly to evacuate the stomach contents. They can be barbied on long skewers or deep-fried like über-large whitebait.

MINNOW – *Phoxinus phoxinus*
This small inhabitant of many of our rivers, brooks, and canals is one of the best known fish species, by name at least, but it also tastes good when cooked up like a large whitebait (see safety note opposite). Generally found in the same sort of habitats as trout it sometimes swims in shoals, preferring clear water, and shallow sands and gravels; certainly when spawning around June. This minnow species (there are others across Europe) ranges in size from 6 to 10 cm, perhaps a little longer – or about the size of an anchovy. Around spawning time the male's belly and under parts become pink coloured, although the natural coloration is a white belly and the head and back of a mottled dusky olive, these markings sometimes forming into roughly shaped stripes. It has a somewhat short snout and feeds on aquatic plants, worms, and small portions of animal substance, so a little piece of worm on a hook may catch you some with a rod and line. Alternatively, construct a soda-pop bottle minnow trap and fish for them passively.

BITTERLING – *Rhodeus amarus*
European bitterling (*Rhodeus amarus*) is a small fish found across most of western Europe to Russia, being an introduced species in the UK (though I am uncertain how widespread). It is small, growing to a maximum of about 9 cm (more often 4 to 5 cm), and somewhat minnow-like in habitat and appearance. There are around twenty other bitterling species one of which used to be quoted as a key bitterling species, *Rhodeus sericeus*. However, this is more of an east European species. *Rhodeus amarus* will be found in streams with clear, slow-flowing, water with sandy bottoms, but also ponds, lakes and muddy backwaters, and waters with lots of weeds in them. Both *R. amaraus* and *sericeus* are mostly found where freshwater mussels exist, since these play an active role in their breeding cycle. They feed on plant material as well as small bugs, worms, and so on.

STICKLEBACKS – *Gasterosteus aculeatus / Pungitius pungitius*
The two species of sticklebacks that have the widest distribution across Europe are the three-spined (*Gasterosteus aculeatus*) and the nine-spined (*Pungitius pungitius*) types. They are both very small fish, and for food are cooked like whitebait. The three-spined form grows from 4 to 10 cm long, and gets its name from the three spines running along the back. Although it inhabits lakes and rivers this variety is also found in riverine habitats close to the sea, appearing to tolerate brackish waters. From this point of view, if you were going to man-manage sticklebacks as a food resource, then it may be possible to move live specimens as fish-stock between these two types of water. During the mating season the male develops a pinky-red underside, with the remaining scales taking on a green iridescent hue. The 9-spined variety is a smaller species, lives in similar habitats and, despite its name, may have between seven and twelve spines running along its back. Both species live on a diet of worms, crustacea and insect larvae.

SMALL FISH SAFETY
It is common for small fish such as whitebait to be cooked or deep-fried without gutting them, since they are so small and the intestinal contents insignificant. In a post-disaster world, where there may be contaminants at play, my own view would be that it will be safer to catch minnows, sticklebacks and sandeels, then keep them unfed in a holding net immersed in water and allow existing gut contents to passively work through.

MACKEREL – *Scomber scombrus*
Mackerel is one marine fish species that is also accessible from the land, providing you can cast a line from a harbour wall, jetty, river mouth or coastal rock formation, hence its inclusion among the other fish species here. Growing about 40 to 60 cm long when mature, mackerel has small, smooth, scales, a brilliant iridescent blue-green striped pattern along the upper body, and a silvery underside. It's a sleek machine in the water; its shallow body and sharply angular, cleft, tail fin and other aerofoil-like fins, making it a fast mover. Mackerel is a voracious feeder, and will bite at any bait that looks like a small

fish – which is why anglers use fish-shaped lures to catch them. However, there are stories around that they will 'take' simple silver foil lures round a hook. The best time to catch them from the shore is during the May-June breeding season when shoals of mackerel come inshore to feed. During the winter they tend to retreat into deeper water.

APPROXIMATE TIMES FOR FISHING

If the seasons of a particular year are exceedingly hot or cold** then they are going to have a bearing on the activity of individual fish species, so the following details will vary.

JANUARY. Pike, chub, roach. Middle, or warmest part, of the day. Weather still and the water clear.

FEBRUARY. Perch, carp, chub, roach, pike. Middle, or warmest part, of the day. Mildest days preferable, in eddies and near banks.

MARCH. Pike, carp, perch, roach, dace, chub, gudgeon, minnow. Middle of the day, in eddies and shallows.

APRIL. Species from March, above, plus trout and tench in rivers, barbel, bleak, eel in shallow waters and sharps.

MAY. All sorts of fish bite well this month. Eels, night and day.

JUNE. Often the main spawning season so not a favourable angling month as fish out of condition. Trout may be taken.

JULY. Post-spawning, all sorts begin to take a variety of bait again.

AUGUST. Fish begin to bite more. Best times, morning and evening.

SEPTEMBER. Barbel, roach, chub, and dace in deep waters till Spring. Shot baits to reach bottom.

OCTOBER. Roach and chub in bottoms. Not a good month for ponds or still waters.

NOVEMBER. Roach, pike, and chub if weather good. Middle, or warmest part, of the day.

DECEMBER. Not favourable as waters thick and often frozen. Roach, chub, pike may still bite.

** Largely speaking, the best times to fish are when waters have either warmed up, or cooled down, depending on season and species. Spring snows / frosts need to be out of the way, then fish will start to bite mid-morning, becoming more active around midday. In summer it might be best between 5 and 9 am and 5 to 9 pm, when the sun is not high and then dips down in the evening. As cooler autumn comes along then the warmer part of the day is around mid-morning to midday, to late afternoon / early evening. In the winter months really only the warm parts of a day will be useful.

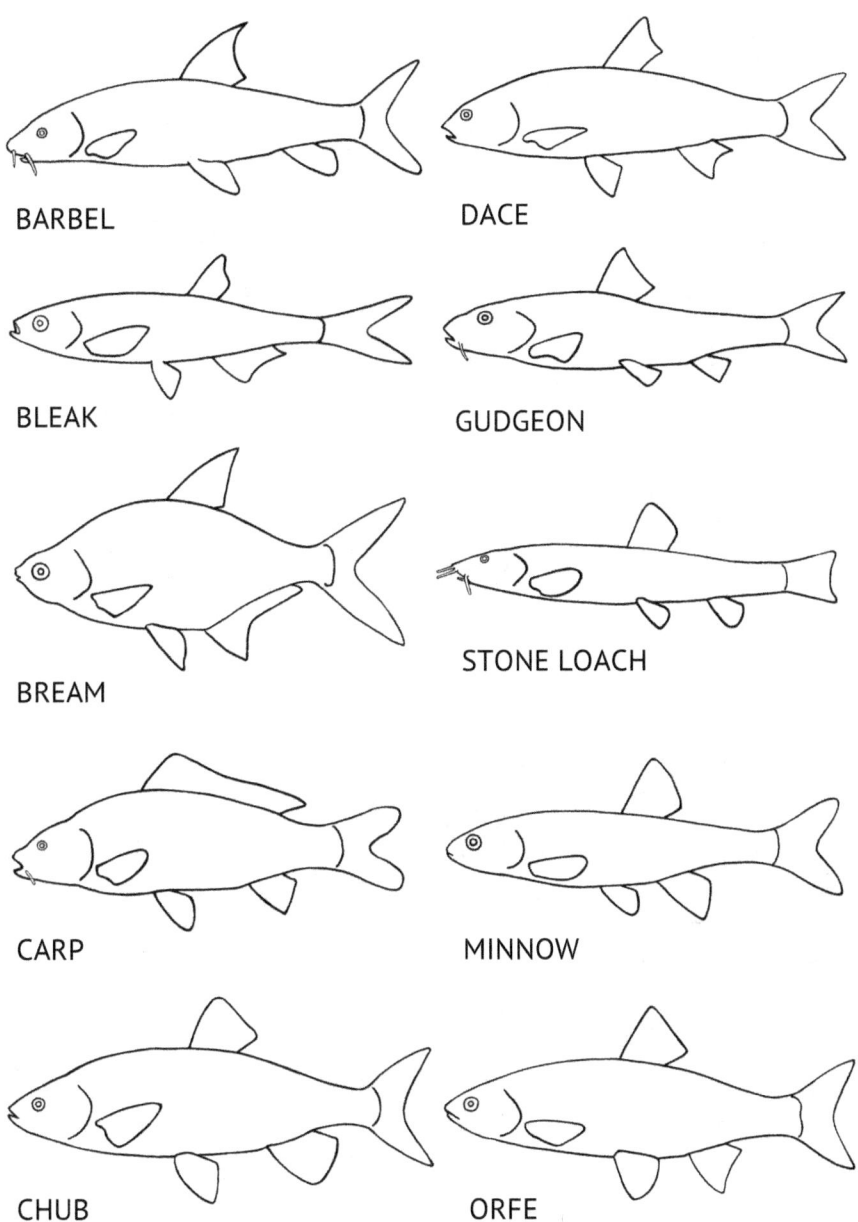

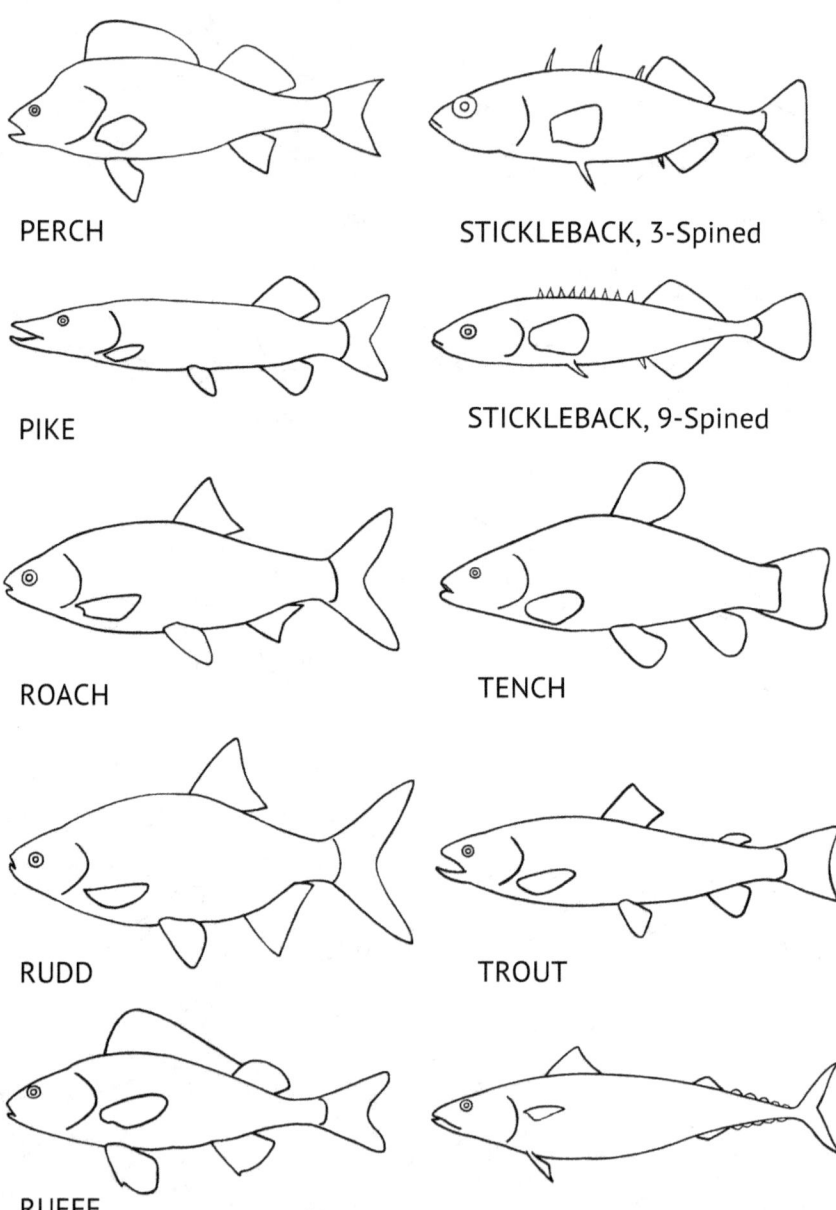

GOOD SPOTS TO FISH

Successful fishing or angling eludes even seasoned fisherfolk sometimes, and they are folks 'in the know'. If you are not familiar with casting a line (or even trapping fish), here are a couple of visualizations of some good spots to hunt for fish – freshwater ones.

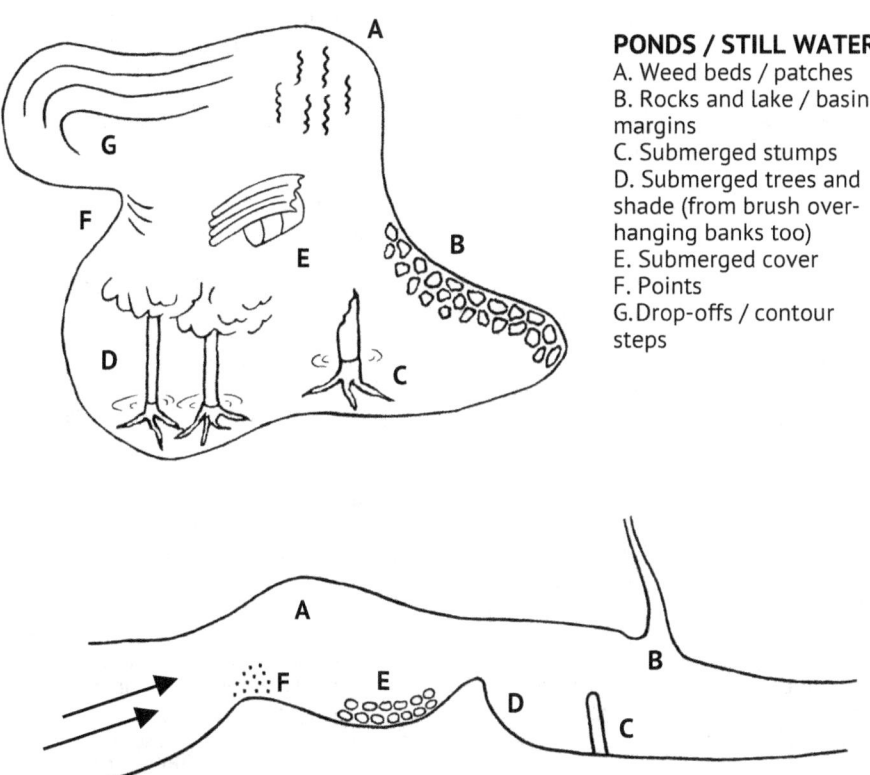

PONDS / STILL WATER
A. Weed beds / patches
B. Rocks and lake / basin margins
C. Submerged stumps
D. Submerged trees and shade (from brush overhanging banks too)
E. Submerged cover
F. Points
G. Drop-offs / contour steps

RIVERS
A. Deep river bends and undercuts
B. Mouths of feeder streams
C. Behind wing dams and fallen trees
D. Eddies and backwash pools
E. Riprap stone banks
F. Holes below riffles and behind rocks

PASSIVE & SIMPLE FISHING

Throughout this book there is reference to *economy of effort* when it comes to true survival, since any effort is likely to need feeding with calorific food intake. *Cost of acquisition* is another related aspect of food sourcing; weighing up the risks and energy expended, among other things, to acquire a food resource. Fishing is one area that both of these concepts apply to. Yes, it is possible to have a hook and line, and spend hours attempting to catch your dinner, perhaps getting sunburnt or frozen to death in the process as you are exposed to the elements while casting your line.

A much better option is passive fishing, where there is minimal effort involved in hunting your prey and catching it, though it is not the purpose of this book to delve seriously into hunting and trapping techniques for all the animal species covered. Essentially we are talking about *trapping* fish here, and in some countries there are strict limitations on trapping, particularly in freshwater areas.

Perhaps one of the best known passive fish traps is the 'minnow trap', frequently referred to in survival books, which can be made in less than a minute by cutting off the neck and crown of a plastic soda-pop bottle then placing the inverted Y-shaped neck section back into the base of the bottle and fixing in place. The main drawback with this design is that it catches small fish with little calorific value, though the funnelling concept is used in many commercial fish traps but scaled up.

The pages that follow show some representations of fish traps (generally passive) used successfully in various parts of the world. In nearly every case there is an initial personal investment of time and effort required to fabricate the trapping hardware, but after that only occasionally maintenance, the fixing of problems, and collecting the daily catch.

The first example (pictured below) is my personal variation on a simple Vietnamese trap used for catching eels in paddy fields. The real version is made from hollow bamboo tube about 70 to 90 cm long, and 5 or 6 cm wide, and baited with worms. The bottom end of the tube is solid, formed from the natural joint between two bamboo cells or sections, while the entrance is fashioned from split bamboo slivers formed into a removable funnel shape, the inner opening just large enough to allow an eel to squirm through.

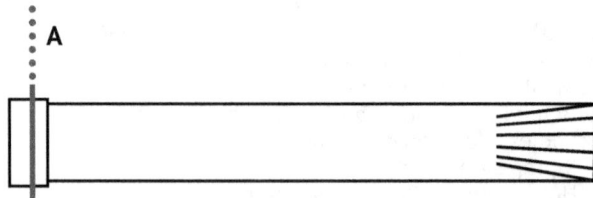

In my personal twist on this trap the tubing is made from 5 or 6 cm PVC drain pipe. The bottom end where the bait is placed, has a removable mesh or gauze cap (the gaps helping the smell of the bait circulate in the water) fixed in place with a piece of wire, while a cone shaped funnel made of stiff plastic strips from a PTFE soda-pop bottle is inserted into the open end and permanently fixed in place with wire or clips. So in my version it is the baiting end which is removable and not the funnel. The dotted line at 'A' in the diagram represents a variation on the paddy field trap, in that the Vietnamese trappers use a fine long bamboo cane to both fix the funnel in place and also act as a 'marker' for the trap, the bamboo cane projecting above the paddy water level.

The next example pictured below depicts the principle behind a fish trapping technique used in the paddy fields of Cambodia but could be adapted for small channels in estuarine environments or dykes known to contain fish. In the example seen an active flow irrigation channel about one metre wide (A) was partly blocked (A^1) then the mouth of the catchment net pegged into place across the remaining channel width. The full length of net extended about three metres with the end simply tied to a single post in the paddy field, and consisted of nothing more than a coarse (so porous) plastic sacking material that allowed irrigation water to pass through (B), was open at the top like a gutter but with the far end tied off, and dipping slightly in shape to contain the fish in a mass.

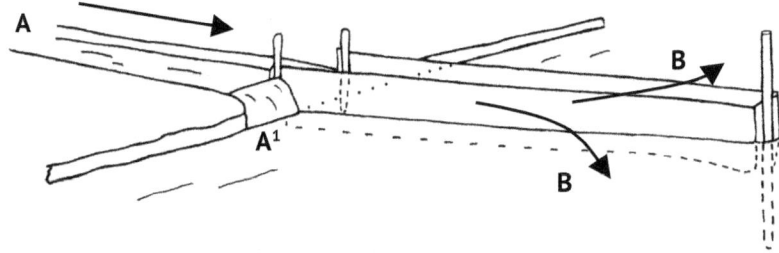

Also from Cambodia, specifically the area of Tonle Sap lake, is the passive barrage fish trap represented in the diagram below. The traps used by the artisan fishermen are made from bamboo or reeds sewn together and then staked into the muddy bottom of the lake, the long curtain section being anything from 50 to 100 metres in length. The theory (which obviously works in practice since the lake is full of similar traps) is that fish encountering the curtain wall are forced to follow its length towards the funnels which trap them. Tonle Sap lake floods annually with a huge migratory fish population moving with the incoming and receding water levels, and these traps appear to be placed to catch fish on both the inward and outward phases of the annual flood.

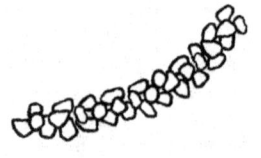
A variation on the curved catchment trap method (left) is used in coastal areas of the Arabian Gulf where the intertidal waters are shallow; being a wall of stones about 50 to 70 cm high and about 10 to 15 metres long, and placed close to high tide level. This is a traditional fishing method in the area, catching fish in the curved trap as the tide recedes.

The next two examples of passive traps from a coastal area (and made with hurdle-like latticework), show how varied localized fishing philosophy can be. In the left hand example with the more triangular catchment enclosure the trap faced outwards towards the sea and was so designed to trap fish on the ebb of the tide, while the right hand set-up was arranged to trap fish on the incoming tide. In both cases a straight central barrier curtain aims to divert fish towards the penning area. The dotted lines represent a variation on the two chambered trap seen in a rocky reef-like area; the structure being made of piled rocks though having no central straight guide but instead two guiding arms, one of them curved to deter fish from returning to the sea if they turn the wrong way upon encountering the barrier.

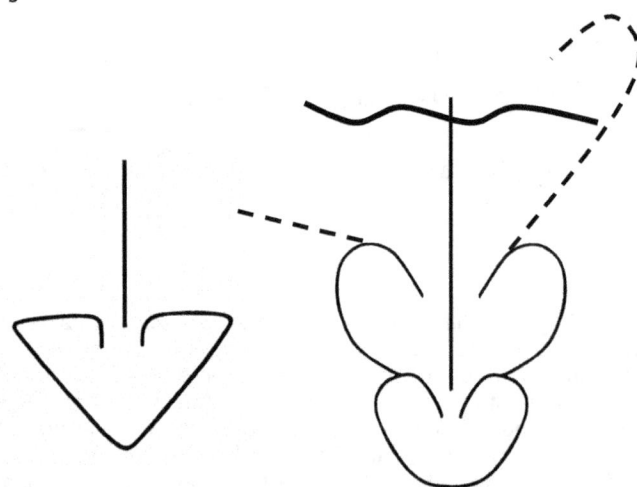

The example below comes from central Europe where this virtually omni-directional set-up is used for trapping in lakes; the main trap curtain and guides constructed of woven or stitched reeds, although twigs could be used.

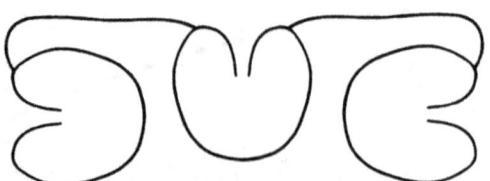

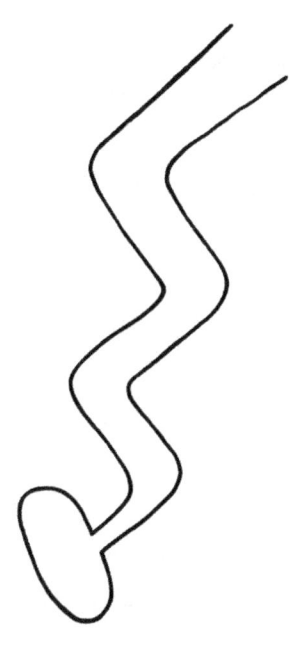

Left: Another example from central Europe for trapping fish in lakes. A passive funnel trap made of stitched reeds.

Right: From Tonle Sap lake, a series of relatively large chambers made of interlinked bamboo canes, and leading to a trapping pot (about 120 to 140 cm long).

Below right: A complex array of chambers for trapping in the direct line with the flow of river water.

Below: Another river design, the concept of which is a barrage of traps across the water flow, interlinked by guiding hoops; so traps are added at X and Z too. Made of twig and branch hurdles.

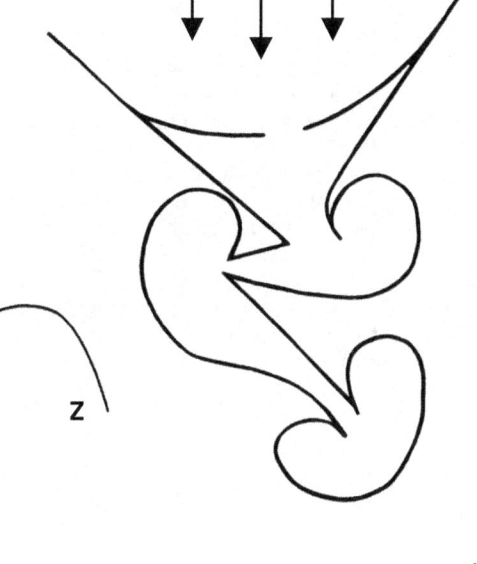

The next item is a take on the 'dip net' concept and is used for catching crabs; a piece of bacon being fixed to the centre of the netting. The net is then lowered into the water in a position where it may be observed, and when crabs start to clamber on-board it is lifted quickly out of the water and the crabs harvested. In size you are looking at a dimension of roughly 50 to 70 cm square.

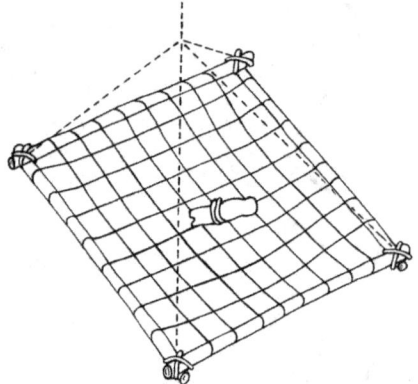

There is always some slack given in the net, rather than it being held taught, though designs which are used to catch fish have netting slackened to create a basin-like dip that helps retain fast moving fish which could disappear with the swish of a tail as the net is lifted. I have heard tales of crabs being caught (with the bacon bait) using an old bicycle wheel suspended from a rope in a similar manner, the spokes acting as a netting substitute.

In some parts of the world the square dip net design above is a key method of fishing. For example, in the Kerala region of India, and other Asian countries, large nets 10 to 15 metres square are suspended from cantilevered frames and lowered into lagoons, estuarine areas, and large river systems. Those operators clever enough have the rear cantilevered part weighted with stone blocks so that little effort is required to raise the net. Less sophisticated folks use teams of men to haul on ropes to lift the catch. In a much smaller single-man operation I have seen nets about 2 metres square simply lifted out of the water with the aid of a cut branch.

Finally, a handy little wheeze for trapping prawns that one of the SERE instructors I work alongside experimented with when on exercise, and involves one of the tough plastic press-lock bags issued in the 24-hour ration packs.

To begin with, the bag (they are almost A4 in size) has a corner cut off – about 2.5 cm wide (A), and then the remaining corner of the bag is pushed inwards to create a funnel (B). Some attractive prawn-luring bait is placed in the bag, and then a suitable sized stone inside (C); not only to weigh the bag down in the rockpool but also create a cavity big enough to hold captive prawns. Seal, walk away and leave this simple passive trap to work its magic.

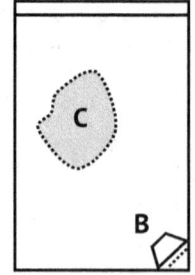

GUTTING A FISH

There is no 'precise' method of gutting a fish (not a flat fish like sole or plaice); individual anglers having their own variation on the process described below. However, the core principles are worked through, and over time you will develop your own preferred technique.

Wash the fish to remove any slime as it makes for easier handling, even lightly wipe the skin dry to allow for a better hold for the first few times that you gut fish.

Begin by placing the fish on a firm surface and then de-scale it; holding the tail and scraping towards the head with a scraper or back of a knife. Then rinse the fish to wash off any scales clinging to the skin surface. Check the fish over and remove any remaining scales that you missed. If the fish has really sharp-spined fins then they are best removed prior to scaling to prevent injury.

Not all fish require scaling, and to a certain extent it depends on whether you are going to steam, boil, bake or pan-fry them. Indeed, the skin and bones are easiest to remove once the fish has been cooked.

Place the fish back on the work surface. Starting at the anal opening (1), begin to open the belly with the tip of a clean, sharp, knife, stopping at the jaw or 'chin' below the gills (2). Until you get used to gutting fish it's best to do this unzipping with the cutting edge of the knife facing outwards so that you don't puncture the internal organs, and also cut away from your body in case the knife slips. Spread the fish open, and reach inside with your fingers to remove all the internal organs.

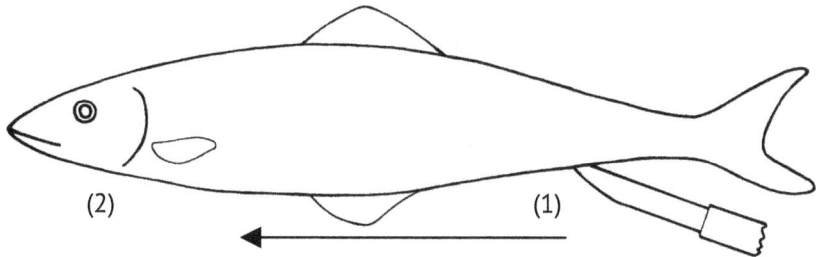

Next (pictured overleaf), raise the pectoral fin (3) behind the gills and make an angled (tilted at 45°, for example), curved cut right behind the fin (3a), down through the body towards the spine. When you feel the blade run up against the spinal bone stop cutting downwards, but trim round towards the belly of the fish which should create a visible flap (3b).

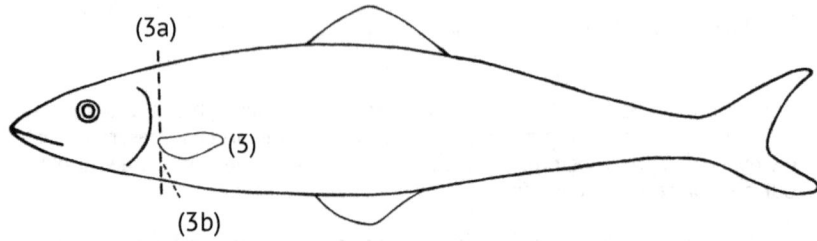

Flip the fish over and repeat exactly the same process on the other side. Make one final short cut through the spine which should entirely release the head and gills with any remaining bits of viscera attached.

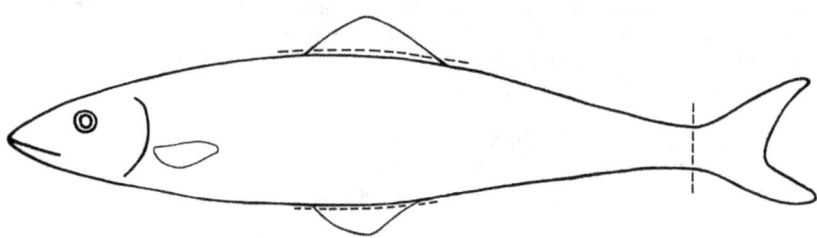

(4) All that remains to do is to is cut off all the remaining fins close to the body (some folks remove the fins before commencing gutting itself especially if they are sharp), and squeeze and scrape away the dark red bloodline in the bottom of the cavity of the fish, and then give the fish a final wash in clean water. The tail fin is often left on, allowing quick handling of the fish and also a potential means of hanging the fish for cooking over a fire.

Well done. You now have food to cook!

FILLETING A FISH

There are a couple of ways to fillet fish. For a small fish begin by lifting the pectoral fin behind the gills and making a cut downwards at right angles to the spine, following the contours of the gills. It is not necessary to gut the fish first.

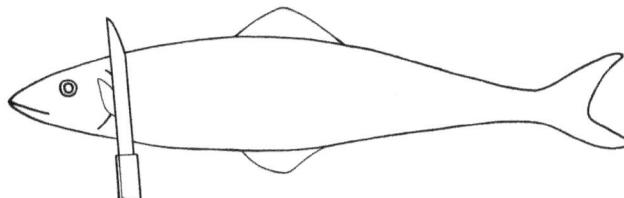

When you reach the spine twist the knife through 90° so that it is parallel with the spine, then cut backwards toward the tail; keeping the edge of the blade at a shallow angle to the spine but cutting against it all the way.

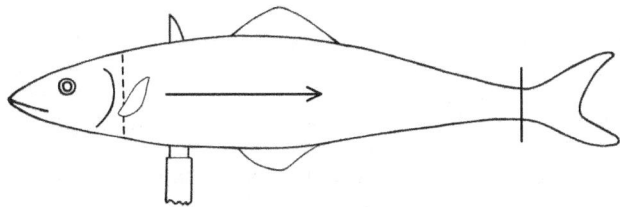

Although the method above is straightforward, it can leave meat on the bones where the flat edge of the knife does not quite reach. So, an alternative is the method below, used for filleting large fish but also, in my view, leaves less valuable meat on the spinal bones of smaller fish.

When I fillet fish this way, in my mind's eye I am dealing with four quarter segments of the fish, although each of the two fillets is left whole. Make the first cut behind the gills as previous, then insert the knife into the fish on the nearside of the top (dorsal) fin facing you [A] with the knife facing out (figure below). Extend the cut forwards to the head [A1], and back towards the tail [A2]. Then swivel the fish through 180° and repeat at the bottom; first making an incision with knife on the nearside of the lower (pelvic) fin facing you, and then cutting towards the front and back.

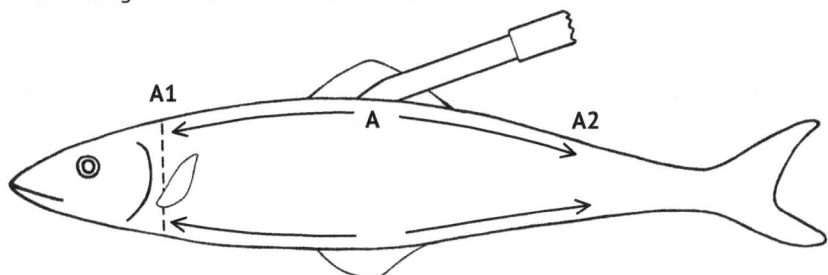

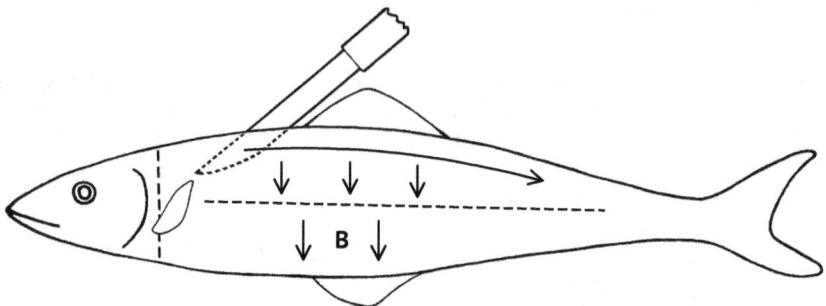

The next step (above) is to cut towards the centre of the spine, from the front to the back of the fish; keeping the knife quite shallow and slanting your cuts against the bones. In essence you have now released the first quarter segment of fish meat. However, don't cut the first fillet in two just yet... as you have two stylistic options:

The first is to continue cutting onwards ('B' above) from the straight edge of the exposed spine, till you reach the bottom of the fish, OR you can swivel the fish round 180° (below) and repeat the process from the bottom side working towards the spine until the fillet is released whole. The whole process now needs to repeated on the other side of the fish to cut away the second whole fillet. Again, the fish does not need to be gutted for this filleting to take place.

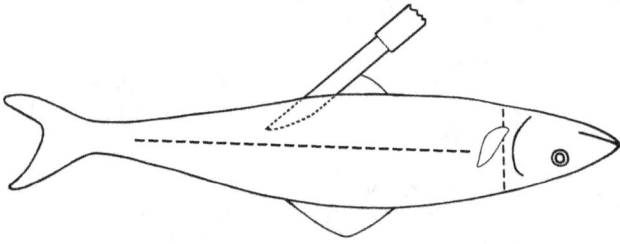

The final task of filleting is to remove a series of small 'pin' bones that run along the centre of each fillet. Gently run your fingers down the meat to locate these bones then with the knife make cut a sharp 'V' shaped cut downwards on either side to cut them out. You should now have a couple of boneless fish fillets for cooking up.

NOTE: Don't throw away the backbone and head sections of your filleted fish. Put them in a pan of suitable size with just enough water to cover the bits, and then simmer for 30 minutes or so to make a basic fish stock which may be transformed into a soup, or perhaps a tasty sauce to go with your fish fillets.

MARINE MOLLUSCS

What is the definition of a mollusc you may ask? Well it is a soft-bodied invertebrate (that is an animal without a backbone), generally protected by a hard protective shell. So if it's soft and squidgy and surrounded by a hard shell it is likely to be an invertebrate that you are looking at. A differentiation needs to be made between those molluscs found in freshwater habitats, and those from the sea and shoreline. Freshwater mussels I have always been led to believe, are non-edible, possibly toxic, and I still have not found a definitive research paper, resource, or confirmed report of human usage that absolutely convinces me they will do no harm; despite whatever populist TV pundits may prattle about them. In a post-disaster world freshwater molluscs may become absorbents of whatever toxins end up in rivers and streams. As far as I am concerned only certain coastline molluscs make satisfactory and safe food. However, I have listed at the end of this section a number of freshwater mussels that it is claimed have been eaten in the past (in the 1800s).

The two main Classes of Mollusca that concern us are the *gastropods* which generally have hard, coiled shells (like the snail), and *bivalves* the shells of which are composed of two parts connected by a hinge, or 'ligament' as it is technically known; mussels being a well-known example. While some bivalves like the mussel are permanently attached to rock other species like the scallop can be highly mobile.

Harvesting shellfish from the shoreline carries with it health risks even at the best of times, let alone following some natural disaster which has released or spread contaminants. You need to be vigilant about the quality of the seawater all around your harvesting area. The most obvious pollutant would perhaps be untreated sewage released from dysfunctional treatment plants, but there is also agricultural run-off, and both of these may contain nasty bacteria and viruses harmful to human health. There may also be chemical or heavy-metal pollutants around following damage to industrial infrastructure.

Another major consideration will be *algal blooms* that produce toxins in filter-feeding molluscs. In peacetime there are monitoring services and warnings of imminent harmful algal blooms. In a post-disaster world these checks will not be in place to protect you, so the best piece of advice is perhaps to follow that very old maxim of not collecting shellfish when the is no 'r' in the month. It may not protect you entirely, but that harvesting philosophy was developed centuries ago when there was no science to help solve the mysteries of the universe – certainly not cyanobacterial poisoning – and they simply learned by experience that something contaminated shellfish during the hot summer months, when algal blooms tend to develop, while the colder months (those with an 'r') caused less of a problem – because the blooms had not formed out at sea. In the worst cases the algal blooms release neurotoxins or biotoxins which lead to very serious food poisoning in humans, even death in the worst cases.

So before you start harvesting shoreline shellfish, closely observe the local waters, and avoid areas that look dirty or are in close proximity to shoreline outflows. And take into consideration any rainfall carrying contaminants from inland areas into your harvesting zone.

Consider observing where other people harvest from; although this might bring you into conflict over precious resources, and they may also not fully understand the health and safety consequences as you do.

If you have a track record of being tripped up, healthwise, by eating shellfish, then it may be wiser to avoid eating specimens harvested in the uncontrolled environment of a post-disaster world.

Finally, when cooking shellfish they should be alive before cooking. Snail-like specimens will usually react to being touched, even if they are curled up inside their shell, while the best rule for bivalves is that when tapped they will respond by closing up, but then open during cooking. So, an open (after tapping) uncooked fresh bivalve must be discarded, and a closed cooked one should also be tossed away. And although some shellfish may be eaten raw, in any post-disaster circumstances that you find yourself in you should cook all shellfish to kill harmful bacteria.

On a non-food safety slant, do take care when foraging from the shore as it can be a dangerous place. Work out the tide times so that you do not become stranded out in the shallows, or become marooned on rocks. Be very careful when you are approaching wet muds and sands – there may be quicksands and soft bottomless mudflats which are almost superfluid because of moisture. When clambering among rocks to get at your harvest area, wear non-slip footwear, and be particularly careful when clambering among seaweeds which can hide nasty crevices between rocks that could break an ankle.

COMMON / EDIBLE COCKLE – *Cerastoderma edule* syn. *Cardium edule*

Species widespread. Found in and or sandy muds of mid-shore to just below the low water line. Often in estuarine areas. Shell about 5 cm wide, with 24 or more radiating ribs.

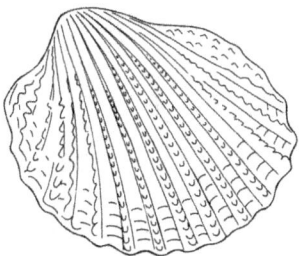

Collected by raking through the top few centimetres of sand at low tide. Best collecting period is in the autumn when the cockles have fattened up, while in the summer months they should be avoided, allowing the colonies to spawn.

Place collected cockles in salt water to allow system to clear through, then disturb the cockles – any that have shells remaining open should be discarded as they have probably died. When cooking, eat only those where the shells open up.

In Wales cockles were cooked with ham, also put into pies with chopped chives and a layer of bacon lining the bottom of the dish. Another way was to fry the cockles with oatmeal and chives, or turn them into soup. Simplest of all, cook in their shells over a fire.

LIMPET – *Patella vulgata*

Widespread species with an oval, conical, shell, of a greyish-yellow to greenish-brown colour. Up to about 5 cm wide. Active during the night period.

They adhere tightly to shoreline rocks but can be harvested by giving a quick rap with a small stone then dislodging them, or sliding a knife under one side of the shell and prizing off the rock.

Limpets can be a bit rubbery when cooked. Simply place the shells on a griddle over the fire or embers, and cook until the water boils off – the flesh will have separated from the shell. Another way to cook them is to place the shells on the sand or shingle, cover them with dry grass and set fire to this.

An old 19th century recipe for limpet soup is as follows (but does require ingredients you may not have in a survival situation): Parboil the limpets and then remove them from their shells. Next, chop some parsley and put with a knob of butter in a pan and fry. Add a ½-litre of water and bring to the boil. Add the limpets, a teaspoon of anchovy sauce, season with pepper, and bring to the boil and then simmer for half an hour. If preferred, stew your limpets before adding to the soup base.

Other cooking methods included frying large sized limpets with butter, pepper and vinegar, while the smaller ones were reckoned better boiled, and then eaten with vinegar and pepper. Personally, I cook my limpets on an open fire, then slice them thinly and slow cook in soup or as a shellfish chowder or stew.

Other limpet species used are: *Patella caerulea* / Rayed Mediterranean Limpet, *Patella ulyssiponensis* (=*aspera*) – Rough limpet / China Limpet, and *Patella rustica* (=*lusitanica*) / Rustic limpet.

COMMON WHELK – *Buccinum undatum*

Widespread species, growing about 10+ cm long, and found in sand, rock and muddy low-water habitats. Shell varies in colour, but is ovate, with a number of whorls and a large aperture.

The modus operandi of this mollusc species is to bore a hole through the shells of other mollusc species and then devour the contents. Jolly! For this reason I think whelks (as carnivores) should be passively purged before they are cooked. Use a wicker or other type trap baited with offal to catch them. Generally they are best around August-September. If whelks are not to your taste use them as bait for line fishing.

There are various methods of preparing whelks, but generally they are boiled first, so as to allow the flesh to be removed from the shell, and then processed further...

The boiled whelks can be fried with butter of fat till browned. For a seashore soup fry off some sliced onion then add a good handful of sea-beet (see plants section) and a small clutch of young alexanders (*Smyrnium olusatrum*) leaves if in season, some old bread crusts broken into pieces, and a ½-litre or so of water. Season with pepper, and allow to simmer for an hour. Meanwhile, fry off some whelks and add to the soup, allowing the mixture to gently boil for a few minutes. Another option is to make up a roux-like base then stir in water or milk, and finally the whelks. Bring to the boil and simmer for 30 to 40 minutes. Generally I think whelks are better slow-cooked.

COMMON MUSSEL – *Mytilus edulis*

Widespread, wedge-shaped, equivalved species found on rocky outcrops and sea defences; growing to about 10 cm in length in some instances, but generally around 5 to 6 cm long. Shell coloured greyish blue to dark blue-black.

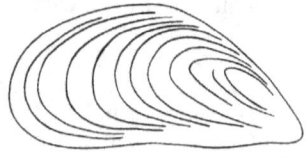

I doubt that many readers of this book will not be aquainted with mussels, so I will not give any recipe details. Mussels can be simply steamed in a pan with a little water (wine is better) until the shells open. As with cockles, if the shell of any uncooked mussel remains open after being agitated, then discard it. And after cooking, any mussel which remains closed-shelled should be discarded. As a filter-feeder it is essential the quality of the local sea water is good.

Other mussel species eaten where available:
Mytilus incurvatus and *achatinus* (both tougher than *Mytilus edulis*)
Mytilus modiolus (Faroe Isles)
Mytilus minimus (Mediterranean)
Mytilus galloprovincialis – Mediterranean Mussel
Mytilus trossulus – Northern Blue Mussel

PERIWINKLE – *Littorina littorea*
Widespread on rocks of the middle and lower shore, but always near the edge of the tide, the spiral shell having 6 or 7 whorls, a sharp apex, and an aperture almost round in shape. Periwinkles vary in colour – from almost black to olive-green, to pale greenish-white. They are collected at low tide. Sometimes they hide on the shady / dark sides of rocks.

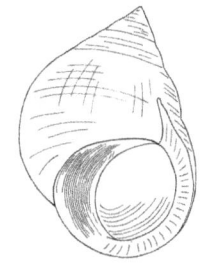

My preference is to let winkles passively purge their gut contents before cooking them – generally in a soup or seaside chowder-type concoction. First boil the winkles in water and, using a pin, tease the flesh out of the shell; nipping off the hard disk of the *operculum* before proceeding with a recipe. The Small Winkle / *Littorina neritoides* which is found widespread, and inhabits upper shoreline crevices, is edible too.

RAZOR CLAMS – *Ensis ensis* syn. *Solen ensis*
In the past both the filter feeding *Ensis* (=*Solen*) *ensis* and the very much bigger *Ensis* (=*Solen*) *siliqua* (up to 20 cm in length) were regularly used as food. Another species *Solen marginatus* is also consumed. A mature *Ensis ensis* grows to about 10 to 12 cm long and has a slightly curved shell, while *Solen marginatus* [European Razor] grows slightly larger, has a straight shell and similarly inhabits from the mid to extreme low-tide mark, living buried in the fine moist sand.

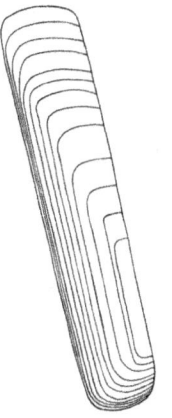

All three species will be found on the very lowest shoreline and in shallow water, living in vertical holes burrowed in the sand. The classic way to catch razor clams is to identify their burrow holes and then drop some salt into the gap. The mollusc rises up to expel the salt, at which point a gloved hand poised by the hole grabs hold of the clam. Alternatively, a spade resting on the sand just beside the hole is pushed into the sand immediately the razor rises to briefly block the retreat of the mollusc to allow it to be plucked from the sand. Yet another way (in the 19th century at least) of catching razor clams was to take a long narrow wire (such as metal coathanger), give it a small centimetre long bend at one end, and then sharpen the tip. This barbed wire was then thrust into the sand where a razor shell had been identified; passing between the shell halves, given a half twist to fix the mollusc on the barb, and then pulled to the surface.

Razor clams can be steamed just like mussels, or placed on the embers of a fire to cook. Other old ways of cooking them were to boil them for 10 minutes, remove the flesh from the shells, then fry in butter or lard and seasoned with salt and pepper. A further cooking method involved stewing them in milk till tender, then adding salt, pepper and butter – though instructions are unclear as to whether this was eaten as a 'stew' or the stewed razors were removed from the pot and then butter and seasoning added.

SOME OTHER 'LOCAL' EDIBLE MARINE MOLLUSCS

SAND GAPER – *Mya arenaria* / BLUNT GAPER – *M. truncata*
The sand gaper burrows into sands and muds from the low-shoreline down to 70 m, so may entail some paddling in shoreline water to reach them. It also lives in estuarine habitats, and is found from the Baltic and North Sea, to Atlantic and English Channel.

The blunt gaper (*M. truncata*) is found from mid-shore to 70 m, but not in estuaries, and has a dirty cream-white-fawn shell colour. A common filter-feeding mollusc, it too inhabits sandy mud and sands, burrowing down to about 20 cm, and is found from Norwegian waters to Biscay.

GREEN / EUROPEAN ABALONE – *Haliotis tuberculata*
A species growing to about 9 cm, found from the Mediterranean to NE Atlantic European shores; living in shallow water and under stones on the lower shoreline.

COMMON PIDDOCK – *Pholas dactylus*
This shellfish can reach up to 15 cm in length, and is found on British Atlantic shores, in the Mediterranean and English Channel. Found in shallow water and lower shoreline habitats it bores holes into soft rocklike shale, chalk or sandstone, or finds a home in firm sand and clay, or even wood. This habit can induce coastal erosion. *Pholas dactylus* secretes a luminous blue dye when irritated.

Most of the species listed above are reasonably accessible to the beach forager. However, there are more edible molluscs like the ones listed below which are available close to the shoreline but they may not be practicable for shoreline harvesting; often requiring deep dredging or paddling or hand dredging in shallows:

OYSTERS – *Ostrea edulis* is perhaps the best-known oyster species, but dotted round northern temperate Eurasia there are other edible species, namely *Ostrea cyrnusi* and *O. stentino*.

There are also a number of other shellfish species commonly called 'oysters' that are edible too:
Rayed Pearl Oyster – *Pinctada radiata*
European Wing Oyster – *Pteria hirundo*
European Thorny Oyster – *Spondylus gaederopus*
Giant Cupped / Portuguese Oyster – *Crassostrea gigas* (=*angulata*)

SCALLOPS – *Pecten* (=*Aequipecten*) *maximus* & *opercularis*
The Great Scallop / *P. maximus*, is the scallop best known to us in restaurants, but the Black Queen Scallop / *Aequipecten* (=*Chlamys*) *opercularis*, and the White Queen Scallop / *Chlamys varia* are also eaten. A sedentary bivalve, *P. maximus* is found at water depths down to 60 m in Atlantic and English Channel waters, where it likes thin muddy sand and gravelly sea bottoms. *Chlamys varia*, or the Variegated Scallop, is found down to depths of 80 m in the waters of the North Sea to the English Channel, the Mediterranean, and in the east Atlantic from southern Norway to the waters off Senegal. It averages 4 to 5 cm, with a maximum of 8 cm in size. *Pecten jacobaeus*, and *Crassadoma* (=*Chlamys*) *multistriata*, the Little Bay Scallop, are also eaten.

PRICKLY COCKLE – *Acanthocardia* (=*Cardium*) *aculeata* (=*aculeatum*)
A larger species than the traditional edible cockle, growing 9 to 10 cm in size, the brownish-pink shells having long spines on each rib. Inhabits muddy sands in shallows down to 40 m. Found from southern UK through to the Mediterranean.

PRICKLY COCKLE – *Acanthocardia* (=*Cardium*) *echinata*
Grows to about 6 cm, the yellow to red-brown shells rounded with striated spined ribs. A very common filter-feeding bivalve that partly buries itself in muddy sands and gravels, and fine sand, and is found from shallows down to 200 metres. Distributed from Iceland and Norway in the north, through to the Mediterranean.

RED NOSE / TUBERCULATE COCKLE – *Acanthocardia* (=*Cardium*) *tuberculata* (=*tuberculatum* = *rusticum*)
Long used as food, particularly in Mediterranean countries, this bivalve produces a strong heavy shell growing to about 8 or 9 cm, of a red-brown colour, occasionally banded with white, with the ribs having wide-spaced tubercules along their length. Burrows in low-water sands and gravels, but inhabits down to 100 metres. Found from Irish Sea and southern UK through to Mediterranean waters.

SMOOTH COCKLE – *Laevicardium crassum*
A smooth-shelled variety of cockle growing to about 7 cm, being coloured white with external pale reddish-brown mottling. And the shell ribs not projecting outwards as with most other cockles mentioned. A burrower of muddy sands, sand and gravel, and inhabiting depths from 10 to 100 metres (so a dredging species).

HEART-SHELL / OXHEART CLAM – *Glossus humanus* syn. *Isocardia cor*
Found from Norway to the Mediterranean, this filter-feeder shellfish (once confusingly called Pecten) has a thick dark brown to yellow-white shell that grows to about 10 cm, and is heart shaped when viewed from the side. However, this clam burrows into the seabed mud and sand from about 10 m which rather puts it in the dredged shellfish league.

BITTERSWEET CLAM / DOG COCKLE – *Glycymeris glycymeris*
A thick-shelled bivalve with a round shell of a dark chocolate or ochre brown, with white striations, found from the Baltic and north Atlantic to the Mediterranean. It reaches from 4 to 6 cm in size (maximum 8 cm), and finds a home between the extreme shallow-water mark and 80 m, making shallow-ish burrows below the surface of muddy gravels and clean sands. This species will need a careful, sustainable, harvesting regime as it grows slowly.

CHICKEN VENUS / STRIPED VENUS – *Chamelea gallina*
A common filter-feeding bivalve growing to about 4 cm, the shell of a pale yellow / dirty white colour, usually with three red-brown surface markings. Inhabits clean or muddy sands where it burrows shallowly. Found from Norwegian waters through to the Mediterranean and Black Sea.

WEDGE SHELL / TRUNCATE DONAX – *Donax trunculus*
A bivalve with a roughly wedge-shaped shell, of a yellow-light brown colour, and growing to 2 to 3 cm, maximum 5 cm. A very agile species, it inhabits sands in exposed lower shoreline shallows to 6 m. Older specimens gravitate to lower tide levels while young individuals inhabit high tide levels. Found from Norway and European Atlantic to the Mediterranean and Black Sea.

WARTY VENUS – *Venus verrucosa*
This bivalve is found in the coarse sand and gravel in the shallow waters of the extreme low shoreline, down to 100 metres. At the low tide region it can be dug out from sandbanks, particularly during low Spring tides. It inhabits eastern Atlantic waters from the west of Scotland, and NE of there, down to waters west of Angola, through the English Channel, and into the Mediterranean. A good specimen can reach 6 cm in size.

DECUSSATE VENUS – *Venerupis* (=*Ruditapes* =*Tapes*) *decussata*
Also known as the grooved carpet shell this filter-feeding bivalve species has a yellow-light brown shell, sometimes streaked brown, that grows to about 7 cm. Inhabits sand and muddy gravel where it burrows shallowly, and is found round southern UK regions to the Mediterranean.

SMOOTH / BROWN VENUS – *Callista* (=*Venus*) *chione*
Despite the fact that this filter-feeding species can grow up to 9 cm, it can burrow very quickly in the sands that it inhabits. Older specimens have a polished shell of a chestnut-red-brown colour, often with darker streaky markings, while juveniles are colour-banded or spotted. Found from sandy shallows to 100 m deep, *C. chione* is often gathered during the low Spring tides. Distributed from southern Britain through to the Mediterranean.

SMOOTH BUTTER CLAM – *Venerupis aurea* syn. *Paphia aurea*
Bivalve growing to about 4 cm, with the shell coloured a cream-white to yellow-light brown, usually with reddish-purple-brown markings. Burrows into soft sands of lower shoreline and shallows. Found from Norwegian waters to those off NW Africa, to the Mediterranean.

GOLDEN / PULLET CARPET SHELL – *Venerupis* (=*Tapes* =*Venus*) *pullastra*
A shallow burrower of the sandy lower shoreline to shallows, growing to 5 cm. The shell is a cream-light fawn, to brown, and unevenly shaded. Found from northern Norwegian waters to NW Africa, to the Mediterranean.

BANDED CARPET – *Venerupis rhomboïdes*
This is a burrowing bivalve with a sandy brown shell with radiating stripes, growing to around 4 or 5 cm (maximum 7 cm). It inhabits coarse sands, gravels and muddy sands between the shoreline down to 50 m, and is found in eastern Atlantic waters from Norway and through to the Mediterranean.

TROUGH SHELLS – *Mactra* sp.
The trough shells belong to the *Mactridae* family, and over many decades there have been various re-classifications, so in the examples below I have bundled other family members (*Spisula* and *Donacilla*) together, although from their names they may appear to come from different backgrounds.

Mactra corallina / Rayed Trough Shell is a bivalve, growing to about 7 cm, the shell having bands alternating yellow and brown, and with *Mactra glauca* / Grey Rough Shell will be found in North European and Mediterranean waters.

Mactra stultorum is a burrowing filter-feeder, the shiny shell cream coloured with a purple hue, and growing to about 5 cm. Found in sands from Norwegian waters round to the Mediterranean and Black Sea.

Donacilla (=*Mactra*) *cornea* / Banded Wedge Shell, is quite small, growing to about 2 cm in somewhat exposed beaches of medium-coarse sand. Found along European Atlantic coasts, in the North Sea round to the Mediterranean.

Spisula (=*Mactra*) *solida*, the Atlantic Surf Clam, is a related burrowing, filter-feeding, species within the *Mactra* family, the bivalve having a thick, fast-growing shell. Of a dirty white-yellow coloration, growing to about 4 cm, and inhabiting sands close to the low tide mark down to 50 m. Found in European Atlantic waters down to west of Morocco.

I do have a reference to *Spisula ovalis* / Thick Trough Shell being used as food but have not been able to track down any further information, though it might have changed names. Nor have I been able to track down *Mactra helvacea*, quoted in an old research paper as being edible. There is also the edible Grey Trough shell (*Mactra glauca*), but this is rare.

QUAHOG – *Mercenaria mercenaria*
This appears to have been an introduced species (from the US) that is finding a home in this part of the world. It grows to about 10 cm, the shell having a dirty white-gray to light brown colour. It prefers gravelly and shingle-type substrata for its burrowing activities. Found from the waters of western France, and in the North Sea around Belgium and the Netherlands.

BLUNT TELLIN – *Arcopagia* (=*Tellina*) *crassa*
Bivalve, growing to about 6 cm, the almost oval shell having a yellow-white-fawn coloration, sometimes with pale orange-red to brown markings. Burrows in shell gravels, muddy and coarse sands from the lower shore to 100 m. Found from Norwegian waters down to somewhat beyond the Iberian Peninsula, and widely in the North Sea although it is not a very common species. Look out also for *Tellina tenuis* in similar waters, *Tellina fabula* in north European areas, and *Tellina albicans* / Glossy Tellin in the Mediterranean area.

OTTER SHELL – *Lutraria magna*
This is a big beast of a mollusc, growing to around 13 cm in size. Of a yellow-white-fawn colour, sometimes tinged with a purple-pink hue, the elongated shell gapes at the ends rather than closing entirely shut. A filter-feeding bivalve it burrows in shell-like gravels, and is found at the lowest shoreline down to 100 m or more. It is distributed from Norwegian waters down to the Mediterranean, though only round the southern waters of the British Isles. Some old references have a related *L. elliptica* (= *L. lutraria*) also used for food. The Narrow Otter Shell (*L. angustior*) may also be eaten.

FRESHWATER MUSSELS
As mentioned in the pre-amble to this section I have a reluctance to consider freshwater mussels as a foodstuff since there seem to be very few recent contemporary reports of long-term consumption of these molluscs, at least on UK shores. There is also the thought that as they are inhabiting riverine conditions, subject to all sorts of water quality, then as filter-feeders they may be concentrating all sorts of nasties. Of the older references I came across the following species were said to be eaten: *Anodonta cygnea* (in County Leitrim), *Unionae* shell roasted or scalloped with breadcrumbs in southern Europe, with *Unio requienii* and *Unio litoralis* specifically identified for culinary use in Spain, though both species were said to be tough. Finally, *Arca Noe* and *Arca barbata* were said to be eaten in Spain and Italy. All the names may have changed since they were first written about.

OTHER EDIBLE BIVALVE & GASTROPOD MOLLUSCS

North America [See note below]

Amiantis callosa - White venus
Anomia peruviana - Peruvian jingle
Argopecten irradians - Atlantic bay scallop
Argopecten purpuratus - Peruvian calico scallop
Argopecten ventricosus - Pacific calico scallop
Cerastoderma edule - Common edible cockle
Chione fluctifraga - Smooth venus
Chione succincta - Hard-shell cockle
Chione undatella - Frilled venus
Chlamys islandica - Iceland scallop
Clinocardium nuttallii - Nuttall's cockle
Corbicula fluminea - Asian clam
Crassadoma gigantea - Rock scallop
Crassostrea corteziensis - Cortez oyster
Crassostrea gigas - Pacific cupped oyster
Crassostrea rhizophorae - Mangrove cupped oyster
Crassostrea rivularis - Suminoe oyster
Crassostrea virginica - American cupped oyster
Donax californica - Wedge shell
Donax laevigata - Bean clam (quite rare)
Gari californica - Sunset clam
Gari edulenta - Sunset shell
Haliotis rufescens - Red abalone
Laevicardium elatum - Giant eggcockle
Littorina littorea - Common periwinkle
Macoma nasuta - Bent-nose macoma
Macoma secta - White-sand macoma
Mercenaria mercenaria - Northern quahog
Modiolus rectus - Straight horsemussel
Mya arenaria - Sand gaper
Mya cancellata - Boring softshell clam
Mytilus californianus - Californian mussel
Mytilus edulis - Blue mussel
Mytilus galloprovincialis - Mediterranean mussel
Nuttallia nuttallii - Purple clam
Ostrea edulis - European flat oyster
Ostrea lurida - Olympia flat oyster
Panopea abrupta - Pacific geoduck
Panopea generosa - Geoduck
Parapholas californica - Scale-sided piddock
Patinopecten yessoensis - Yesso scallop
Pecten fumatus - Australian southern scallop
Penitella penita - Borer piddock
Perna perna - South American rock mussel
Pinctada margaritifera - Black-lip pearl oyster
Placopecten magellanicus - American sea scallop
Pododesmus macroschisma - Rock oyster
Protothaca staminea - Pacific littleneck clam
Ruditapes philippinarum - Japanese carpet shell
Saxidomus giganteus - Butter clam

Caribbean Basin [See note below]

Americardia media - Atlantic strawberry cockle
Anadara notabilis - Eared ark
Arca imbricata - Mossy ark
Arca zebra -Turkey wing
Argopecten gibbus - Calico scallop
Argopecten irradiana amplicostatus - Atlantic bay scallop
Asaphis deflorata - Gaudy asaphis
Atrina rigida - Stiff pen shell
Atrina seminuda - Half-naked pen shell
Atrina serrata - Sawtoothed pen shell
Charonia tritonis variegata - Atlantic triton's trumpet
Chicoreus brevifrons - West Indian murex
Chicoreus pomum - Apple murex
Chione cancellata - Cross-barred venus
Chione paphia - King venus
Cittarium pica - West Indian top shell
Codakia orbicularis - Atlantic tiger lucine
Conus mus - Mouse cone
Conus regius - Crown cone
Crassostrea rhizophorae - Mangrove cupped oyster
Crassostrea virginica - Eastern oyster
Ctenoides scabra - Rough lima
Cymatium femorale - Angular triton
Cymatium parthenopeum - Giant hairy triton
Cyrtopleura costata - Angel wing
Dinocardium robustum - Atlantic Giant-cockle
Diodora listeri - Lister's keyhole limpet
Donax denticulatus - Common Caribbean donax
Donax striatus - Striate donax
Euvola ziczac - Zigzag scallop
Fasciolaria tulipa - True tulip
Fissurella balanoides - Rayed keyhole limpet
Fissurella barbadensis - Barbados keyhole limpet
Fusius closter - Philippi's spindle
Geukensia demissa - Ribbed Mussel
Heterodonax bimaculatus - Small false donax
Iphigenia brasiliana - Giant false donax
Isognomon alatus - Flat tree oyster
Laevicardium laevigatum - Common egg cockle
Latirus infundibulum - Brown-lined latirus
Leucozonia nassa - Chestnut latirus
Lithopoma tecta - Imbricated star-shell
Lithopoma tuber - Green star-shell
Lyropecten nodosus - Lion's paw
Macrocallista maculata - Calico clam
Macrocallista nimbosa - Sunray Venus
Mactrellona alata - Caribbean winged mactra
Melongena melongena - West Indian Crown conch

85

North America cont'd.
Saxidomus giganteus - Washington clam
Saxidomus nuttalli - California butterclam
Semele decisa - Clipped semele
Siliqua lucida - Transparent razor
Siliqua patula - Pacific razor clam
Solen sicarius - Sickle jack-knife clam
Spisula solidissima - Atlantic surf clam
Strombus gigas - Pink conch
Tagelus californianus - California tagelus
Tellina bodegensis - Bodega tellin
Tivela stultorum - Pismo clam
Trachycardium quadragenarium - Pricklycockle

NOTE: List drawn from both sides of N. America.

South America
Argopecten irradians - Atlantic bay scallop
Argopecten purpuratus - Peruvian calico scallop
Argopecten ventricosus - Pacific calico scallop
Aulacomya ater - Cholga mussel
Choromytilus chorus - Choro mussel
Crassostrea corteziensis - Cortez oyster
Crassostrea gigas - Pacific cupped oyster
Crassostrea rhizophorae - Mangrove cupped oyster
Haliotis rufescens - Red abalone
Mytilus chilensis - Chilean mussel
Mytilus edulis - Blue mussel
Ostrea chilensis - Chilean flat oyster
Perna perna - South American rock mussel
Strombus gigas - Pink conch

Oceania
Aulacomya ater - Cholga mussel
Cerithium coralium - Coral cerith
Cerithium echinatum - Spinose cerith
Cerithium nodulosum - Giant knobbed cerith
Crassostrea gigas - Pacific cupped oyster
Crassostrea rhizophorae - Mangrove cupped oyster
Littoraria scabra - Rough periwinkle
Mytilus planulatus - Australian mussel
Pecten fumatus - Australian southern scallop
Pecten novaezelandiae - New Zealand scallop
Perna canaliculus - New Zealand mussel
Perna viridis - Green mussel
Pinctada fucata - Japanese pearl oyster
Pinctada margaritifera - Black-lip pearl oyster
Pinctada maxima - Silver-lip pearl oyster
Pseudovertagus aluco - Aluco vertagus
Pteria penguin - Penguin wing oyster
Rhinoclavis aspera - Rough vertagus
Rhinoclavis fasciata - Banded vertagus
Rhinoclavis sinensis - Obelisk vertagus
Rhinoclavis vertagus - Common vertagus

Caribbean Basin cont'd.
Mercenaria campechiensis - Southern Quahog
Modiolus americanus - Tulip mussel
Modiolus squamosus - False tulip mussel
Mytella guyanensis - Guiana swamp mussel
Mytella strigata - Strigate mangrove mussel
Nerita peloronta - Bleeding tooth
Nodipecten nodosus - Lions-paw Scallop
Oliva reticularis - Netted olive
Oliva sayana - Lettered olive
Periglypta listeri - Princess venus
Perna perna - South American rock mussel
Phyllonotus margaritensis - Margarita murex
Phyllonotus pomum - Apple murex
Pinctada imbricata - Atlantic pearl oyster
Pinna carnea - Amber pen shell
Pitar dione - Royal comb venus
Polymesoda aequilatera - Equilateral marsh clam
Polymesoda arctata - Slender marsh clam
Pteria colymbus - Atlantic Wing-oyster
Pugilina morio - Giant hairy melongena
Rangia cuneata - Common rangia
Scapharca brasiliana - Incongruous ark
Solen obliquus - Antillean razor clam
Strombus costatus - Milk conch
Strombus gallus - Roster-tail conch
Strombus gigas - Queen conch
Strombus pugilis - Fighting conch
Strombus raninus - Hawk-wing conch
Tagelus plebeius - Stout tagelus
Tellina fausta - Faust tellin
Tellina laevigata - Smooth tellin
Tellina listeri - Speckled tellin
Tellina radiata - Sunrise tellin
Thais deltoidea - Deltoid rock shell
Thais haemastoma floridana - Florida rock shell
Tivela mactroides - Trigonal tivela
Trachycardium isocardia - Even cockle
Trachycardium muricatum - American yellow cockle
Turbinella angulata - West Indian shank
Turbo canaliculatus - Channelled turban
Turbo castanea - Chestnut turban
Vasum capitellum - Spiny vase
Vasum muricatum - Caribbean vase
Ventricolaria rigida - Rigid venus
Voluta musica - Common music volute
Voluta virescens - Green music volute

NOTE: The term Caribbean Basin refers here to the area encompassing southern US states to northern South America, and from the central American isthmus across to the Caribbean islands.

Saccostrea commercialis - Sidney rock oyster
Saccostrea echinata - Spiny oyster
Tectarius grandinatus - Hailstorm prickly-winkle
Tectarius pagodus - Pagoda prickly-winkle
Tridacna derasa - Smooth giant clam
Tridacna gigas - Giant clam

Mediterranean

Acanthocardia tuberculata - Tuberculate cockle
Bolinus (=Murex) brandaris - Purple dye murex
Cerastoderma edule - Common cockle
Cerithium vulgatum - Common cerinthe
Chamelea gallina - Striped venus
Chlamys glabra - Smooth scallop
Chlamys proteus - Proteus scallop
Crassostrea angulata - Portuguese cupped oyster
Donax variegatus - Smooth donax
Lithophaga lithophaga - Date mussel
Littorina littorea - Periwinkle
Mytilus edulis - Common mussel
Mytilus galloprovincialis - Mediterranean mussel
Nassarius mutabilis - Changeable nassa
Ostrea edulis - European flat oyster
Pecten jacobæus - Great Mediterranean scallop
Phyllonotus trunculus - Banded murex
Solen spp - Razor clams
Tapes decussatus - Grooved carpet shell
Tapes pullastra - Carpet shell
Tellina planata - Flat tellin
Tellina incarnata -Feshy tellin
Venerupis aurea - Golden carpetshell
Venerupis rhomboides - Banded carpetshell
Venus verrucosa - Warty venus

Mediterranean – East & Southern

Anadara natalensis - Arc clam
Cassidaria echinophora - Helmet shell
Chama pacifica - Pacific jewel-box
Donax semistriatus - Half-striated donax
Donax trunculus - Wedge shell / Truncate donax
Gafrarium pectinatum - Comb venus
Hexaplex trunculus - Banded dye-murex
Lithophaga lithophaga - Date mussel
Mactra corallina - Rayed trough-shell
Monodonta turbinata - Turban shell
Patella caerulea - Mediterranean limpet
Patella rustica - Lusitanian limpet
Patella ulyssiponensis - China limpet
Pinctada radiata - Rayed pearl oyster
Ruditapes decussatus - Carpet shell
Spondylus spinosus - Red thorny oyster
Strombus persicus - Persian conch
Thais lacera – Rock shell
Tonna galea - Tun shell

Asia

Anadara granosa - Blood cockle
Argopecten irradians - Atlantic bay scallop
Cerithium coralium - Coral cerith
Cerithium echinatum - Spinose cerith
Chlamys farreri - Farrer's scallop
Chlamys nobilis - Noble scallop
Clinocardium nuttallii - Nuttall's cockle
Corbicula fluminea - Asian clam
Corbicula japonica - Japanese corbicula
Crassostrea belcheri - Lugubrious cupped oyster
Crassostrea gigas - Pacific cupped oyster
Crassostrea iredalei - Slipper cupped oyster
Crassostrea madrasensis - Indian backwater oyster
Crassostrea rivularis - Suminoe oyster
Haliotis discus - Japanese abalone
Haliotis diversicolor - Small abalone
Haliotis tuberculata - European abalone
Mactra veneriformis - Globose clam
Meretrix lusoria - Japanese hard clam
Meretrix meretrix - Asiatic hard clam
Mya arenaria - Sand gaper
Mytilus coruscus - Korean mussel
Mytilus edulis - Blue mussel
Nodilittorina pyramidalis - Pyramidal prickly-winkle
Ostrea edulis - European flat oyster
Panopea generosa - Geoduck
Paphia undulata - Undulate venus
Patinopecten yessoensis - Yesso scallop
Perna indica - Indian brown mussel
Perna viridis - Green mussel
Pinctada fucata - Japanese pearl oyster
Pinctada margaritifera - Black-lip pearl oyster
Pinctada maxima - Silver-lip pearl oyster
Pseudovertagus aluco - Aluco vertagus
Pteria penguin - Penguin wing oyster
Rhinoclavis aspera - Rough vertagus
Rhinoclavis fasciata - Banded vertagus
Rhinoclavis sinensis - Obelisk vertagus
Rhinoclavis vertagus - Common vertagus
Ruditapes decussatus - Grooved carpet shell
Ruditapes philippinarum – Japanese carpet shell
Saccostrea cucullata - Hooded oyster
Saccostrea echinata - Spiny oyster
Scapharca broughtonii - Inflated ark
Scapharca subcrenata - Half-crenate ark
Sinonovacula constricta - Constricted tagelus
Tectarius pagodus - Pagoda prickly-winkle
Tridacna derasa - Smooth giant clam
Tridacna gigas - Giant clam
Venerupis pullastra - Pullet carpet shell
Villorita cyprinoides - Black clam

CRABS & PRAWNS

The rocks and crevices of the shoreline present more coastal foraging opportunities in the form of crabs, shrimps and prawns, although crabs are generally a little more difficult to reach than prawns and shrimps.

EDIBLE CRAB – *Cancer pagurus*
With its distinctive black-tipped pincers the edible Brown Crab, as this species is also known, is found in eastern Atlantic waters from northern Norway down to northern Morocco and waters around Portugal, and has been reported in the Mediterranean Sea. The main body shell (carapace) which is somewhat reminiscent of a crimped pie crust round its edges, is broadly oval in shape, of a reddish-brown colour, and generally ranging in width from 15 to 25 cm (very occasionally 30 cm). Specimens under 10 cm in width should be returned to the water. Habitats range from the rocky shoreline shallows – where specimens are younger and so tend to be smaller – down to depths of 100 m, though 6 to 40 m is a more general range of depth. Although they are found in open areas from coarse gravels to muddy sands, fissures in rocks and between boulders are a more frequent habitat. Generally, they are caught in baited pots which are lifted every one to two days, the bait often being dogfish, remnants of skate, plus horse mackerel. The brown crab is largely nocturnal and is essentially a carrion scavenger, but also hunts for shellfish such as mussels, razors, cockles and whelks, and smaller crabs, including of its own species.

SHORE CRAB – *Carcinus maenas*
A considerably smaller crab species than the brown crab, the carapace of *C. maenas* may only reach around 9 to 10 cm in width. Unlike the brown crab it can tolerate relatively long periods out of water and will be found around the shoreline, often hiding under clumps of overhanging seaweed or beneath rocks. It is an edible species, and is also a scavenger.

VELVET SWIMMING / DEVIL CRAB – *Necora puber*
Growing to about 8 or 9 cm wide (the carapace) this is a commonly found species among the rocks, substrata and shallows along European Atlantic coasts, though its range extends to western parts of the Mediterranean. There are two helpful identifiers with this edible crab, in my view. First are the eyes, which are bright red (perhaps why the species was also called the Devil Crab), and second, the upper surface of the carapace (which is much more flattened than the edible crab) has a blueish tinge and a covering of reddish-brown velvety hairs – hence the official common name. It is also a very aggressive species, so watch your fingers, and is also a fast-moving (swimming) species. For its diet is feeds on everything from smaller crabs to brown algae according to some research.

EUROPEAN / SPINY SPIDER CRAB – *Maja squinado*
As the name suggests, this large species of crab has long legs and a carapace that is more triangular in shape when compared to the broadly oval shape of the edible brown crab. And while the shell of the former is largely smooth, that of the spiny spider crab is covered in sharp spines. Found from north-eastern Atlantic waters round to the Mediterranean, the meat in the long legs is edible, and tasty. However, this species inhabits the clean sandy shallow waters and beyond, only migrating to shallows during the breeding season, so for the shoreline forager this may not be a practicable food source.

FLOWER / BLUE CRAB – *Portunus pelagicus*
This species will be found in the Middle-Eastern waters of the Mediterranean, although it is widely met with from east Africa through to southeast Asia and the Pacific region. A relatively large crab, the carapace reaching widths of 20 cm, its' habitats are the sands and muds of intertidal estuaries. Smaller specimens are often eaten as 'soft shell' crabs while older specimens are processed like traditional hard shell crabs.

KILLING AND COOKING CRABS
As with any animal that you kill for food its despatch should be humane and dignified, and the following is recommended.

Keep the crabs alive until they are required for cooking, and indeed they do need to be cooked to remove any pathogens and bacteria that may lurk within or on them (remember most of the ones mentioned scavenge or prey on other animals, and also live in habitats where there may be pollution). To kill the crab a knife or spike is pushed into the carapace just above the mouthparts where the brain or nerve centre is located. Death is quick, though perhaps not immediate. The crab is then dropped into boiling salted water (note, at the boil, and continued boiling) with the cooking time varying from 20 minutes for a smaller individual with larger crabs requiring up to 30 minutes.

COMMON PRAWN – *Palaemon serratus* (= *Leander serratus*)
This is perhaps the most common prawn species encountered around UK shores; growing about 5 or 6 cm long, and being almost transparent olive-grey (until cooked). The head has a forward facing, upward curving, spine (rostrum) between the eyes, and two pairs of antennae. The forward legs have tiny pincers for holding food, while the tail comprises five overlapping plates, each fringed with fine stiff bristles along the edge. This species tends to live in small groups among the crevices of rocks and in rock pools of the lower shore, often among seaweeds. So if you spot one specimen there may be a colony of others nearby. They are night feeders, and a pretty effortless way to catch them is to bait a weighted trap or net with offal and leave out overnight.

COMMON SHRIMP – *Crangon vulgaris* syn. *Crangon crangon*
In general the shrimp resembles the prawn but it carries no toothed spine (rostrum) on its head, while its front legs have claws instead of pincers, the legs being shorter generally than those of the prawn. Although the shrimp's body can change colour to match the local sand colour, it also partially burrows into the sand, fanning up the grains which then settle over it. Like prawns, shrimps are night feeders, mostly hiding by day, their diet being worms and small crustaceans. This species is also much smaller than the prawn above, generally growing some 3 to 5 cm in size (sometimes larger) and is found in brackish river estuaries as well as shallow shoreline waters and pools; often under the green grass-like seaweeds attached to piers and jetties as it wavers in the tidal water.

SANDHOPPERS
Sandhoppers (*Talitrus saltator* is perhaps the best known around UK and northern European shores) are not traditionally used as food and are included here as a possible additional resource BUT with a very large *safety* caveat. The reason for this is that these *very* small shrimp-like creatures (they are the jumping flea-like animals which often emerge when you kick over some rotting seaweed on the beach) are scavengers feeding off rotting animal and vegetative garbage stranded around the high tide mark which is where they generally live. If there's the slightest doubt about the contamination of any animal or seaweed debris washing up on a shore then personally I think it wiser to avoid sandhoppers. In any case they are tiny creatures although they can be caught in swarms (perhaps why they get their common name sand-fleas) and thereby can produce a volume of food. However, there's really nothing to them in terms of body mass so they are best cooked, pasted and then sieved to provide a flavouring stock. Given their scavenging nature my preferred way of preparing sandhoppers is to wash the collected ones then store them for a few hours or overnight to purge them, then wash again before going through the cooking process mentioned.

In any disaster situation you will quickly need to develop a foraging, food and water gathering strategy specific to the habitat type and resource availability of a local area. Upstate knowledge of an area or region and its resources is going to put you in a much better position than if you have to make ad hoc evaluations.

OTHER EDIBLE CRAB SPECIES

It must also be pointed out that many of the scientific names given below are in *transition* as species reclassification takes place, so you may need to use these as *synonyms* to make species linkages when doing your own local background researches.

Additional Mediterranean
Carcinus aestuarii - Medit. green crab
Charybdis longicollis - Swimming crab
Eriocheir sinensis - Chinese mitten crab *
Eriphia verrucosa - Warty crab
Maja squinado - Common spider crab
Portunus pelagicus - Blue swimming crab

North America [See note (1) below]
Arenaeus cribrarius - Speckled swimcrab
Callinectes ornatus - Shelligs crab
Callinectes sapidus - Blue crab
Cancer (Metacarcinus) borealis - Jonah crab
Cancer irroratus - Rock crab
Carcinus aestuarii - Medit. green crab
Chionoecetes bairdi - Tanner crab
Chionoecetes opilio - Snow crab
Eriocheir sinensis - Chinese mitten crab *
Libinia emarginata - Nine-spined spider crab
Paralithodes camtschatica - Red king crab

Caribbean Basin [See note (2) below]
Arenaeus cribrarius - Speckled swimcrab
Calappa gallus - Yellow box crab
Callinectes bocourti - Blunttooth swimcrab
Callinectes danae - Dana swimcrab
Callinectes exasperatus - Rugose swimcrab
Callinectes larvatus - Masked swimcrab
Callinectes ornatus - Shelligs crab
Callinectes sapidus - Blue crab
Callinectes similis - Lesser blue crab
Cardisoma guanhumi - Blue land crab *
Charybdis hellerii - Indo-Pacific swimming Crab
Libinia emarginata - Nine-spined spider crab
Menippe mercenaria - Stone crab
Ucides cordatus - Ghost crab *

NOTE 1: List drawn from both sides of N. America.
NOTE 2: The term Caribbean Basin refers here to the area encompassing southern US states to northern South America, and from the central American isthmus across to the Caribbean islands.

Oceania
Birgus latro - Coconut crab *
Cardisoma carnifex - Brown land crab *
Cardisoma hirtipes - Blue land crab *
Gecarcoidea lalandii - Purple land crab *
Ocypode ceratophthalma - Horned ghost crab
Ocypode cordimanus - Common ghost crab
Portunus sanguinolentus - Flower crab
Portunus trituberculatus - Gazami crab
Scylla oceanica - Philippine king crab
Scylla serrata - Brown mud crab
Scylla tranquebarica - Mud crab

Asia-Pacific
Birgus latro - Coconut crab *
Callinectes sapidus - Blue crab
Cardisoma carnifex - Brown land crab *
Cardisoma hirtipes - Blue land crab *
Chionoecetes bairdi - Tanner crab
Chionoecetes opilio - Snow crab
Eriocheir japonicus - Mitten crab
Eriocheir sinensis - Chinese mitten crab *
Eriphia verrucosa - Warty crab
Gecarcoidea lalandii - Purple land crab *
Ocypode ceratophthalma - Horned ghost crab
Ocypode cordimanus - Common ghost crab
Paralithodes camtschatica - Red king crab
Portunus pelagicus - Blue swimming crab
Portunus sanguinolentus - Flower crab
Portunus trituberculatus - Gazami crab
Scylla oceanica - Philippine king crab
Scylla olivacea - Orange mud crab
Scylla paramamosain - Green mud crab
Scylla serrata - Brown mud crab
Scylla tranquebarica - Mud crab

* These species are land or mud crabs which spend a large part of their life living close to the shoreline or in mangrove swamps.

OTHER EDIBLE PRAWN & SHRIMP SPECIES

Depending on which part of the world that you live the vernacular names for some *prawn* or *shrimp* species may be differentiated. European languages do make a differentiation, while North American English generally bundles them all together as 'prawns'. Some of the scientific names given are in *transition* as reclassification takes place, so you may need to use these as *synonyms* to make species linkages when doing your own local background researches. The original list for this section contained more than 200 species and has been narrowed considerably for space reasons to those with habitats down to about 10 metres or have juveniles which inhabit closer to the shoreline.

West / Northern Europe

Lysmata seticaudata - Monaco shrimp
Palaemon adspersus - Baltic prawn
Palaemon elegans - Rockpool prawn
Palaemon longirostris - Delta prawn
Palaemon varians - Atlantic ditch shrimp
Pandalus montagui - Aesop shrimp
Pasiphaea sivado - White glass shrimp
Processa edulis - Nika shrimp

Mediterranean

Lysmata seticaudata - Monaco shrimp
Metapenaeus monoceros - Speckled shrimp
Palaemon adspersus - Baltic prawn
Palaemon elegans - Rockpool prawn
Palaemon longirostris - Delta prawn
Palaemon varians - Atlantic ditch shrimp
Pasiphaea sivado - White glass shrimp
Penaeus semisulcatus - Green tiger prawn
Processa edulis - Nika shrimp

Caribbean Basin

Acetes americanus - Aviu shrimp
Alpheus heterochaelis - Bigclaw snapping shrimp
Alpheus sublucanus - Coral snapping shrimp
Atya innocous - Basket shrimp *
Atys scaber - Camacuto shrimp *
Macrobrachium acanthurus - Cinnamon river prawn *
Macrobrachium carcinus - Painted river prawn *
Macrobrachium jelskii - Agar river prawn *
Macrobrachium ohione - Ohio river prawn *
Macro. olfersii - Buchura river prawn *
Macro. tenellum - Longarm river prawn *
Penaeus (Litopenaeus) setiferus - Northern white shrimp

North America

Crangon alaskensis - Alaska shrimp
Crangon franciscorum - California shrimp
Crangon nigricauda - Blacktailed shrimp
Crangon nigromaculata - Bay shrimp
Crangon septemspinosa - Sand shrimp
Heptacarpus brevirostris - Shortspine shrimp
Macrobrachium ohione - Ohio river prawn *
Palaemon macrodactylus - Migrant prawn
Pandalus hypsinotus - Coonstripe shrimp
Pandalus montagui - Aesop shrimp
Pandalus platyceros - Spot shrimp
Penaeus (Litopenaeus) setiferus - Northern white shrimp
Penaeus brasiliensis aztecus - Northern brown shrimp
Penaeus brasiliensis - Redspotted shrimp
Penaeus duorarum - Northern pink shrimp
Sicyonia brevirostris - Rock shrimp
Sicyonia dorsalis - Lesser rock shrimp
Trachypenaeus constrictus - Roughneck shrimp
Xiphopenaeus kroyeri - Atlantic seabob

Caribbean Basin cont'd.

Penaeus brasiliensis - Redspotted shrimp
Penaeus duorarum - Northern pink shrimp
Sicyonia brevirostris - Rock shrimp
Sicyonia dorsalis - Lesser rock shrimp
Sicyonia typica - Kinglet rock shrimp
Trachypenaeus constrictus - Roughneck shrimp
Trachypenaeus similis - Yellow roughneck shrimp
Xiphopenaeus kroyeri - Atlantic seabob

* Freshwater tolerant, sometimes in brackish areas. Other species may live in estuarine and shallow habitats.

EDIBLE WILD PLANTS

Outside the influence of some apocalyptic event the pure availability of wild edible plants for survival food depends ultimately on soil type, regional temperature differences, moisture, sun aspect, and so on. Often these variables will overlap in their effect, as can terrains. Where some catastrophic event has taken place then there may be (a), displacement of wild plant resources because they have been physically destroyed by the event, or (b), they are *contaminated* as a consequence of the event.

For anyone unfamiliar with plants and botany the task of learning about the many edible wild plant species available can be daunting, if not off-putting. So, for this largely Northern Temperate edition of the book I have selected around 30, often commonly found, wild plants which are largely perennial, or have a prolific annual habit (such as shepherd's-purse [*Capsella bursa-pastoris*] and chickweed [*Stellaria media*]), that makes them act almost like perennials. The species have also been selected to try and represent a variety of terrain or habitat types. There is an additional clutch of pretty readily recognizable edible seaweeds too, which would extend your resources in coastal areas. Not included in my lists are fungi since, in my view, the poor nutritional gain they offer balanced against the risks of poisoning does not stack up favourably.

There could also possibly be available specimens of commercial crops which still remain in field systems – potatoes and carrots, for example, cereals, oilseed rape, mustard, and kale. Sometimes odd remnants of these crops will be found in the hedgerows or borders of fields, so it is worth scavenging round for them. You should also consider all the edible ornamental and garden plants that may exist in urban areas. To a certain degree most of the ornamentals in gardens are useless providers of food. If they had been useful food sources then they would no doubt have found their way into commercial usage. A short section on ornamentals with edible parts will be found in a following section.

My list of edible *wild* plants is by no means exhaustive, deliberately so, but it will provide you with a good basic variety of edible species. Indeed, you do not need to have a mastery of botany, or knowledge of all edible plants found in the wild, to forage for real. As long as you can correctly pick out the species useful to you, then you can jettison the irrelevant non-edible species. Not all species in my list are illustrated. Also, when moving to a new foraging area and before setting up camp, take a few moments to evaluate the location and weigh up its foraging potential or limitations (including soil-borne pathogens) and plan accordingly.

FIELDS / PASTURE / MEADOW
Black Mustard – *Brassica nigra*
Couch Grass – *Agropyron repens* syn. *Elymus repens*
Dock, Curled – *Rumex crispus*
Dock, Broad-leaved – *Rumux obtusifolius*
Thistle, Creeping / Field – *Cirsium arvense*

Thistle, Nodding – *Carduus nutans*
Thistle, Spear – *Cirsium vulgare*
Greater Plantain – *Plantago major*
Salad Burnet – *Poterium sanguisorba*

OPEN ARABLE / GARDENS / ALLOTMENTS
Borage – *Borago officinalis*
Charlock – *Sinapsis arvensis*
Fat-Hen – *Chenopodium album*
Chickweed – *Stellaria media*
Shepherds-purse – *Capsella bursa-pastoris*
Smooth Sow-Thistle – *Sonchus oleraceus*
Nettle, Stinging and **Small** – *Urtica dioica* & *urens*
Sorrel, Sheep's – *Rumex acetosella*
(1) **Oilseed Rape** – *Brassica rapa* ssp. *oleifera*
(2) **Wintercress** – *Barbarea vulgaris*

HEDGEROW / HEDGE BANKS
Ramsons – *Allium ursinum*
Sorrel, Common – *Rumex acetosa*
Dandelion – *Taraxacum officinale*
Ground Ivy – *Glechoma hederacea*
Goosegrass – *Galium aparine*

MOORLAND
Bilberry / Whortleberry – *Vaccinium myrtillus*

RIVER / FRESHWATER / MARSHY
Thistle, Marsh – *Cirsium palustre*
Cat's-tail / Reed-mace / Bulrush – *Typha latifolia* & *angustifolia*
Ribwort Plantain – *Plantago lanceolata*
Opposite-Leaved Golden Saxifrage – *Chrysosplenium oppositifolium*
Watercress – *Nasturtium officinale*
Bittercress – *Cardamine pratensis* & *hirsuta*
Brooklime – *Veronica beccabunga*

SEA / COAST
Buck's-horn Plantain – *Plantago coronopus*
(3) **Fennel, Common** – *Foeniculum vulgare*
Sea Aster – *Aster tripolium* syn. *Tripolium vulgare*
Sea Beet – *Beta vulgaris* ssp. *maritima*
Sea Buckthorn – *Hippophae rhamnoides*
Sea Kale – *Crambe maritima*
Orache – *Atriplex patula*
Scurvy-Grass – *Cochlearia officinalis*

(1) Though not a wild plant, escapees of this commonly grown crop can exist in farmland post-cropping. Younger leaves can be eaten as a vegetable green.

(2) Wintercress is an old salad-like cress that was once grown as a food and may exist in some areas as a legacy plant species so is worth looking for in these areas. Old watercress production areas would also be worth seeking out to see if there are legacy plants still around, but watercress growing in streams should be regarded with caution, and is safer cooked.

(3) Fennel is not covered in the main descriptive texts that follow since it is such a well-known culinary flavouring plant. However, fennel may sometimes be found growing among the sand dunes and small patches of shingle near the beach, so there may be an opportunity to harvest the frothy young leaves, or the later seeds, if you like the anise-like aroma. This is not the florentine fennel species of culinary use.

If habitat conditions are favourable then species often pop up in environments where you do not expect to find them. Closer inspection of the spot may show a micro-environment or micro-climate exists that allows the specimen to take hold.

By the same token, if you are in a rural area then plants that have been grown in the cottage gardens of hamlets and village communities sometimes find their way into the surrounding countryside, often remaining as legacy species in the hedgerows and lanes long after they have disappeared from gardens themselves.

In a long-term survival scenario then there may come a case for planting various wild plant weed species as many seem to be extremely tenacious and very hardy in their growth characteristics, and need little maintenance. There is a Wild Food School occasional paper available on the subject (*Cutting Your Food Bills*) which outlines the philosophy of essentially cultivating a number of wild plants species – mainly perennials – in everything from window boxes to large and small back yards, and suggests species that could be usefully grown in a temperate climate.

Foliage of both domestic and edible wild plants that is discoloured and yellowing should not be eaten. In the Outdoors if a plant in its natural habitat has yellowing, unnaturally curling, or dying leaves it could indicate that poisons are at work; on the other hand the plant may have simply reached the end of its annual growing / foliage cycle.

BITTERCRESS – *Cardamine hirsuta, amara, flexuosa & pratensis*

Hairy bittercress (*C. hirsuta*) is a herbaceous annual found in moist habitats, generally on open ground. The base leaves are usually in a rosette form, with the plant growing from 15 to 45 cm in height, and has small white flowers. The related large bittercress (*C. amara*) has a similar habit as the previous species, and is also found along riversides, in moist meadows, and watery places. A herbaceous perennial, the large bittercress is frequently taller in height than *Cardamine hirsuta*. There's also a wavy bittercress (*C. flexuosa*) which, again, likes damp soils.

Perhaps the most familiar species of this group of plants is the Cuckoo-flower or Lady's-Smock (*C. pratensis*), a lilac-white flowered perennial which appears during the Spring, and is also found in low-lying areas bordering streams and rivers, marshy ground, and water-meadows. The peppery leaves of all four may be eaten as a salad item, or cooked – which destroys the spiciness.

BLACK MUSTARD – *Brassica nigra*

This is a close relative of the cultivated mustard (*Brassica alba*) and was once widely cultivated for its mustardy seeds. For this reason remnant specimens may be found in cultivated areas, but also on hedge banks, field waysides, coastal cliffs, waste areas and woodland margins.

This is a herbaceous annual species growing about 30 to 120 cm in height, the leaves are somewhat greyish-green in colour, and generally hairless (certainly when compared to *B. alba* and the related charlock (*Sinapsis arvensis*). The yellow flowers of *B. nigra* appear around June to August. Black mustard seeds may be used for their flavour, as may also the whole seed pod when in its green state. In their young state the tender green leaves may be eaten, and also have a slight mustardy flavour. Older leaves get pretty dreadful quality-wise. If you ever come across legacy specimens of related oilseed rape (*B. napus*) in arable fields then the leaves of young specimens of those may also be used for food.

BORAGE – *Borago officinalis*

This bristly herbaceous biennial will be found growing in the wild having become naturalized after centuries of cultivation in herb gardens, and thence escaping into farmland, waste places and hedgerows. Borage is sometimes grown as a crop for the herbal medicine industry too. From my own experience you therefore tend to find borage in the vicinity of human habitation but not generally in the deepest arable and country terrains.

Apart from its bristly foliage and stems, which makes borage quite uncomfortable to handle, a key distinguishing feature of this plant are the vivid blue, stalked, flowers with purple-black anthers at their centre. Some varieties of borage have somewhat white-ish flowers.

From a food point of view borage has the advantage of tasting mildly like cucumber flesh – assuming you like cucumber. To get round the bristles dip the leaves in batter and briefly fry them, or scrape the down off the hollow stems and use those. Cleaned-up stems may also be pickled or cooked, and the flowers may be added to salads. Borage can grow quite prolifically so could be a handy plant.

BROOKLIME – *Veronica beccabunga*

Brooklime is a common, semi-aquatic, species generally found in a submerged state in association with streams, lakes, ponds and rivers, but also in moist silty soils close to such habitats. Young brooklime shoots are upright, becoming prostrate with time.

The oval leaves are relatively smooth and slightly succulent, and are generally lightly toothed. From experience it appears that young and early season leaves possess little indentation of the leaf margin. In early summer brooklime produces tiny blue flowers on short stalks.

Leaves of early growth have little bitterness and may be eaten raw (brooklime has a good vitamin C content), but older leaves get disappointingly bitter. From a survival point of view the plant can be easily propagated; stems lying in contact with water or moist soil quickly developing small rootlets at the leaf joints, which would make the plant a good candidate for transferring to a pond system for larger scale production.

BUCK'S-HORN PLANTAIN – *Plantago coronopus*

This is one member of the plantain group and grows in gravelly, barren, coastal and maritime habitats, but may also be found inland in similar habitats.

The leaves are quite distinct, being deeply cut, slightly downy, have a single midrib, and form a rosette of leaves on the ground.

In its young state the downiness of the leaves is not so pronounced and they can make a reasonable raw survival food in salad. Older ones require cooking as they become somewhat bitter.

CAT'S-TAIL / REED-MACE / BULRUSH
– *Typha latifolia* & *angustifolia*

Both species of reed-mace can be used interchangeably. Technically 'bulrush' is the incorrect name but it is the one that many people call these two species by. Both reed-maces are associated with ponds, lakes and pools, and aquatic habitats where there is peaty soil and relatively slow-moving water (personally I have not encountered *Typha* growing in fast-flowing riverine situations – although that is not to say that reed-mace might be able to survive in such habitats).

The greater reed-mace (*T. latifolia*) can reach over 180 cm in height when flowering, the individual bluish-green leaves being some 90 to 120 cm long. The lesser reed-mace (*T. angustifolia*) is a smaller plant in stature and leaf size but, as mentioned above, can be used interchangeably with *T. latifolium*.

In terms of survival foraging the roots provides a starch source; individual starch grains being held in a matrix of fibrous filaments. Dislodge the starch by bashing the roots with a heavy-ish stick then wiggling the root in cold water to draw out the starch granules (which can then either be dried, or used like corn starch).

The young shoots and internal foliage makes a quite reasonable cooked green (I always cook aquatic plants unless I can verify the cleanliness of the water source). The soft lower parts of the flower stems too are a good cooked vegetable. What eventually becomes the male and female parts of the flower can be boiled up and stripped off the woody stalk, but they aren't great food. Lastly, each flower head produces about a level teaspoon of pollen which may also be used as food.

CAUTION: Reed-mace grows in similar watery habitats to toxic yellow iris (*Iris pseudacorus*) the roots of which are pale pinkish-lilac colour inside. Be sure to know the difference! Reed-mace roots also absorb heavy metals – BEWARE!

ALSO, read the section on waterborne diseases in relation to *Typha*. My personal preference when sourcing *any* edible plants from aquatic habitats is to cook them unless the purity of the water can be assured or verified.

CHARLOCK – *Sinapsis arvensis*

Charlock (wild mustard) is a somewhat rough annual plant that prefers sandy cultivated, arable land, open ground and waste places. Once grown for its seeds as a condiment, before commercial mustards, it may remain as a legacy plant in suitable farmland.

The plants grow about 45 cm high, and have quite coarsely toothed, often rough, leaves; the base ones having short stalks while the upper leaf stalks are very short, without actually clasping the stem. Cross-shaped, yellow petalled, flowers are much larger than the common mustards, being about 1 cm in diameter or slightly larger. These give rise to long slender seed pods.

Young leaf specimens of charlock can be used as a cooked vegetable green, being too rough as a salad ingredient in my view. The seeds may also be used as a condiment, and young green seed pods in salads.

CHICKWEED – *Stellaria media*

Chickweed is a common annual weed species, but because it self-seeds many times in a year it provides an almost perennial survival food resource; only disappearing during the coldest months. As a rather delicate plant chickweed finds it difficult to compete against grasses and compact herbaceous foliage, so it is rarely found in cultivated fields (the margins and bare ground excepted).

The species is low-lying and rarely exceeds a few inches high, and depends on open soil and areas of cultivation for its existence, not being able to compete amongst grasses. Leaves are ovate and set in pairs on a round stalk which has a single line of delicate hairs on one side. The small white flowers are some 4 to 5 mm in width.

The youngest chickweed sprigs can be eaten raw as salad, but with age they need cooking. Indeed, if individual leaves become large (as in 1 cm long) then they will need to be individually removed for use since the stalk at that stage is full of inedible fibre.

DANDELION – *Taraxacum officinale*
Dandelion is unlikely to need an introduction other than to say that there are many micro-species of the plant across Europe (in fact there are hundreds), but they can all largely be used in the same way.

As a foodstuff large dandelion leaves are bitter but this can be removed by shredding the leaves and soaking for several hours in tepid water to draw out the bitter white latex, and then steaming the pieces if you want them hot. Cooking the leaves is a bit like cooking lettuce leaves in that they collapse into an unappealing heap.

If you are in a static situation then you can cover over dandelion plants with a bin-liner (or some other item that can block out the light) and light-blanch the leaves which taste much milder; not unlike the mild bitterness of lettuce in fact. Root material may be slowly simmered and used as a root veggie but again there is bitterness and you may want to throw away the cooking water. If you can dry and then bake/roast the roots you can obtain an excellent coffee substitute which is much better than acorn coffee.

DOCK, BROAD-LEAVED & CURLED – *Rumux obtusifolius* and *R. crispus*
Broad-leaved dock is a common perennial species growing to around 1 metre in height; able to grow in peaty soil, but also clay soils, waste ground and near aquatic habitats.

Older leaves are bitter to the point of being gross, but if (as a perennial) you can identify colonies of broad-leaved dock and use the young Spring leaf growth (leaves no larger than about 2 cm long) then these can be cooked and used as food, though you may want to throw away the cooking water. Truly this is a survival food rather than pleasant fare, but it is a vigorous and persistent weed species making it useful in survival terms. The leaves are also slightly laxative.

While the stalked leaves of the broad-leaved dock (right) are large and oblong, or almost lance-shaped, those of the curled dock (*R. crispus*) [below] are narrower, come to an acute leaf point, and have wavy leaf edges.

The curled dock is a plant found along roadsides and in field borders, but also natural broken ground, and is a native of seashores. Also a perennial species, curled dock grows from about 60 to 120 cm high, and the very young leaves make a more pleasant survival green than those of the broad-leaved variety.

FAT-HEN – *Chenopodium album*
An annual plant species common to bare waste-land and cultivated ground such as allotments, gardens, arable fields, and manure heaps. Fat-hen is a quite varied species, expressing different forms which can make ID difficult.

Generally speaking the main lower stem leaves have a flat, rhomboidal, appearance, with the leaf edge indented by a few blunt teeth. Upper flower stem leaves are almost lance-shaped in their appearance. The leaves also have the appearance of being dusted with a fine white powder (harmless), particularly in the early stages of growth.

Whole stem sprigs of young plants may be cooked (the upper leaf cluster is the most tender), while individually collected large leaves of older specimens should be boiled. Fat-hen makes an excellent spinach-type vegetable and is rich in vitamins. As an *annual* it is important to let some specimens go to seed.

GOOSEGRASS / CLEAVERS – *Galium aparine*

Cleavers (right) is one of the best-known hedgerow plants, perhaps not by name but certainly from its ability to stick to clothing and animal fur; a feat achieved through the masses of small backwards facing prickles that cover the stems.

Commonly found in hedgerows, field margins, and waste ground, cleavers is an annual plant; its straggling growth can reach over 120 cm in length as it sprawls over hedgerow shrubbery. It prefers sand-like and sand-loam soils, but will also tolerate more clay-type soils too. Physically it has a stringy square stem around which are circular arrays of 6 to 8 leaves at intervals along the stem length. Nondescript greenish-white flowers give rise to bristly seed pods which also stick to clothing, and become purplish as they mature then brown as they dry out. Cleavers can seed prolifically.

For food, the *very youngest* seedlings and plants may be cooked up in the spring months. After that stringy fibres develop in the stem which make them gross to eat. At this point transfer your attention to the smallest leaves near to top of the plant, and the unopened top or just opening top leaf clusters. All foliage should be cooked. Some folks bake the seed pods in their purple state as a form of coffee. In my personal view, don't bother and save your precious fuel resources. Not a gourmet wild green!

GREATER PLANTAIN – *Plantago major*

This is one of several plantains useful to the survival forager, and contains high levels of pro-vitamin A. Frequently found by footpaths and roadsides, grassy areas of pasture and waste ground, this species generally grows from 5 to 15 cm tall. It is a perennial plant and pretty persistent.

The leaves are characteristically ovate with a series of distinct tough 'ribs' on the leaf underside, and are slightly downy to the touch.

Old leaves are leathery and very bitter, but young leaves (up to about 2 cm in length) picked in the Spring can make a reasonable survival vegetable when cooked (they are even tolerable raw in their very youngest state). Small leaves of specimens found on *stony* ground are generally tough and bitter, and only have small foliage because of poor nutrient and water levels. Young seeds that have not ripened can also make a useful survival food addition.

GROUND IVY – *Glechoma hederacea*

Ground ivy is a low, creeping, trailing hedgerow species belonging to the mint family, but will also be found tucked away along the edges of fields out of reach of the plough and combine harvester. The leaves are almost kidney or heart-shaped with blunt teeth around the leaf edge. The flowers are blue-purple in colour. From personal experience, ground ivy can be quite variable – in exposed, dry, sunny habitats the plant may take on a purple tinge and the leaves become quite downy, while in dark sheltered habitats the leaves are a rich green with just a slight downiness.

Ground ivy leaves are full of vitamin C and so a useful ingredient. However, it is probably wise to use them in moderation as they may contain odd chemicals. Personally, I only add small clutches to other wild greens rather than use them as a vegetable leaf. The leaves can be used as a pleasant tea-like beverage (fresh or dried), and for stuffing meat.

NETTLE, STINGING and SMALL – *Urtica dioica* & *urens*

Nettles need little introduction, other than to say both the above species are edible; *Urtica dioica* [pictured] being the perennial, common stinging nettle, while the small nettle (*U. urens*) is an annual species frequently encountered in gardens, allotments and arable ground where the seeds can find open soil for germination. Perennial *dioica*, is able to compete with other perennials in grassland, hedgerows, etc. *Urtica dioica*, in particular, likes nitrogen-rich soils.

For food select just the top 2 or 4 leaves of a vivid fresh green colour (ignore the lower leaves) between about February-March through to May-June. After that you will need to harvest similar leaves from nettles which have been cut back during the summer months to produce secondary growth, or hunt down specimens which have been growing in shadowy areas or sheltered by over-hanging tree canopy. The very youngest Spring foliage and stems – up to a few centimetres tall – can be used in their entirety. New grown seedlings have no sting and may be eaten raw.

As a rule of thumb look for nettle specimens that have green stem material (even those later in the year which grow as a result of being cut back in the summer) rather than plants tinged with purple or brown (signifying that the plant is beginning to mature or has matured).

Providing you pick the best foliage the leaves can be wilted just like spinach rather than boiled, and make a very good vegetable green. Older leaves (such as fresh green secondary growth) will need an extended cooking period. I personally never boil nettles, rather stewing or simmering them gently, and use them wherever I would want to use spinach as a food ingredient. Nettle leaves may also be dried for later use (though they crumble easily), and also be used to make a 'tea'.

OPPOSITE-LEAVED GOLDEN SAXIFRAGE
– *Chrysosplenium oppositifolium*

OLGS, as I term it in my own mind, is a small aquatic plant (about 5 to 15 cm tall) with tiny yellow flowers that grows in shady moist and damp areas – streams, brooks, and soils readily oozing with moisture.

As a foodstuff the small springtime sprigs of leaves / stalks can make a wonderfully fresh salad item (note, however, potential concerns over waterborne disease). In my experience, the quality of the plant (in terms of bitterness) varies considerably, even though specimens have been picked at the same developmental stage in similar habitats. It may be that OLGS is sensitive to too much sunlight, or that certain chemicals in the soil nutrient-base, or water, are converted into bitter principles. To overcome this simply nibble a sample or two from any OLGS colony you find, and then decide how to use them do. The young leaf sprigs may also be steamed or boiled. *C. alternifolium* may be similarly used.

COMMON ORACHE – *Atriplex patula*
Annual orache is found both by the coast, and on cultivated ground, waste places, dunghills and the like, and is of a deep mealy green colour (though specimens in coastal areas sometimes appear to have more fleshy leaves and be less mealy). It is an upright plant growing from about 10 to 90 cm tall, with furrowed stems striped with red, and branched. The lower leaves are opposite, triangular and taper towards the leaf-stalk. The non-descript flowers give rise to seeds sand-wiched between two green, slightly toothed, leafy bracteoles.

Orache is one of a number of related species, and the leaves of this particular one make a very good cooked vegetable item akin to spinach. Towards coastal areas and in salt marshes the leaf material seems to take on a salty taste from the saline conditions. The annual spear-leaved orache (*A. hastata* syn. *prostrata*) is another good edible member of this family, having triangular spear-shaped leaves, and distinctive, toothed, seed pods. This species grows in cultivated areas, waste ground, and I have found it in salt-marsh areas.

RAMSONS – *Allium ursinum*
Perennial ramsons grows from an elliptical bulb, and is widespread throughout the British Isles and most of temperate Europe, although it can be a very *localized* species. Generally, ramsons grows along shady lanes, in damp wood-land, copses, and shady corners of fields. That said, I have come across clumps of it surviving in exposed areas in the full glare of the sun, and also clusters quite close to the shoreline where there was a lot of fresh water running off the land. Such are the foibles of nature. Every part of ramsons may be used to provide a garlic flavour (mostly lost once heat is applied).

Ramsons (pictured overleaf, left) produces long spear-shaped leaves and clusters of small, star-like white flowers on single stems, almost triangular in cross-section. **Do not mistake** ramsons for lily-of-the-valley (*Convallaria majalis*) which has similarly shaped leaves, though is stiffer and more upright in its posture, produces red berries, and has no smell of garlic (pictured overleaf, right)

As a species lily-of-the-valley is more or less confined to woodland, although it is grown in shady corners of gardens for its fragrant flowers (no garlic odour!), and reaches about 15 cm in height, which is generally shorter than ramsons. It prefers humus-rich lime soils, and has a creeping rhizomous root-stock, which is again a good ID indicator since ramsons has elliptical bulbs which smell of garlic!

RAMSONS

LILY-OF-THE-VALLEY

RIBWORT PLANTAIN – *Plantago lanceolata*
Ribwort is yet another edible plantain, this particular species found in grassy pasture, waste ground, road verges and near rivers. From personal experience it would appear that ribwort is fond of soils that contain a good deal of moisture, growing well in such environments. In its pre-flowering state ribwort has a characteristic rosette of long, spear-shaped, leaves with long tough ribs running along the underside, and growing some 5 to 30 cm long. It is a perennial.

In my experience some ribwort specimens have much longer masses of flowers than those pictured right. Whether these are a hybrid cross between the true ribwort plantain variety and greater plantain (*P. major*) I am uncertain.

In its very youngest state the leaves of ribwort make a reasonable cooked green, and are even palatable raw, though, like other plantains, they become bitter and tough with age. Ribwort is particularly handy during the winter (at least in my experience) in that when most other plants are dead and brown new ribwort growth can be appearing where there is warmth in the climate. Cook the small leaves that appear at this time. One great attribute of unopened ribwort flower bud clusters is that they have a flavour reminiscent of mushrooms (assuming that you like mushrooms).

SALAD BURNET – *Poterium sanguisorba* syn. *Sanguisorba minor*

Growing to about 60 cm in height (frequently much less in porous soils) salad burnet is a leafy perennial plant that likes chalk and lime-rich soils and grassy habitats, and is just sometimes found growing alongside sheep's sorrel (see later).

The foliage smells and tastes a bit like cucumber skin (and is sometimes bitter too).

The advantage to the survival forager is that this plant species can, if the conditions are right, continue producing foliage through the winter months (a time when almost every other edible green has died away). The youngest pale green leaves – particularly as they are just unfolding – make a reasonable salad ingredient. This young foliage can be encouraged to grow by cutting back the plant. Older, darker, leaves really need to be cooked – as in added to stews, soups, and the like.

SCURVY-GRASS – *Cochlearia officinalis*

Common scurvy-grass is not always the most palatable edible plant, but it does provide good amounts of vitamin C which may be important in a survival scenario (scurvy being a physically debilitating disease).

Scurvy-grass is largely associated with coastal terrains, whether it is among sand dunes, shoreline cliff faces and tops, or even in muddy tidal rivers. In the 17th and 18th centuries scurvy-grass was grown in inland gardens too (with the help of a little salt sprinkled on the soil), so it could be possible to re-invent the wheel on this species if needs be.

Avoid using leaves of older plants in flower (and even in flower-bud mode) as the foliage seems to develop a phenolic-like taste which is revolting, and appears to be concentrated even more when cooked. On the other hand, the young foliage of pre-flowering specimens has little, or none, of this chemical taste and makes a quite tasty, pungent, horseradish-like condiment. The plant is full of vitamin C and so would be an important plant in long-term survival.

SEA ASTER – *Aster tripolium* syn. *Tripolium vulgare*

Sea aster is a member of the daisy family and will be found growing in saltmarsh and muddy estuarine habitats. In appearance the flowers look somewhat like those of a michaelmas daisy, having a yellow centre and lilac-purple outer petals.

The leaves are quite succulent, lance-shaped, and up to about 15 cm long (base leaves). Sea aster grows from about 30 to 90 cm high and tends to retain an upright posture through the annual cycle.

Young leaves may be eaten raw as a salad item while older leaves are best steamed or otherwise cooked. Since sea aster is a member of the daisy family (and the insecticide pyrethrum is derived from another member of the daisy family) it may be wise not to consume sea aster in large quantities or too often.

SEA BEET – *Beta vulgaris* ssp. *maritima*

With a thick perennial rootstock sea beet inhabits maritime and coastal places; from muddy areas to sand spits and shingle beds right by the shoreline. I have also come across it three miles inland on an estuarine river. Sea beet is perhaps the best of all the edible wild greens (as far as this writer is concerned).

In the early months of the year sea beet forms as clumps of bright, glossy, green leaves. Initially somewhat triangular in shape, the leaves mature to provide hand-sized foliage more rhomboidal in outline shape. Upper leaves of the flowering stem are more lance-shaped. The foliage is quite thick and fleshy. As the plant ages and sends up its flowering stalk the stems tend to become prostrate, giving the plant rather an untidy appearance. The best foliage is around April to August. Sea beet can be very bitter in its raw state, but boiling removes the bitterness, although older leaves may need two changes of salted cooking water.

SHEPHERDS-PURSE – *Capsella bursa-pastoris*
A weed well-known to gardeners, farmers and horticulturalists, shepherd's purse is an annual plant species that produces several generations each year. The seeds need an open soil to germinate, hence it is a plant of arable land and cultivated ground, rather than areas of grass.

The shape of the base leaves, which can reach about 10 to 12 cm in length, are highly variable in appearance, and look somewhat like a small dandelion leaf. The flower stem can reach over 30 cm in length, but in poor soils may only be a few centimetres tall.

As a survival foodstuff the leaves are quite tasty; the youngest leaves being almost as thin as lettuce leaves, but cooking up with the consistency of a thin cabbage.

SMOOTH SOW-THISTLE – *Sonchus oleraceus*
There are a number of sow-thistles which have edible parts though this is the only one which can really *rate* as a survival food. Ignore the others unless there is absolutely nothing else available. The alpine blue sow-thistle (*Cicerbita alpina*) has edible leaves but it is an endangered species in some localities and should be avoided.

The *smooth* sow-thistle grows in waste places, among earthy gravels, and cultivated areas. As a somewhat delicate annual it can struggle where dense vegetation and grasses dominate. It is easy and quick to grow from seed.

Smooth sow-thistle has hollow stems which immediately ooze a bitter white sap when broken. The soft, flat, pale green (when young), toothed leaves have a distinctive, almost triangular, end lobe. Pale yellow, dandelion-like, flowers form in clusters on single stalks. Young leaves raw, but better cooked. Old leaves are generally too bitter to eat without being doctored with a sauce.

SORREL, COMMON – *Rumex acetosa*
One SERE instructor trainee group I was working with a several years ago nicknamed this plant their *survival sweety* since the leaves provide a rhubarb-like acid flavour. I call this sorrel species my 'pudding plant' although the leaves are quite edible in their raw state.

Common sorrel [right] is usually found in pasture, meadows, grass verges and woodland margins. Lower, long-stalked leaves are almost arrow-shaped in their appearance, having two backward facing 'ears' at the base of each leaf. Flower stalk leaves are more lance-shaped. Young leaf material is a fresh pale green, while older leaves become darker and sometimes quite glossy.

Sorrel makes an excellent hot pudding (wilt the leaves like spinach) and add some raisins from your trail-food. Young leaves can be used in salads, or eaten on the hoof as a thirst-quencher while walking. Always use *non-reactive* cooking utensils as the acid in the leaves is oxalic acid. In large quantities that is toxic to humans so consume sorrel in small handful-size quantities and not too often.

Speaking of toxic matters... Common sorrel has a poisonous look-alike: Cuckoo-Pint or Lords-and-Ladies (*Arum maculatum*) [pictured right] which can grow in similar habitats if the conditions are right, and has similar shaped leaves when in their young state. The *Arum* produces bright scarlet berries in the autumn, and has a peculiar-looking flower in the early part of the year. If you are uncertain of the ID of sorrel walk away from the plant and find something to eat that you do recognize with certainty.

SORREL, SHEEP'S – *Rumex acetosella*
Sheep's sorrel (opposite, top) is essentially a sand-loving perennial plant (whereas common sorrel prefers moist clay-like soils), and will be found growing among dry pasture, heaths, rocky soils and knolls, and even on hardened off sand dunes from experience. In range it grows up to the low arctic regions of temperate Europe.

The lower base leaves are spear-shaped with two sideways facing ears at the base which give rise to the plant's common name. Leaves on the smooth, single, flowering stem are stalkless and simply spear-shaped. Overall, sheep's sorrel will grow about 45 cm tall, but can often be very stunted.

As with common sorrel the leaves contain oxalic acid and so provide a pleasant tasting acid-tasting wild green. The same precautions should be observed with this species as with common sorrel. Generally, sheep's sorrel leaves are very much smaller than the common variety and make a reasonable substitute, and as they mature take on a quite distinctive red flush.

THISTLE, CREEPING – *Cirsium arvense*

Being one of the most common thistles in the British Isles and temperate Europe the first of our edible thistle species (below, right) is probably better known to readers by sight, rather than by name.

This is a perennial species (troublesome to farmers) with a creeping rootstock that will be found in waste places, fields and pasture, and beside roads, and growing some 60 to 120 cm high when mature. It often grows in colonies thanks to that creeping root network.

As a foodstuff it is the generally the smooth stems of young plants (use a knife to scrape away any spiny material and attached leaves) that are used, as well as the roots of young specimens. The roots of the latter should be simmered in water over a slow fire rather than baked, since they become tough that way. The youngest field thistle stems can be boiled, simmered, or gently stewed as a reasonable, though rather tasteless, vegetable, and even eaten raw.

THISTLE, MARSH – *Cirsium palustre*

Personally, I rate the marsh thistle as the best edible thistle species listed here (pictured overleaf, top). In parts of the Italian countryside it is used as food, which perhaps reveals its potential as something more than a mere survival foodstuff, while in parts of central Europe the brook thistle [*Cirsium rivulare*] would be a substitute foodstuff.

Potentially growing more than 180 cm high the perennial marsh thistle inhabits ground which is either quite wet or certainly moist or damp, though it appears not to like its feet in standing water. So expect to find it *near* rivers, ponds, stream banks and water meadows. The stem and foliage frequently develops a brownish-purple tinge as the plant matures. One of my past instructor students nicknamed this plant the 'burnt thistle' as the brownish-purple tinge almost looks as if it has been flashed by flames.

As a foodstuff the best part to use is the pre-flowering flower stem (preferably before the flower buds appear) stripped of ALL spines, then boiled, steamed or otherwise cooked. If the outer rind is peeled off the youngest stems the internal pith can be eaten raw. The stems become hollow as they age, and are useless at that point.

THISTLE, NODDING – *Carduus nutans*
Also called the musk thistle, this herbaceous annual or biennial species will often be found close to human habitation, on waste ground and rubbish heaps; often where the soils are sandy, sand-based, or even have chalky subsoils, and in sloped areas that offer favourable drainage conditions (one presumes) for the plant.

As with other thistles the leaves are spiny, but in this instance the whole plant is somewhat cottony too. One of the most striking visual recognition points is that musk thistle flowers are usually solitary in number on the stalk, and droop down. From experience the flowers also tend to be of a red-purple coloration, rather than deep purple.

The parts used are young pre-flowering bud stems and young leaf stalks, stripped of all external spines and cottony material, and then cooked. I have never attempted to use the roots – at the time of writing at least.

THISTLE, SPEAR – *Cirsium vulgare*
The biennial spear thistle (pictured opposite, top) is found in virtually every waste ground and field habitat, but has an affinity for both clay and sandy soil, and also sand-loam. In my own experience I have not generally come across it in watery habitats – unless a micro-terrain has produced a dry-ish soil base.

The foliage of the whole plant is somewhat cottony or bristly, with the leaves having a distinct pointed end lobe from which, by all accounts, the species derives its name. The flowers tend to form in spaced clusters.

From a survival foraging point of view first year and early second year roots can be stewed slowly in water as a root vegetable. Leaf midribs, when the plant is in its' ground-hugging rosette form, can be stripped out and eaten raw or cooked – providing it is a young specimen. Like the other thistles here, the young pre-flowering flower stems stripped of all spiny material may then be steamed, boiled or otherwise cooked.

WATERCRESS – *Nasturtium officinale*

A common and widespread aquatic species that is probably known to most readers – at least from supermarket shelves. Although it generally grows submerged in wet habitats watercress can survive in saturated muds or sedimentary shingles right alongside the main watery habitat. So you could well find it in watery ditches as well as streams and riverine habitats.

It is a creeping plant the stems of which, if allowed to grow unhindered, can reach 90 to 120 cm in length. The oval to egg-shaped leaves grow in opposite pairs on a common stalk, with a solitary leaf at the end of each stalk. The true watercress produces seed pods with two rows of somewhat flattened seeds. Watercress, like brooklime, readily sprouts new rootlets at leaf joints submerged in water, so this may provide you with the opportunity to propagate the plant in other suitable locations.

Because of the potential for waterborne parasites and disease I think it wiser to cook <u>all</u> watercress found in the wild unless the purity of the water source can be determined; I certainly do.

IMPORTANT – The harvesting and consumption of edible plants from the wild needs to be done in relation to waterborne and soil-borne pathogens. Be sure to familiarize yourself with that topic.

113

FLOWERING TIMES

For use as food the general rule of thumb is that the foliage of a plant species is only useful *before* it produces flower buds or flowers. By that point the specimen will be quite old and full of fibres, and you will be wasting your personal energy in harvesting it, and then precious fuel energy to cook it. Admittedly it is hard for the novice forager to be able to recognize plants in their early stages of growth, but the more often you can get outdoors and do a bit of practice plant-spotting the better.

The following table shows the *average* (any shifting seasons and regional variance will also have their effects) flowering period of the species previously covered. To get the very best foliage you need to be gathering it some 4 to 6 weeks before the months shown (though laggard and straggler specimens should also be looked for around any older plant colony). Indeed, where you see an edible species in flower look nearby for young plant specimens that have not yet fully grown and may be tender enough to eat. Vice versa, where you are having difficulty making a positive ID on a very young plant or leaves, look nearby for a flowering mature example and use that to help provide positive ID.

As mentioned, flowering times are flexible so when you have to harvest vegetative greenery 'for real' do not depend on the flowering times as indicators of when a plant will be available. Instead, observe what you see among the general plant foliage around you to determine what seasonal changes are happening (heavy frost or snow can shift the growing season 4 to 6 weeks, while exceptionally warm weather combined with moisture may accelerate the flowering time).

Bittercress *Cardamine pratensis* (1) *C. hirsuta* (2) *C. amara* (3) *C. flexuosa* (4)	(1) April - June (2) February - November (3) April - June (4) April - September
Black Mustard – *Brassica nigra*	June - August
Borage – *Borago officinalis*	May - September
Brooklime – *Veronica beccabunga*	May - September
Buck's-horn Plantain – *Plantago coronopus*	June - August
Cat's-tail / Reed-mace *Typha latifolia* & *angustifolia*	June - August
Charlock – *Sinapsis arvensis*	April - October
Chickweed – *Stellaria media*	March - October
Dandelion – *Taraxacum officinale*	March - September
Dock, Broad-leaved – *Rumux obtusifolius*	June - August
Dock, Curled – *Rumex crispus*	June - October
Fat-Hen – *Chenopodium album*	July - October

Fennel – *Foeniculum vulgare*	July - September
Goosegrass – *Galium aparine*	May - September
Greater Plantain – *Plantago major*	May - November
Ground Ivy – *Glechoma hederacea*	June - September
Nettle, Stinging and **Small** *Urtica dioica* & *urens*	June - September
Opposite Leaved Golden Saxifrage *Chrysosplenium oppositifolium*	March - July
Orache – *Atriplex patula*	July - October
Ramsons – *Allium ursinum*	March - May
Ribwort Plantain – *Plantago lanceolata*	June - October
Salad Burnet – *Poterium sanguisorba*	May - June
Scurvy Grass, Common *Cochlearia officinalis*	April - August
Sea Aster – *Aster tripolium* syn. *Tripolium vulgare*	July - October
Sea Beet – *Beta vulgaris* ssp. *maritima*	June - October
Sea Buckthorn – *Hippophae rhamnoides*	April - May
Shepherd's-purse – *Capsella bursa-pastoris*	February - November
Smooth Sow-Thistle – *Sonchus oleraceus*	June - October
Sorrel, Common – *Rumex acetosa*	May - August
Sorrel, Sheep's – *Rumex acetosella*	May - July
Thistle, Creeping / Field – *Cirsium arvense*	June - September
Thistle, Marsh – *Cirsium palustre*	July - October
Thistle, Nodding – *Carduus nutans*	May - August
Thistle, Spear – *Cirsium vulgare*	July - October
Watercress – *Nasturtium officinale*	June - August

Remember, the above details are *average flowering periods* and any specimen will be past its 'sell-by' date at the flowering time, even when in bud for some species. So look for young specimens of the species in the near vicinity to any in flower.

PLANT ID SOURCES

On the matter of edible wild plant identification and uses, Wild Food School has a number of free downloadable plant ID eBooks available via the website www.wildfoodschool.co.uk, and also publishes under the Wild Food Wisdom banner a number of specific *Cooking With Weeds* eBooks at very low cost, and also a number of wild food cookbooks in digital format.

OTHER NORTHERN HEMISPHERE / EUROPEAN PLANTS

The subject of edible wild plants is enormous, and when you factor in a global dimension, the vast complexity of the subject becomes clear, and would take up volumes of paper. Bearing that limitation in mind, I have put together a few plant species that you could look out for in some other corners of the northern hemisphere if you got stuck there; the lists being a mixture of some species covered in the earlier text of this book, plus the odd specific localized item (that you will need to personally research to find out more about).

I have NOT identified which parts of the plants may be used as food for space reasons, but it is important that you understand the parts of any plant that may be used as a foodstuff since one part of a species may be edible while another part is deadly toxic.

The other thing to point out is that where any of the temperate species are found in hotter or colder regions they are likely to be located only in areas where the conditions mimic temperate habitats. Another point to consider is that some of these species may ordinarily be 'protected' in their respective regions of the world so should not be harvested at times outside of the occasion when they are required as emergency food for your doomsday kitchen.

Eastern Mediterranean / Near East
Bitter-Cress – *Cardamine hirsuta*
Black Mustard – *Brassica nigra*
Blackberry – *Rubus fruticosus*
Borage – *Borago officinalis*
Chickweed – *Stellaria media*
Dandelion – *Taraxacum officinale*
Dock, Curled – *Rumex crispus*
Goosefoots – *Chenopodium album, murale & rubrum*
Goosegrass – *Galium aparine*
Mallow, Common – *Malva sylvestris*
Milk Thistle – *Silybum marianum*
Mustard – *Sinapsis arvensis, alba*
Nettle, Small – *Urtica urens*
Nettle, Stinging – *Urtica dioica*
Orache – *Atriplex tartarica*
Plantains – *Plantago lanceolata, major*
Reed-mace – *Typha* sp.
Shepherd's-Purse – *Capsella bursa-pastoris*
Smooth Sow-thistle – *Sonchus oleraceus*
Sorrel, Common – *Rumex acetosa*
Sorrel, Sheep's – *Rumex acetosella*
Dandelion – *Taraxacum officinale*
Plantains – *Plantago major / lanceolata*

Southern Mediterranean [1]
Amaranth – *Amaranthus caudatus, graecizans, hybridus*
Black Mustard – *Brassica nigra*
Camel Thorn – *Alhagi graecorum*
Charlock – *Sinapsis arvensis*
Christ-thorn – *Ziziphus spina-christi*
Dates – *Phoenix canariensis, dactylyfera*
Fennel – *Foeniculum vulgare*
Field Eryngo – *Eryngium campestre*
Field Poppy – *Papaver rhoeas*
Goosefoots – *Chenopodium album, murale*
Henbit Dead-Nettle – *Lamium amplexicaule*
Hoary Cress – *Cardraria draba*
Jute – *Corchorus olitorius*
Mallows – *Malva parviflora, sylvestris*
Milk Thistle – *Silybum marianum*
Oleaster – *Eleagnus angustifolia*
Pistachio – *Pistacia atlantica*
Plantains – *Plantago major, ovata, coronopus*
Prickly Pear – *Opuntia ficus-carica*
Reed-mace – *Typha domingensis*
Rocket – *Sisymbrium irio*
Rosy Garlic – *Allium roseum*
Sahara Mustard – *Brassica tournefortii*
Sea Beet – *Beta vulgaris*

North Mid-Mediterranean
Alexanders – *Smyrnium olusatrum*
Common Mallow – *Malva sylvestris*
Cotton Thistle – *Onopordum acanthium*
Greater Burdock – *Arctium lappa*
Holy Bramble – *Rubus sanctus*
Milk Thistle – *Silybum marianum*
Nettle-leaved Goosefoot – *Chenopodium murale*
Plantains – *Plantago major, lanceolata, coronopus*
Prickly Pear – *Opuntia ficus-carica*
Sea Aster – *Aster tripolium*
Smooth Sow-Thistle – *Sonchus oleraceus*
Spear Thistle – *Cirsium vulgare*
Stinging Nettle – *Urtica dioica*
Stonecrop – *Sedum acre, album*
Yellow Sorrel – *Oxalis corniculata*

Low Arctic Europe
Arctic Bramble – *Rubus arcticus*
Cloudberry – *Rubus chamaemorus*
Cowberry – *Vaccinium vitis-idaea*
Crowberry – *Empetrum nigrum*
Lady's-Smock – *Cardamine pratensis*
Northern Bilberry – *Vaccinium uliginosum*
Roseroot – *Sedum rosea* syn. *Rhodiola rosea*
Scurvy-Grass – *Cochlearia officinalis* and others
Seabeach Sandwort – *Arenaria peploides*
Sorrel, Common – *Rumex acetosa*
Sorrel, Mountain – *Oxyria digyna*

Eastern United States
Blackberry – *Rubus fruticosus* agg.
Borage – *Borago officinalis*
Broad-leaved Dock – *Rumex obtusifolius*
Burdock – *Arctium lappa / minus*
Chickweed – *Stellaria media*
Curley Dock – *Rumex crispus*
Dandelion – *Taraxacum officinale*
Dead-Nettle – *Lamium amplexicaule / purpureum*
Dead-Nettle, White – *Lamium album* [NE]
Garlic Mustard – *Alliaria petiolata*
Great Nettle – *Urtica dioica*
Hairy Bitter-Cress – *Cardamine hirsuta*
High Mallow – *Malva sylvestris*
Lady's Smock – *Cardamine pratensis*
Lamb's Quarters – *Chenopodium album*
Mallows – *Malva neglecta/sylvestris* [not SE]
Plantains – *Plantago major / lanceolata*

Southern Mediterranean cont'd.
Small Caltrops – *Tribulus terrestris*
Small Nettle – *Urtica urens*
Smooth Sow-Thistle – *Sonchus oleraceus*
Tartar Orache – *Atriplex tartarica*
Wild Turnip – *Brassica rapa*

Iberian Peninsula
Three-Cornered Leek – *Allium triquetrum*
Marshmallow – *Althaea officinalis*
Chicory – *Cichorium intybus*
Goosegrass – *Galium aparine*
Ground Ivy – *Glechoma hederacea*
Honey Locust – *Gleditsia triacanthos*
Mallow – *Malva sylvestris*
Cotton Thistle – *Onopordum acanthium*
Prickly Pear – *Opuntia ficus-carica*
Purslane – *Portulaca oleracea*
Bladder Campion – *Silene vulgaris*
Milk Thistle – *Silybum marianum*
Salsify – *Tragopogon porrifolius*
Cat's-Tail – *Typha* sp.
Nettle, Stinging / Small – *Urtica dioica, urens*

Northern United States
Bearberry – *Arctostaphylos alpina / rubra*
Bilberry – *Vaccinium myrtillus*
Cat's-Tail – *Typha* sp.
Common Reed – *Phragmites communis*
Curly Dock – *Rumex crispus*
Dandelion – *Taraxacum officinale*
Golden Saxifrage – *Chrysosplenium americanum* [NE]
Horseradish – *Armoracia rusticana*
Lamb's Quarters – *Chenopodium album*
Mallows – *Malva neglecta/sylvestris* [not SE]
Miner's Lettuce – *Montia perfoliata*
Miner's Lettuce – *Montia sibirica* [NW]
Nettles – *Urtica urens / dioica*
Oleaster – *Elaeagnus angustifolia* [NW]
Orache – *Atriplex patula*
Plantains – *Plantago major / lanceolata*
Scurvy-Grass – *Cochlearia danica / officinalis*

117

Eastern United States cont'd
Sheep's Sorrel – *Rumex acetosella*
Smooth Sow-Thistle – *Sonchus oleraceus*
Sorrel, Sheep's – *Rumex acetosella*
Spear Saltbush – *Atriplex patula*
Stickywilly – *Galium aparine*
Thistle, Nodding – *Carduus nutans* [not ME and VT]
Thistles – *Cirsium vulgare / arvense* [E&NE]
Wild Cherry – *Prunus pennysylvanica*
Wild Cherry – *Prunus pumila*
Wild Plum – *Prunus alleghaniensis* [NE]
Wild Plum – *Prunus angustifolia*

Western United States
Bilberry – *Vaccinium myrtillus* [+NW]
Cat's-Tail – *Typha* sp.
Cherry – *Prunus avium* [+NW]
Common Reed – *Phragmites communis*
Curly, Dock – *Rumex crispus*
Dandelion – *Taraxacum officinale*
Dead-Nettle – *Lamium amplexicaule / purpureum*
Lamb's Quarters – *Chenopodium album*
Mallows – *Malva neglecta/sylvestris* [not SE]
Miner's Lettuce – *Montia perfoliata*
Nettles – *Urtica urens / dioica*
Oaks – *Quercus dumosa / Kellogi*
Plantains – *Plantago major / lanceolata / coronopus*
Serviceberry – *Amelanchier utahensis*
Smooth Sow-Thistle – *Sonchus oleraceus*
Sorrel, Sheep's – *Rumex acetosella*
Thistle, Milk – *Silybum marianum*
Thistles – *Cirsium vulgare / Carduus nutans*
Tumbleweed – *Salsola kali*
Whitlow Grass – *Draba verna*
Wild Rice – *Zostera marina*
Wintercress – *Barbarea vulgaris*

Southern United States
Cat's-Tail – *Typha* sp.
Common Reed – *Phragmites communis*
Crab Apple – *Malus angustifolia* [+SE]
Curly Dock – *Rumex crispus*
Dandelion – *Taraxacum officinale*
Dead-Nettle – *Lamium amplexicaule / purpureum*
Ground Cherry – *Physalis ixocarpa = philadelphica*
Ground Cherry – *Physalis pubescens*
Jute – *Corchorus olitorius*

Northern United States cont'd
Serviceberry – *Amelanchier alnifolia* [NW]
Smooth Sow-Thistle – *Sonchus oleraceus*
Sorrel, Garden – *Rumex acetosa*
Sorrel, Sheep's – *Rumex acetosella*
Stonecrop – *Rhodiola rosea = Sedum roseum*
Tamarack – *Larix larcina*
Thistle, Marsh – *Cirsium palustre* [NE&NW]
Thistle, Nodding – *Carduus nutans*
Thistles – *Cirsium vulgare / arvense*
Tower Rockcress – *Turritis glabra*
Wild Plum – *Prunus nigra*
Wintercress – *Barbarea vulgaris*

Central United States
Black Walnut – *Juglans nigra*
Cat's-Tail – *Typha* sp.
Common Reed – *Phragmites communis*
Curly Dock – *Rumex crispus*
Dandelion – *Taraxacum officinale*
Dead-Nettle – *Lamium amplexicaule / purpureum*
Lamb's Quarters – *Chenopodium album*
Mallows – *Malva neglecta/sylvestris* [not SE]
Mulberry – *Morus nigra*
Plantains – *Plantago major / lanceolata*
Smooth Sow-Thistle – *Sonchus oleraceus*
Sorrel, Sheep's – *Rumex acetosella*
Spear Saltbush – *Atriplex patula*
Thistles – *Cirsium vulgare / Carduus nutans*
Wild Cherry – *Prunus pennysylvanica*
Wild Cherry – *Prunus pumila*
Wild Plum – *Prunus americana / hortulana*
Wild Rice – *Zizania aquatica*
Wintercress – *Barbarea vulgaris*

Southern United States cont'd.
Lamb's Quarters – *Chenopodium album*
Mallow – *Malva neglecta / sylvestris* [not SE]
Milk Thistle – *Silybum marianum*
Mulberry – *Morus nigra*
Nettle, Small – *Urtica urens*
Oak – *Quercus undulata* [SW]
Oak, Live – *Quercus virginiana*
Passionflower – *Passiflora incarnata*
Persimmon – *Diospyros virginiana* [SE]
Plantains – *Plantago major / lanceolata*
Prickly Pear – *Opuntia ficus-carica*
Smooth Sow-Thistle – *Sonchus oleraceus*
Sorrel, Sheep's – *Rumex acetosella*
Thistle, Nodding – *Carduus nutans* [not FL]
Thistles – *Cirsium vulgare / arvense* [SW]
Tumbleweed – *Salsola kali*

[1] The data for the southern Mediterranean area essentially relates to the coastal region and immediate hinterland of the North African countries that border the Mediterranean. Behind that immediate hinterland is generally desert which supports very little plant life of use as food. This is an immense stretch of land with a generally quite different set of plants, with the species mentioned barely scratching the surface of what is available.

In any of these parts of the world keep a look out for localized domestic and cultivated species that can randomly appear in the wild. So in the Mediterranean region you may well come across almonds, figs, lemons and oranges (there will be olives too but these need processing), while in the US you may similarly come across citrus fruits and almonds in the outback of warmer regions.

In any disaster situation you will quickly need to develop a foraging, food and water gathering strategy specific to the habitat type and resource availability of a local area. Upstate knowledge of an area or region and its resources is going to put you in a much better position than if you have to make ad hoc evaluations.

TREES WITH EDIBLE PARTS

From a food standpoint trees, apart from those which provide nuts (viz. sweet chestnut, hazel, walnut and oak) or fruit do not really make any significant contribution towards the doomsday kitchen, other than supplying fuel or being utilized for the construction of kitchen utensils or furniture. The tree species listed below present, as far as I am concerned, the ones which offer something useful albeit in a limited way.

While there is a common notion that during the growing season trees have a higher water / moisture content this is not generally the case. And while foragers tend to harvest saps from trees in Spring when the sap is on 'the up', one hypothesis is that the abundant movement of the sap at that stage is due to major root activity combined with closed leaf buds which bottles up the sap under pressure so making it readily available for collection. When that pressure is relieved through leaf opening (and evaporation) the natural rhythm of sap flow settles in. Although there is this Spring variation, timber cut in the growing season has as much moisture content as that cut in winter. If, as popular notions have it, the tree sap was 'down' in the winter months then logs cut at that period of time should theoretically be lighter than those cut in summer, but experiments show that this is not the case.

BEECH (*Fagus sylvatica*) – leaves / nuts / ?sap
Found across much of Europe (with the exception of northern Scandinavian climes) beech likes well-drained soils, often shallow but fertile, and thrives well in chalky soils. The soft springtime leaves, just as they emerge, can be used as food, while the two or three nuts (masts) contained in the small, spiky brown, capsules that ripen around September-October are edible and contain about 20% oil which can be extracted and used for cooking or lighting. A hot summer is often rewarded the following year by a bumper crop of the masts. Somewhere I came across one reference to the spring sap being harvested, though that is the only reference I have come across relating to sap usage, and I have not personally tried harvesting it. The wood makes a good fuel.

OAK (*Quercus robur* & *Q. petraea*) – nuts (masts)
There is little point in describing oak since it, and the acorns produced, should be well known. What is not well known is that the acorns are edible, and there's more about that in the section on nuts. Only a couple of points need to be made. First, the Common English Oak (*Q. robur*) is usually found in rich, well-drained, soils with good moisture levels. It is sometimes called the 'Pedunculate Oak', the peduncle bit referring to the long stalks upon which the acorns mature. The second species referred to above, *Q. petraea*, is called the Sessile Oak, 'sessile' referring to the fact that the acorns are virtually stalkless and almost hug the twigs upon which they mature. It grows in the same sort of habitats as the first species, and the two sometimes produce hybrids.

LIME (*Tilia europeae* syn. *T. vulgaris*) – leaves / dried flowers / sap
There are a couple of dozen lime species, and I am uncertain whether all can be used for doomsday kitchen purposes. This species is a large deciduous one, and it is the young springtime leaves which can be used as a food, and later on the dried flowers as a herbal tea. This is another tree species where there is just one old mention of the sap being harvested in spring, and again which I have not tried to extract personally. However, both the lime, and beech above, are reasonably benign trees (as in not containing toxins), so their sap could well be a viable proposition as a cooking liquid. If you are concerned, then the liquid could be distilled to extract the water element alone.

WYCH ELM (*Ulmus glabra* syn. *U. montana*) – immature fruits
Often living near water wych elm is found from north and central Europe, across to western Asia. The immature fruiting bodies of the wych elm can be used in salads; the seed pods being flat and green with the embryo part of the circular mass having a pinky-red hue. On my shelves I have an early 18th French botanico-herbal book that mentions the leaves of 'elm' being used in pottage, and currently I am trying to ascertain whether that was drawn from even older 16th or 17th century European reference sources or if it was something conjured up locally by the writer. It is also unclear which elm species is being referred to. However, if the detail is correct then it adds another food use for elm.

SILVER BIRCH (*Betula alba* syn. *B. pendula* syn. *B. verrucosa*) – sap
A medium size tree species that is found right across temperate Europe, favouring the dry, light, soils of heathland, gravelly scrubland, peaty moorland and hills. The key use of this species is the sap harvested from the trees during the spring months before the leaves sprout from their buds. Traditionally, a small hole was bored about eighteen inches or so above ground level and directly below an overhanging branch. Then a small drip-tube was inserted and the sap collected in containers. In Russia a birch leaf bud tea was used, in conjunction with the *chaga* fungus (*Inonotus obliquus*) that grows on birch, though I cannot say that is something personally attempted on my part. On an entirely different tack, the bark is quite resinous and makes very good fire-lighting tinder. The inner bark, or *cambium*, can be boiled and eaten, or boiled, dried and added to flour for baking, but it is more desperation food.

SYCAMORE (*Acer pseudoplatanus*) – sap
Almost certainly known to many readers this tree species is common right across central parts of Europe, and down to some of its southern reaches. Very commonly found in woodlands, hedgerows, parks and managed grounds, sycamore thrives in rich soil. Again, it is the sap that is harvested here, in the spring. One further item that may be worth further exploration is whether the aromatic flower clusters that appear around May might possibly be infused in hot water to give a fragrant beverage. On the non-foodie front, sycamore wood burns slowly and gives out a good heat. Very large sycamore leaves make useful 'plates' to perch small morsels of food on.

WHITE WILLOW (*Salix alba*) – young leaves
Many readers may be familiar with willow as being one of the plant species which contains aspirin-type compounds in the bark used as an analgesic. This willow species is found right across temperate Europe near streams and other low-lying wet habitats. There are lots of willows but the leaves of this one are a silvery grey-green, their undersides having a particularly silky-white down on the surface. The very youngest, infant, leaves in the spring can be boiled and eaten. Given the medicinal compounds found in the species I do not feel it wise to consume these too often or in large quantities to be on the safe side.

Also:

HAZEL (*Corylus avellana*) – nut
SWEET CHESTNUT (*Castanea sativa*) – nut
WALNUT (*Juglans regia*) – nut / sap
ALMOND, SWEET (*Prunus dulcis* syn. *P. amagdylus* = *P. communis*) – nut
CHERRY (*Prunus avium*) – fruit
HORNBEAM, EUROPEAN (*Carpinus betulus*) – sap
MULBERRY (*Morus nigra*) – fruit
SCOTS PINE (*Pinus sylvestris*) – inner bark
POPLAR, WHITE (*Populus alba*) – inner bark / sap / young leaf buds
NORWAY SPRUCE (*Picea abies*) – young leaf shoots

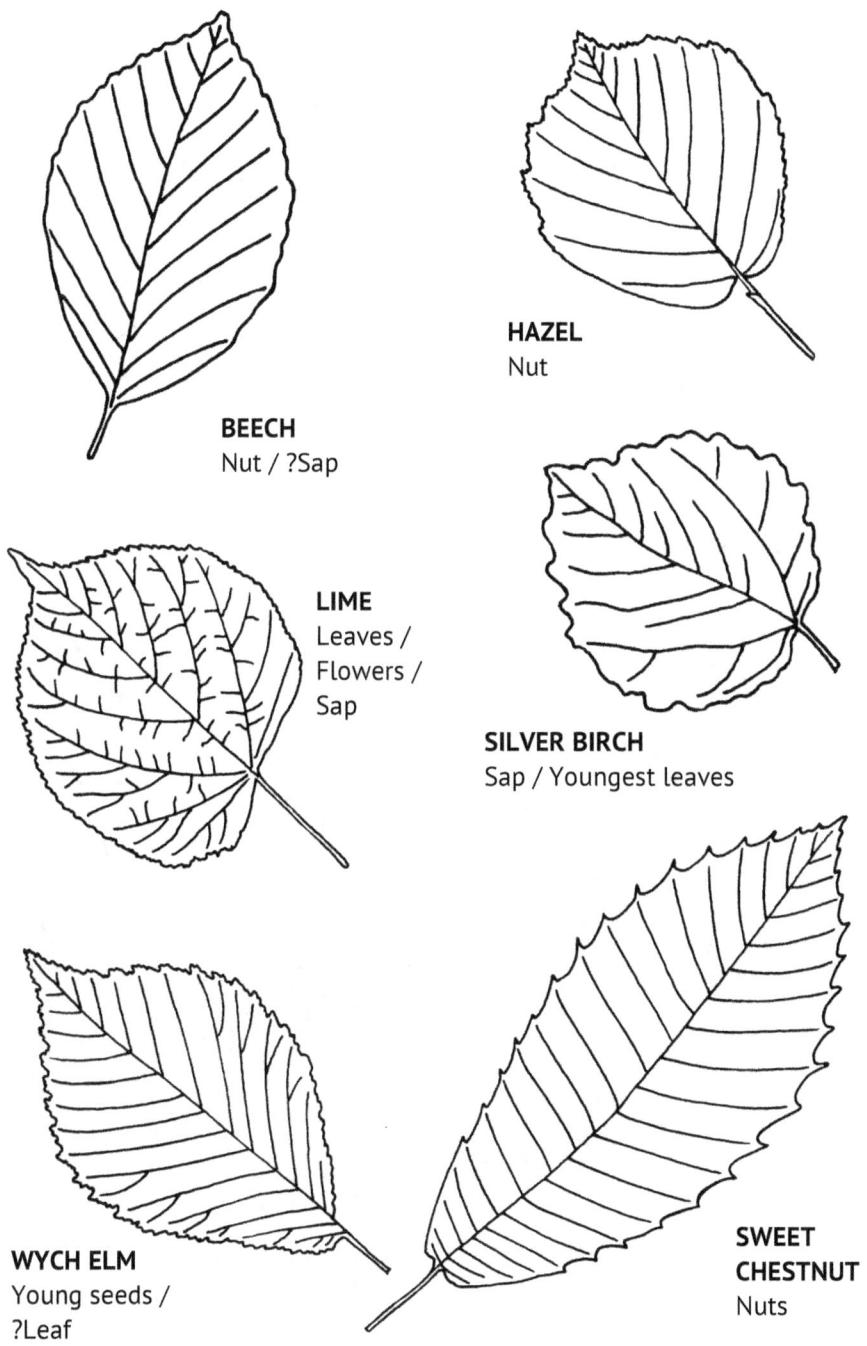

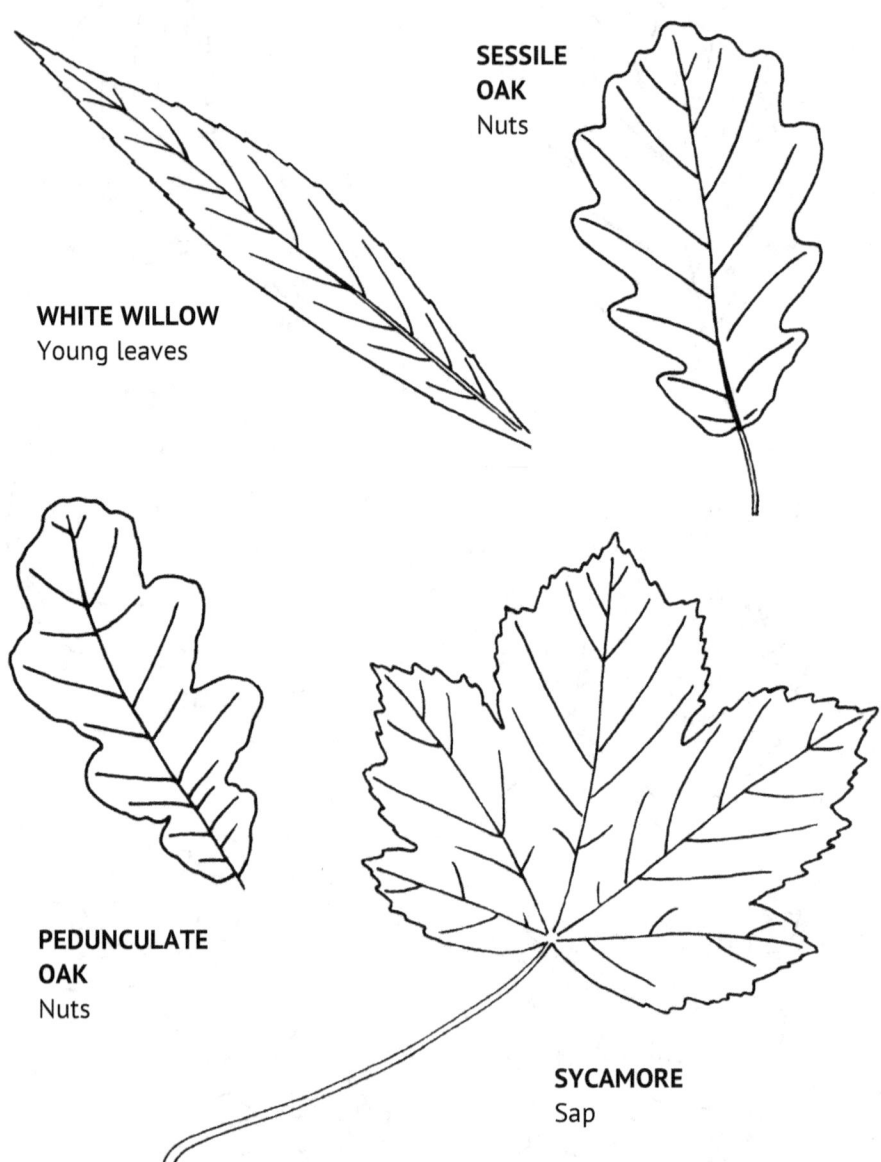

WHITE WILLOW
Young leaves

SESSILE OAK
Nuts

PEDUNCULATE OAK
Nuts

SYCAMORE
Sap

PLANTS - ORNAMENTAL, ESSENTIAL

The number of ornamental plants in domestic gardens – both exotics and those natives – is enormous, and way beyond the scope of this book. Listed below are just some of the ornamentals that have edible or useful culinary parts. Your best option for this subject area is to work through the many gardening manuals, catalogues and books which are available and compile a list of useful plants from those. On a gardening note, do not forget all those legacy domestic kitchen-garden plants that may still lurk somewhere – everything from currants and gooseberries, to apples, plums, and perpetual spinach in allotments.

Red Valerian – *Centranthus ruber*
Fuchsia – *Fuchsia* sp.
Ceanothus – *Ceanothus americanus*
Pyracantha – *Pyracantha angustifolia / coccinea*
Broom – *Cytisus scoparius*
Cornelian Cherry – *Cornus mas*
Stonecrop, Biting and White – *Sedum acre / alba*
Houseleek – *Sempervivum tectorum*
Quince – *Cydonia oblonga*
Barberry – *Berberis thungbergii (atropurpurea)*
Amelanchier – *Amelanchier laevis / rotundifolia / lamarckii*
Fig – *Ficus carica*
Mulberry – *Morus nigra / alba / rubus*
Oleaster – *Elaeagnus multiflora*
Oregon Grape – *Mahonia aquifolium*
Monkey Puzzle Tree – *Araucaria araucana*
Stag's-Horn Sumach – *Rhus typhina, glabra* and *coriaria*
Medlar – *Mespilus germanica*
Common Whitebeam – *Sorbus aria*
Garden Nasturtium / Indian Cress – *Trapaelum majus*
Dwarf / Morello cherry – *Prunus cerasus* (bitter)

ESSENTIAL PLANTS

In my view there are a small number of domesticated plants that it would be essential to grow in a longer-term disaster recovery world. My first priority would be potatoes since these provide you not only with a basic vegetable, but can also be transformed into bread, pure starch extracted from them, and can be dried for storing. Potatoes can grow in a wide variety of soils, although they are susceptible to various bugs, diseases, and excess moisture. In the absence of a garden they can be grown in car tyre 'gardens' – two or three tyres stacked together and filled with soil.

Next, would be turnips since they provide both a root vegetable and also vegetable greens in terms of their foliage. The downside is that they are biennials, though they are quite fast growing. Swedes are another bulk vegetable root that would be worth considering.

Also, on the rootcrop front, would be sugar beet, although not a readily available domestic vegetable. Sugar can be extracted from the root while the residual pulp from that process could be eaten at a push if desperate. However, sugar extraction from sugar beet is not a straightforward affair and requires considerable expertise to get rid of bitterness in the juice extract.

Although not a garden ornamental, one other vegetable plant species that would be worth looking out for in old allotments and waste ground would be the Jerusalem Artichoke (*Helianthus tuberosus*). In the right soils this can grow like wildfire, and can even become a nuisance weed for those who grow it for the edible bulbs. In a post-disaster world this might be a useful plant to try and propagate for food. Another tasty rootcrop that I have found easy to grow is biennial salsify (*Tragopogon porrifolius*), which has quite reasonable keeping properties once 'lifted' and stored in dry sand, and does not take up too much room.

Beans, and to a much lesser extent peas, are useful since they not only provide a daily vegetable, but may be dried for long-term storage and also be transformed into bread. Peapods also have their own culinary uses.

For something entirely different on the culinary flavour front, the grated roots of the herbal plant elecampane (*Inula helenium*) provide you with a spicy, ginger-like, food flavouring though the roots themselves are not eaten as a vegetable.

Finally, consider poppies, particularly the one which is frowned upon for its drug constituents, the opium poppy (*Papaver somniferum*), although there are hybrids grown for breadmaking purposes, while some species are toxic. Poppies are relatively easy to grow – even on pretty rubbish soils – and what you are after from a food point of view is the seeds, both fresh ones and dried, and not just for sprinkling on bread. Fresh seeds may be made into a sort of porridge (not wonderful tasting in my personal view), while mature dry seeds may be ground and the slightly nutty paste used as a filling for biscuits and cakes (and so might stand in as a nut substitute for those craving for nuts in the post-disaster world), also ground as a sauce thickener, and very young seedlings up to 5 or 6 cm tall eaten as a salad ingredient. There is also a recipe for obtaining poppy seed oil later in the book, and this can be used for cooking with. So the humble opium poppy is quite a versatile food plant, and each seed head produces hundreds of seeds for further propagation.

SEAWEEDS

For coastal survival situations seaweed adds another dimension to your doomsday kitchen larder. They are one group of wild edibles that most folks should be able to tolerate as a food since many domestic processed foodstuffs contain gelling agents based on the algenins and carrageenans derived from seaweed.

Despite what you read in survival books about all seaweeds being edible I think it wiser to limit the species range to the ones included here (which are very common in northern temperate Europe), since some seaweeds are now regarded as containing 'suspect' chemicals. Be aware, also, that seaweeds can absorb radio-nucleotides from seawater. Being full of nutrients and minerals you only need small amounts of seaweed as part of your diet.

Indeed, I think it probably wiser to consume seaweed as a small part of your diet, and not as the major component or too frequently, since many seaweeds are supercharged with lots of iodine which, if consumed in excess, is detrimental to your health. We normally associate iodine deficiency with the development of goitre, but an *excess* of iodine can also inhibit thyroid function, again resulting in goitre. There are also suggestions that there might be an increased risk of thyroid cancer, and thyrotoxicosis (a build-up of of thyroid hormones in the bloodstream) from excess iodine intake.

Interestingly, a study of US Peace Corps personnel working in West Africa (Niger) for an extended period of time in the late 1990s, and who were dependent on iodine-resin ceramic filtration systems to purify their daily water (for up to 32 months in some cases), found that more than one third of the volunteers medically checked had developed goitre. Many of the volunteers were consuming more than 50 mg/day of iodine through their filtered water consumption, five or six times the US RDA. In the light of that, I think it is probably wiser not to depend on seaweed as a major component of a coastal diet.

BADDERLOCKS – *Alaria esculenta*
Where it is anchored in deep rock pools off the low water mark this seaweed can reach 3 to 6 m long, and has a light olive green colour which is retained upon drying. From the holdfast (root) grows a single stem which develops into a midrib at the centre of a delicate, long, lance-shaped frond.

The part which was generally eaten is the cartilaginous mid-rib stripped of its' outer membrane, but also the substance of the delicate leaf area.

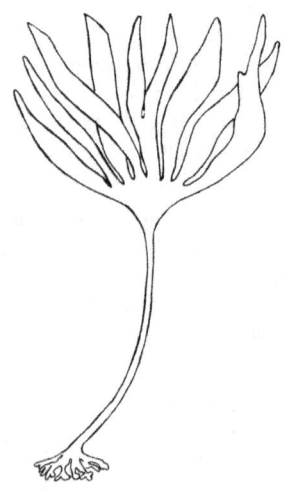

TANGLE / OARWEED – *Laminaria digitata*
A common, deep water, perennial seaweed of olive-brown colour. It can become a really tough and woody plant as it ages; having tapering woody stalks reaching about 1.5 m long, which expand outwards at the top to produce an array of deeply cleft, flattened, leathery fronds which can range from 60 cm upwards in length. Stalks of very young specimens, and the young frond material also, may be eaten. For sustainability reasons take sections of individual fronds, or complete fronds, only.

DULSE – *Palmaria palmata*
Dulse (not pictured) is a very common seaweed with dull-purple to brownish-red fronds which are broadly wedge-shaped and irregularly cleft; supple when young but leathery when old. It is found attached to rocks in the sea and immersed rocks, the preferred growth being on rocks near the low-water mark as these are smaller and more tender.

Dulse is eaten fresh from the sea as a sort of salad addition once it has been washed, but may be dried and eaten raw as a snack or trailfood, and was sometimes cooked and served with dripping or butter. In its dried state it will store pretty well.

SUGAR KELP – *Saccharina latissima*
Another very common perennial seaweed found rooted in deep water, and made quite distinctive by the wrinkly, ribbon-like, appearance down the centre of the fronds (sometimes across the whole frond) and also the wavy, curled, edges.

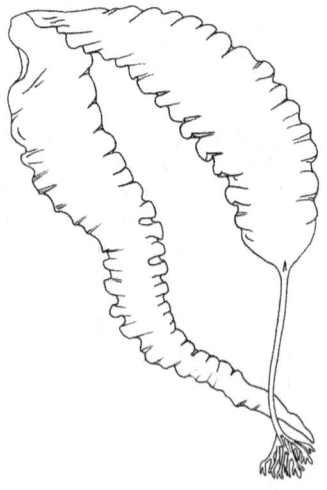

With its fronds ranging from an olive-brown to somewhat yellow-brown colour, sugar kelp can grow to about 3 to 3.5 m in length, and over 30 cm wide (though the stems are short compared to frond size). However, in my experience these large specimens tend to be too tough and chewy as food, and I concentrate on smaller specimens up to about 60 cm long which are much more tender, having a sort of cartilaginous texture that is quite pleasant once cooked.

IRISH MOSS – *Chondrus crispus*
This is a somewhat variable seaweed and is, strictly speaking, not a true sea-vegetable but used, rather, for the gelling or thickening quality that it provides. A purple-red perennial, growing from a small disc-like holdfast (root base), and with an unbranched stem, this plant can grow about 25 cm long. Generally this seaweed is found in rocky habitats close to the lower shore and in rock pools near high water mark. Where it is exposed to lots of sunlight it can be more greenish.

The densely tufted fronds turn a translucent yellow-brown when dried. These, along with fresh fronds, produce a jelly-like mass when boiled in water.

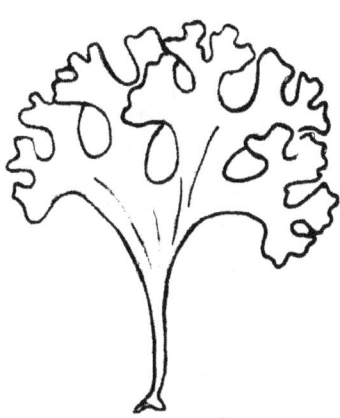

LAVER – *Porphyra* sp.
Various types of *Porphyra* exist around the shores of northern temperate Europe including *P. laciniata* and *P. vulgaris*. The fronds of annual *laciniata* are deeply and irregularly cleft, being about 10 to 20 cm long, generally of a purple colour when fruiting (but can be a dark green at other times), and is found in the sea and on shoreline rocks and stones within the tidal reach. The ragged *P. vulgaris* is a much bigger species, the fronds reaching more than 30 cm long, 5 or 7 cm wide, and having a more simple spear-shaped frond that is often wavy. It will be found in similar habitats to the previous species.

The substance of the fronds in both species is delicate. Stewed gently they are served with butter, vinegar and pepper. Extended boiling produces a gelatinous pulp which, when mixed with oatmeal, becomes 'laver bread', and is usually sliced and fried in fat.

SEA LETTUCE – *Ulva lactuca* & *latissima*
Sea lettuce (*U. lactuca*) is one of the annual edible seaweeds having thin, almost translucent, pale yellow-green fronds of 7 to 20 cm in length; narrower at the base than at the top. The species tends to grow on rocks and stones in pools (which can be a good way of finding this seaweed at low tide), but can also be

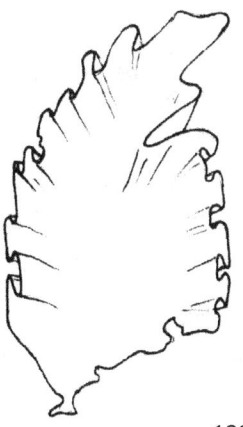

found on rocks out of water and in the sea. Best quality in spring / early summer.

The texture of sea-lettuce is a little gelatinous but it may be eaten raw (carefully) and also cooked. I frequently wrap fish in the thin leaves (a bit like dolmades) and then steam the bundles.

The second sea-lettuce species mentioned before, *Ulva latissima*, is a somewhat bigger annual species, of a darker green, and a little more glossy. It too may be eaten. NOTE: sea lettuce has an affinity for water contaminated with nutrient-rich effluent!

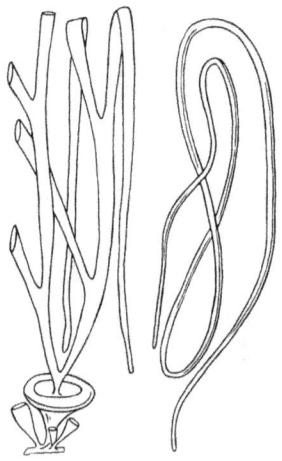

SEA SPAGHETTI / THONGWEED
Himanthalia elongata (syn. *H. lorea*)
This olive-green seaweed (left) is commonly found on rocky lower shores and rock outcrops in shallows. Individual fronds grow from small green mushroom-like disks which adhere to rock surfaces; initially the disks are about 2 to 3 mm in diameter but reach a couple of centimetres wide as the plant matures. The fronds can grow to about 3 m long.

In its very young state, the fronds up to about 30 cm long make a tender seaweed vegetable with a slight crunchy texture. As they age they become dreadfully tough and rather rough in texture, and I personally pass them by at this stage as they are not worthy of eating. One writer of old says that a ketchup-like sauce to accompany fish or poultry could be made from the disks attached to rocks, though I cannot say that I have attempted any such adventure myself.

GUTWEED – *Enteromorpha intestinalis, linza, compressa*
The name gutweed relates to some green, almost grass-like, seaweeds which grow on or among the shoreline rocks (in my experience, frequently towards the higher tide mark).

E. intestinalis (which can also be found in the first reaches of tidal rivers) has simple, elongated, rich green, tubular fronds that contain air-sacks which help the fronds float upright in water. Size varies from a few centimetres long to more than 60 cm; the stem at the base tapering towards the tiny root. Fronds of *E. intestinalis* are mostly unbranched. *E. linza* (pictured) can again grow 60 cm long but differs in that the somewhat crinkly fronds have two membranes between which small air pockets are sandwiched holding them upright in water.

The fronds of *E. compressa* tend to be branched, are about 15 to 30 cm long, and often of a more yellow-green.

All three *Enteromorpha* species can be eaten cooked – better chopped up than in their natural stringy form. They are easily dried for storage and later use.

In any disaster situation you will quickly need to develop a foraging, food and water gathering strategy specific to the habitat type and resource availability of a local area. Upstate knowledge of an area or region and its resources is going to put you in a much better position than if you have to make ad hoc evaluations.

OTHER LOCALIZED EDIBLE SEAWEED SPECIES

North America

Alaria esculenta
Alaria fitulosa
Alaria marginata
Egregia menziesii
Enteromorpha linza
Fucus gardneri
Gracilariopsis sjoestedtii
Halosaccion glandiforme
Laminaria bongardiana
Laminaria groenlandica
Laminaria longicruris
Laminaria saccharina = Saccharina latissima
Laminaria setchelli
Mazzaella splendens
Nereocystis luetkaena
Palmaria hecatensis
Palmaria mollis
Palmaria palmata
Porphyra abbottae
Porphyra cuneiformis
Porphyra fallax
Porphyra perforata
Porphyra psuedolanceolata
Porphyra torta
Porphyra umbilicalis
Ulva fenestrata

Caribbean & Central America

Acanthophora spicifera
Caulerpa racemosa
Caulerpa sertularoides
Enteromorhpa flexuosa
Eucheuma isiforme
Gayralia oxysperma
Gracilaria cornea
Gracilaria crassissima
Gracilaria domingensis
Laurencia papillosa
Porphyra spiralis
Ulva fasciata

South America

Callophyllis variegata
Durvillaea antarctica
Gracilaria domingensis
Macrocystis pyrifera
Porphyra acanthophora
Porphyra columbina
Porphyra spiralis

Other North & West Europe

Gracilaria verrucosa
Laurencia pinnitifida
Porphyra umbilicalis
Scytosiphon lomentaria
Undaria pinnitifida

Additional Mediterranean Basin

Codium taylori
Laurencia obtusa
Laurencia pinnitifida
Sargassum filipendula
Ulva rigida
Ulva pertusa

South-East Asia

Acanthophora spicifera
Asparagopsis taxiformis
Betaphycus gelatinum
Calaglossa adnata
Caulerpa lentillifera
Caulerpa peltata
Caulerpa racemosa
Caulerpa sertularioides
Caulerpa taxifolia
Codium bartletti
Codium edule
Codium fragile
Codium tenue
Codium tomentosum
Colpomenia sinuosa
Enteromorpha compressa
Enteromorpha intestinalis
Enteromorpha prolifera
Eucheuma denticulatum
Eucheuma gelatinae
Eucheuma muricatum
Gelidiella acerosa
Gelidium anansii
Gelidium latifolium
Gracilaria asisatica
Gracilaria changii
Gracilaria coronopifera
Gracilaria eucheumoides
Gracilaria firma
Gracilaria fisheri
Gracilaria heteroclada
Gracilaria salicornia
Gracilaria tenuistipitata var. liui.

Oceania [+ Hawaii]
Asparagopsis taxiformis
Caulerpa racemosa
Codium muelleri
Durvillaea antarctica
Gracilaria coronopifera
Gracilaria parvispora
Hypnea nidifica
Meristotheca procumbens
Undaria pinnitifida

Southern Asia
Caulerpa racemosa
Gelidiella tenuissima
Gelidium pusillum
Halymenia discoidea
Hydroclathrus clathratus
Hypnea pannosa

East Asia
Alaria crassifolia
Capspsiphon fulvescens
Caulerpa lentillifera
Caulerpa racemosa
Chondria crassicaulis
Chondrus ocellatus
Cladosiphon okamuranus
Codium fragile
Ecklonia cava
Ecklonia stolonifera
Enteromorpha clathrata
Enteromorpha compressa
Enteromorpha grevillei
Enteromorpha intestinalis
Enteromorpha linza
Enteromorpha nitidum
Enteromorpha prolifera
Eucheuma cartilagineum
Eucheuma gelatinae
Gelidium anansii
Gloiopeltis furcata
Gloiopeltis tenax
Gracilaria bursa-pastoris
Gracilaria lemaneiformis
Gracilaria verrucosa
Grateloupia filicina
Hizikia fusiformis
Laminaria coriacea
Laminaria (syn. Saccharina) japonica
Laminaria angustata
Laminaria diabolica

Continued across page...

South-East Asia cont'd.
Gracilaria verrucosa
Grateloupia filicina
Halymenia durvillaei
Hydroclathrus clathratus
Hypnea muscoides
Hypnea pannosa
Hypnea valentiae
Kappaphycus alvarezii
Laurencia obtusa
Porphyra atropurpurae
Porphyra crispata
Porphyra suborbiculata
Porphyra vietnamensis
Sargassum aquifolium
Sargassum crassifolium
Sargassum oligosystum
Sargassum polycystum
Sargassum siliquosum
Scinaia moniliformis
Ulva lactuca
Ulva reticulata
Ulva fasciata

East Asia cont'd
Laminaria longissima
Laminaria ochotensis
Laminaria religiosa
Meristotheca papulosa
Monostroma latissimum
Monostroma nitidum
Nemacystis decipiens
Nemalion vericulare
Pelvetia siliquosa
Porphyra arasci
Porphyra haitanensis
Porphyra kuniedae
Porphyra seriata
Porphyra suborbiculata
Porphyra tenera
Porphyra yezoensis = Pyropia yezoensis
Pterocladia capillacea
Sargassum fulvellum
Sargassum horneri
Scytosiphon lomentaria
Undaria peterseniana
Undaria pinnitifida
Ulva pertusa

NB. Many of the scientific names above are in *transition* as reclassification of species takes place, so you may need to use these as *synonyms* to make species linkages when doing your own background researches.

WILD BEVERAGE PLANTS

Beverages and teas do not really count as *food* in my view, however the sip of a hot drink can often lift your spirits, so I have included a number of wild plants that you can try out in this respect. Also, the word 'tea' is used in the following text as a general term for water-infused plant parts, actual domestic tea often being a dried fermented leaf.

Another point that should be borne in mind is that around the world there are literally hundreds of plants which are used as tea and coffee substitutes, however many of these are used for their *medicinal herbal* qualities and from a personal viewpoint I do not think it wise to take medicines unless a need arises. So where you ever see a reference in any literature to a plant used as a *tea* do a bit of research to check on its safety for use as a daily pick-me-up beverage. Even some of the following ones mentioned are on the verge of the herbal side.

BLACKBERRY & BLACKCURRANT
Dried green blackberry leaves can be used as a tea. Raspberry leaves can similarly be used (don't use either during pregnancy). Blackcurrant leaves also have a fruity flavour that can be extracted as a beverage flavouring.

CRAB APPLE (*Malus* sp.)
The small fruits, halved and then boiled in lots of water until the fruits become pulpy, then strained and sweetened, makes a pleasant drink.

DANDELION (*Taraxacum officinale*)
If you have permission to dig up dandelion roots then these make an excellent coffee substitute once roasted, and is infinitely superior to acorn coffee.

GROUND IVY (*Glechoma hederacea*)
Either the fresh or dried leaves of this bitter, aromatic plant (belongs to the mint family), makes a pleasant tea when sweetened with a little honey.

MEADOWSWEET (*Filipendula ulmaria*)
The open clumps of flowers of the meadowsweet – which particularly likes moist habitats – make an interesting beverage when infused for 1 or 2 minutes in hot water. Sweeten with honey.

LIME (*Tilia* sp.)
Dried flowers of the lime tree made a tea known as Linden Tea in former times. It's got some herbal qualities so it's probably best to drink this in moderation.

OTHERS
Although it's not something that I have tried, the leaves and flowers of mountain ash or rowan (*Sorbus aucuparia*) have been used to adulterate tea in the past so there might be some scope there for experimentation.

The use of dried blackthorn / sloe (*Prunus spinosa*) leaves as an adulterant for Indian tea was a very common event, however I am not sure whether a diet of pure blackthorn leaf tea would be deleterious to health or not. Indeed, other tea 'adulterants' (when tea was expensive and highly taxed) were the leaves of beech, plane, sycamore, horse-chestnut and poplar. Personally I would not touch most of these as a tea alternative, certainly not horse-chestnut which contains saponins. The leaves were simply used by the unscrupulous to dupe the unwitting into parting with their money in the belief they were drinking real Indian tea.

Three other plants which can provide a 'flavoured' beverage are the crushed, whole, flower bud masses of ribwort plantain (*Plantago lanceolata*) which have a mushroom-like flavour (bruise and steep in hot water), and then the flowers of the pineapple weed (*Matricaria discoidea*) which, as the common name suggests, suggest a pineapple flavour. Occasional use of crushed sorrel leaves (*Rumex acetosa*) might also be used though ingesting the oxalic acid compounds that provide the rhubarb-like taste over a long period will probably cause problems, while oxalic acid ingested in quantities is toxic.

Elder (*Sambucus nigra*) flowers may be dried for later use as an infused beverage.

Tea-like beverages have also been made from:

Bilberry (*Vaccinium myrtillus*) – leaves
Borage (*Borago officinalis*) – flowers and dried shoots
Dog Rose (*Rosa canina*) – leaves
English Elm (*Ulmus campestris*) – leaves = Warsaw Tea
Fennel (*Foeniculum vulgare*) – leaves, stalks, fruits
Gorse (*Ulex europeae*) – fresh flowers
Hawthorn (*Cratageus oxycantha*) – leaves
Mountain Avens (*Dryas octopetala*) – leaves = Swiss Tea
Mugwort (*Artemisia vulgaris*) – leaves
Nettle (*Urtica dioica*) – leaves
Norway Spruce (*Picea abies*) – young leaf shoots
Pennyroyal* (*Mentha pulegium*) – leaves, upper parts
Raspberry (*Rubus idaeus*) – leaves
Rock Cinquefoil (*Potentilla rupestris*) – leaves = Siberian Tea
Southernwood (*Artemisia Abrotanus*) – leaves
Strawberry (*Fragaria*) – dried leaves
Sweet Cicely (*Myrrhis odorata*) – leaves, immature seed pods
Sweet Woodruff (*Asperula odorata*) – dried leaves (as additive)
Water Mint (*Mentha aquatica*) – fresh leaves
White Dead-Nettle (*Lamium album*) – flowers
Wood Avens (*Geum urbanum*) – bruised roots (in wine too)

* A 'protected' species in some countries.

APPLEADE
Four large apples, unpeeled, sliced. Place in a pan with 1 litre of water and 5 or 6 gm sugar (or substitute honey). Simmer gently till the fruit is soft then strain the liquid off. Pulp can be eaten too.

APPLE PEEL TEA
If you find the peel of an apple too tough to pleasantly chomp through, or apples are required peeled for a doomsday recipe, do not discard the peelings. Dry them and store for later use as a tea. When required boil peelings in water for 10 to 15 minutes, then strain off and use.

ROSE HIP TEA
3 or 4 gm rose hips
1 litre tepid water

Place hips in tepid water then bring them to a gentle boil and simmer for an hour. Strain and serve sweetened with honey or sugar. The large, ripe, hips of *Rosa rugosa* with their slightly sweet taste are good for this. Young leaves of wild / dog rose (*Rosa canina*) may also be used for an infused beverage.

LIME BLOSSOM TEA
Place a tablespoon of lime blossoms in a pan. Pour 1 litre of boiling water over, bring just to the boil, then take off the heat and allow the 'tea' to draw for 10 minutes. Strain, and sweeten to taste. Another refreshing addition is some sorrel juice added to the cold blossom tea or, indeed, two or three sorrel leaves added during the boiling phase.

PEPPERMINT & BLACKBERRY LEAF TEA
The peppermint leaves can be from dried reserves or fresh. Blackberry (bramble) leaves want to be gathered from the fresh green growth early in the year, not old ones which are dark green. Pour boiling water over a tablespoon of the mixed leaves. Allow to draw for 5 to 10 minutes, then strain and sweeten to taste.

FIR (SPRUCE) TEA
This is more of a medicinal tea to correct (or supply) vitamin C in cases of deficiency. The needles of the branch tips and the young cones, gathered around March-April for the best brews, are boiled in water. A little sweetening added will help mask the slightly turpentine aromatics.

SWEET CICELY TEA
Sweet cicely (a perennial) has the unusual quality of tasting somewhat like aniseed, so if you like that flavour then you can make a tea from the seed pods (best) or the leaves. What's more the plant even tastes slightly sweet, which might be welcome in a world without processed sugar.

BERRIES / FRUITS

Berries (seeds too) have a knack of concentrating strange, often toxic, chemicals in their make-up, so if you are ever unsure about the ID of a berry leave it well alone. You are trying to survive, not be a foolhardy pioneer destined for the graveyard.

In this section I want to look at half a dozen wild berries that offer an additional resource to common species like blackberry, and also raspberry and gooseberry (which are found as wild forms, as also are pears). The ones I have selected are variously found in upland, coastal and general hedgerow habitats.

Be on the lookout too for any domesticated fruit species, and fruits which have entered 'the wild', as garden escapes or sprung up from a discarded apple core or fruit stone. Those are fair game too for your armageddon menu.

BILBERRY – *Vaccinium myrtillus*

Sometimes referred to as a whortleberry this short, shrubby, species (to about 45 cm tall) is typically found on heathland terrains where the soil is peaty and humus rich. Frequently it is found in association with heather species in upland regions and moors. Occasionally small colonies of bilberry may be found growing on the tops of high banks surrounding fields, the habitat at the summit of those banks mimicking heath conditions in microhabitat form.

Bilberry leaves are oval to egg-shaped with some serrations along the leaf edge, the flowers pinky-red, drooping and waxy looking, and giving rise to a small blue-black fruit that develops a greyish surface bloom.

The berries should be cooked, though in small quantities may be eaten raw. Being very astringent they can be used to help with diarrhoea.

CRAB APPLE – *Malus sylvestris*

Crab apples (pictured overleaf, top) are the wild equivalent of the domesticated apple bought off your supermarket shelf. However, the true variety (which has a green skin) produces a fruit about the size of a walnut, while domesticated hybrid crabs are even smaller, often being less than 2 cm in diameter. These hybrids often have a different colour too, sometimes being quite red, orange-yellow, and even pale green tinted with a red flush.

The true wild crab is also very bitter and cannot be eaten like a domestic apple, though I have come across a small red variety which was passable eating raw. Essentially the way of using these wild apple varieties is to cook them to a pulp, then sweeten and consume. Also, if the crabs are stewed for a long period in water, then an apple tasting beverage can be produced. Again, it will almost certainly need sweetening somehow.

WILD CHERRY – *Prunus avium*
Gean (below right), as this deciduous species is known in some places, is commonly found in northern Europe, often in parks and gardens (although there are domesticated cherry species which you can also take advantage of for food), but also in mixed deciduous woodland. Quite large white flowers, which appear around April, give rise to clusters of 3 to 5, long-stalked, fruits that vary in colour from yellow-bright red, to dark red. These ripen by June-July usually. Taste, too, varies, some fruits being sweetish others bitter. *Prunus cerasus* (syn. *Cerasus sylvestris* of old) is a sour wild cherry form that is regarded by some botanical writers as synonymous with *P. avium*.

DAMSON – *Prunus domestica* syn. *P. insititia*
It is doubtful that damsons require any introduction if you are familiar with the Outdoors. They are a personal favourite, and although most people will stew the dark purple, plum-like, fruits (about the size of a medium to large-size grape) with sugar, or make pies or jam with them, they can also be eaten raw provided the flesh is fully ripened and the skin is peeled off. It is a rather tedious process because damsons are so small, but it appears that it is the purple skin which harbours damson's tart and astringent qualities.

DEWBERRY – *Rubus caesius*
Looking a bit like a bramble, dewberry (pictured opposite, top) is a low, prostrate, shrub species found in thickets, hedges and damp places (I have encountered it in heathy, sandy conditions too). The plant, however, is much more slender than bramble.

Generally flowering around the summer period the berries which form are smaller than blackberries and develop a greyish-blue bloom. They are absolutely delicious tasting (often regarded as better than blackberries) and may be eaten raw or cooked.

ROSE HIPS – *Rosa rugosa*

The berries (hips) of this introduced species of wild rose – it's actually called the Japanese Rose, sometimes Beach Rose – are the only rosehips that I consider worth the effort of picking since their considerable size provides a good return on effort expended to harvest them (the hips can be the size of cherry tomatoes). Hips of the Dog Rose (*Rosa canina*) I do not normally consider as worthy of picking simply because they are too small; though that might change in an emergency situation.

Rosa rugosa is a species which frequently grows near shorelines, often in the shady areas adjacent to the shore (sometimes intermixed with sea buckthorn shrubs – see below).

Rose hips cannot really be considered as a *food* but as a source of vitamin C in a time of survival they could be useful.

SEA BUCKTHORN – *Hippophae rhamnoides*

Sea buckthorn is a small-ish, prickly, shrub (reaching a maximum of about 2 to 2.5 m high) found on sandy land close to the shoreline. On occasion I have come across it in thicket-like quantities, yet frequently you find just a few specimens huddled together on the shoreline.

The leaves of sea buckthorn are thin and silvery green, and the shrub eventually gives rise to a small orange to orange-red berry that has a lovely acid-sour taste when ripe, but is rather too sour when unripe. Mixed with some sugar you can make a refreshing drink with the juice, or use the acid berries in any old recipes where barberry (*Berberris vulgaris*) might have been called for.

NUTS

As you enter a time of true survival you will inevitably be saying goodbye to nut favourites such as peanuts, almonds, pistachios and the like, unless you happen to be in Mediterranean climes. Instead, you are going to have to make do with whatever nut species are found naturally in the wild; essentially acorns, beech masts, hazel and sweet chestnut (horse chestnut should not be regarded as safe to eat – despite some of the nonsense you see about them on the internet – as they contain saponins which may cause haemolytic breakdown if they get into your bloodstream).

You do sometimes come across walnut trees in the wild but frequently they are near, or in, domestic locations where they have been deliberately planted. The walnut mast may obviously be eaten when it is ripe, but the young, green, unripe fruits may also be pickled (though they are not to everyone's taste).

ACORNS – Processing & Preparing
As the fruits of oak species are so well known I think we can dispense with a botanical description. In their raw state acorns are not good news for your body system, and I would suggest that acorns, even when processed, should be used as a small part of a varied diet that includes vegetable greens. The main problem with acorns is that they contain large amounts of tannin, and therein lies the problem... though this is one easily solved by leaching your acorns with water – exactly the process we go through when making a cup of tea. However, processing acorns is more time-consuming and requires lots of water – which may be a problem in a survival situation where precious water is at a premium.

Many of the preparation details and procedures which follow come from Wild Food School distance-learning course materials with little amendment (and in itself adapted from the *Essential Acorn, Hazelnut, Chestnut &c Cookbook.* ISBN 0 9544158 7 6). Anyway, they should get you up to speed with your own experimentation on this long-forgotten potential food resource.

1. Select windfall acorns that have started to brown, rather than green ones picked off a tree (although those *may* be used too). And avoid acorns that are sprouting, since there may be chemical changes going on which are deleterious to health [though I have personally included a few acorns with minor emerging root sprouts among unsprouted ones and, having removed the sprouted bits, do not seem to have come to any harm].

2. Wash, and then pick over, your gathered acorns, removing any 'caps' still attached and discarding acorns which have insect holes / bores.

3. The next step is to remove the shell to get at the pale inner meat, and this can be done in two ways... The first is to place the acorns in a heavy-duty bin-liner, or similar, and batter the contents with something heavy. Although there are reports of American Indians doing something similar this is NOT a favoured

method since fragments and slivers of the tough outer shells end up in the final processed acorn and are troublesome to pick out.

The second, and better, method is to make a cut into the shell with a sharp knife. If you use a small paring knife hold each acorn against the blade and 'roll' the acorn from top to bottom whilst pressing it against the sharp edge. You need to watch your fingers, but after a while you pick up momentum and the process speeds up. You could also possibly use a nutcracker to split the shells but that would be a dreadfully slow process.

4. Next, put the acorns in a bucket or container and pour scalding or boiling water over them. Leave for about an hour, during which time the skins will have expanded and partly softened enough for you to 'peel' your acorns. Discard any masts that are discoloured or worm eaten. As mentioned, preparing acorns is not a fast process.

5. The next stage of the process is to remove the tannins, and here there are various routes or options you can choose, depending on your urgency to get to the end product. There is no hard and fast rule as to 'how' to process the masts. The only key factor is tannin removal so pick and choose from the techniques below...

If you are not in a hurry and want 'whole' acorns – noting that some acorns will disintegrate during the boiling process – then return the acorns to your bucket to start the leaching process. Pour more hot water over and leave for several hours. The tannin-stained water can then be discarded and more hot water added. Repeat this process several times over a day or two, leaving one last water change overnight. Next day strain off the water and place the acorns in a pan. Place on the fire, pour boiling water over and allow to boil for a couple of minutes before steeping for 30 or 40 minutes beside the fire. Then replace the tainted water with more clean boiling water. Allow the mush to settle each time before pouring off the top cooking water, otherwise you will lose a lot of your precious acorn material. Repeat this process [which may take several hours] until the cooking water is clear or only very slightly coloured. At that point most of the harmful tannin should have been removed. The pre-soaking regime draws out a lot of the tannin prior to boiling. Also, during the boiling process, do not add cold water to the pan as it seems to coagulate a dark tannin coat on the surface of the acorns.

If you are in a real hurry to get at acorn flour/mush then you can adopt another method; crushing, grinding or milling the hulled acorns with some water. This process provides more surface area for the soaking/boiling water to act upon, speeding up the leaching process. What you end up with is a beige coloured slurry rather reminiscent of lumpy hummus.

You now have two options... a fast route or a slower one. The slower method follows the slow and repetitive pre-soaking regime mentioned previously, but because of the increased surface area the pre-soaking time is shorter and more effective. To fast-track your acorns put the slurry in a pan and add boiling water, and allow to come to the boil. It is most important if going down this route to keep the contents of the pan stirred or paddled for the first 10 to 15 minutes [or as long as it takes], since the ground acorns will congeal on the bottom of the pan and burn, and burnt acorn is foul! Once you have passed the 'sticky zone' as I like to call it, then the pan only needs stirring from time to time. Replace the water every 15 to 20 minutes until the leaching water is virtually clear. Again, so that you don't waste acorn when replacing with fresh boiling or hot water, allow the mush to settle in the pan before pouring off the top leaching water.

6. Once you have reached minimal coloration of the leaching water, strain the contents of the pan. Congratulations! You are the proud owner of acorn mush with which you can cook and experiment with.

7. You may use the mush immediately, but if you want to preserve it the next step is to dry the mush; spreading it out on porous surface and drying in a very low temperature oven or the warmth of a fire.

The end product can then be stored in an airtight container. I tend to double-bag the end product in polythene bags. For very long-term survival mode storage this would be essential since oaks do not produce acorns every year, and there may be a two year gap before the next flourish – a very similar situation with beech masts.

There is yet another method, but one which I have not used personally. This involves shelling the acorns, drying out the untreated masts then grinding them down to a fine meal or flour which is then stored. When needed the flour is then mixed with water and leached until the tannins have been removed.

Note that acorns, both cooked and raw, will go off if left exposed to the air for too long.

BEECH MASTS – *Fagus sylvatica*
Although tasty, the main drawback with beech masts is that they are *very* fiddly to shell, and it can be hit and miss in terms of nut quality and content. The surest way to guarantee success every time you hull a mast is to choose ONLY those masts which appear to have slightly distended hulls, indicating the nut inside is well developed. Do not waste your time with any masts which appear to have concaved sides, have a small bug hole in the side or, indeed, are dark brown. The latter ones are frequently rotting or have fungal growth inside. The masts can be nibbled on raw while lightly toasting then really brings out a pungent nutty flavour.

HAZEL – *Corylus avellana*
Hazelnuts and filberts probably rank as some of the tastiest hedgerow articles the forager has the opportunity to harvest, although getting to the nuts before the squirrels can be something of a race.

Hazelnuts may obviously be consumed as nuts, but they can also make a hazel equivalent of almond milk that was a common kitchen ingredient in wealthy medieval households in the days before refrigeration was available to keep milk cool. Windfall hazels that are not quite ripe are good candidates for making hazelnut milk too, but you might like to try them in a home-made hazelnut praline. Another potential product is hazelnut oil expressed from the ripe nuts.

To preserve hazels for winter use, and beyond, gather when the cup surrounding the nuts turns brown and they fall into your fingers as you touch the nut clusters on the tree. Transfer the nuts to a box of dry sand, layering sand and nuts, and removing any residual husk material, then store in a cool place. In the old days it was suggested burying the nuts in sealed, earthen pots, about 30 to 60 cm deep in gravelly or sandy ground, though I cannot say that I personally have tried this.

SWEET CHESTNUT – *Castanea sativa*
Chestnut trees thrive in rich sand-loam soils but struggle in habitats with heavy soils. The nuts that they produce are the same as those roasted chestnuts that may be bought from street vendors in winter months.

WARNING: Chestnuts will explode if they are cooked without piercing the outer skin first – the cooking steam builds up inside eventually rupturing the skin.

ROASTING in an oven is a bit of an inexact art but requires the oven to be pre-heated. Where the oven is very hot they may take just 7 or 8 minutes, but in a cooler one about 15 or 20 minutes. Water content and freshness may vary so test a couple of chestnuts from a batch before doing a whole lot.

Use a sharp paring knife to make cuts in the rounded side of the chestnut, then place on a suitable-sized tray and put in a preheated oven. The outer skin and inner pellicle should easily separate from the chestnut kernel when cooked sufficiently. One tip that I came across is that if a single uncut chestnut is included with the knife-scored batch, when it explodes then the rest should be done.

For BOILING, make an incision in the rounded side of the shell then place in a pan of cold water. Bring to the boil and cook for about 4 or 5 minutes. Take off the heat, allow to cool down in the cooking water until they can be handled, then shell and peel.

If you are not too worried about the physical condition of the chestnuts – for example, where they are required chopped or mashed in a recipe – then cut the chestnuts in half and drop into a pan of boiling water. Cook for a few minutes until the kernels start to slip from their shells, then take off the heat, drain, and allow to cool enough to peel without discomfort. The kernels should then be cooked more properly for further use in recipes. If the kernels are cooked too long, however, they will crumble and become more mealy – though maybe that is what you need.

Chestnuts may also be <u>STEAMED</u>, although I have not tried this. Again, the chestnuts are cut in half, steamed for about 10 minutes, then drained and allowed to cool so that the kernels may be removed from the shells.

While some of these same nut species are available in North America that part of the world has some additional species which can broaden the range of nuts available; such as the American Beech (*Fagus grandifolia*), Pecan (*Carya illinoiensis*), Shagbark Hickory (*Carya ovata*) and Pignut Hickory (*Carya glabra*). Although not a 'nut' the seeds of the American Hornbeam (*Carpinus carolineana*) may be eaten.

LOCATING THE DOOMSDAY KITCHEN

In your keenness to provide food for yourself and fellow survivors, you may overlook some important things when settling down for a fry-up. Permanent or temporary campsites will be chosen for all sorts of reasons, and the doomsday cook may have to make do with whatever situation prevails, ideal or not. The longer you stay in an area then the more comfortable you can make your surrounds as you adapt them. A few points to throw into the mix are:

Locate near to a stream, spring, or lake, or in an area where ground water is available by well digging. However, on that same note, do not locate your doomsday kitchen too close to the edge of that water source – pond, lake or stream – in case water levels rise and flood both your fire and precious food. Running water is a better source than a static lake, and certainly the water in an isolated pond will almost certainly need to be distilled if it is contaminated. Consider potential sources of contaminants from below as well as above ground (as in leakage from latrines, or your waste-water pit).

For the kitchen cooking area select a well-drained patch of ground, possibly on a gentle rise (provided there is not too much exposure to turbulent wind that will make cooking with fire a problem) so that rainwater drains away and not towards the fire or food area. If the earth is clayey or relatively non-porous then trench round the fire / food area and arrange channels for water soak-away to avoid getting flooded. Wet food preparation areas should also be avoided for reasons of disease. Try to avoid setting up in hollows or depressions as these may prove damp and chilly, which can affect fire performance, particularly on frosty Spring mornings. Chilly hollows, however, may prove good places to store food provisions providing they do not flood.

Consider, also, if the area is good for collecting deadwood and fallen timber for your fuel source, saving time and energy in harvesting it (*economy of effort*). If you are isolated and on your own then this aspect of your doomsday kitchen routine is potentially going to become a key task that will rank almost as importantly as finding food or water.

Open sunny and airy spaces are better for insect and mosquito prevention, though one of the best places for a fire is under lofty tree canopy, from both a combustion and rain shelter point of view. For long-term situations factor in prevailing winds and airflows when constructing a permanent cooking facility. Being chased round a fire by smoke is a pain, while smoke inhalation is positively deleterious to your health. Basing your kitchen area (or camp) in the direct line of winds on a northerly aspect is going to make life pretty chilly, and possibly also take the heat out of your cooking fire. Daylight will also be rather gloomy on a northerly aspect. Conversely, being exposed to blistering sunshine on a southerly aspect in the summer could become thoroughly uncomfortable, and no doubt increase your personal requirement for precious water.

Keep the area around your food preparation zone free from garbage / refuse, and fallen meal scraps. Animal skinning and plucking should be done in a designated area away from the main food / cooking area. Kitchen refuse should be disposed of in a designated pit. Food remains in bottles and cans can attract flies and should be stored, burnt or buried with the other kitchen detritus (bones, parings) with a layer of soil thrown over to prevent flies. Lidded plastic garbage bins would also do wonders.

Dirty dishwater should be disposed of in a waste-water pit rather than thrown on the ground. If there is the luxury of some sort of disinfectant being available then the waste-water pit should be regularly disinfected. In long-term situations dig an underground brick-lined soak-away pit, but make sure it lies well below the water-table, and well away from your own water supply.

Purely on a fire safety note, if based in coniferous areas where there are beds of old pine needles, light the fire on rocks since the fire could creep under the ground in these conditions. The construction of more substantial fireplaces or storage huts requires firm ground. Keep the cooking fire a good distance from your personal shelter, bedding, or other fire hazards such as clothes, and consider the circulation of airborne cinders / ashes when the wind blows.

For creature comfort, place the table or eating area close enough to the fire for convenience, but not close enough to be smoked out. Get everything in the kitchen area organized and 'in place', as this saves on time when you need a utensil or other kitchen item.

Food provisions need to be stored both securely (if there are scavengers around) and hygienically. Consider tree-caching (pictured opposite) if necessary, or in urban areas hanging provisions from guttering, lamp-posts and street signs; while tins, abandoned microwaves and old ovens can keep food away from flies and scavengers. If you are near to running water then food can be kept cool by placing in watertight bags or containers and submerging in the running water. Another alternative is a coolbox (a lidded metal dustbin, for example) buried in shaded dry ground, but placed so the lid is above the water table level.

STORING FOOD AWAY FROM SCAVENGERS

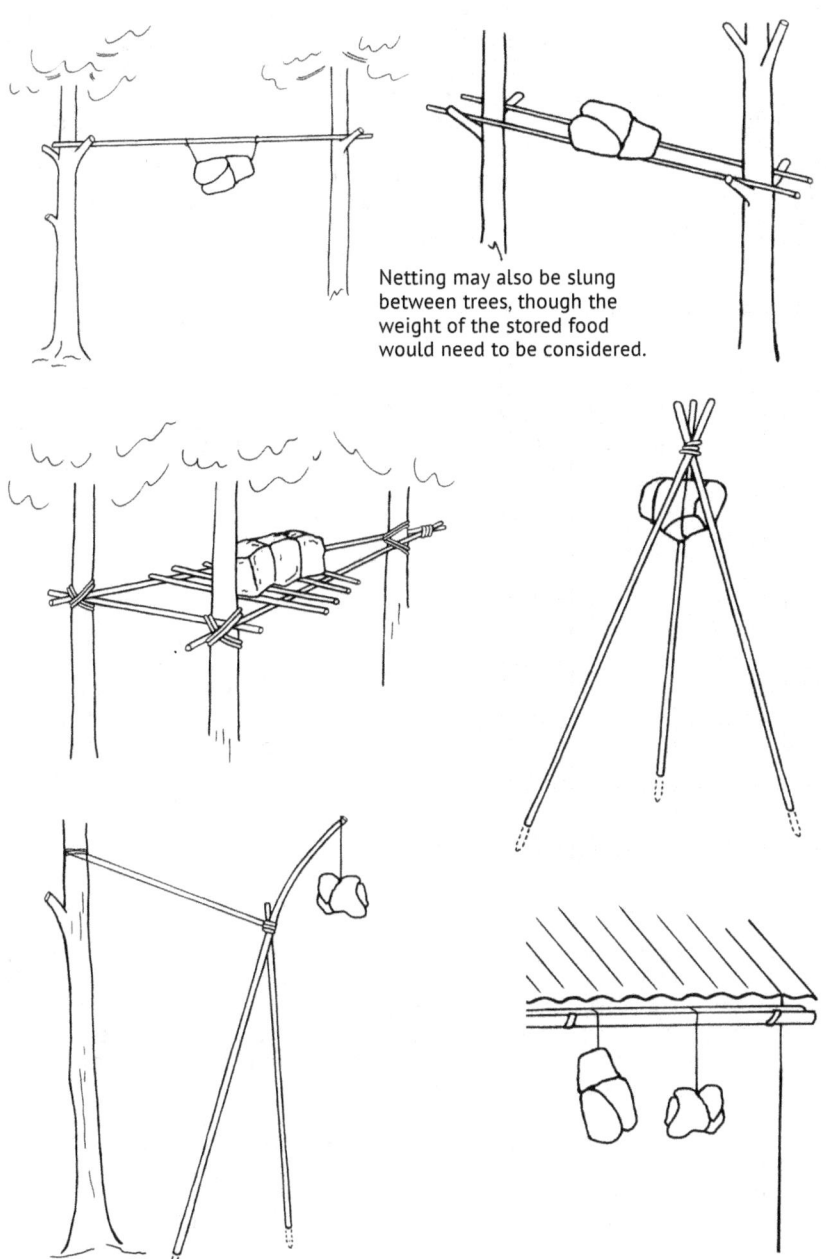

Netting may also be slung between trees, though the weight of the stored food would need to be considered.

MEAT & FOOD SAFES

Ground-based meat safes will be of use if you are in a permanent or semi-permanent environment. In an urban area it would be possible to utilize an old fridge, oven or microwave oven to lock food away from scavenging animals, be they small rodents or dogs. Given that some animals do find their round fridge door locks, as some pet owners will attest, it may be worth adding a secondary fixing such as a piece of rope or wire. At a push, a secured metal dustbin (assuming that it can be thoroughly cleansed by fire and / or bleach) could act as a food safe. Vehicles do not make good food safes as they are often porous to insect life and mice.

In rural areas a structure made of interlocked logs can be fashioned, with heavy stones placed around the base to prevent animals digging, and the roof similarly weighed down with stones or a metal plate / sheet.

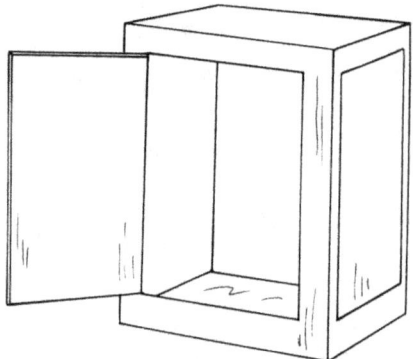

For keeping flies off meat a traditional *meat safe* with metal mesh or fabric gauze walls could be constructed from an old cupboard, and used in either outdoor or indoor situations provided the conditions are cool.

If such a set-up is not conveniently possible then an old fridge or oven with no door could have a gauze-covered framework attached or tied to the front of the empty cabinet. However, with no lockable door, such designs would be more susceptible to scavenging animals able to trace the scent. For venison, the deer carcass kept intact with its' tough protective membrane still in place, and suspended over the cooking smoke, will keep pretty well.

Another option for storing food would be an oil drum, the top cut out and suitably cleaned inside. Some sort of lid (with or without ventilation depending on the intended purpose) would need to be made, and some means of securing the lid to prevent scavenging animals getting at the food inside.

KEEP THE HOMEFIRE BURNING

In this section I do not intend to dwell upon *general* lighting of fires, apart from pointing out some useful, practical, points from a cooking point of view. If you want to learn about lighting fire by friction, or whatever other manual means, then I suggest that you head towards a specialist in the skill. With experience it is possible to light fires even in wet conditions.

Heat of various means (frying, boiling, steaming, baking, for example) is needed to make most non-salad leafy foodstuffs fit for food, and this is very much the case in a post-disaster situation where there is likely to be an added contamination problem.

To get good heat out from a wood source thick pieces need to be split so that they burn more rapidly. However, there is no point on having a mass of raging flames that waste heat energy. So, have just enough fuel burning to achieve the cooking task required, and no more; adding frequent small portions of wood as is necessary to maintain the fire at a constant level, or boost heat output. Conversely, heat can be reduced by removing fuel (when using long branch material). In this way you save on wastage and have much better control of your precious fuel resources.

Where wood is exceptionally dry and burning too fast, then a trick that is sometimes used is to dampen it slightly. However, this can produce more of that unwanted, unhealthy commodity, smoke. Rapid burning twigs and small branches can similarly be dampened to slow down the burn rate.

There is a balance to be struck here, however, between dampening the wood fuel to prevent excess loss of energy through too rapid burning (more heat escaping than doing the job of cooking food), while the dampening process reduces the combustive heat output – making the cooking time slower, though slowing down the rate of fuel consumed. But, fuel wood in a post-disaster world will be a precious commodity (as will any fuel) that needs to be carefully used.

Behind the combustion of wood in a fire there are some rather complex processes going on that it is good to understand from a fuel efficiency point of view. Let us assume that you have got a fire started, and that you add a new log to the pile. What happens when that wood hits the flames is that it begins to decompose in the high temperatures, producing volatiles (a mixture of aerosols of gas, vapour and liquid droplets) which burn as flames, while at the same time developing charcoal areas that also begin to burn. So, in effect, there are two sources of fuel burning simultaneously. If you are familiar with the charcoal making process then this separation of volatiles and charcoal is self-evident. The task for the cook is to utilize the radiated heat (charcoal) and convective heat (from flames and hot gases) to efficiently heat the cooking pot and food.

Obviously air is part of that efficient burning process, so any wood needs to be placed in the fire so there is plenty of air freely available. However, too much air (especially when cold) cools the *heart of the fire* to a point where there is insufficient heat to ignite the volatiles, and the wood fails to burn properly. Too little air and combustion is also incomplete and the fire simply smokes, unable to reach a temperature where the volatiles can burn.

My emphasis here on non-combusted *volatiles* is deliberate because they make up the greater part of the wood being burnt. About 25 to 30% of a piece of wood is charcoal material, most of the rest of the heat content (omitting the ash component) comes from the volatiles. So if they fail to ignite and burn, and simply waft into the air, then you are losing huge amounts of available heat energy. Is that really what you want as a pay-off for hours of collecting precious fuel wood? I did read somewhere that in open fires perhaps up to 50% of volatiles fail to be burnt, though whether that is correct I am uncertain.

The trick, then, is to create the right dynamics where as much as possible of the volatile component of the wood gets burnt: lots of heat, minimal smoke, and as near complete combustion as practicable with little wastage.

A key to this is something referenced to above: *the heart of the fire*. It is a concept the SERE instructor's that I work with always emphasize when delivering their lessons on fire. Once you get enough heat in the core, or heart, of the fire then wood fuel added to the fire will, or should, burn. The *heart* needs to be *maintained*, so wood fuel is added at regular intervals in quantities that do not suffocate the fire. Nor is excessively damp wood thrown on as this cools down the heart. Where damp, or even wet wood, is only available then the best way of tackling this, in my view, is to burn long sticks of wood. One end is fed into the fire, the heat from that burning end drying out, and driving off, the moisture in the sections of wood following immediately behind the burning section. A further advantage of burning long wood pieces is that less energy is expended in cutting it into log-like sections (*economy of effort*).

On a common-sense tack... Build your fire just large enough to cook with; out in the open and not against a tree, shrub or bush. Scrape away, or remove any foliage or debris in quite a wide sweep around the fire area. This is very important if the season has been dry and there is windy weather at the time. Just build a small fire and keep some water handy. Finally, the best practice is never to leave a fire unattended or out of line of sight if you are on your own. As annoying as it may be, it would be safer to douse a fire with earth or water if you need to leave the fire.

OTHER ISSUES

When a cooking pot is placed over a fire it becomes hot through a combination of both convection and radiated heat, the efficiency of that heat transfer to the food mass down to the thermal conductivity of the pot itself (metal having better thermal conductivity than ceramics).

If a large pot is moved in too close to the flames of a fire then its effect can be to deny sufficient airflow to burn the wood volatiles, so the heat in the fire slowly ebbs away. In a worst case scenario the fire may go out. So pot position / height needs to be adjusted to balance the need for heat transfer while maintaining the fire's efficiency.

A good rule of thumb is to create a fire that is suited to the diameter of the cooking pot. A small pot over a large fire simply wastes valuable energy and may unnecessarily evaporate precious cooking water, while a small fire trying to heat the contents of a large pot may never bring the food to the critical boiling point or cooking temperature, although it may be adequate for simmering. In every case, covering the pot with a lid improves efficiency during the early cooking or heating phase.

The sides of a pan, not just the bottom surface, are important in transferring heat, so where possible hot gases should be channelled around the sides of the pot too. If designing and building a stove (mud, oil drum or hobo) then consider recessing the level upon which the pots stand, leaving about a fingerwidth of space around the pot for the gases to rise. If this is not possible consider making some sort of 'collar' from a piece of sheet metal that can be used to drive the hot gases up the sides of the cooking pot.

So, as a general rule, it is best to construct a stove to the size of the main everyday cooking pot to get the best thermal transfer. Where the bottom of a pot is larger than the top dimension of the stove, and simply blocks off the hot gases and causes heat stagnation, lift the pan with three or four *risers* placed between the pot bottom and stove top surface. The risers allow the heat to flow over the whole of the pot bottom (while the addition of a collar could improve heat conduction through the pot sides as mentioned).

Where you have an open fire, such as a three-stone, or three-point fire, then consider constructing some sort of shielding from the wind. As mentioned previously, cold air and draughts can cool down a fire to a point where there is insufficient heat generated to burn fuel. However, another action of gusting wind is that it the added levels of airflow can cause the fuel to burn more quickly, while at the same time cooling the hot gases produced and blowing them away from the cooking pot, so losing their heating potential.

For the SERE team that I work with 'survival' scenarios are not just a fantasy but built into the job description, and during my wild food travels with them one thing that I have noted when out on exercise is the orderly way in which the campfire is kept alive / burning, day after day, with seemingly little effort.

A couple of logs about 20 to 30 cm in diameter and a metre long ['A' on diagram below] are drawn up side by side (some survival books talk about arranging two logs to form a 'V' shape, which can be helpful in really windy conditions, and also provides a pot resting area where the two logs meet). Once the fire is underway members of the team will gather larger logs and place them behind one of the horizontal logs to form a dry line, or drying line of timber [B]. Sometimes sawn lengths of branch are placed at 'A'. Either way this means there is a ready supply of dry-ish timber which burns hotter, and with less smoke. A cross-stacked pile of smaller branches [C] for re-lighting the fire, or giving a little extra rapid burn, is placed nearby. There is usually a pile of feather-sticks drying out nearby too. Each scran / crib time a mesh grille is simply placed over the logs and the meal cooked. The two horizontal logs at 'A' are somewhat sacfricial and gradually burn away, though at night they can be rolled over so the burnt surfaces face the ground protecting the glowing embers overnight, and ready to effortlessly re-kindle the next morning's breakfast fire.

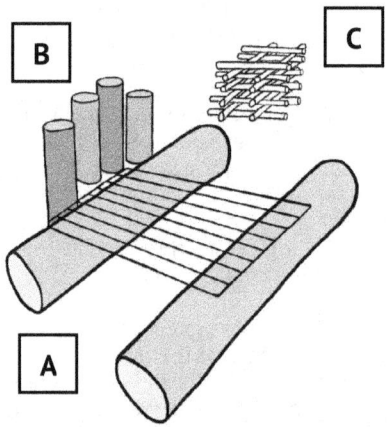

The one thing that these survival professionals insist upon is prepping their fire-building materials before even considering getting out the means of lighting the fire. So there will be some tinder, and then a range of size-graded twigs and kindling (from matchstick to slightly larger than pencil size thickness) all laid out ready for use as soon as the tinder is kindled on a platform of small branch pieces. This procedure rapidly creates a 'heart' which can support the first large pieces of wood fuel. Never have I seen this method fail first time, nor has it failed me. There's no huffing and puffing air into the fire, or having to re-light it (something that you may not have a chance to do in a true survival scenario, which is why these guys insist on prepping everything first).

Where an area has little timber available and there is rather too much wind blowing around for comfort (remembering that the wind will take heat out of your fire), then scoop out a small hollow and create the fire in that. More elaborate trench fires can be created, and scaled up or down according to requirements.

Where regular gusting wind is a really serious issue that prevents day-to-day maintenance of a fire, then you can consider creating what is known in survival circles as a Dakota stove (outline concept shown below). Despite its name North Americans do not, in fact, have exclusivity over this concept, and you will see similar sheltered fires in use by nomads across the windswept plains of Mongolia for processing their yak milk, although the stoves are bigger since large wok-like pans are in use.

In my view the effort required to create a Dakota stove really isn't worth it unless you are going to be permanently based in a place for a short while at least. The dimensions shown in the diagram are for guidance only, with the size of fire egress hole [A] depending on pot size, and air intake hole [B] big enough to enable fuel to be added to the fire. In this respect the air intake hole can be angled downwards, but I would suggest starting with a smaller size hole, and then widening if it is found there is insufficient airflow getting to the fire. Although the Dakota design is an excellent solution for maintaining a fire in windy environments, it has the drawback of filling with water if the terrain or soil are ill-suited. You may need some support for your pot at [C]. If the pot is wider than the dimension of [A] then it will be a good idea to provide some sort of pot 'risers' so that hot air from the fire flows over the whole bottom part of the cooking pot. If the fire chamber is sealed over then the heat flow will stagnate and not provide efficient heating of the pot. A small gutter or trench [D] is a useful addition to allow ashes to be scraped forwards and scooped out.

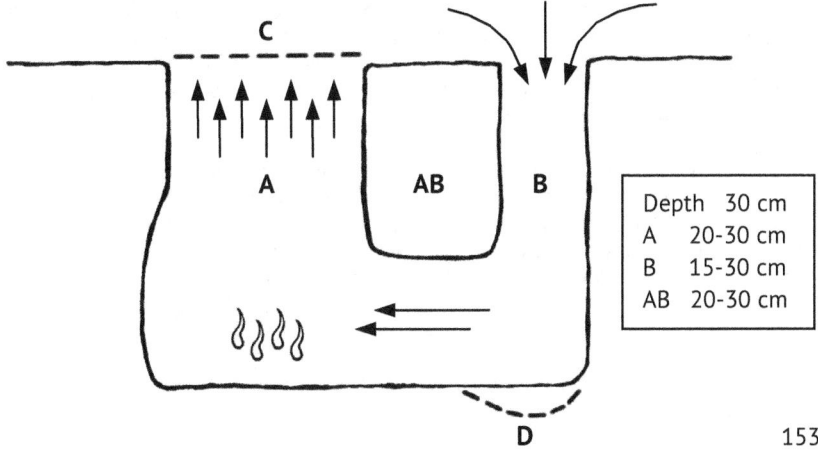

BASIC COOKING FIRE DESIGNS

When you look at primitive cooking facilities and strategies around the world, the majority employ a '3-point principle' somewhere in their design. This theoretically provides stability, and also act as natural 'risers' (modern terminology for a feature that has almost certainly been understood for thousands of years) for the cooking vessel. As you will read elsewhere 'risers' are an important part of cooker design because they allow hot combustion gases to flow across more of the surface area of the cooking vessel and effectively transfer heat. The concept of three cooking pot 'support points' is almost, but not always, universal where fire is used to cook with.

The simplest way of combining three point support with a heat source is to place the cooking vessel between the ends of three (and sometimes more) burning logs or branches (below, left) – a cooking method commonly seen throughout the developing world and poorest communities.

However, the three stone fire (below, right) is perhaps the most commonly observed, simple, method of cooking in undeveloped and poorer societies. Fuel, in the form of branch and twig material, is simply fed into the fire through the gaps between the non-fixed stones.

The supporting stones can vary in size. Large ones are used to support bigger, rounded, cauldron-like cooking pots, and also recycled oil drum type cooking vessels which are usually placed on top of the stones. Smaller stones are frequently used for smaller pots, but not always; the 3-stone cooking method having the advantage of allowing the cook to adjust spacing of the stones and, indeed, rotate the stones to achieve an optimum support position for the cooking pot size / shape.

In fact pot stability is one of the major disadvantages of this type of cooking arrangement, and is a serious hazard faced by countless millions of people who cook this way, and who have very limited access to medical help. A situation similar to any doomsday-kitchen scenario, so be careful! The 3-stone method can be highly inefficient fuel-wise, having something in the order of only 10% efficiency.

The Yukon stove (pictured right) is one of the survival classics, comprising a cylindrical chimney constructed of mud and stones, and heated by a fire which is usually placed in a small, wind protected, slit trench beneath the chimney. Often the chimney would be built with the lower internal surface funnelling inwards as it rises and then bending outwards towards the top. It is a design that draws air inwards and helps the fire generate lots of heat. Indeed, once the structure heats up it provides a very good source of radiant heat, as well as a means of cooking food.

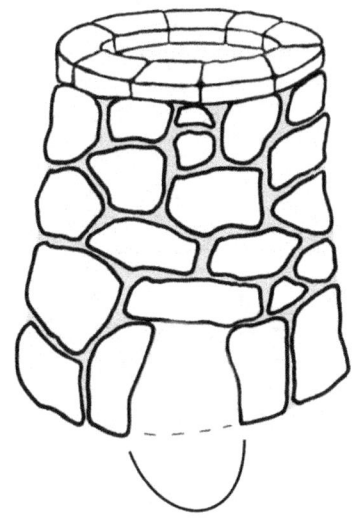

The version pictured has been built with an upper rim of turf, with the main structure of mud or moist clay and stones. Exposed grass and roots in the turf will eventually be scorched and burnt away by the fire, but the pliable layer provides a more stable base than stones upon which to rest pots, pans or support bars. The proportion of clay / thick mud to stone for the walls really depends on what is available to you to make the stove.

Building a Yukon stove purely with grass turves is entirely possible, but a little more tricky unless the turves are reasonably wide. If you can find a few pieces of wire to sort of staple the grass layers together then the structure will have greater stability. And, of course, you could simply build something out of bricks or cinder blocks cemented together with mud. Once the structure is completed allow the mud or clay filler to partly dry out and then help solidify the structure by giving the stove a good firing before actually cooking on it – building up the heat gradually.

Converted oil drums frequently appear where there are large families or groups to cater for, or where volume processing of foodstuffs is involved. The example seen right was observed in southern Malaysia and is a standard 50 gallon oil drum conversion at its least sophisticated. With the top removed, and an opening cut through the metal for fuel wood to be loaded into the base, the fire simply blasts large concave wok-shaped vessels the cook used with this stove. There is no ash grate nor are there any pot risers, so this would be very inefficient to run.

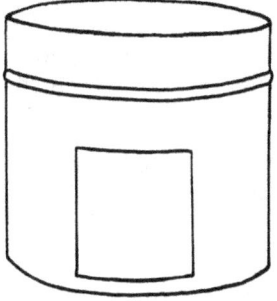

Although 'risers' are sometimes seen on metal oil drum cookers (below left) they are not so frequently found as in mud and clay stoves. Quite simply, it takes a lot of time and effort to sculpt the risers when cutting round an oil drum. Also, simple metal risers cut from normal thickness metal would not bear the weight of over-heavy cooking pots, so something like the reinforced folded riser configuration below centre would help. Personally, I would try and fashion some sort of clip-on risers which can be added or removed as required. Another possible adaptation is that of a removable grille plate (below right).

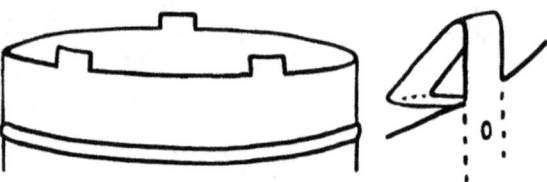
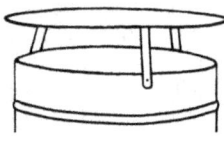

The paint can stove design (right) is simply an update on the hobo stove found in many survival books. It is not the sort of thing you would expect to carry in a rucksack. The triangular top notches are simply punched with a beer bottle opener – more holes cut round the top than the bottom – though one could do away with the notches and simply fashion three 'risers' to do the same job, although that might be more troublesome than using the can opener. The wire grid at the bottom is made out of a series of metal coathanger wires – fitted through holes punched in the side of the paint can and the ends bent down to avoid snagging. The components for this are likely to be easily found in a post-disaster debris field, but would need firing before use to destroy any nasty chemicals that might get into cooked food.

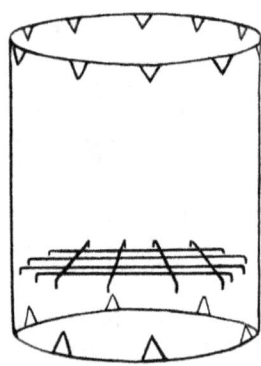

Made of building materials (either standard bricks, or cinder blocks for a much larger stove) that you may find strewn across a debris field is the 6-brick design opposite (top); the bricks laid on their end in a circle and then held in place with two wraps of wire tightened round the upper half to provide rigidity. The gaps between the bricks in the circle may be 'cemented' with mud or clay, with the potential for banking up earth all round the structure for a more permanent cooking facility. Half a brick is used on the sixth side of the circle, supported by two flat-topped pieces of stone, and again 'cemented' into place. Sticks are fed into the bottom of the fire chamber, with a stone placed in front of the gap to raise the fuel wood and provide more air circulation for better combustion.

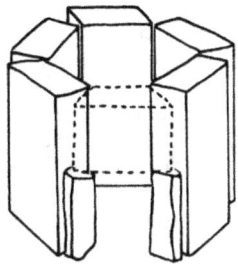 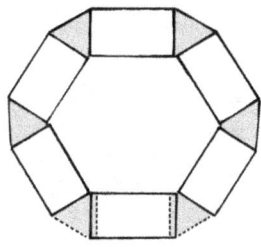

The quick and dirty 15-brick design below provides a quite substantial cooking facility if the bricks are cemented with mud or clay as it is put together. Although this 15 brick set-up is designed for typical UK brick shapes it could be easily adapted to longer adobe-type bricks.

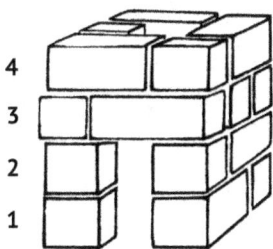 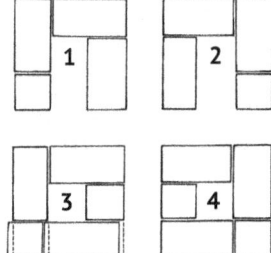

Without any sealant between the bricks heat will escape through gaps. To provide the 'arch' over the fuel filler gap the front two bricks in the 3rd layer (from the bottom) are displaced by about 1 cm, with the final 4th layer of bricks following the original alignment. On the other hand, a flat metal strip of appropriate length and width could be used allowing a snag-free construction, there being no protruding front brick to get knocked out of alignment.

Another design made from brick type components is pictured to the right. You might term the design the 'cinder block rocket stove'. This basic, makeshift, design uses those twin-hollow concrete building blocks commonly found on building sites. The lower, intact, block has part of the dividing wall removed – a hole about 10 to 12 cm wide – which allows fuel to be added to the main fire chamber. A smaller hole / notch is cut into the end wall as an air intake (a flat stone or small slab of concrete is used to cover the top of the outer chamber).

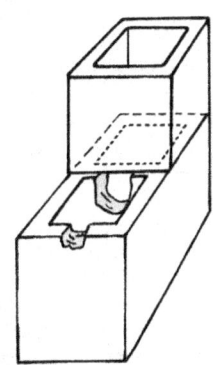

The flue/chimney is made of half of a second block, being placed directly over the fire source. Clay or mud can be used between the two surfaces to prevent heat escape. The design won't be particularly thermally efficient, though probably more efficient than an open fire, and the square hole will leak heat around the sides of curved cooking pots with a diameter smaller than the diagonal of the internal chimney. Risers could be added where large pans are used to distribute the heat flow. Still this design makes for a convenient cooking facility if you happen to find cinder blocks amongst debris fields.

The coathanger pot-rest (right) is constructed from three bottom sections of metal coathanger (approx. 40 cms long), the curvature at the ends of the hanger forming natural 'feet'. Permanent sections of thick folded aluminium sheet form hinges that allow the segments to be folded back for stowage, while the third piece is slotted and acts as a 'catch' [A]. Narrow gauge copper tube could also be used for the hinges. This design will not take very heavy pots but is adequate for many small cooking pot operations. Using heavier gauge wire, welding rod or rebar with modifications to the hinges and catch could make a substantial pot rest.

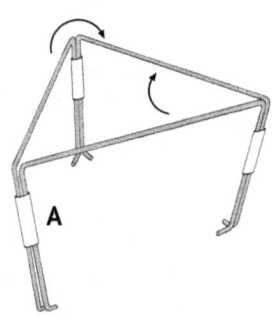

CLAY OVENS

First, select a site that has a firm subsoil and is not susceptible to flooding or excess groundwater seepage. Clear off the surface debris and then dig down a few centimetres and level off the ground. Next, put a thick layer or sand or gravel 2 or 3 cm thick onto this, and level off (this layer is to help provide a little insulation from the cold of the earth and reduce heat from the fire being dissipated into the cold earth). In the precise circle area of the oven (plus an overshoot of 15 cm) cover this in a single layer of stones, preferably ones that are igneous. Fill the gaps in between the stones with soft clay and then tamp the mass down till reasonably level. Add another 2 or 3 cm of clay on top of this and beat down and smooth off. This will become the oven 'bed' upon which the fire will made and bread dough be placed.

In the days while the base dries off a little, collect up enough earth or sand to 'form' the interior shape of the oven space, and also puddle some clay containing as few stones as possible in water until it has the consistency of a very thick bread dough. You will need about 12 to 15 cm depth of clay covering the entire surface of your 'former'.

Form the collected earth (damp sand will do too) [A], and then cover with newspaper; dampening if required to help the paper take the shape of the former [B]. Thin cotton material, or even hessian sack or cardboard would do at a push, but synthetic material must NOT be used as this layer needs to be burnt away during the first firings of the oven, and synthetic hydrocarbons will irreparably taint and contaminate the oven interior and the foods cooked in it.

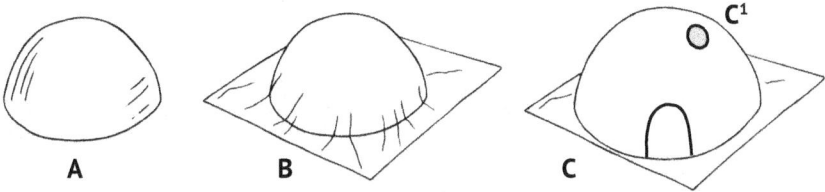

Next cake on the clay over your former, building up successive layers until a depth of 12 to 15 cm of clay is achieved [C]. If it looks as if you have underestimated the mount of clay required distribute what you have evenly, then acquire more clay and add it to the existing layer while it is still moist. Allow the clay to dry off for several days (protect from rain should any come along), and then cut out a door shape in the side of the mass, and remove the clay debris. Allow to continue drying off for another week then excavate the soil or sand used to form the shape, and allow another week for excess moisture to evaporate from the interior. After that, light a succession of small fires inside the oven to drive off more moisture, and then finally a larger one when the oven appears to have largely dried out. Meanwhile, construct a thick wooden door plate that fits *exactly* into the hole that you cut into the side. It should not leak heat from ill fitting edges. Although it is not absolutely essential a small vent (C^1) can be added which helps create a draft when the fire is burning, but is then stoppered up to conserve the heat when baking takes place.

When not in use keep the oven covered against the rain since it is not made from 'fired' clay and will dissolve in excessive rains. Where cracks develop in the external surface they should be filled with a bit of clay slurry, having first moistened the existing crack surfaces with water. Although, there may be a temptation to reinforce the clay dome with metal or twigs it is better to let the structure be self-supporting, since internal metal will expand and contract in the heat at a different rate than the clay and gradually cause the oven to crack. Wood also has the same problem but to a lesser degree, but if the clay-encased timbers start to decompose through carbonisation then there's the possibility of gas pockets building up, potentially exploding, and again loosening up the clay structure.

The oil drum oven (anything from a 5 to 50 gallon size) pictured overleaf, is not very thermodynamically efficient, but is perhaps more so than a plain metal drum exposed to the air; providing the earth that it is buried under is not moist and so absorbs heat too. In an ideal world the drum would be earthed up in a sand or sandy-loam, and be covered over when not in use to prevent the soil becoming sodden, so reducing any thermal insulation qualities. A hole is cut at the back for smoke to escape, and a wooden or metal sheet door constructed to fit over the front. Internally, some sort of racking system needs to be wedged across the diameter of the drum, and below this coals or embers provide the heat source.

While on the subject of oil drums for cooking, the schematic below represents a quick and dirty oil-drum oven seen in use among desert dunes. In essence, it's almost a desert hangi; a mass of fuel wood is burnt in the bottom of the drum and when reduced to coals a grille is inserted, loaded with food, a lid placed over the top, and then everything covered with a mound of sand. The ambient heat of the desert maintaining a high sand temperature is one reason why this is probably successful.

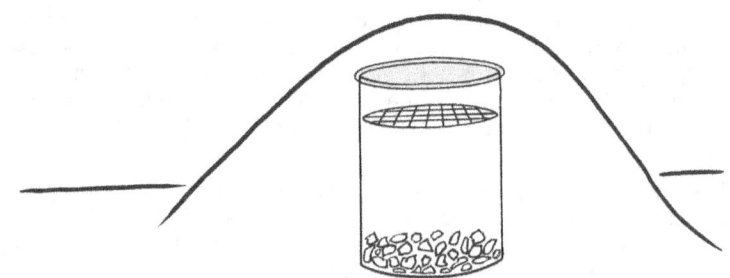

In the absence of something to bake in – as in a Dutch oven – you might consider a temporary oven made from a big biscuit or cake tin, which has a thick layer of mud / clay and pebbles at the bottom. While this layer may help reduce the metal warping in the flames it's main aim is to provide a distribution of heat more akin to a baking environment, and avoid the cooked item burning on contact with the thin metal base of the tin. The 'oven' can be immersed in embers (over or beneath), but care will be required not to melt the thin steel. If the lid is very tight fitting then a small hole will need to be pierced in the side to allow expanding air to escape.

In a more permanent doomsday kitchen you might want to construct a contained hearth structure – the walls made of turves / stones, and then a chimney stack of logs which can draw the smoke upwards naturally (pictured left). The spaces in between the logs are filled with clay or mud intermixed with moss (moss on its own may catch fire if the heat is too great). A very quick alternative chimney design to the logpile would be sheet metal or plywood cut into sections to form a similar funnel shape. This design is useful for smoking foods in the chimney-stack, as well as providing you with a fire protected from the elements.

This upright log fire design is one of the solutions to fire construction where there is ground-lying snow. It is also handy because it *projects* radiant heat at an elevated level which is useful when using a reflector oven for cooking with (see below).

Reflector ovens – more of a 'grille' than an oven – are made from polished aluminium sheet (a schematic of the component parts can be seen below). An upright back plate improves heat reflecting efficiency, but makes for a more fiddly assembly. The joints may be clipped together for use or permanently hinged. The only drawback with the concept behind these ovens is that they tend to be rather heavy since they need to be made of thick aluminium sheeting, and the reflecting surfaces need to be kept polished for optimum reflective efficiency.

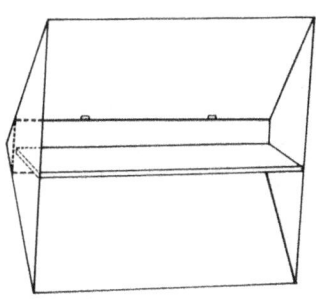
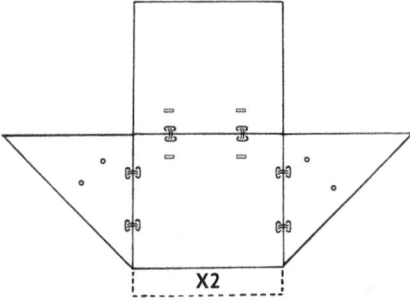

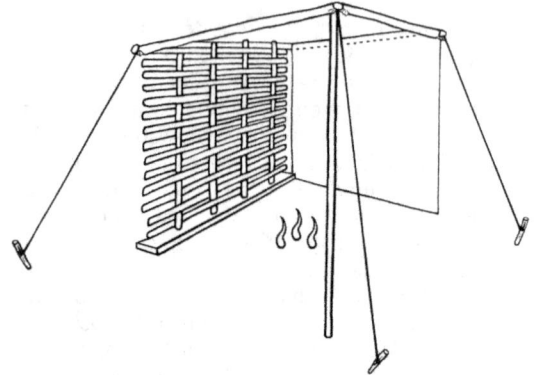

Where a doomsday kitchen may be of temporary use, setting two movable hazel (or other wood) hurdles at right angles to one another can provide some control over gusting winds, while allowing enough airflow for satisfactory combustion of fuel.

Fixing a tarpaulin overhead would also provide a surface for rainwater harvesting, but also prevent heavy downpours of rain from damping the fire. However, the flames and heat of the fire must never be close or hot enough to cause ignition of the tarp. Furthermore, in an ideal world, a small hole to allow the upward drifting smoke to escape would be a good idea, but that rather depends on how precious the roof material is. Likewise, the hurdles need to be placed sufficiently far enough from the fire to prevent scorching, although the lattice can be dampened down with water.

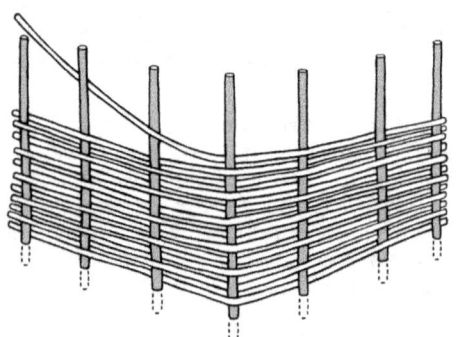

Once you have decided on a permanent base for your doomsday kitchen then more rugged structures can be added. So, instead of lashing together movable hurdles, a proper hurdle that is embedded in the ground can be built, and perhaps even on three sides of the fire too. Consider spacing from the fire / fire size in relation to the wood scorching.

Pot rigs may simply be formed from sticks lashed together to form a 'V' shape, or the natural 'Y' cleft of a stick utilized. For stability the stick ends need to be embedded well in the ground. Ideally, even the two-stick design could do with a further support in case it slips laterally. For any structural pot-holders placed near the fire it is best to use moist greenwood branches.

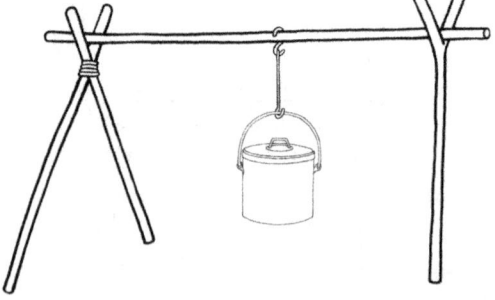

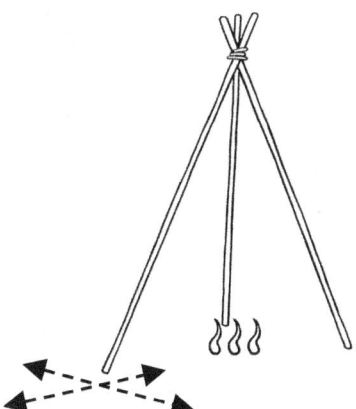

An A-frame pot-holder (left) is made from three poles lashed together, and the pot manoeuvred over the fire through leg movement. Although this type of structure can support the weight of quite heavy cooking pots when made of greenwood, the chain, cord, or other type of pot support and its hook also needs to be strong enough to carry the pot weight.

In the absence of a pot chain or natural rope with which to suspend a pot over the fire, then a double-hooked pot holder may be made from two greenwood branches (thickness depending on the pot weights to be suspended), which are notched, as shown to the right, and then tied into place with strong cordage such as the roots of pine. One thing to note about this design is that over a period of time there may be shrinkage due to the heat driving moisture out of the sticks and cordage, and this slack will need to be re-adjusted for.

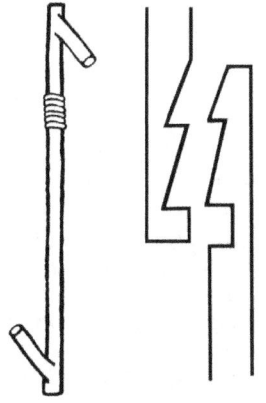

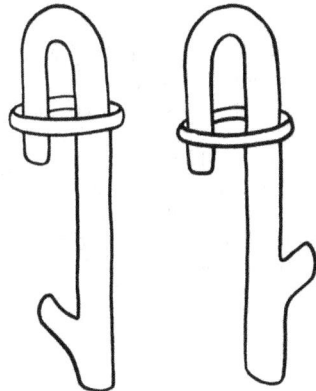

A variation on the wooden pot-hanger above is the one pictured left, where green sapwood branches are bent over and bound with natural cordage (pine root, for example) to form a loop from which it can be suspended. The area which is curved needs a little material to be whittled away to prevent the wood snapping. One disadvantage with this design is that the loops are permanent, which might be inconvenient where you want to take the pot-hanger offline on a regular basis.

The very simplest sort of pot-holding rig comprises two Y-shaped sticks (see below, left), the lateral one moved in / out, or up / down, to place the pot above the heat. A heavy stone secures the tail end, but must be at least as heavy as the weight of the cooking pot and contents. Variations of this design sometimes affix the tail end of the lateral stick by rope / cordage to a wooden stake embedded deeply in the ground.

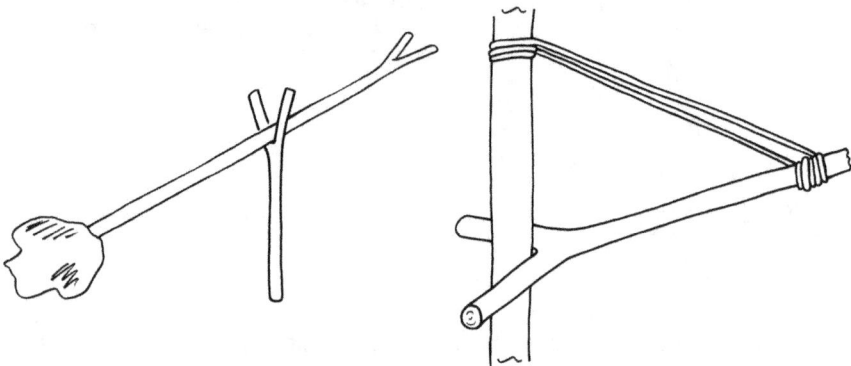

The version above right is an *adjustable* pot rig; the upright stick well embedded into the ground near to the fire. The 'Y' of the lateral stick forms the base of the cantilevered pot-holder, with pine roots (or other strong cordage) taking the strain. The root wrapped round the length of the Y-stick is wrapped around a shallow, recessed, groove cut into the green wood so the root does not slip. The root wrapped round the upright stick stays largely in place simply from tension. To slip the pot-holder up and down the upright piece of root is slackened off and the coil slipped up or down the stick, along with the 'Y' support, to adjust the cooking pot to the right height over the fire. For safety, adjustment must obviously be done without the weight of the cooking pot attached, and is best suited to boiling kettles of water or small pots of food (similarly with the design previous, and the one that follows)

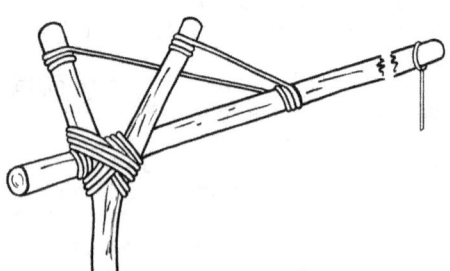

Although, on initial viewing, this simply looks like another version of the previous adjustable pot-holder it is not. The end of the lateral branch has to be well and truly tied down, otherwise the weight of the cooking pot on the end of the stick will force it through the binding and collapse into the fire, so this design has limitations.

FUEL CONSERVATION

Scarcity of fuel is likely to be a major concern for an indeterminate period, post-disaster. Not only is electrical power likely to be absent, but fuel for running generators may also be unavailable. So, whatever fuel you need for cooking or keeping warm will need to be physically sourced. That sourcing may take up to two thirds of the day (certainly it can in parts of the developing world where immediately local resources have been picked clean), which is both time-consuming and also diminishes the physical energy of individuals tasked with fuel gathering at a time when they may need to conserve their physical strength. There will also be the problem of *resource territory* as diminishing local fuel resources are used up and the survivors have to travel further into areas where other established survivor groups have set up camp and who want those same resources for themselves. Resource conflict, which brings up other entirely different communications and negotiating skills, is outside the sphere of this book.

So, the *careful* use of what fuel you have will be important, and here are some thoughts from the doomsday kitchen perspective. Having constructed a mud stove, tin oven, or whatever cooking facility, it needs to be *understood* in the way that it consumes fuel, or how the fuel can be conserved – I am thinking here of excess air current that would cause fuel to burn too quickly. Are there perhaps ways in which the stove design could be modified to burn more efficiently, or to use less fuel? Remember, someone has to go and get that fuel – perhaps you – so the fewer trips required would probably be welcomed.

At the extreme, the simplest way to conserve fuel is not to use it. But in a post-disaster situation you may need hot food and drinks to keep you going and your morale up, so it is unlikely that a campfire for cooking will be absent. Drinking water will also need to be boiled (refer to *waterborne disease* section). One way of getting the most out of your fuel resources is to plan the cooking of food ahead of time (assuming adequate ingredient resources). Can several meals, pots of food, and the kettles, all be cooked over the fire at the same time? If you have constructed some oven facility, then think how bread, pies, stews and dried pulses could share the same, single, firing, or the oven be filled up with lots of bread, or whatever. Those items required for the day's use will be immediately available to you while there is now food ready for use over the forthcoming days (remembering food safety issues) which can be eaten cold or simply re-heated as required.

Don't *heap* fuel on your open fire as this can smother it. What's more, if a large amount of added fuel really 'gets going' then it may produce a volume of heat and flames that make it virtually impossible to cook with, and will take time to die back to a usable point. At that point you have just wasted your valuable fuel, with no gain on the food side. A much better way is to add smaller amounts of fuel to a fire to reach the heat output that you want and then continue adding small amounts of fuel to maintain that output.

NOTE: Try to resist burning plastics as fuel, although they may come in handy for fire-lighting. Smoking hydrocarbons are not good for you, and some burning plastics release toxic fumes. Furthermore, if molten plastic touches skin very nasty burns can result. Not what you need in a medically deficient post-disaster world.

FUEL TIMBERS

Perhaps it may sound obvious to say, but as a general rule the age, dryness and quality of a wood all have a great deal to do with its heating properties; old timber that has been 'seasoned' lasting longer on the fire and heating more strongly, than younger sapwood. In an ideal world cut timber should be stacked and protected from the weather and exposure to excess moisture for a year before it is used. Rotten or decaying wood makes poor firewood. Conifers, with their resins, burn quickly and often fiercely, so do not produce a fire that lasts. However, some conifer wood can be useful to get the *heart* of a fire going in its initial stages (dead gorse [*Ulex europaeus*] branches are another good fire starter). Another very generalized observation is that the wood of trees that grow in rocky dry soils tends to be hard and compact, while that from trees growing in moist conditions tends to be more spongy, and softer in comparison.

ASH wood burns well but quickly, even when green (unlike most others), and does not produce too much smoke. It grows on soils of a clay type often to a large size and produces excellent, long-grained and pliable timber, though on poor light soils the timber can be brittle.

BEECH timber makes excellent fuel – perhaps the best – producing a lasting, even, heat. Likewise charcoal made from beech produces a good heat, while destructive distillation of beech wood will produce acetic acid and acetone among the substances output. Beech is often found where there is a chalky subsoil, often poor and dry soil, or a sandy loam.

BIRCH has a close-grained and tough timber that makes good firewood, and also charcoal. However, the wood is somewhat rapid-burning and does not generate a lot of heat output. As a species it is one of the first tree colonisers of waste ground, being able to live in poor gravely and rocky soils.

ELM is not regarded as one of the best firewoods, being a slow burning timber. However, once alight it makes a lasting fire.

HAWTHORN timber makes very good firewood, producing a decent heat output, not a great deal of smoke, and burning slowly. It has a hard and close-grained structure that also make the wood valuable for manufacturing articles.

HAZEL rods (as in coppiced stems) burn well but they are not always available in quantity.

OAK from seasoned sources is a good fuel timber, though the smoke is hard on the throat.

The timber of **LONDON PLANE**, planted in so many metropolitan areas, also burns well; producing lots of heat from a lively, relatively clean, burn. For best results winter-felled timber needs partial seasoning. Plane thrives best in rich, damp, loam soils.

SYCAMORE wood is close-grained, but not hard, and burns slowly giving out a reasonable heat.

Although it is not a tree species shrub-like **GORSE** (*Ulex europaeus*) makes good kindling; the volatile compounds in the dead branches burning rapidly and fiercely.

NORTH AMERICA
In North American some of the best fuelwoods come from the following species (though burning live species that provide you with food is going to be self-defeating):

Apple (*Malus* sp.), Green Ash (*Fraxinus pennsylvatica*), White Ash (*Fraxinus americana*), Honeylocust (*Gleditsia triacanthos*), Black Locust (*Robinia pseudoacacia*), Mulberry (*Morus* sp.), Red Oak (*Quercus rubra*), White Oak (*Quercus alba*), Osage Orange (*Maclura pomifera*), Black Walnut (*Juglans nigra*).

Other good ones are the Kentucky Coffeetree (*Gymnocladus dioica*), Douglas Fir (*Pseudotsuga menziesii*), Hackberry (*Celtis occidentalis*).

Also consider the Black Ash (*Fraxinus nigra*), Blue Ash (*Fraxinus quadrangulata*), Black Birch (*Betula nigra*), Yellow Birch (*Betula alleghaniensis*), Black Cherry (*Prunus serotina*), Slippery/Red Elm (*Ulmus rubra*), Bitternut Hickory (*Carya cordiformis*), Shagbark Hickory (*Carya ovata*), Rocky Mtn. Juniper (*Juniperus scopulorum*), Red Maple (*Acer rubrum*), and Tamarack (*Larix larcina*).

FURTHER TIPS ON TIMBER
If you are not familiar with timber or trees then the following notes might help you avoid some pitfalls in harvesting and keeping wood for firewood. To begin with, timber logs or branches are said to have a sapwood and heartwood. The outer sapwood is involved in the movement of nutrients and food storage for the tree but eventually becomes INFILTRATED with resins and LIGNIN and so turns to heartwood, the cells of which are dead and merely provide strength for the tree. This heartwood (tree trunk for example) is the part that finds its way into use as general timber, furniture, construction and firewood.

Depending on the size and age of a tree the sapwood may be anything from a matter of millimetres to 3 or 4 cm thick, and if you were attempting sap extraction from a tree then it is this layer that you want to tap into. When it comes to making clean-burning fires then the more this sapwood layer can be dried out (or removed) the better the heartwood will burn.

When it comes to storing your harvested fuel wood then there are some considerations to be taken into account. For example, the dead heartwood is more resilient to moisture / water absorbtion than the sapwood but will still absorb moisture. So if your doomsday kitchen is in a damp environment then removing (or drying out) the sapwood from logs will give the heartwood a better chance of burning. That said, any unprotected dry wood is going to absorb moisture from damp air, and vice versa in dry air. Also, the sides of a timber length give up moisture less rapidly than the end grains, and also in relation to whether it is sapwood or heartwood. So if you have a large log it may be better to cut it into several smaller sections to allow moisture to escape.

IMPORTANT

PRESUME that anything near an open fire is going to be *very* HOT. It does not matter whether you are going to lift a kettle lid, move a pot, or turn over a broiling steak, protect yourself from burns by using some implement, or covering your hands with protective material. A small burn can painful, but without medical attention in a survival situation that burn could become infected and cause problems. A *major* burn in a survival situation would not only incapacitate, but could become life-threatening if harmful pathogens get past the skin's defences. Be careful with your fires.

Also consider wearing cotton or wool clothing when cooking around an open fire as flammable synthetics and manmade fabrics (footwear too), may melt with the heat or, worse still, catch fire. Molten synthetics on human skin is painful!

HAY-BOX COOKER

Where fuel economy is of major consideration then hay-box, or fire-less, cookery can be a valuable tool in your doomsday kitchen. You may never have heard of a hay-box cooker, but if you think of the basic concept behind vacuum flasks – insulation – then you'll get a rough idea of what this is about, although there are no vacuums involved.

At its basis your food is cooked to boiling point (so this cooking method is very good for stews) then placed quickly in an insulated environment where the residual heat in the food and cooking pot continues to cook the food over a long period – away from cold draughts and the natural cooling effect of air-metal contact.

It is, however, important to bare in mind two things: first, the contents of the pan or casserole must be absolutely boiling when put into the hay-box. Second, the food will almost certainly need a short re-heating before it is served, though you will have saved using your valuable fuel supplies during the main cooking period.

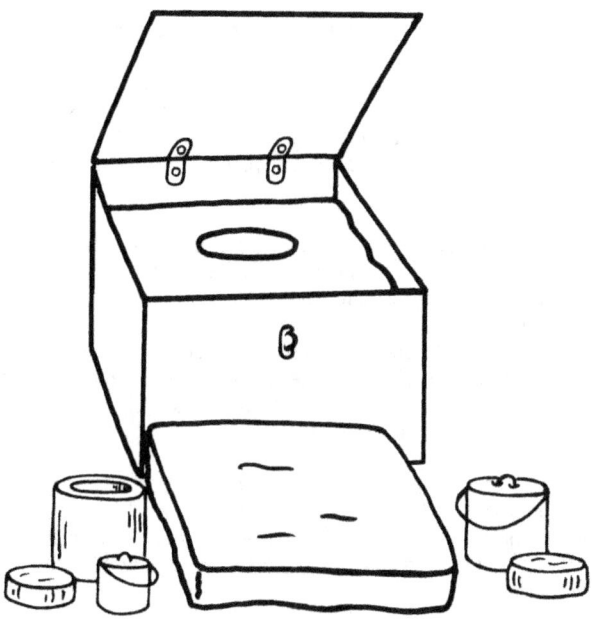

To make the hay-box find (or make) a well-made wooden box constructed of heavy boards and with a lid, which must be attached by hinges and have a firm fastener/s. Wooden barrels can provide hay-boxes for very large pots, however the hinging may not be as robust and the lid will need to be held down tightly with weights.

First line the box and lid with some heavy paper or fabric if there are any gaps in the wooden seams. Next, place a good layer of hay or mass of soft dry grass on the bottom of the box – about 12 to 15 cm deep – pressing down to compact it to a minimum of 10 cm depth. This is the platform on which your cooking pot/s will rest. You could, incidentally, use hard polystyrene foam, other inert insulation material, or mineral wool as an alternative to hay (which, in any case, will absorb moisture during cooking, as would sawdust). There must be no thermally leaky pockets of air or spaces anywhere in your cooker construction.

If you intend to use only one size of pot in your cooker then construct a cardboard collar that fits around it – leaving a space no wider than one centimetre on either side of the pot circumference and as high as the pot is tall – then fix the ends of this cardboard sleeve together securely. Pots, incidentally, need to be straight-sided to achieve best efficiency and have tight fitting lids. Good, heat-retentive, thick, pot walls are an advantage too, while those with overhead handles are slightly easier to retrieve than those with side handles – unless these are placed at the top edge of the pot.

Next, place the pot in the middle of the base platform, slip the card collar over and then pad the surrounding finger-space gap with newspaper or cloth to provide some support during the main cavity packing process. Next, fill the cavity extending from the card collar to the box walls tightly with the insulating material, and up to the full height of the sleeve. For good insulation ideally you want 10 to 12 cm of packing material in every direction around the pot at the centre of the cooker.

Holding the card collar in place, remove the temporary padding from around the pot, then the pot itself, to reveal the pot recess. The next stage is to place a wad of flannel at the bottom of the pot recess and then cover all the exposed packed surface and card collar with cotton or jute-type material to keep everything in place. In the early stages of cooker operation you may prefer to use paper since the packing will almost certainly settle and need topping up a little. Paper also has the advantage of being easily replaced if becomes stained or marked by food spills. Your choice.

Next, you need to make a 'cushion' of cotton-type material the exact size of the upper box space and stuff it with plenty of hay. Not only should this be large and thick enough to entirely fill the space beneath the box lid, but a little over-filling that provides some upward pressure against the covering wooden lid is advantageous.

If you want to use smaller cooking pots in a hay-box designed for larger ones then you have two options: either design a double-chambered box unit to accommodate the different pot sizes, or construct a padded 'space adjuster' and supporting cushion to raise the smaller pot. Cooking with a nested small pot in a large cavity does not produce the thermal efficiency required to cook the food through thoroughly.

A space adjuster can be made from two smaller card cylinders, taped or bound together and filled with more packing material, while the cushion to raise the smaller pot can simply be fashioned out of cotton-covered packing material made just wide enough to fit snugly inside the base of the space adjuster.

SUGGESTED HAY-BOX ALTERNATIVES

If finding a suitable wooden box or metal container presents a problem then similar fireless cooking properties may be achieved by using leaves and, potentially, a bale of hay. For the leaves (they must be bone dry) place a large square of tarpaulin on the ground, say 180 by 180 cm, and then pile the dry leaves to about 30 cm depth and also to about 30 cm from the edges. Have some rope / cordage ready too, plus some extra dry leaves for filling gaps. Place the pot of cooked food in the centre of the leaf pile and then gather up the corners of the tarp (you may need assistance) so that the pot is cocooned in a mass of dry leaves all round, top included. Use the extra leaves to plug any thinly packed parts or gaps. Then tie up the top with the cordage. The only drawback with this method is that some heat is lost during the scramble to package the leaves and tarp round the pot.

Another alternative, if you have bales of hay available, is to hollow out the centre of a tightly packed bale to the size of the cooking pot (actually it's quite a hard task to chop a hole even with a sharp knife). Essentially, this option mimics the rigid structure of a wooden hay-box cooker, but uses the structural integrity of the tightly bound hay to hold the shape. A second bale used as the 'lid' and placed over the hollow top cavity will make an excellent thermal barrier. And don't forget garden water butts and other large barrel-like vessels.

HAY-BOX COOKING

The success of hay-box cooking depends on the *retention* of heat, so the *volume* of food being cooked is also an important factor in success or failure. The larger the amount of food to start with, the higher the temperature will be at the end of a given length of time, while smaller amounts of food or partially filled pots do not retain their initial heat and will often fail to cook through properly. So a litre of food is going to cool down sooner than 5 litres of foodstuff.

All food for the hay-box must be brought to a boil and then boiled for a certain time after reaching boiling point to ensure it is thoroughly heated to the centre of its mass. So larger and denser items (such a hams or pot-roasts) require longer boiling, while less compacted, chunky, food is more easily penetrated by heat and will be boiling hot nearly as soon as the surrounding water. Such foods need only be given a brisk boiling for a few minutes before being put into the hay-box.

Cooking times will obviously vary with size of the item involved, and thermal efficiency of your hay-box, but the times below offer a good starting point...

	Boiling time (Mins.)	Hay-Box time (Hours)
Fish	5	1½ hrs
Boiled meat	24	4
Stews	20	3
Peas / Beans	10	2
Cabbage	10	3
Cauliflower	10	2½
Potatoes, whole	5	2¾
Suet pudding	30	3

Finally, two other key things to factor in with hay-box cooking: have the hay-box as near as possible to the fire or stove so that transfer of the boiled food is a quick as possible (have the lid open and cushion removed already), while it is essential that the hay-box lid remains *tightly closed* from the moment the food is put into it until the end of the cooking time.

If for any reason the box is opened before cooking time is up, then the food must be reheated to boiling point before being replaced and resuming cooking in the hay-box. To a certain extent, the heat decay involved is similar in principle to that of a hangi, so don't be in a hurry to unpack the hay-box as food left in the cooker longer than required will not burn.

A key advantage of fireless cooking from the survivalist's point of view is that once the food is in the cooker then it can be left without fear of it burning, or the fire having to be tended, so freeing up time for other important doomsday kitchen tasks to be dealt with.

One final point in hay-box operations... In your haste to move the boiled food to the cooker and lowering it into the pot recess, DO be careful as you do not want scalds and burns.

SOLAR COOKERS
Solar energy is another potential form of heating for food, but in northern temperate climes it will not generally be a useful energy resource because of the intermittent nature of that vital ingredient sunshine. For that reason I will say but few words about solar.

The two main aspects of solar in my mind are a blackened, heat absorbant, container (for heating water or food), and a parabolic shape reflective source that can focus the sun's rays on the cooking container. If that heat can also be trapped within the cooker then the added thermal efficiency will help boost temperatures. Where solar could provide a useful input would be in pre-heating water (so saving precious fuel) that was going to be used for cooking, or washing; containers painted matte black and simply left out in hot sunshine (added reflector material would boost efficiency) can work very efficiently. In the past I have solar-heated water in a coiled 8 mm copper tube painted black with very good results. In fact, when no water flow was applied through the copper coil, and the water column was left for thirty minutes in hot sun, it came out almost scalding hot.

So, solar has its uses but will not be of great benefit in areas where the sun spends more time hiding behind clouds than revealing itself. A lot of experimental work on solar cooking has been done by NGOs in Africa and Asia, so if you are interested in finding out more about the subject then that is where to start looking for data and cooker design instructions.

DOOMSDAY KITCHEN UTENSILS

Imagine for a moment that your domestic kitchen and all the utensils and culinary paraphernalia that you need for normal food preparation have been swept away, or hoovered up by a tsunami. What would you cook with and store your food in? The answer almost certainly lies in the detritus and debris strewn all around you, though you may fortuitously come by a cooking pot, coffee cup, or sealable container which will make life infinitely easier (*economy of effort*, right?).

When urban habitats have been smashed apart by an earthquake, tsunami, or huge explosion the one thing that tends to happen is that many manmade artefacts get pulverized, zipped apart, and their components sometimes exposed, often to the minimal component level. Many of these normally hidden bits may prove useful for your doomsday kitchen.

So now is the time to start scavenging round debris fields for old tin cans and serviceable polythene bags – both of which can also provide you with water storage containers.

Pick over metal cans you find to provide (1) a boiling vessel – such as catering size baked bean can, (2) tins for cooking food in, (3) tins for drinking, &/or eating from, (4) tins suitable for storage of food items such as animal fat, and (5) smaller, shallower, tins that can be transformed into a strainer by having tiny holes punched in the base. Look, also, for suitable gauge wire for making handles for pots – metal coathangers, brass picture wire, and stripped electrical wiring which can be braided. Don't use sardine cans for storing food because of their large surface area, though they can provide you with a very small cooking and frying surface.

Other useful items for your doomsday kitchen are plastic bags – for storage and to cook in. In terms of storage any small-ish bag which can enclose food to prevent it being contaminated is ideal. Press-lock or press-and-seal ones would be even better, obviously. Also of use are those small plastic foil-lined bags used for potato crisps or peanuts, even boil in the bag or microwaveable types. Bin liners can be used to protect larger items such as butchered meat.

There are two important considerations for any tin cans and plastic bags that you scavenge: (1) contamination (both on the surface itself, and possible chemical leakage into your food from a plastic substrate), and (2) their thermal integrity. You do not want to start cooking in a tin can or plastic bag only to find that it cannot take the heat and breaks open. Food in a post-disaster world is too precious to waste!

So, for the cans, I suggest that before they are used in anger they are suitably scrubbed inside and then put into a really hot fire to burn off any paint and plastic lining material. Out of preference I would always choose cans with pure steel walls and NO liner whatsoever. In any case I would *fire* any new can before use to kill off bugs in the seams and burn liner chemicals. If the cans come unstitched at the seams during this test-firing then you now know that they would have failed in real use – so avoiding any wasted food or, in the case of water, putting out the emergency fire that you may have struggled to get going in the first place.

As for the plastic bags, they too need washing out; if necessary turning them inside out so the inner surfaces and corners can be properly cleaned. The next thing that I suggest you do is investigate which bags can be cooked in by putting a pot of water on the boil (with an inert mat on the bottom to prevent plastic-hot metal contact), and then filling various bags with water and placing these into the boiling pan. If the bags distort or break then obviously they would not have passed muster for cooking in. Keep an eye too, on any shedding of plastic (both in the hot and cold state) that might get into your food. Obviously micro-waveable bags and oven chip bags are chemically suited to being in contact with food (being 'food grade'); some of the other types that I mentioned might not be. Ultimately you will have to make your own 'needs be' hygiene and usability decisions based on what you discover at the time.

Where you are concerned about the quality of the water available to you, then both tin cans and plastic bags provide vessels in which to boil food in a water bath, while keeping the food out of water's reach. It is very likely that any ground water you find in a post-disaster scenario is contaminated, so this 'boil in an inner vessel' method would be advantageous.

One other trick where the plastic bags come in handy is that they allow you to cook two or three items separately, but in the same cooking pot without mixing the foods (pictured right). I've spotted that in Africa where a cook had a bin liner of meat or fish cooking inside a cauldron of bubbling mealy pap. Great idea, saving the effort of maintaining fires under two pots, and also helping conserve valuable fuel. So *economy of effort* AND *fuel resources* in that case.

On a shoreline you can consider collecting shells of a decent size for measuring, scooping, or scraping, and scallop-like shells for putting food on, while broken, strong, large shells may provide you with a cutting edge.

As you walk through rubbish or debris keep an eye out for anything else that may help furnish your doomsday kitchen. Many everyday items that we see only in the role for which they were manufactured, can have other uses. If you want to train your eye and imaginary senses regarding re-purposing of junk, take a walk around a landfill site. Remember that notion mentioned in the Introduction, *flexibility of mind*?

For example, old disposable razors, the tops of which can be hacked or melted off, can be fashioned into makeshift cutlery handles, if you can find other bits / scraps to make spoons, forks etc. to attach to the handle stump.

The blades of garden shears might be useful for chopping/hacking up lumps of meat. Ditto lawnmower blades. Shovels or spades can be scoured, polished, and then cooked or fried on.

Debris fields will almost certainly be strewn with microwaves and fridges in former urban areas. Strip out the innards and plastic of a microwave and you might have the basis for constructing a rudimentary oven, or use it as a place to store precious food away from flies and vermin.

Doors of white goods appliances could furnish you with flat surface upon which to fry or griddle (making the assumption here that the painted surfaces are burnt off to get to the raw metal beneath). It may be possible for you to transform those same doors by bending them into large water storage pots, or simply bowls for washing up in. Heavy industrial footplate metal too is ideal for frying on as the metal is usually heavy duty and quite thick. Similarly, the side panels of tower PCs could be utilized although they are rather thin and will not hold heat.

Car hubcaps can be used as plates, providing they are solid, have no perforations integral to their design, and plastic attaching spigots are removed. The side windows removed from cars can provide you with a clean flat surface upon which to prepare food. Car aerials can become handles for those tin cans that you've been scavenging, while seat material might be transformed into protective oven mits, or into fire bellows. Suitably cleaned up, the pipework from a car exhaust may provide an opportunity to distil water.

Beach balls (even water wings and inflatable beach paraphernalia) may be used to store water once the valves have been removed.

Plastic buckets have all sorts of possibilities; for carrying water, storage, or perhaps salting of food (pickling might be out of the question if the plastic was not of food grade quality). But then that is a situational 'call' that has to be made at the time.

Suitable bits of wood for skewering meat, or bendy twigs of greenwood can be transformed into kitchen tongs – similarly with strips of bendy steel that you find lying around. Short lengths of log can be split and transformed into a supported cutting surface (below). A piece of wooden plank similarly split may provide you with a temporary clean working surface, as may ceramic floor tiles.

Plastic milk containers, and other PTFE bottles, can provide storage; or cut the bottom off and use the body as a funnel. Two-litre milk containers can even be used to fashion a makeshift spoon and plate (pictured below), although the spoon is more of a 'scoop', but it saves on the effort of carving out an eating implement from a piece of wood. The other distinct advantage of using these plastic containers is that they are obviously food grade, and if you were in a situation where your hands or other conditions were dirty then the ability to hygienically eat food without holding it in your hands could be useful. The cap holds about 20 ml of fluid.

Grilles or wire trays which can be sandwiched together as a rotisserie-type cooking facility. Refrigerator shelves may provide grilles once the plastic coating has been burnt off and the metal taken down to base.

The skeleton of a short metal stool can become the tripod-type framework that you cook over the fire with, the seating part having been removed. Where the stool is long, then consider burying part of it in the ground to adjust the height. The metal frame of a kitchen table might be transformed into a drying platform once a latticework of wires has been strung between the steel bars.

A cake or biscuit tin with a lid can become a water boiler (assuming there's not too much shape warping under heat stress. All lidded tins can be used for food storage, while all marmalade jars with intact lids offer some opportunity to *bottle* items for preservation.

Paint cans, and anything similarly used for industrial products, I personally would avoid cooking in. What I would consider, however, is using them as 'heat baths' (once they had been fired to burn off any nasties). The following technique (see next two diagrams) also applies to tins that have holes in the bottom, and where you have not been able to find any form of metalware to cook or boil water in.

The left hand image represents a shoreline scenario where a rusty, but holed, can has been found plus an empty plastic drink bottle. The holes are partially blocked with flat stones, then a thick layer of damp sand placed at the bottom. The plastic bottle is inserted (containing your food or water) then the remaining space filled with more damp sand and tamped down. The can and contents are then heated *slowly over embers* to boiling point (not a raging fire). In this set-up damp sand is no doubt providing better thermal transfer to the plastic bottle (in itself not a good thermal conductor) than would soft dry sand. In the second example (below right) the holes are roughly patched over with a piece of sheet metal (cut from a fizzy drink can, for example), and the cavity surrounding a thick-walled plastic bag (flimsy ones may melt) filled in with thick, claggy mud, and again heated over hot embers.

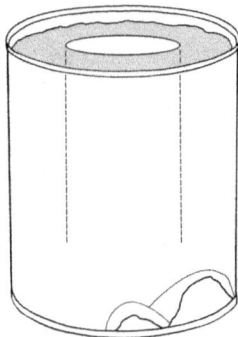 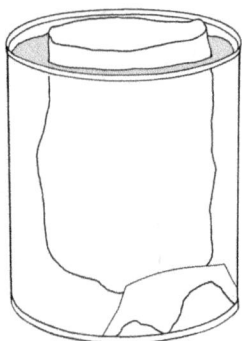

The filament of an electric fire, stretched out and wound round a frame, could make you a trivet / wire rack to cook lightweight items on. Coathanger wire or the spokes of a bicycle would support heavier items.

Another trivet design could be made from woven wire coathanger, with the feet / legs made from redundant pins of an electrical plug; the wire passed through the holes normally reserved for electrical wire, but the screws tightened on the coathanger metal instead. The only drawback with this is that repeated heating and cooling is likely to loosen the screw's grip, probably requiring re-tightening from time to time.

Cut sections of a hard steel wire, such as metal coathangers, bicycle spokes, and so on, can be bound together to form a whisk for beating eggs; alternatively use fine birch or hazel twigs bound together.

Use small metal doorhandles as lifting handles for large pots; attaching with nuts and bolts or wire as circumstance dictates. Don't use plastic or plastic covered handles as they are likely to melt.

Polystyrene panels or blocks of insulation material (associated with packaging TVs etc) that you find might be transformed into the lining for a homemade cool box. Line a very large biscuit tin for small items, while an old wooden cupboard could offer a bigger cool storage space.

Feathers (sterilized in boiling water before first use) can be used for brushing melted fat over roasting items, or wherever the *brushing* of food with something is required.

When collecting items for your doomsday kitchen try and apply the philosophy of 'can it have than more than one purpose?' So a single polythene bag may be used (1) to cook in, (2) to store water in, (3) to carry things in. If on the move then this means that you have less to carry; *economy of effort* being an important aspect of survival.

Cut the top of a 5-litre plastic bottle and there's the potential for devising a makeshift bucket (right) once a handle made of greenwood, or strong dead wood, has been inserted. If the container was one of those designed to hold liquids for the catering industry then you have food grade plastic to work with.

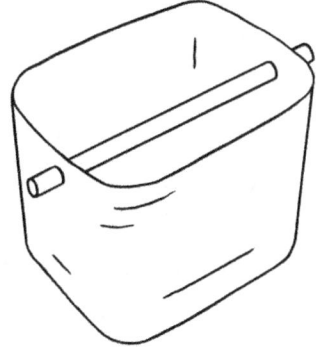

Paper (particularly waxed, or discarded laser label sheets with a shiny, slightly water-repellent surface on one side) can be used to make those paper cups that we made as kids. More permanent cups may be fashioned from thick plastic sheet (something of damp-proof course material consistence, for example). A dab of sticky tape here and there will make the structure even more robust. Since instant paper cups aren't something that adults make on a regular basis – if ever – I have included the small refresher diagram below....

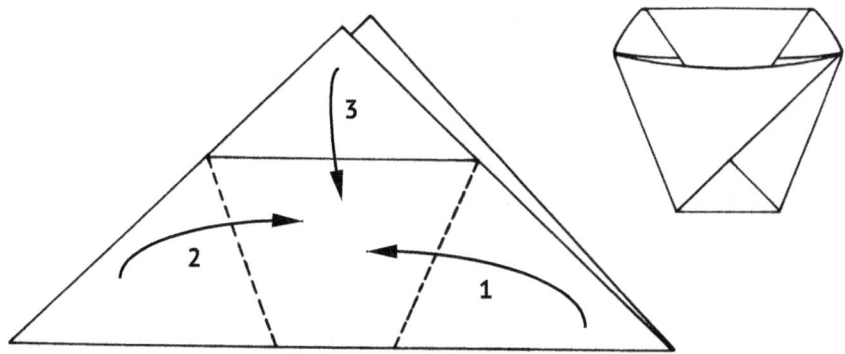

A number of survival and bushcraft resources go to elaborate lengths in describing the making of funnels from pieces of cone-shaped birch bark or other materials. That all seems very laborious when a funnel can be quickly fashioned from a square of material (paper or plastic of various thickness depending on the item to be funnelled and what is at hand).

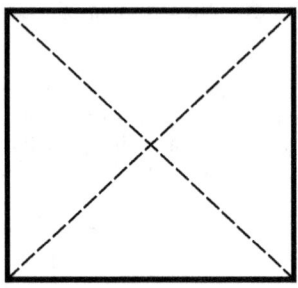 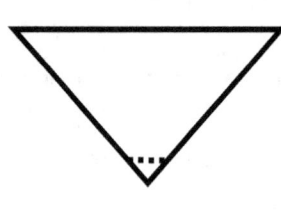

The method is simple, but then in times of stress the human mind can overlook simple and obvious things. Square off your material then fold diagonally twice till you get the triangular shape pictured above. Nip out the apex (start small and widen as required), then separate out one of the material folds and push the others aside. You now have the basis for a funnelling. Using absorbant paper this same process will provide you with a proper paper filter. Your funnel can be supported by a nest of woven or braided greenwood twigs. At the most simple level, the corner of a plastic bag can be nipped out and used as a funnel when supported somehow. *Economy of effort*, remember?

Although sand and grit can be used for filtering purposes, keep aside a few handfuls for scouring rust, food and grease from pots and utensils. In a related manner, cutlery can be pushed into the ground (particularly sandy soils) to remove excess gunge from cutlery before it is washed.

Glass bottles can become rolling pins, as can short sections of hard PVC pipework. Stoppered with polystyrene, cork, or other suitable material short lengths of PVC pipe can become storage containers.

Fine metal gauze could be transformed into a doomsday kitchen sieve, while more chunky mesh could become a colander.

Look, also, for firelighting items that may help get your doomsday kitchen fire started: old cigarette lighters for their flints (and perhaps a bit of gas fuel too); old battery and wind-up torches to ignite steel wool placed across the terminals; old cotton garments (not synthetics) which can be turned into charcloth; soft toys, which may have flammable stuffing which makes good tinder.

Consider, also, the volumes of common items for measuring... a flip-top cigarette packet for example. A 20 unit packet with external dimensions of

22 x 55 x 85 mm will give you an internal volume just below 100 ml, or somewhat short of a ½ cup measure (125 ml); though as long as the slightly deficient measure was used for all ingredients then the error would be relative. Spirit bottle and wine bottle tops vary in size between manufacturers but you may get 10 or 15 ml in a cap. And the typical ¾-inch crown caps for beer bottles (previously crimped but with the 'kink' pushed flat and internal liner removed) will give you a measure of slightly under 1 teaspoon. A very slight heaping of any solid material measured in the top would bring it nearer to the official teaspoon measure, while pushing out the bottom of the cap could achieve the same for liquid measures.

Damaged PTFE bottles, perhaps with a hole in the bottom or a split crown, and of no use for storing water, may provide you with low strength plastic cordage or fixing. To do this, cut the bottle column into a continuous ribbon about 5 mm in width, continuing round the bottle circumference until enough length of material has been obtained. To take some of the curve out of the strips warm then near the fire and stretch the pieces before plaiting three pieces into the plastic cordage.

A two-litre PTFE bottle can also provide you with a form of outer cooling jacket for water distillation. With the bottle in a horizontal position insert the metal 'worm' tube through the bottle neck then make a small hole in the bottle base to allow the worm tube to pass through, finally sealing any gaps around the tube as best you can. Then in the top wall of the bottle cut a hole that allows it to be filled with cold water and become a condenser.

Small greenwood branches can be made to hold meat over the fire for grilling (below) – although skewering the meat might be simpler – with the ends held in place with a greenwood loop. Wire coathangers can be fashioned into tongs to pick up hot food or flip your doomsday burgers. However, coathanger wire is not very strong and any tongs made from this wire will be no match for the proper kitchen gear.

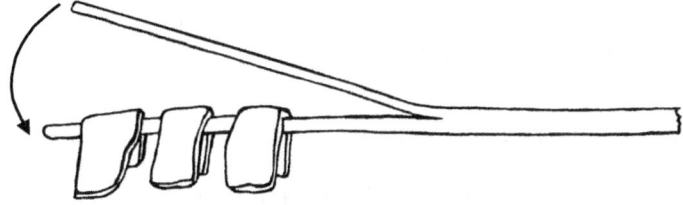

While on the subject of wire coathangers, a section of wire, or a knitting needle, or spoke of a bicycle wheel can be used for forming macaroni pasta shapes – to remind you of old times. Roll pasta into cigarette size shapes then press the wire into the raw material and roll it again until a tube forms. Release the pasta from the wire, cut into macaroni size pieces and then cook them. Your pasta will cook more quickly this way, so possibly save on precious fuel.

DOOMSDAY BINLINERS / TRASH BAGS

One of the keys to any survival kit carried with you is that items should, where possible, have more than one use. The humble bin-liner or trash bag, normally dismissed in everyday life, has a multiplicity of uses, and I suggest that carrying a few of them in an emergency situation would / could be very handy.

In the doomsday kitchen refuse bags might be handy for:

- Protecting food (and other perishable items) from contamination
- Foraging bag
- Providing a clean food preparation surface
- Collecting food waste and rubbish (their normal occupation)
- Plastic tinder for fire-lighting
- Eel trap (black bags preferred)
- Light-blanching plants such as dandelion to make them more palatable
- Water reservoir, water collection, and transpiration bag (if made of white or clear plastic). Where the plastic liners are thin they may need to be doubled up. There's more on water harvesting later.
- Cup – being cradled in a woven twig lattice lined with a cut section of bin-liner to hold the fluid
- Wrapped around a *former* (a broom handle, for example) a crude piece of pipe can be made for transferring liquids with a low energy flow (secure the pipe shape with bits of sticky tape or some form of glue).

Other uses:
- Cut into strips and braided as a low-strength fastener
- Ground to air signalling (white bags preferred)
- Shelter – emergency roof or storm shelter
- Bedding – filled with dried leaves as a mattress and/or leaf duvet
- Waterproof clothing – a hole cut in top for head, slits in sides for arms, or bottom of a bag slit and tied round waist as over-trousers, or bound as leggings round lower legs, or as waterproof head protection.

Some of these useful attributed could also be applied to those plastic foil emergency blankets, which have the additional advantage of being a good signalling aid, and heat reflector on hot days.

Flexibility of Mind

PRACTICAL COOKERY WITH FIRED OVENS / OPEN FIRES

There is (*was*, too) a definite knack to cooking with a wood or coal-fired cooker, not least in dodging wafts of choking, swirling, smoke. Cooking with, or by, fire is a skill that we have forgotten about in the industrialized world, but it is a skill that will have to be mastered in any post-disaster world where electricity and gas are no longer conveniently available. We can learn much from kitchen tips and recommendations of past cooks and the section which follows draws together some cooking wisdom trawled from countless old texts.

If you are going to bake bread in a brick or clay-type oven then heat it with proper blocks of wood rather than lots of brushwood and twigs. Start by virtually filling the cooking space with 90 to 120 cm split branches, piled cross-ways to each other, and then keep on feeding with more wood material so it has burned for about an hour. Then rake the embers across the whole of the oven floor, before pushing them to one side. To test the heat of an oven for bread-making (white floured bread) an old trick was to hold your hand inside the cavity, and if you could count to forty then it was at the right temperature. Items were also baked in sequence according to the declining oven temperature – brown bread first, then white, pies, cakes / puddings, and then custards and quiches. As a treat the final items that might be put in would be a dish of apples to gently bake.

For the folks who baked bread on a large scale then the operation was similar. With a mass of brushwood and kindling lit, and an intense blaze achieved, more fuel was added and then continued to be added until a sufficient heat mass developed. The whole burning process might take an hour, by which time the heat would be sufficient to raise the bread to full height, cook through to the loaf centre, and give it a nice crust. A general rule for many bakers was to light the fire at the same time the bread dough was being started.

The fire was thought sufficiently hot when strong embers sparkled and the smoke had dissipated. One particular test for a baking oven was when the point of a long wooden stick was forcibly rubbed against the interior brickwork it would leave a trace of black charcoal which would burn off in a few moments. The embers were then either drawn out or pushed aside, the floor of the oven cleaned off, and the loaves or loaf tins loaded in the oven with a *baking peel* (a long pole with a flat board at the end). The oven door is then sealed with the loaves baked in 1½ to 2 hours depending on the loaf size.

Where a dinner or major meal was to be prepared (with boiled meat, for example) then the whole cooking process would need to begin 3 or 4 hours before the event. The kitchen 'range' needed to develop a good and steady fire that would keep going throughout the whole cooking session without too much maintenance (cooks of old used terms such as *sharp*, *brisk*, of *slow* fire to describe the heat and combustive energy of their fire).

Timing, too, was perhaps a very important skill in successful cooking in the past. For example, soon after breakfast had finished a cauldron of cold water containing the meat joint would have been hung on the crane over the fire.

If, after an hour or two, the water was boiling then the pot for cooking suet and other puddings could be hung up. An hour or so later a whole cabbage might have been tipped into a cooking pot to start boiling, and then at half hourly intervals carrots and small turnips, parsnips and potatoes be pitched in according to their cooking time. If all the pyrotechnic wizardry worked out then everything might be ready to serve up at the same time.

There were also quasi-technical rules for *roasting*. For example, to roast a joint of meat then the fire needed to be 7 to 10 cm longer at each end of the joint being cooked, while it was regarded as crucial for the fire to burn equally throughout – otherwise thermal hotspots could develop that either overcooked or undercooked the meat in patches. And sand and water were the only permitted cleansers for the spit itself, which was one of the first items prepared.

The cooking fire was mostly made up about 30 minutes before roasting commenced, with the volume or size of the fire relative to the size of the piece of meat being cooked (there was no point in wasting valuable fuel – something that would be of concern if you needed to gather it yourself). Where meat was thin or very tender then a small, quick, fire was recommended.

With the exception of ribs it was recommended never to salt the roast before it was put in front of the fire. Similarly, and contrary to the image that we perceive of cooking over kitchen fires, lots of skewering of the meat was frowned upon since it punctured the body of the roast allowing internal cooking juices to potentially escape and the meat to dry out. A dripping-pan was always placed under the cooking meat, initially with a little lard or fat which was allowed to melt and get very hot and then used for the first few bastings of the meat. As the roast progressed the volume of liquid in the pan would increase, and then 15 minutes before the roast was served some water (30 ml, perhaps more) was added to the dripping-pan to make the gravy. Flour might also be added as a thickener.

It was recommended to keep the meat at a moderate distance from the fire, not place it right on top of the heat. The larger the joint, the greater the distance from the fire at the *start* of cooking – which meant that the outer layers of meat didn't shrivel up and harden before the middle was cooked.

Some roasts started off at a distance of 45 cm from the fire, others closer depending on size and type of meat. When the meat was nearly done the roast was moved closer to the fire to crisp and brown the outside. And all the time the cook needed to continually turn the meat to ensure even cooking, and also regularly baste it, and maintain that steady fire.

Meat was never exposed to a fierce fire at the start of roasting; the fire being stoked so that it burned bright, strong and clear (just think of a big mass of hot, perfectly glowing and burning embers), and as smoke-free as possible – certainly the front portion of the fire facing the meat joint. To maintain a constant, good, heat draughts and cold air needed to be excluded as much as possible. If you were a sophisticated cook then you might have a tin *meat screen* while others would make do with clothes or washing slung over the back of chairs to prevent draughts. Metal meat screens also had the advantage of reflecting heat back.

Every now and then the cook would temporarily draw both the roast and dripping-pan back from in front of the fire (to avoid smoke and cinder contamination) to allow new red-hot coals to be raked forwards from the back of the fire to the front, and new fuel to be added at the back. In this way a constancy of heat was, hopefully, maintained during the roasting process.

The rough rule of thumb for timing a roast was 15 to 20 minutes (or slightly longer) per half kilo of meat when the fire produced a good heat. A 4½ kilo chunk of beef would roast for 2 to 2½ hours, starting at 45 cm from the fire. Veal and mutton took slightly less time to roast, while lamb took a shorter period than mutton but was recommended to be well done, so placed 35 cm from the fire. Fat pork and veal joints took longer to roast than lean meats, leg joints longer than loin or breast meat cuts. Pork was always recommended to be well done.

For roasting fowl and poultry three quarters of an hour was reckoned as good for a large chicken-type bird, with a small one done in twenty minutes. A small turkey or goose might be roasted for an hour and a quarter, but longer if the bird was larger. In all cases of roasting poultry the caveat of *properly* or *thoroughly done* was observed at all times, and not reliance on mere timings.

The state of the weather also played a part in the cooking time, as did the age of the animal killed. Meat was expected to be *hung* sufficiently before it was cooked – a couple of days in hot weather being regarded as doing what a week of cold weather hanging would do. Excess fat would be trimmed off the meat prior to roasting, since the fat was regarded better in the form of suet for making puddings, than as dripping.

When it came to *boiling meat* the recommended practices somewhat diverge. One school of thought was that the meat should be dropped into boiling water, while others preferred to place the meat in cold water and then bring that to the boil, the reasoning being that the gradual heating process produced a more tender end result. Of the many old texts I have analysed my perception is, on reflection, that the '*cold boilers*' outweigh the instant boiling water brigade.

Meat to be boiled was covered with just enough water to submerge it and no more. During the boiling process any scum which formed was carefully removed since that could cake or stick onto the meat and give it an unappealing look. A little salt thrown into the cooking pot would help more scum rise to the surface, while a little cold water added to the seething, bubbling, pot would briefly reduce the heat to allow easier skimming.

Once the large majority of scum had been removed then the meat was allowed to boil gently and steadily until it was cooked, with no sudden increase or reduction in heat. This could cause the meat to expand and/or contract, helping break it up, whilst a harsh heat would harden the meat and dry up the juices within the joint. In relation to this, a kettle of boiling water was always recommended to be kept at hand to top up the cooking water as it evaporated.

As in cooking hams or bacon joints today, salted meats often needed prior soaking in water to remove excess salt or brine pickle. Since brining, salting and smoking of meats (see the various recipes later) were key methods of preserving food for the winter months then one imagines that most boiled meats must have needed to go through some washing or soaking process to remove excess preservative prior to boiling. One curious recommendation that I came across was that if you believed your salted meat to be *under salted* then it was to be cooked very slowly in water because that process would *freshen* the meat up.

As with roasted meat no exact *boiling time* rule could be given since meat freshness played a part (a well hung mutton leg, for example, was cooked for a shorter time than a fresh one), as did whether the meat was a solid chunk or a joint (the latter taking less time, assuming equal weight but less thickness), while salted meats took longer also. An old culinary maxim for boiling meat in the past was: a quarter of an hour, and two pints of water, to every pound of meat to be boiled. As with roasting, however, there were variables which needed to be taken into consideration.

Once the meat had finished cooking it was recommended that it be removed from the cooking pot to prevent it becoming sodden and waterlogged, then placed on a trivet or some other similar device and both put over the cooking pot so the meat would keep warm until served up. Of course the liquor remaining from the boiling process was used as the foundation for soups and gravies (though not that from salted meats), so waste was limited. And that in a post-disaster scenario is something to be avoided as food may be very scarce.

Regarding the making of a good broth or soup; other than from using the cooking liquor from boiled meat mentioned above, past wisdom recommended the slow stewing or gentle simmering of soups – for three to six hours – while it was suggested that broths and soups were made the night before they were wanted so that the fat could be more easily removed.

Boiled puddings are a simple enough way of cooking food, whether sweet or savoury, and judging by the number of 'pudding' recipes in ancient books they appear to have been a highly popular way of cooking food, either boiled in a greased basin (sometimes covered over with paper and tied), or wrapped in cotton cloths and cooked.

Recommendations from the past suggest that any cloths used for boiling food needed to be thoroughly scalded and dried after use, and be stored in a dry place (obviously mildew, and cotton rotted by moisture, wouldn't have been very healthy). When it came to using a cloth the dry material was to be buttered and floured before it was filled.

Furthermore, to prevent crusts or pastry sticking to basins in which a pudding was to be boiled it was rubbed with butter. Where pastry itself was a key part of the dish then a minimal amount of water or milk was mixed with the flour – just enough to make the pastry happen.

It was recommended that the water must be boiling before the pudding was lowered into the pot, and if being cooked in cotton muslin then the pudding should be kept moving to prevent it sticking to the bottom of the pot. With the exception of suet pudding, which gained flavour from being boiled in the same pot as meat, then puddings were to be boiled in plenty of water on their own. Cooking time for a pudding would range from 2 to 3 hours, though size was ultimately the determining factor.

Broiling (read barbeque) has also been around for a long time, and I imagine most readers will be familiar with the backyard barbie process. Much of past cooking wisdom relating to broiling should be pretty familiar, although there are a few interesting nuances.

As with our experience today a good, clean, and hot fire was regarded as essential. Before broiling, the coals were to be broken up so that a clear fire was obtained. Kitchens were expected to have two gridirons or griddles, one for meat and poultry, and the second for fish (whether these were of differing grades of metal I am not sure). Once the griddle was hot it was rubbed with a piece of fresh suet where meat was to be cooked, or with chalk if fish was being broiled. Cooks were instructed that a used gridiron should be rubbed clean immediately after use and never put back in storage with grease or soot attached. Like today, a pair of tongs to turn the food with were regarded as indispensable.

Frying needs little explanation but old cooks recommended that any butter, suet and dripping used for frying ought to be clarified, as this had a better taste. When frying fish the suggested method of testing whether the pan was hot enough was to dip the tail of the fish into the boiling fat. If it quickly became crisp and hard, then the fat in the pan was ready.

IMPORTANT
PRESUME that anything near an open fire is going to be *very* HOT. It does not matter whether you are going to lift a kettle lid, move a pot, or turn over a broiling steak, protect yourself from burns by using some implement or covering your hands with protective material. A small burn can painful, but without medical attention in a survival situation that burn could become infected and cause a problem. A major burn in a survival situation would not only incapacitate but could become life-threatening if harmful pathogens get past the skin's defences. Be careful with your fires.

Also consider wearing cotton or wool clothing when cooking around an open fire as flammable synthetics and manmade fabrics (footwear too), may melt with the heat or, worse still, catch fire. Molten synthetics on human skin is painful!

COOKING WITH CLAY

Some readers of this book may have heard of tales about country folk baking hedgehogs in clay. Cameron [*Wild Foods of Great Britain*, 1917] notes that farm labourers regarded the taste of hedgehog as a 'delicacy', the cooking instructions being: *'Clean, but do not skin, wrap the hedgehog in a ball of clay and roast in the ashes of a wood or peat fire. This should take from 10 to 20 minutes, according to the heat of the ashes. When done the ball is broken open and the skin comes away with the clay.'* Of course, hedgehogs are rightly protected by legislation because of their dwindling numbers, but Cameron's description identifies the concept behind cooking in clay – encapsulation – and both feathered poultry and fish may be cooked in a similar manner.

There are different ways of enclosing food in clay for cooking, but several points need to be considered: First, where is your clay source in relation to ground level? If the clay is too deep to dig economically (remembering *economy of effort*) then it may not be a worthwhile method, yet in other terrains clay may be less than a foot below ground level, even in a garden. In open country, check streams to see if the water flow has exposed clay strata, similarly in rivers (though be aware of the increased dangers of working in riverine locations). Any exposed clay that you mine from the ground needs to be free of organic matter and debris that might taint the food.

Second, is the plastic quality of the clay – too much sand and it cannot be shaped without cracking, while sticky clays can be used for coating some foods with little extra preparation but are often subject to shrinkage and consequent cracking. To test the plasticity roll a little clay to a pencil thickness and then bend it. If it cracks rather than bends then it is unlikely that you will be able to use it in a pastry-like envelope to cook food without difficulty, however not all is lost, as you will read further below.

The third aspect of clay is that you are unlikely to be able to bake it in a campfire to the temperatures required to make it impervious to water, as in pottery. Basic fired earthenware is somewhat porous to water and stains easily, and even that stage of firing would require lots of fuel to achieve high enough temperatures. Do you have fuel to waste?

Despite these one or two negative aspects of clay, the bottom line is that when you have no cooking pots or facilities to spit your food for roasting over a fire, then clay cooking does give you additional cooking options. So, how to cook with clay now we understand the limitations?

Assuming the clay is of a plastic-like consistence that may be rolled or patted out with your hands to the thickness of a pencil, then the food (a gutted but unskinned fish, for example) can simply be laid on one half of the rolled clay, then the other half of the clay folded over, pressed onto and around the fish, then excess trimmed off but leaving enough edge for it to be crimped closed. Small birds can similarly be wrapped, and so can potatoes. If using other ingredients to flavour the wrapped item (thinking here of pigeon wrapped with bacon – if available to your doomsday kitchen) then wrap those items first in non-toxic, non-bitter, vegetation, before wrapping in the clay.

Where the clay is of a sticky consistency then it is better for smearing onto food; mainly feathered birds, but even rabbits or rodents with the skin intact, provided they have been gutted and thoroughly washed out. You may need to apply two coatings, allowing the first layer to partly dry out before adding more sticky clay. This can also be achieved with fish if the skin has been dried off first (otherwise the clay does not always get a really good hold). In my view this method, and the clay envelope one previous, are for cooking in fire embers.

A further development of sticky clay is to make it into an actual slurry in which the food to be cooked is dipped and then suspended over the fire. For this, firmer clays too can be thinned with water, and sandy clays that cannot be rolled or bent may also be usable. The slurry wants to be the consistency of a really thick, gloopy, batter. While this can be used for unplucked animals, it is also good for plucked and dressed poultry or other de-furred animals, however all items may need dipping three or four times to build the thickness up to a point where flames licking the suspended food will not scorch the contents of the package. For this slurry method, batches of the clay gloop should be made up as needed, and any leftovers of the batch in which food has been dipped, discarded. This is for safety – in case bits of organic animal matter left in the gloop ferments or it develops nasty bacteria that might be transferred to your food.

Where really large pieces or hunks of meat are being cooked then the clay layer needs to be 2 to 3 cm thick and, in my view, a lot of your precious fuel will be wasted in heating up the vast inorganic mass of clay even before the basic meat ingredient starts cooking. However, it is another cooking option when you are down to bare basics.

One of the advantages of this clay cooking technique for anyone living in a coniferous area is that clay encapsulation allows you to keep some of the resinous flavours imparted by burning pine wood away from your food.

Another doomsday kitchen potential for clay is that of making a baking plate or hob to provide a means of cooking flatbreads and bannocks, rather than having to cook them directly in ashes or embers. As mentioned before, however, your campfire will never be able to generate enough heat to make proper ceramics so the baking plate will be porous; but then that should not be a problem when cooking flatbreads.

To make your 'plate', clear a piece of ground with a reasonably porous soil (this helps prevent the clay mixing and adhering to the ground), then place a solid mass of clay on this and beat it down to about 2 to 3 cm in depth. As much air as possible needs to be removed otherwise airpockets in the clay will expand in the heat of the fire and cause breaks. Ideally, if there is time, then a thick clay slurry can be moulded in a 'former' and allowed to dry out over two or three weeks – a similar drying off time for the beaten clay mass too. Shape the layer into a suitable size cooking surface area while still soft then, once the 'plate' looks visibly like it is free of moisture, introduce it gently to the heat of your fire, before finally baking it on embers to drive off the last of the locked-in moisture. Because the plate is not a true ceramic it will always need to be handled with great care due to its fragile nature, but it still provides you with a baking surface area. It is possible to reinforce the baking plate with something like chicken wire, however that has a drawback in that the thermal expansion properties of the metal and clay will be different and over time cracks will develop. That said, where clay is abundant then this may not present a problem.

Quite recently I was reading somewhere that in ancient South America they once used clay balls to cook maize-like ingredients, perhaps in the same way as heated igneous stones can be used to boil water where you do not have a fire-resistant cooking pot or boiling vessel. It was not clear from the write-up whether the clay balls (about 2 to 3 cm in diameter in the picture) had actually been fired to a hard ceramic or were plain earthenware status. Still this concept might provide you with another doomsday kitchen option if you could suitably bake or fire clay, and no stones were available.

One thing I have never done with clay slip cooking, and *must* put on my 'to do' list, is to use the process for cooking animal ears (pig, lamb, calf), since that ability of the clay to fix the ear bristles in a fire-hardened matrix could make the need to singe the ears, pre-cooking, unnecessary. It might also work for cow's udders too in this respect.

SOIL TEXTURE AND MOISTURE

In the process of putting this work together finding a natural position in the subject order for a few words about soil texture and moisture has been a little problematic. Soil may sound like an odd inclusion, since this book is about food and related topics, but soil texture and moisture not only affect both plant growth and habitat, but are also relevant to certain types of water harvesting methods, which we will be coming to shortly, and also the drainage properties of the ground where you establish your doomsday kitchen. From a plant growth perspective it is not only the nutrients in the soil base, or the chemical influences of underlying rock strata such as chalk, sandstone, granite, or whatever, but also the water holding and permeability properties of the soil structure which come into play. The subject of soil mechanics is a heavyweight science in its own right so all I want to do here is highlight a few pointers that could aid you in obtaining water for your doomsday kitchen.

For example, if you were considering digging a hole in the ground with the idea of making a solar still for use on a sunny day, then understanding the moisture content of the soil beneath your feet might help out in your design considerations because the very moisture contained in that soil may become a valuable resource. Similarly, if you identified that there was a shallow-lying rock strata, or perhaps an impervious clay hardpan, covered by a porous overlying subsoil, then instead of randomly digging a gypsy well in the vague expectation of obtaining water you can make an informed decision before you expend lots of effort digging (*economy of effort*, again). An understanding of soil texture might also help you identify mystery water drainage problems in areas you seek to harvest water from. If you are a soil engineer or geologist then you probably do not need to read through this section.

Soils are generally made of a mixture of components – gravels, sand, silt, clay and organic matter – unless, that is, you are in a desert, clay pit, or mudflat, where the component exists in a pure, or almost pure, form. In an ideal world a good *soil structure* is one that has a variety of soil particle types bound together by lots of decomposed organic matter such as leaf mulch, rotted wood, and so on. This sort of 'ideal' soil generally holds good amounts of moisture. The next key attribute of a soil is its *texture* which, in technical-speak, defines the proportions of the different sized particles that make up the soil. The coarsest are gravels, followed by sands, then by silt, and finally clay particles, and it is these particle types which help or hinder water absorbtion, water holding capacity, the permeability of the soil to water, and also the erodability of the soil. Soil with a fine texture will hold more water than a coarse one. Because of the fine particle size of clays a given volume of clay will have a greater particle surface area than an equal volume of sand and can hold large amounts of moisture. That said, clay is almost impermeable (just think of how long it takes for a rain puddle to disappear through clay), and where the clay bed is thick there is every possibility that pooled water will 'evaporate' long before it can be absorbed. Silts fall somewhere in the middle of sand and clay, their physical structure making them permeable but not as porous as sand, and, unlike clay do not generally become sticky and claggy when wet.

The bottom line then, is if you can get a bit of an understanding of soil texture then you will be better prepared when it comes to making decisions on harvesting water from the land while it should also help you in understanding more about the type of terrain in which you might be hunting for edible plants.

The diagram below is my über-simplified rendition of a soil texture chart devised by the United States Department of Agriculture (USDA) in the 1960s and which has been through various iterations since. Widely used around the world as the model for describing soil texture the chart shows the interaction of different particle sizes to produce the soil type, while the influence of organic debris in the form of humus asserts itself in the loam soil portion. As mentioned, this is a gross simplification of a quite complex chart, but hopefully it will give you an overall picture, an overview, of what makes up a soil. And all of this has importance in the water holding capacity, or not, of a soil and about which we will be dealing with shortly.

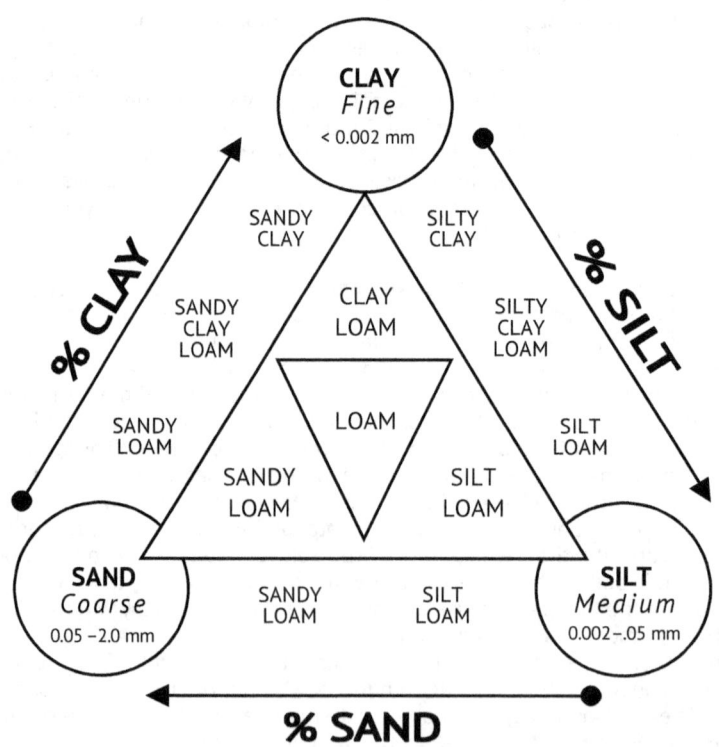

IDENTIFYING SOIL TEXTURAL CLASS

Being able to determine the make-up of a soil sample and put a finger on the soil texture type can be rather daunting at the beginning, but the more you investigate and practice ('soil spotting' as opposed to 'plant spotting') then the easier it becomes. Below and overleaf are two different methods of getting a feel for the texture of the soil under your feet.

In the first instance, take a sample of the soil (a really good handful) and place in a clear bottle or pickle jar then add water to submerge the soil. Shake the container well and then leave the contents to settle for a day, potentially two days, until the particle layers separate out, particularly the fine clays. If you have a mathematical bent of mind then it would be possible to measure the layers and work out rough percentages of the particle size layers, but overall the method should provide you with a good visual grasp of the soil type you are dealing with.

The diagram below shows the sort of results you might obtain for a sandy, loam and clay soil respectively. For the sake of simplicity fine sand has not been indicated on each sample, nor have any gravelly pebbles that would sink to the bottom with the sand, while the organic component may be a mixture of debris in suspension or floating on the water surface. In the case of the loamy soil then there is likely to be a significant amount of debris mixed in with the water.

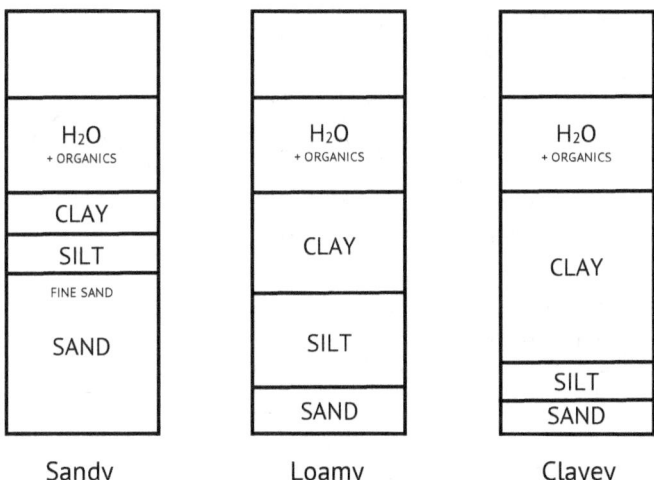

Overleaf is another way of establishing the texture grade of the soil, using both tactile and visual cues. As soil porosity decreases the soils become more plastic and water retentive, allowing a sample to be shaped and formed in the hand.

DECREASING POROSITY / PERMEABILITY ⟶	**SANDY** Soil particles loose and separated, gritty when dry. Can only aggregate into a slumped pyramid form.	△
	SANDY LOAM Initially almost velvety to the touch but become gritty on rubbing. A soil with enough silt and clay to become sticky and able to form a ball that fissures readily when pressed flat.	○
	SILTY LOAM Similar to sandy loam but more firm; slightly sticky but no grittiness. Holds shape when rolled into a small, sausage-shaped, cylinder but fissures when pressed flat. Smooth, floury, texture when dry.	⬭
	LOAM Sand, silt and clay particles in almost equal amounts. May be rolled into a weak cigar-like cylinder but breaks when bent.	⬭
	CLAYEY LOAM Additional clay to loam, which makes the soil more sticky and plastic, and firm. A cigar-shaped cylinder does not fissure if *gently* bent into a U shape. Hardens to quite crush-resistant clods with some grittiness to the touch.	⌒
	FINE CLAY Smooth, sticky, plastic soil. A formed 'wire' can be bent into the shape of a circle, but shows some cracks, or does so when moderate force applied.	◯ (with cracks)
	HEAVY CLAY Smooth, plastic, soil; a 'wire' able to be shaped into a circle, without showing fissuring.	◯

IDENTIFYING SOIL MOISTURE CONTENT

Having identified the type of soil you can now make a decision as to whether to dig a well, gypsy well or natural water collection pond. For example, while moisture will rapidly sink in sandy soil through the force of gravity and may 'pool' where it meets clay or an impermeable rock strata, in my view there's little point in expending valuable personal energy in digging a water collection hole unless bedrock or clay hardpan is close by. A clay loam (and to a lesser extent a sandy loam) would present better options since the organic matter in the soil will help it retain moisture – and hopefully you would be able to dig downwards to reach an impermeable barrier where water sinking by gravity can be collected. If the topsoil has a high clay content then pure clay layers may be present not far below, and in this case may offer an opportunity to create natural collection ponds. However, wet clay is heavy going to work with, particularly if excavating through tens of centimetres of the stuff to create a deep pond. On the upside, the clay spoil from your dig could be used to construct a second collection pond on the surface of the ground, or even a clay oven or clay stove (see page 159).

At ground level, a comprehension of the type of soil should also help you understand the futility of constructing flood defences or water diversion systems from the wrong types of soil. Clay, or clay with some sand content, is generally a good soil for this sort of work, particularly if layered with grass sods to prevent the scouring activity and erosion potential of fast moving water.

The next associated step in digging water collection holes is recognizing the water capacity of the various types of soil. From time to time some soils are going to become saturated and the water will be highly visible, yet there may be occasions where a soil layer always seems to maintain a constant high moisture level, perhaps being fed through water travelling along wrinkles in the underlying rock strata. In which case if the soil feels quite moist then it may be worth conducting a test hole to see if any water sinking by gravity can be harvested.

Another option, where there isn't enough moisture to be physically collected through the pull of gravity is to get at that moisture content through solar evaporation / distillation, digging a 'solar distillation pit' details of which will be found in most decent survival books. This can work well where the soil is dark (so readily absorbing the sun's energy) and relatively moist, though in northern temperate climes my personal view is that this type of solar distillation is hardly the makings of a regular 'water supply' but is, rather, available as a water harvesting technique for emergencies. However, in warmer Mediterranean countries this method could be a useful option.

Overleaf is a table that will help you determine the percentage moisture in a soil sample, relative to the texture grade of the soil. Make a rough ball of the soil – the size of an egg – place in the palm of your hand and then squeeze it tightly. Upon opening your fingers pay special attention to how much particulate adheres to your fingers, finger impressions in/on the sample surface, and any sign of moisture or water on your fingers.

Available Moisture	*Fine* **Silty-Clay Loam**	*Medium* **Sandy Clay-Loam to Silt-Loam**	*Moderately Coarse* **Sandy Loam to Fine Sand Loam**	*Coarse* **Fine Sand to Loamy Fine Sand**
100%	Wet. Surface water when squeezed. Sticky, thick coating on fingers. Forms soft ball.	Wet. A little water exudes on pressure. Medium-heavy coating on fingers. Forms soft ball.	Wet. A little water exudes on pressure. Medium-heavy coating on fingers. Forms soft ball.	Wet. Quite heavy soil-water stains on fingers. Forms weak ball leaving outline stain on hand.
75 - 100%	Wet. Medium to heavy soil-water coating on hand. Easily squeezed between fingers, feels slick. Forms uneven ball.	Wet. Light to heavy finger coating. Extrudes between forefinger and thumb. Finger impressions left in ball surface.	Wet. Some water staining on fingers. Some extrusion properties between fingers. Wet, slightly sticky, ball leaves outline on hand.	Wet. Grains dark from moisture, some remaining on fingers. Heavy water stain on hand. Extrusion mostly fails. Ball is weak, breaks easily.
50 – 75%	Moist. Fingers lightly soil-water stained. Extrusion possible. Ball is smooth and pliable with finger impressions visible.	Moist. Fingers lightly stained with water. Extrusion possible but weak, feels damp. Pliable ball, not sticky; dark with moisture.	Moist. Light water-soil staining on fingers. Ball does not stick; well defined finger marks.	Moist. Some darkened (moist) grains on fingers. Medium water staining. Extrusion not possible. Forms loose grained, weak, ball which breaks easily.
25 – 50%	Slightly moist. No water staining on fingers. Little soil breakaway. Flattens between fingertips. Weak ball with some pliability.	Slightly moist. Very minor grain breakaway. No water staining. Rough surfaced, weak, ball; crumbling with pressure.	Slightly moist. Grains dark (being moist). No finger staining. Weak ball with finger impressions, crumbling with pressure.	Slightly moist. Sand and grains lightly coat fingers. Ball very weak. Finger impressions well defined.
0 – 25%	Dry. Soil particles separate easily. Lumps of soil hard to break between fingers. Appearance is hard, baked, crust-like.	Dry. Soil breaks apart and powders easily. No staining evident. Lumps crumble under finger pressure.	Dry. Ball holds weakly together, grains easily shedding.	Dry. Soil loose but lightly aggregates when immobile; otherwise flows through fingers. Loose particles on fingers when pressure applied.

[Table modelled around USDA Soil Moisture Estimation data.]

FURTHER ASPECTS OF SOIL AND MOISTURE

Where you encounter very dry soil conditions, or there is drought, then soil moisture and the ability of soil to retain moisture may become critical – both in terms of providing moisture for plants to feed upon, but also if you needed to evaporate water for consumption through solar distillation.

After long periods of dryness it is possible for more than a third (I have seen a figure of 40% quoted) of any rainfall that falls on the dried land simply to disappear as runoff. This may be affected by the slope of the ground, or should the rain be too intense, but it is also down to the infiltration, permeability and water holding qualities of the soil. And while the splash erosion effects of individual energetic raindrops hammering the earth will physically dislodge soil particles there is also a sort of subsidiary phenomenon taking place; the fine silt and clay-like particles of the soil being suspended in solution which then block pores between the larger soil particles, thereby reducing the absorbative capacity of the soil and increasing the chances of water and soil run-off. Compacted earth will clearly not help water infiltration either, while sloping terrains can be subject to crusted earth surfaces. In a worst case scenario the bulk of any rainwater would run away over the baked, hard, earth, while moisture remaining in puddles or on plant leaf surfaces evaporates into thin air. A lose-lose situation.

In terms of surface harvesting of water from the natural terrain in dry conditions it may be that you will need to modify the surface soil, which could be stones / gravel or vegetative (as in straw or branches strewn over an area so that the rain gets better contact with the soil). Natural vegetative ground cover is a major controlling influence in erosion and run-off. Not only does the greenery protect the surface soil from the kinetic energy of the impacting water drops (splash erosion), but the matted root systems of the plants help inhibit water run-off, while dead root material increases soil porosity as it shrinks and decays, so enhancing infiltration of water into the soil. Plant foliage itself intercepts part of the rainfall which can evaporate later, after the storm, while the decayed organic matter from those leaves improves soil structure.

In certain terrains it is possible for impermeable *hardpans* to form, either through compacted soil, natural clay barriers, but also poor soil chemistry thanks to excessive saturation. Continual excess moisture in a soil (whether through poor drainage, or low-lying land) can degrade its structure and aeration, as well as cause chemical changes that result in poor vegetative cover or cropping. Such soils often have a mottled appearance, and the chemicals may taint the water in the near vicinity. Hardpans can sometimes be identified by observing surface ponding of water – where water is slow to drain (although in many instances that may be because the water table is high or ground saturated).

WATER RESOURCES

Somehow fire and water seem to make perfect bedfellows when it comes to discussing food and beverage production in an emergency situation, and briefly I want to review some of the background water acquisition issues in a post-disaster doomsday world, and make some suggestions for water harvesting when the piped supply no longer works.

Depending on the events that have taken place, or subsequent events after a main disaster, water supplies and water availability may, or will, be severely compromised. These 'water events' if they can be termed as such are varied in type and will have different effects on available water for drinking and cooking, and therefore need to be individually considered and assessed when it comes to collecting your own water supplies.

TIDAL SURGES
Coastal tidal surges may impact on freshwater availability inland, decreasing not only the drinking-water resources through saltwater contamination, but potentially affecting ecosystems that one might ordinarily use as foraging grounds. I read somewhere that drinking-water, and water for domestic *vegetative* plant irrigation, is simply unusable with just a 5% increase in salt content.

HEAVY PRECIPITATION
Visible outward signs of the effects of very heavy rains and storms are those of extensive area flooding, and also high-energy torrents with potentially destructive energy that cause erosion or catastrophic building damage. Behind these obvious visible manifestations, however, other sinister scenarios may be unfolding: the increased land runoff from agricultural areas may bring biological hazards from animal waste, manure, or nitrates (although that is probably less likely in a post-disaster world). Chemical agents and sanitation contaminants from urban areas may adversely effect surface and groundwater quality too. All or any of these can be discharged into the lakes, stream or rivers that supply water downstream from an urban area.

HOT / WARM WEATHER
Apart from your personal requirement for more fluids during warm periods of weather, heatwaves can have interrelated consequences. First, reduced water flows may impact on water available for efficient sanitation. Second, warm weather can bring increases in algal blooms; not only at sea (which will affect the foraging of marine shellfish), but in inland water stocks too. Typical symptoms for cyano-bacterial poisoning are skin rashes, tingling sensations around the mouth, itchy eyes and throat, possibly slurred speech.

DROUGHT
Racking up general hot weather periods to that of drought status again brings related problems of insufficient water to dilute sewage water, but may also concentrate contaminants and bacterial pathogens in standing water (ponds /

lakes) through evaporation, while at the same time not diluting waste water run-off that normally flows into that same standing water.

Before considering the use of *any* groundwater source (streams, springs or wells) for human consumption, in my view – but I will happily defer to the superior wisdom of any qualified water engineer – you need to understand the catchment area so that possible hazards can be identified. How does water drain, by what means is it conveyed (surface or sub-surface), where the source originates, and how mobile are pollutants? In my own mind, I would never consider using water from an old well. Why is it disused? What chemicals, pollutants or dead animals might lurk in the depths? Standing groundwater too, should regarded as suspect. Furthermore, you would need to consider the long-term viability of the source. Could it dry up for good, or is it subject to seasonal dry periods?

If, in the very long-term, you decide to take groundwater sources then you might consider the old water purification technique of 'slow sand filtration', sometimes referred to as 'biological filtration'. It would, however, involve lots of work in digging pits and sourcing fine sand. Although it's rather dated, check out a World Health Organization paper entitled *Slow Sand Filtration* by Huisman, L. and Wood W.E. (1974) for more insight into this effective but low-tech approach to water purification.

To make water of unknown quality or purity relatively safe for drinking purposes it should be boiled. At sea level water should be brought to, and held at, a boil for a very minimum of 1 minute, and up to 3 minutes for higher altitudes. Where water is suspected of being particularly contaminated with soil-borne pathogens then it is suggested that the boiling point is maintained for 15 to 20 minutes. This, however, will need valuable fuel resources.

SURFACE WATER HARVESTING

Water is a key item for human life to exist, but my main interest is in securing water for cooking with, rather than for drinking and keeping hydrated – although that is an important parallel issue too – and in this section I wanted to run through a few basic concepts and ideas to help you secure surface water, rather than take it from wells, ponds, streams or rivers which may be contaminated. The second reason for looking at surface rainwater harvesting is that eliminates any need to walk to a water source (*economy of effort*) as it can be gathered on the doorstep, as it were. In the developing world collecting water can consume 2 to 3 hours of the day's activities. There will be an initial outlay in man hours to construct a rainwater collecting system, and the need to acquire materials, but after that the benefits should not take long to appear.

In nature water is never 100% pure, and both standing water and rivers may well have contaminants in a post-disaster world where there is no longer control of effluent seepage and land run-off. For this reason surface-collected rainwater may be the best answer, assuming there are no airborne smoke, chemical, or biological nasties. As for standing water, I would generally leave it alone; certainly if it had algal deposits on the surface. That generally shows the water is a 'non moving', or at least very slow moving, source and I personally would regard that as suspect. In fact some of the cyanobacteria species that form toxic algal blooms (found in both freshwater and saltwater environments) are not visible on the water surface, though many are. In farmland areas where animals are active, there all sorts of nasty parasites and bugs that may lurk in the soil, so collection of water in these areas needs to be treated with thought and consideration.

Once you have collected water then it needs to be filtered or purified, and for that there are the options of filtering through granular layers, or by distillation or other evaporative means. Another option is the capillary wicking of water, but this is dreadfully slow and only leaves solid dirt particles behind. Other water purifying techniques which are not totally appropriate to northern temperate climates (unless hot, dry, conditions temporarily exist) are the solar still, and transpiration bags. In freezing weather collecting ice can be useful because suspended dirt particles in water tend to sink when the water is chilled. But, as with general ground water, snow and ice are not to be regarded as sources of pure water.

Distillation is perhaps one of the best ways of obtaining a pure water, but in a post-disaster world the mass of fuel required to accomplish this will be phenomenal if a daily water supply is required. However, if a water source is suspected of having something really nasty in it then distillation may be the only option. In these cases the water produced in the first few minutes should be discarded, and overall only the first 30 to 35% of the water being distilled should be collected, with the rest left behind in the distilling vessel thrown away. If you do not have the means of constructing a 'still' then an emergency method of collecting the water vapour is to place sponges or absorbant cotton material over the steam source, and then wring these out from to time. Be aware, however, that they will be scalding hot.

In the absence, or non-requirement, of distillation then the water is best filtered first; traditionally through vessels with numerous layers of gravels, fine sand, and animal charcoal. That is still very useful, but the filtrate will still need boiling at the end being used as drinking water. Day to day cooking water will still need to achieve boiling point to be safe, but a large amount of any murkiness can be removed by allowing the water to settle for a period of time first. If at all possible then creating a routine water collection-storage-settling regime would be an ideal move.

There are numerous ways of collecting rainwater, and the water harvesting of a tree trunk (pictured right) came about as a result of sitting in on a talk by some survival professionals on sourcing water. In that instance they were using issue paracord to collect drips of water oozing slowly down a cliff face. Transferring the concept to my world of plants the thought occurred that water could be sourced from tree surfaces during rainy periods...

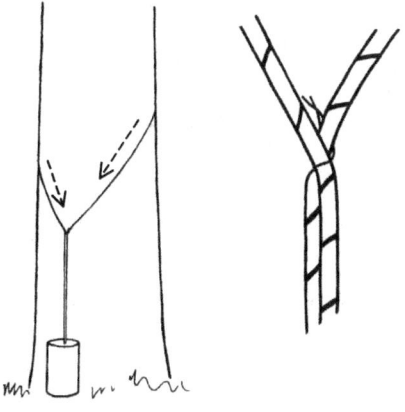

The initial trial was done with a sweet chestnut tree in the early autumn, some of the leaves having shed but a large proportion of them still present. The tree was about 15 to 18 metres high with a trunk circumference (about 120 cm above ground level) of about 140 cm.

A single length of paracord was slung round the waist of the tree – in a lazy loop rather than in a nice tight circle round the circumference. My hypothesis behind this was that water running down the trunk surface was likely to roll straight over cord placed in a horizontal position whereas the sloping cord would present a gentler angle of attack better able to channel away the surface water.

The tie-off point was achieved with a small piece of fine brass wire. In my experiment I pushed the wire through the paracord outer sleeve and tied off the wires in an upward position to try and eliminate any unwanted 'dripping points' (as I call them). This latter point is crucial where using cordage, or any water absorbing material, to surface harvest water. You want precious water to end up in your collection container not be wasted. The tie-off point was about 45 cm above ground level and the two trailing ends simply dropped into the collection container set back a few centimetres from the base of the trunk.

The trial was undertaken in moderately heavy period of rain, but by no means really heavy. Using a 400 ml mug the timings to fill the mug to the brim (over about a 40 minute period) were between 8½ and 10 minutes, with very little debris present in the collected water. If this process was replicated using multiple trees over a longer period of time, then quite considerable quantities of surface water might be harvested given the large catchment surfaces.

There are some important issues and factors involved in this method of collecting water...

First, ONLY use tree species which are harmless to man (the likes of sweet chestnut, sycamore, and so on – not toxic species such as yew and, I would suggest, any of the conifers which could well have resins on their trunks).

Second, and something that one of the survival guys present brought up, tannin. Possibly tannin might leach out of the tree bark into the rainwater and make it bitter. To be truthful I don't know if that would be an important factor, since in a heavy rainstorm there wouldn't be much time for the water to absorb the tannins, and if you were really concerned, then the collected water could be distilled.

Third. The trunks that you use need to be smooth barked, certainly for paracord. If you had natural cordage with lots of fluffy bits, or a much more substantial type of synthetic rope, then you should be able to harvest from trees with rougher barks, and there's always the option of stuffing moss or some other water absorbant material between the trunk and the upper surface of the cordage.

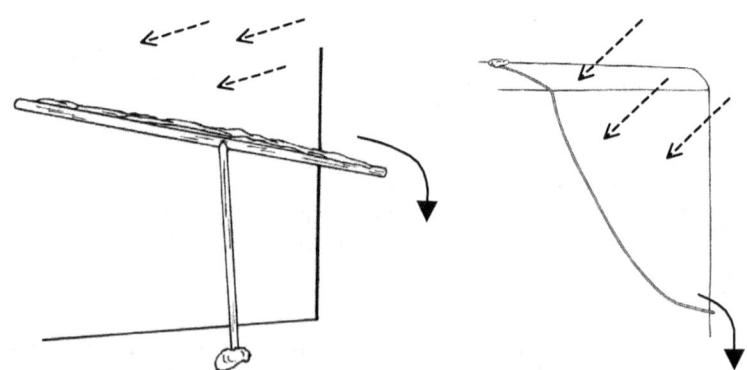

Extending the same concept of surface water harvesting the two examples above show how smooth-ish wall structures, particularly those rendered with cement, can be harnessed. On the left a 'glide' is propped up against the wall and stuffed with moss to take in the water. On the right a piece of paracord is slung over a flat cemented wall, becoming a flexible glide.

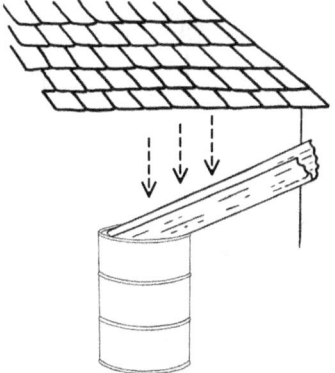

In the absence of guttering on the side of a building structure, place a suitable collecting surface below the roof edge to collect and direct the rainwater.

(Right) Another alternative is to place a 'glide' on the roof to direct the water. Though you may need some packing (cloth, grass, or moss) to prevent surface water running through gaps below the glide.

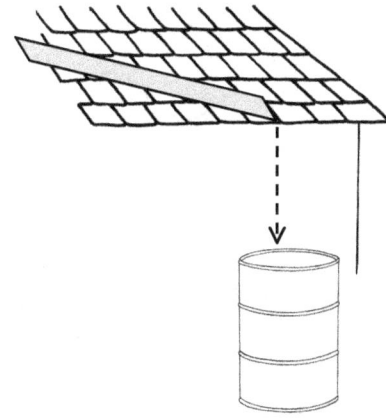

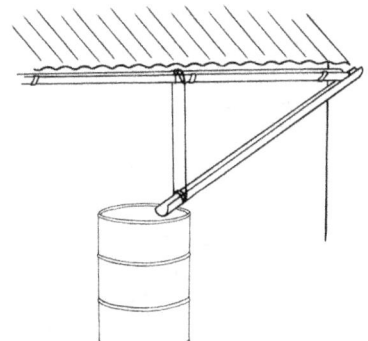

(Left) When guttering is damaged rig whatever collection system is feasible to harvest precious water.

An old gardening trick that you could utilize for bulk water storage (overleaf) is to link a series of collection containers together so that incoming water fills all containers in the chain through a self-levelling system. Each new barrel in the system needs to be primed; so when barrel 1 has collected a decent volume of water, siphon part of it off into barrel 2, keeping both ends of the hose below the water surfaces (weigh the ends down close to the bottom of the barrels). After a short while the water finds an equilibrium in both barrels, and new storage containers can be added to the chain in a similar fashion. It should be pointed out that all containers need to be of a similar size, or raised or lowered to ensure the top water levels are as near as possible equal. An alternative is to interconnect barrels lower down [A] with a system of pipes.

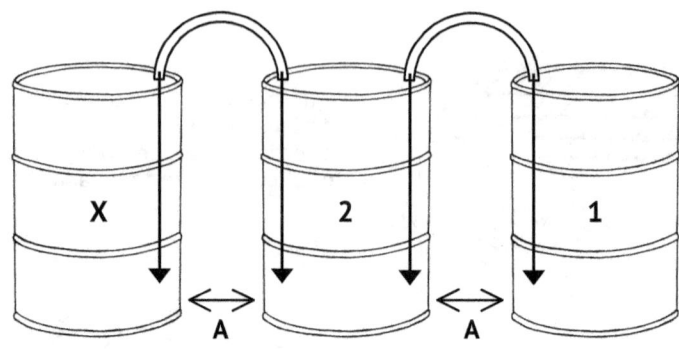

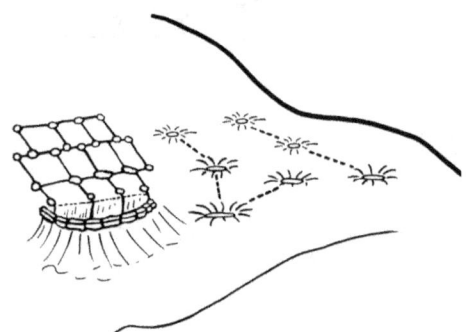

On sloping ground (pictured left) a single large sheet of waterproof material, or weighted bin liners, forms the catchment surface, and feeds a lined, banked, slit trench.

To the right of that individual lined catchment holes can be linked by channels, guttering, or piping so that overfill from higher collection pods is diverted to others in the series below.

Another possibility for harvesting ground water is to adapt a method used in tropical and arid zones of the world (right) where rows of shallow trenches are strung along gently inclined sloping gradients with a bund to help channel runoff. As one trench fills up the excess water cascades down to the next trench and so on. In size the trenches are from 1 to 2 metres long, half a metre wide, 20 cm deep, and spaced 20 to 30 cm apart.

Unless the trenches are lined (they are not in the tropics) then the soil quality needs to be quite clay-like for the water to be retained. Where a clay subsoil is not too far below then perhaps that clay could be puddled and used to line the walls to make them less permeable. The slope gradient must not be too steep since water will erode the earth walls separating each trench, while deeper trenches would require placing further apart so that the dividing walls have sufficient strength to support the weight of water in each capture unit.

Where chanelled water is too energetic then the velocity can be reduced by building stone *check dams* across the water flow, or even barriers of grass sods. Alternatively wooden posts can be driven into the ground (visualize the bristles of a brush) to reduce the energy.

Water flows with a lot of silt or sediment may benefit from a *silt trap* (right) dug in line with the flow. *Check dam* hurdles will not only further reduce energy within the water thereby allowing soil particles to drop out of suspension, but also remove excess debris, though that is not the key intention.

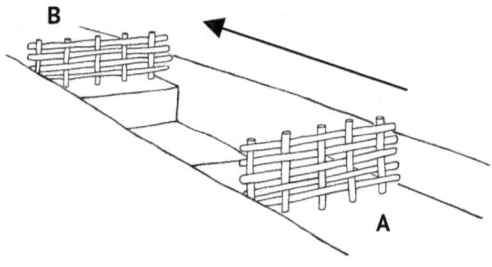

In the example above right the depth of the silt trap is about 80 to 100 cm deep, and about one metre in length. The hurdles (A, B) do not want to be too well woven together, with A placed about 1 metre from the trap edge. The check dam at B, where the water egresses, is not essential by any means but it will remove further energy from the water as it holds up the outflow. That said, you would need to make sure that there is capacity in the system to allow excess water build up to be diverted and not flood the area.

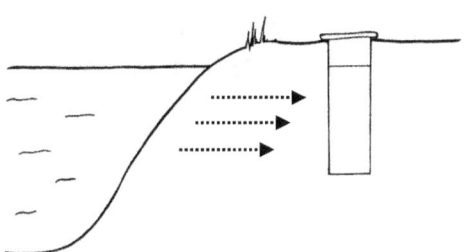

Where a turbid river or stream is the main source then a water-filtration well dug 2 to 3 metres distant from water source will naturally collect and slowly filter the water. Cover the well to keep out animals, debris and insects. However, this technique may not be suitable for water sources contaminated with hydrocarbons as the molecules may simply pass through the layers of soil.

In a large catchment and storage configuration a proper underground cistern could be built, or if excavation equipment or manpower were not available, then a low, log-cabin type, framework similar to the one on page 148 could be constructed with additional support timbers, and then suitably lined.

Quite ordinary domestic objects can become useful water containers once prepared by thorough cleaning or suitably lined with a waterproof inner. Something like the wooden-frame clothes bin (overleaf, top) would need to be checked first to see that it could support the weight of water anticipated. Domestic kitchen bins could be used too, but will need to be lined with a new plastic liner to prevent contamination – given the bin's past use of containing refuse.

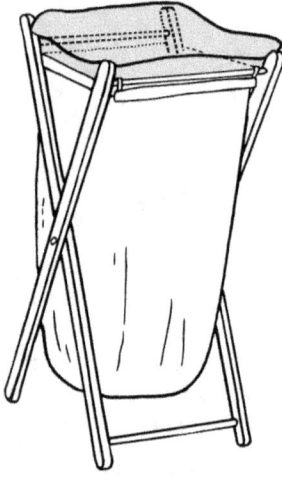

A lined dog basket (below) has the 'door' supported by a piece of wooden board to allow the full volume of the basket shape to be utilized for water storage or collection, while a lined laundry basket (further below, right) may also be used.

A simple cotton shopping bag (below left) can be lined with plastic and then suspended from a tree branch, door or other hook to keep it out of the reach of scavengers or vermin. For ease, water can be accessed with some plastic siphon tube from its hanging position.

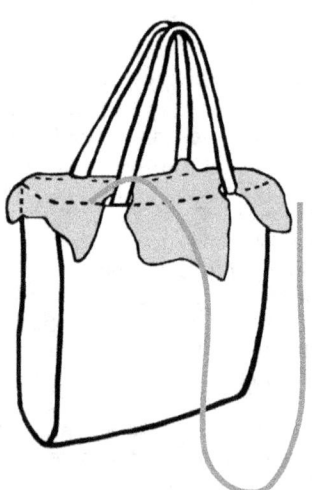

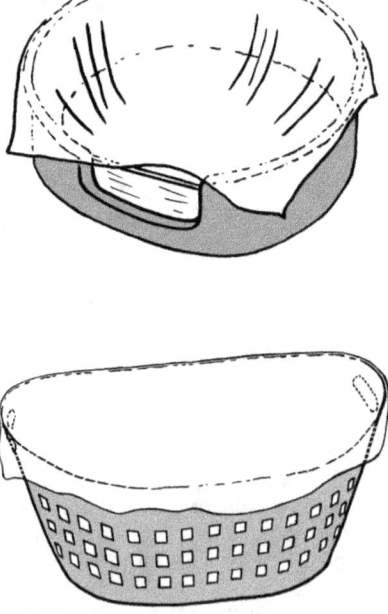

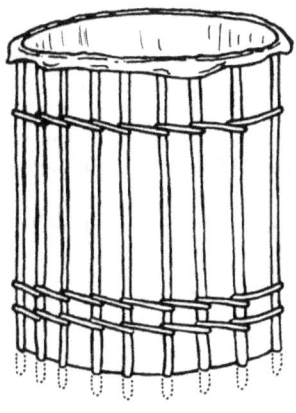

A more permanent 'tank' (left) may be constructed from sturdy upright poles driven into the ground and lashed together with rope or natural cordage (such as pine roots), and then lined with an industrial tarp or thick membrane. Capacity will depend on the strength of the poles and cordage, and their ability to hold the weight of water stored. For a really permanent structure then build out of brick and cement and provide either a solid, or removable, access cover. Another permanent option would be to use reinforcing mesh and concrete construction.

Where water is being collected for long-term storage it should, preferably, be in containers or cisterns that have a covering against light – to help reduce algal growth as well as keep out bird droppings and insects. Evaporation will also be reduced.

Clay, or clay with some sand, well tamped down, is the best natural barrier for retaining water in *ponds*. However, if the clay is bare then the water level in the pond must be maintained, otherwise the clay will shrink and crack when dry, and consequently let water leak. In a dry season (and if water is sufficiently available) then exposed clay could be sprayed every now and then to keep it moist, or perhaps close covered with plastic sheeting. To fill cracks that occur, moisten around the fissure then pour a thick cream-like clay slurry into the gap, topping up as it dries.

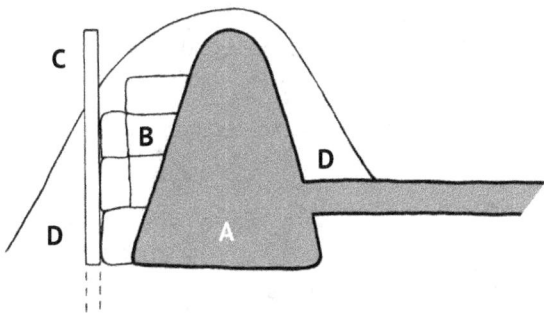

The diagram above shows a cross-section for clay pond construction. The floor needs to be at least 7 to 10 cm thick, and tamped down on good solid ground. The retaining clay barrier wall (A) needs to be sufficiently thick to resist water penetration and the weight of water. Where a large volume of water is being collected additional supporting blockwork (B) may be needed, as might supporting the blockwork with wooden stakes (C) driven into the ground. Cover the retaining clay wall surfaces with tamped earth and a layer of turves to help stop erosion of the clay through rainfall, but also help keep moisture in the clay barrier.

Finally, two additional water catchment methods for use in urban areas. The first (below, left) assumes that you have a house that is built on firm ground or solid foundations and is not likely to subside. Quite simply, a lined storage pond is dug right beside the outside wall to collect rainwater directly from the roof area via the downpipe. This is the sort of method that could be used if you have no access to barrels in which to store water, and will provide for a much larger storage volume than a single barrel. Apart from the subsidence aspect, the downside of the method is that the stored water needs to be protected from domestic pets, airborne debris and rodents, though you have the option of boiling the water (distilling or evaporating too) where it needs to be drunk.

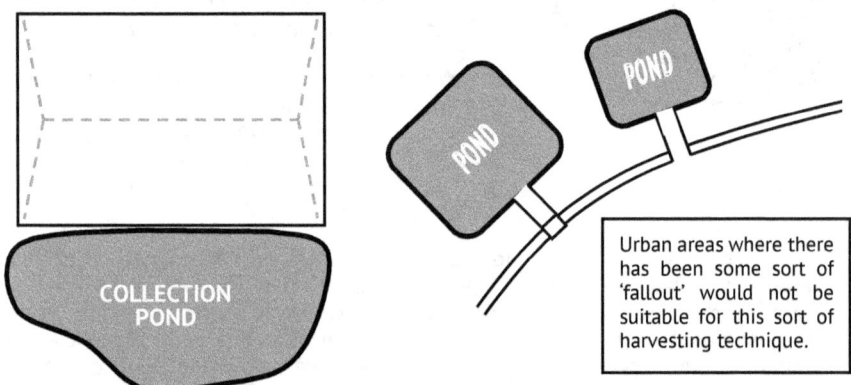

Urban areas where there has been some sort of 'fallout' would not be suitable for this sort of harvesting technique.

The second urban option (above, right) revolves round capturing water diverted from road surfaces through cuttings in curbstones and then chanelled into storage ponds dug behind the road. Once a pond has been filled then the section of removed curb can be replaced and the collected water allowed to settle. Water collected by this means is, however, probably not going to be fit for human consumption given all the oils and other nasties that cling to road surfaces, but it could possibly be solar evaporated, used for bain-marie type cooking or steaming, where food never physically touches the water but is cooked in closed containers. Other than that the water might possibly be used for growing a few veggies.

TIP: Where you want to construct a pond or settling tank that collects the sedimentary sludge settling out of water, build the bottom tank surface (the settling zone [SZ] on the schematic) at an angle of 45° and then introduce some sort of sludge drain at the bottom of the inclined slope to release sludge

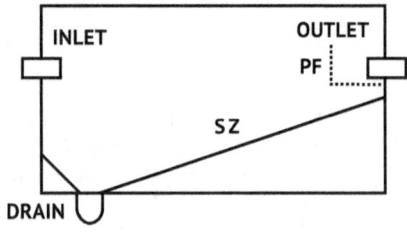

from time to time. The floor area wants to be about 1 to 3 metres long to give solids time to settle out, and the outlet may need a protective filter screen or gauze [PF] should sediments be found to regularly remain in solution.

WATER AND WEIGHING

Using measured volumes of water could allow you to fashion a set of weights with which to measure foodstuffs in the doomsday kitchen. Essentially 1 ml of water weighs 1 gram, so a 1-litre plastic carton will contain 1 kilo / 1000 gm of water, and then that could be further used to calibrate plastic bags of dried sand. You will need to standardize the water source (boffins use pure water at a set temperature), and do the measurements at the same time to harmonize the technical error. Seawater will be more dense than that from a stream. But, it should not be beyond the wit of any reader to work out their set of weights.

WATER CAPTURE CALCULATIONS

A rough and ready approximation of the volume of water that may be harvested from a roof surface or angled tarp can be worked out with the formula, where the *volume caught* (in litres) for a fixed period, is a product of the *rainfall* [R] for that same period unit, times *surface area* [Sa] (*height* by *length* by the *sine* of the roof / slope angle), times the *runoff coefficient* [RoC] of the surface material:

$$\text{Volume (L)} = R \text{ (mm)} \times Sa \text{ (m}^2\text{)} \times RoC$$

The *RoC* for roof tiles is roughly 0.8 to 0.9, for corrugated metal sheet 0.7 to 0.9, while concrete ground surfaces average between 0.6 and 0.8 if you were using the ground as a water capture surface. The ideal material, from a pure water harvesting point of view, would have a runoff coefficient of 1.0, the maximum. Areas of open ground have quite varied coefficients which all depend on the infiltration properties of the soil. Woodland, for example, may fall into a range of 0.05 to 0.25, an uncropped field with sandy soil might be in the range of 0.2 to 0.4, while pasture with sandy soil could be much lower, at 0.05 to 0.25. Compare that with a smooth, bare, packed soil where a runoff coefficient of 0.30 to 0.60 may exist, though that is nothing like the hard surfaces of rooftops and hard asphalt or concrete road surfaces.

For working out the *surface area* contribution to the calculations you will need to know the *sine* of the slope, some common slope angle *sines* being:

1° 0.0175	10° 0.1736	20° 0.3420	35° 0.5736	50° 0.7660	65° 0.9063
3° 0.0523	12° 0.2079	25° 0.4226	40° 0.6428	55° 0.8192	70° 0.9397
5° 0.0872	15° 0.2588	30° 0.5000	45° 0.7071	60° 0.8660	75° 0.9659

By way of example, let us say that we have a 3 by 3 metre square piece of plastic tarp, and it is laid out on ground with a slope of 5°, and that over the last month 125 mm of rain have fallen. Because the plastic tarp is a bit wrinkled we will give it a slightly pessimistic 0.7 runoff coefficient.

Then following the equation the Volume (L) = 125 (mm) x 9 x 0.0872 (m²) x 0.7, or 68.67 litres of water potentially harvested. For readers with a mathematical and organizational mindset, if you know the annual rainfall for an area and how many people need water, then there is potential to calculate the catchment area required plus water storage capacity.

CAPPING NATURAL SPRINGS

A proper 'spring' generally refers to a water source emerging at a single point in the ground, or concentrated water seepage within a small area. Areas of ground that do not provide a focused source may be better suited to the construction of a well or seepage-fed pond.

The first diagram below shows perhaps the most common type of spring, where a water-bearing soil meets with an impervious layer (bedrock or a hardpan) with the water eventually emerging out of the terrain at a single source point (X), or along a seam in the landscape. In the latter case a series of linear trenches (or even common plastic guttering) could be used to concentrate the seepage into a single point source that may then be harnessed. The very lowest point in the water-bearing layer should be tapped since the top of this layer will be subject to capillary action, potentially reducing its water content (this is because a point is reached where the force of gravity pulling down on the water in the strata is counterbalanced by the pores between the soil particles wanting to pull back some moisture).

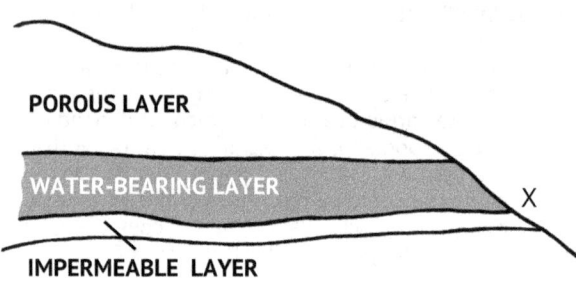

IMPORTANT NOTE: Make sure that there are no contaminants from cesspits and barn runoff which percolate through the porous layer into the water-bearing layer and so pollute it.

The other key type of spring (below) occurs where a pocket of permeable strata (such as gravel) with ground surface exposure to rainfall is surrounded by impermeable strata or hardpans. Where there is a fissure or weakness in the impermeable ground layers then the pressure of the water can force it upwards. Essentially this sort of spring is artesian in nature.

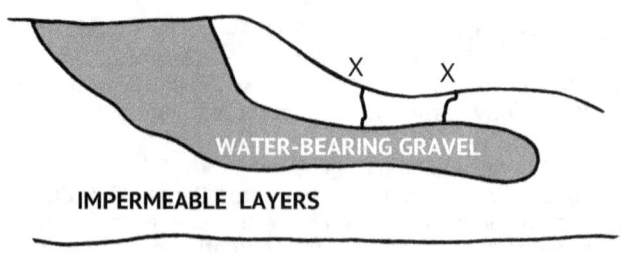

There are two different methods of tapping into the spring resources described. In the case of the first example it can be simply walled in (see diagram below). Where stone and clay walls are used to retain the spring water make sure that the wall and supporting slope is strong enough the hold the volume (read weight) of water. In a real life situation a farmer would normally use blockwork and cement. When conducting this type of spring capping operation make sure to dig right back into the ground until a single point of water can be identified. A diffuse water source could likely work its way round your walling, softening the ground through underflow and so undermine the barrier. Under these circumstances some sort of remedial preparation work will need to be undertaken to try and aggregate the water trickles to a point or drain some of it off. If at all possible cut the ground back to the impermeable layer.

The seeping water passes initially upwards through a layer of medium then small stones, then through a layer of gravel, and then finally through fine sand before being tapped (A). The inclusion of an overflow pipe (B) will prevent water build-up, but make sure this drips onto a hard surface (or is carried away in a long overflow pipe) to prevent the drips eroding away the retaining wall or ground upon which it is built. Another feature that you may need to include is a lined, water-diverting, trench on the slope above the collection tank (C). This is to prevent dirty surface water and debris entering the collected clean water. Some sort of general covering would be good too, to prevent debris, insects or even untreated rainwater falling in the filtered water.

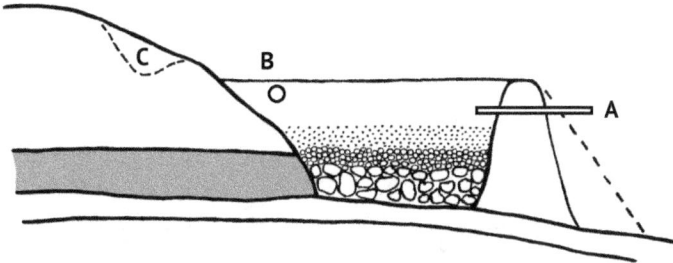

In both the example of capping a spring above, and the one overleaf, it is a good idea to place the water collection point some distance away from the well capping structure so the walls, piping and seals remain undisturbed. This is particularly the case where you may be sharing a field with livestock, in which case the capped water source should be securely fenced off to prevent cattle damaging the spring. Providing sufficient pipework is available then the outlet pipe can be buried in the ground to prevent pipe damage, disturbance to the spring, and also against frost in winter.

The second example of spring capping overleaf demonstrates how you might tackle a spring from an artesian type outflow, rather than a water source emerging along a strata fault-line. The technique is sometimes referred to as 'boxing' a spring. What happens in these cases is that the source of water bubbling to the ground is clearly identified and earth around it removed, then a trench dug and puddled clay tamped down firmly (A). The next stage is to make the 'box' which could be made from a large oil drum with the bottom cut out (as suggested in the diagram below), or four pavement slabs squared off and the seams between the slabs packed well with masses of clay and held in place with strong wire or other suitable fixing. If enough suitable clay-like soil is available then the pavement slabs could even be supported on the outside by ramping up packed earth round the 'box' which should be firmly embedded in the tamped clay. Above the clay could simply be a rammed earth seal, concrete, or even more tamped clay (B); however some sort of layer to prevent rain washing away, or excessively softening, the clay is a good idea. The water flowing upwards passes through a layer of gravel (C) and, potentially a finer layer of sand, with the filtered water drawn off at (D). To divert excess water well away from the boxed spring an overflow pipe (E) is inserted, and a cover (F) provided to prevent contamination from airborne matter.

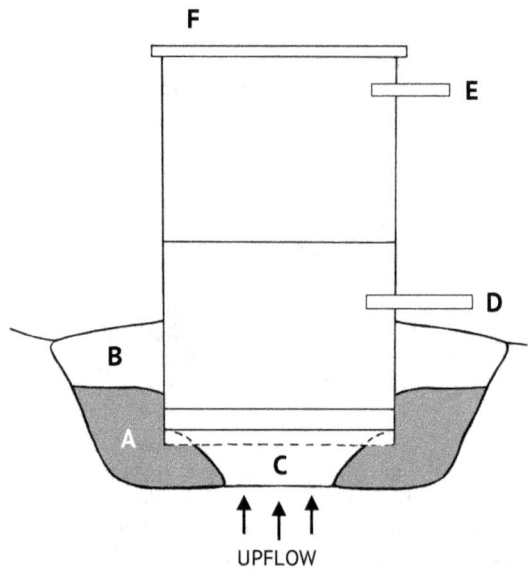

UPFLOW

TIP: Where attempting to harness a spring for a long-term supply then seek and select the water source during a dry period. If water is emerging from strata when there has been minimal rainfall (particularly during an extended dry period) then that source is likely to remain a good provider, whereas a spring identified a couple of weeks after rainfall will not give you a clear picture of the capacity of the soil and water table and could dry out during times of water shortage.

FILTRATION

Turbid rainwater harvested from ground surface sources will almost certainly going to require some sort of settling process before the water can be filtered, while even rainwater may need filtering to remove debris. In areas where rainfall is generally heavy then a horizontal 'baffle tank' or 'storm tank' may be a useful first stage in the collection process; allowing the energy in the water to dissipate before being added to the general water store or settling tank. In the case of a baffle tank water passes through a series of coarse gauzes or mesh layers (the gaps may also be filled with graded gravels), just big enough to remove the largest debris particles such as twigs and leaves (down to pine needle size). Turbidity from finer particles can then be removed by allowing the water to settle properly in a secondary tank (see TIP at bottom of page 208).

There are a variety of basic water filtration methods and two of the most basic are shown below – an upflow sand-charcoal-stone filter and a bio-sand or sand filtration type. Both methods are slow since the water must percolate through layers of sand and gravel, so should not be linked 'in line' with the catchment-settling routine mentioned above but, rather, to process the water once it has settled – post-storage.

With sand-charcoal-stone filtration (below) a constant flow of water from a storage reservoir percolates upwards through compacted layers including one of charcoal. The positions marked with an 'x' should ideally be fitted with a fine screen or gauze that maintains the integrity of the particular filter layer. Although it may be difficult to obtain in a post-disaster world I would personally opt for stainless steel mesh since cloth made of natural fibre might decay, and plastic polymer filters may not be food grade quality. Non-food grade plastic contamination would be the last of your concerns in a post-disaster world however. This system inevitably leads to fine particles settling out in the bottom layers of stones so a flush outlet is included so that every now and then the silt among the stones may be flushed out.

NOTE: Where charcoal is used it must be regularly replaced as bacteria can breed and contaminate the filtered water.

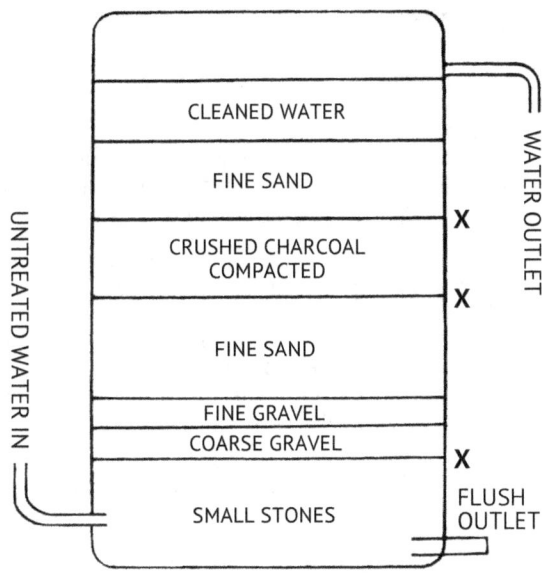

In the second method of filtration (slow, or bio-sand filtration, as it is sometimes known) water is gravity fed through a column of sand to provide potable water from rainwater collected off a clean roof surface. This is important since the sand system does not remove all bacteria and various oocytes that might cause gastro-intestinal problems, though it removes a lot of nasties. And, in my personal view, I would not drink ground-surface water, especially in areas of farmland, that had been through this type of filtration since that water may be so grossly contaminated that the sand is unable to do its work. In any case, where there is doubt, boil water prior to drinking it.

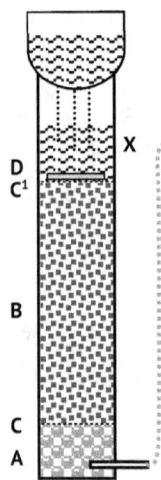

Slow, or bio-sand, filtration works on the principle of harnessing microbes (bacteria and algae) in a top 2 to 3 cm layer of a sand column and slowly trickling water through.

Making one of these filters is pretty easy if the materials are available. In the diagram to the left you are looking at a piece of sewerage type pipe (the plastic version ranges from 20 to 40 cm in width) and about one metre high. The bottom 10 or 12 cm are filled with coarse gravel or small stones – about pea size or slightly less so – and preferably smooth (A). Next, a column of fine sand about two-thirds of the length of the pipe is added (B), separated from the gravel by a gauze, mesh or cotton cloth (C). On top of the sand column another porous mesh is placed (C^1) and on top of this a flat stone, roof tile, piece of slate, or even an upturned plate (D) to absorb the energy of the trickling water from the storage vessel of settled water above. This is important since the biological filter in the top part of the sand (it will *not* look like a green scum) does not want to be disturbed once up and running, while settled water must be used to prevent the trickle holes from blocking up.

At the bottom is the processed water outlet which needs to be run upwards in a pipe to a tap which is placed a few centimetres above the level of the stone at D, say at point X. This is actually most important since the biological layer must be kept moist to maintain its functionality. If the top layer dries out then the whole process needs to be begun over. And, of course, the bottom of the pipe needs sealing watertight!

The system (which can be modified to run in the horizontal position in a sand filled, sloping, clay-lined basin with water output in a trough embedded in gravel at the bottom of the slope) needs to be primed the first time, and run for a week or so before the first drinkable water is available. Essentially this is the time needed for the active processing bacteria to accumulate in the top sand layer. Water used in this priming period can either be returned to storage or used for cooking with, or boiling for drinking.

Last of all, a centimetre or so of the top layer should be removed every few weeks when the water flow starts to slow down. When about one third of the sand column has been removed through this 'topping' process then it is time to clean out the whole system and start again; perhaps once or twice a year.

SOLAR DISTILLATION

The option of solar distillation may be available to you where there is plenty of sunshine available. This low-tech method of water collection allows water of doubtful purity or supply to be processed without the need to use precious fuel resources. The downside is that the process is slow, is sun-dependent, and does not produce large volumes of water. Still, this method could be one part of an overall mixed water harvesting strategy, and does have the advantage of requiring little human attention.

The principle is very simple and is shown in the schematic below: the water reservoir made of black plastic sheeting forms the heart of the system [A]. Above this is a sloping, transparent, plastic sheet [B] upon which condensate forms, and is supported at its apex by a rope or rod [B1]. As sunlight penetrates the clear roof it warms the water in the black reservoir (black towelling or cloth laid on plastic sheeting may also be used); the evaporating water vapour rising and forming beads on the roof surface. These beads trickle downwards to be collected in a gutter [C]. It is important for the design to have some sort of 'drip former' at the bottom [C1] otherwise the water beads will follow the natural line of the plastic sheet and simply be lost in the supporting structure [D] which is made of turves, bricks, stones, or even sand in a shoreline situation. The drip former might be a piece of metal pipe or a thin branch laid on the outside surface of the plastic. Theoretically, a single sheet of black plastic can be used to form the reservoir and collection gutters, using rammed earth the form ridges.

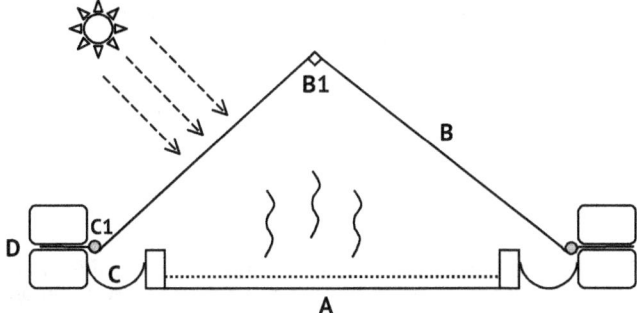

There are some important design considerations when making a solar still. First, that it is a 'sealed' system, so there need to be end walls constructed of metal, plastic or some other non-porous material. If the design is going to be a permanent feature of your doomsday kitchen water supply then the plastic roofing material needs to be made of a UV resistant type, otherwise it will gradually break down in the sunlight over time. You also need to set up an easy means of filling the dirty water reservoir, harvesting the condensate and, in a permanent set-up, how to release the tainted dirty water so the next batch can be processed.

If large sheets of plastic are not available then glass sheet of sufficient size would be an alternative. Where there is no means of creating an apex roof structure then simply use a single sloping surface for the condensate, as shown below.

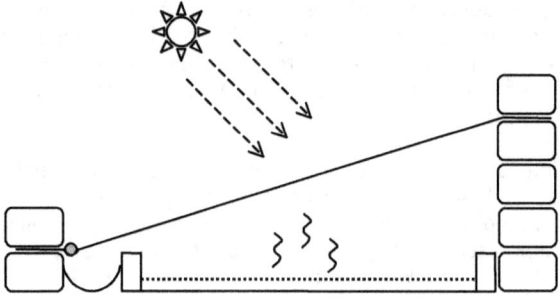

The designs above are more domesticated versions of the solar stills often referred to in survival books, where a hole is dug in the ground and covered over with a sheet of polythene stretched over the hole replacing the condensing 'roof'. A stone placed in the middle of the inverted plastic roof forms the dripping point, while the slope of the 'V' wants to be a minimum of 35°, preferably 45° so that the condensate can run down the surface to the dripping point. As with the designs above the ground solar still needs to be a 'sealed unit', with all the plastic edges held down so that the moist air cannot vent out of the closed system. Having good soil moisture content (see pages 195/6) is important for efficient water output as is sunshine.

BLEACHING WATER

In emergencies domestic chlorine bleach may be used to purify water, but that bleach must be the pure unadulterated stuff, free from colourings, wonder additives and chemical aromatics.

Domestic bleach ranges in strength from about 3 to 5% while you need a concentration of 1% for purifying water; so dilute an amount working on a ratio of 3 drops of the 1% dilute to 1 litre of water. Once added shake or stir the treated water vigorously and allow to stand for at least 30 minutes. Where the water to be treated is cloudy or has solid matter you have two options: 1) allow the water to settle, so allowing the turbidity to subside, then filter / decant before adding bleach or, 2) double the amount of bleach added.

ORGANIZING WATER USAGE

Provided that the atmosphere is free from contaminants, I would prefer to collect and process rainwater over standing water of unknown provenance, and also similarly streams of unknown source. In any case, whatever your water source it will be a precious commodity in a post-disaster world, and you need to carefully plan on the best way of using that resource, and not wasting it. It may be possible to re-use *some* water.

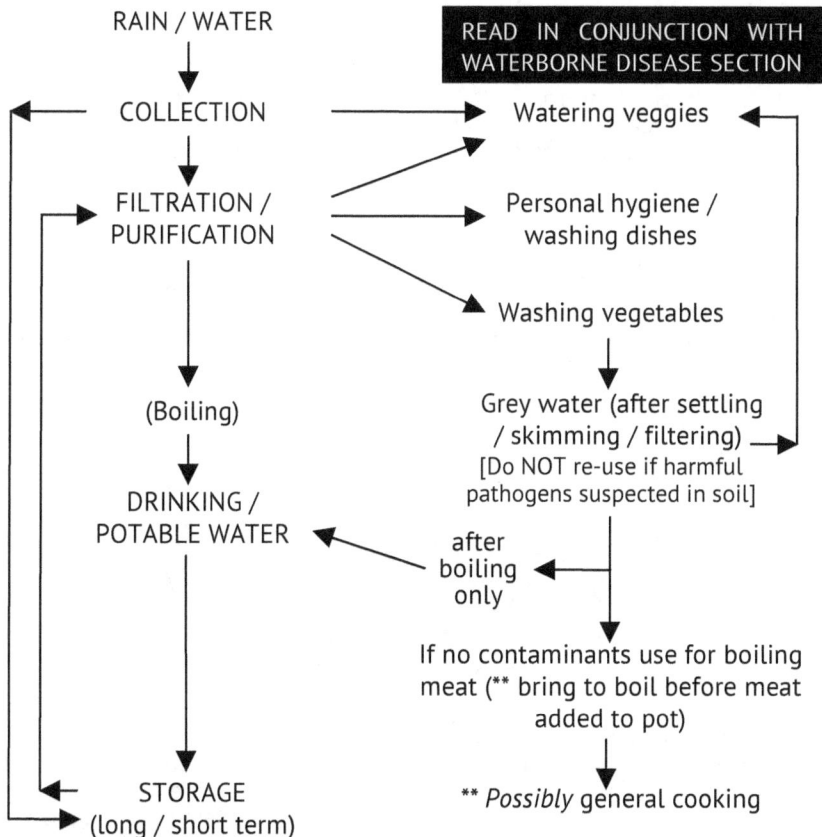

Where the water used for washing vegetables is re-used it should only have light soil contamination, not known contaminants. Water used for cooking veggies should not be used for gardens as sugars in the liquor may ferment and encourage noxious microbial growth. ** Veggie grey water used in cooking must be boiled to eliminate possible pathogens.

WATER-BORNE DISEASE

It is not the purpose of this book to delve into medical matters, but should the water source used in your doomsday kitchen become contaminated with pathogens, there will need to be a re-think on the methods used to harvest, store, and process the water you use in producing food. Below are details of the classic water-borne diseases that you might come across in a northern temperate zone (much nastier diseases lurk in tropical climates). Should any of your party display symptoms of sickness then your water source should be one of the first things to consider putting under the investigative spotlight.

The potential for complete breakdown of water-supply, drainage, sewerage and wastewater infrastructure after any major disaster or extreme event should, I believe, be regarded as inevitable and therefore precautions taken immediately post-event. Diarrhoeal disease from contaminated water and food are likely to manifest themselves among the population of survivors, and in extreme cases this can lead to death.

When reviewing your available water resources you need to be conscious of your situation in relation to the interaction of both humans and animals with those available water sources – call it the *water environment* if you will – since both humans and animals may be hosts and reservoirs of various pathogens which cause waterborne disease.

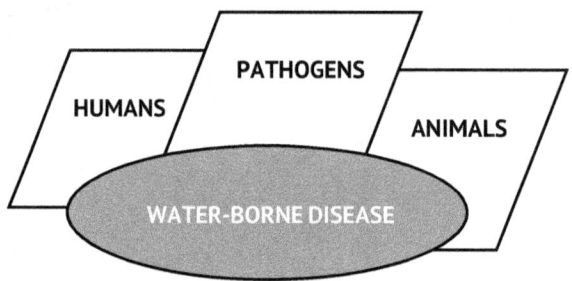

There are numerous water-borne diseases that infect humans, and some of the common ones are listed later. Not all the bugs will be relevant since heat, climate and available moisture/water will all have a relevance on whether they can exist in a locality. In the southern and eastern Mediterranean regions you already start to see diseases with an almost tropical-like nature (bilharzia for example, caused by the blood flukes *Schistosoma mansoni* and *S. haematobium* and treated with praziquantel, hycanthone, niridazole, or oxamniquine), while in cold northern climes another zoonotic pathogen, *Yersinia enterocolitica*, which causes diarrhoea and abdominal pain, and is often associated with raw pork meat, can survive long periods of being frozen and also freezing-thawing cycles.

Perhaps the three key, most commonly encountered, water-borne diarrhoeal diseases associated with bad sanitation and water supply are:

CHOLERA

DYSENTERY

TYPHOID

CHOLERA

This acute intestinal infection, caused by the bacterium *Vibrio cholerae*, is often thought of as a disease of the warmer climates in undeveloped parts of the world, but it can appear anywhere where there are inadequate water supplies, poor sanitation, and poor food safety regimes. Ingestion of contaminated water, food washed with contaminated water, or even undercooked seafood in areas of poor sanitation, or where there is sewage contaminated by infected human faeces, are typical of the means of bacterial entry into the body. Just the sort of situation as might exist after a tsunami or severe flooding.

Symptoms are initially the rapid onset of watery painless diarrhoea, vomiting and nausea. This gradually becomes worse, and in malnourished individuals with impaired immunity (just the scenario of a long-term post-disaster situation) the problems can become deadly, leading to dehydration and death. There's a 50% mortality rate if left untreated. The treatment regime consists of replacing the patient's lost fluids and salts, and recovery normally takes place within a week.

To prevent cholera spreading further:
  Institute a safe drinking water routine
  Insist on proper personal hygiene
  Review food processing and hygiene procedures
  Review disposal of human excreta

DYSENTERY

Dysentery bears some of the signature symptoms of cholera, being another gastrointestinal disease, except the casualty will show symptoms of acute bloody diarrhoea. It is the severe threat of dehydration caused by that diarrhoea wherein the danger lies. In dysentery the stools are watery and contain visible red blood or mucus. There are two forms of dysentery, amoebic and bacillary, caused by an amoeba or bacterium respectively. The amoebic form, caused by the single-celled parasite *Entamoeba histolytica*, is much more of a tropical disease, however the bacillary form is caused by *Shigella* bacteria from which the disease gets its formal name *Shigellosis* (treated with ciprofloxacin, azithromycin, amoxicillin and trimethoprim). The mildest of the bacterial strains is *Shigella sonnei*, which is found in the UK, and then there are the other forms *S.flexneri*, *S. boydii*, and *S. dysenteriae* which produces the severest symptoms.

In the bacillary form the symptoms are mild stomach pains and bloody diarrhoea, possibly also nausea and vomiting, and in more severe cases a fever. The symptoms manifest themselves between one and seven days after infection, and usually last for three to seven days.

Amoebic dysentery symptoms (a more tropical condition as mentioned before, and treated with metronidazole, tinidazole or diloxanide furoate), may take months or years to appear, and sometimes never – an individual being a 'carrier' of the pathogen. In a post-disaster world it might be wise to be made aware of anyone who has recently travelled abroad. The symptoms are similar to the bacillary form but might also include stomach pain and rectal bleeding.

Left untreated, dysentery can be fatal in malnourished individuals (exactly the sort of physical condition that might be expected in a long-term post-disaster scenario), and also children.

Since dysentery is spread as a result of poor hygiene and sanitation you will need to review every part of your food and water processes, utilization and storage to discover where a breakdown in the water-food chain has occurred.

TYPHOID & PARATYPHOID
Although more common in less industrialized parts of the world where there is inadequate sewage disposal and flooding, and unsafe drinking-water, that is precisely the situation that may develop in a post-disaster world. These two diseases are a bit like cholera in that someone becomes infected by coming in contact with contaminated faeces or urine and ingesting the bacteria (*Salmonella typhi* and *S. paratyphi* respectively), whether it is simply drinking water, or eating something handled by an infected person. Indeed, although water is one of the main transmission pathways of these diseases, some people who have had the disease can remain carriers.

The typhoids (paratyphoid is a milder ailment) differ in one key respect from cholera: once inside the body the disease moves from the intestinal tract, where the first symptoms are manifest, into the bloodstream. Those symptoms may not appear for one to three weeks after infection. Infected individuals develop a very high, sustained, fever, and there may be headaches, malaise, constipation or diarrhoea, anorexia, enlarged liver and spleen, while the chest area becomes blotched with rose-coloured spots. In the real world a vaccine is available, although it does not provide full protection, and antibiotics too, but in a post-disaster situation these are likely to be unavailable.

Proper personal hygiene, clean water, and good sanitation will prevent typhoid outbreaks. In event of an outbreak review all water supplies, food handling processes, and sanitation facilities. Those who have been infected should be prevented from future handling of food in case they remain carriers.

So those are the three nasty water-borne diseases, but should any general diarrhoeal and gastrointestinal infection manifest itself in more than one person then you should automatically go into a mode of heightened awareness and review all food and water-related matters.

This is not a medical book but you should also inform yourself about these other food and water-transmitted diseases, some of which are listed more fully in the following table:

Hepatitis A
Algal Cyanobacterial toxins
Campylobacteriosis
Ascariasis
Other zoonotic pathogens (eg. *Cryptosporidium, Giardia, E. coli*)

NOTE. Although many of the pathogens listed are *waterborne* at some stage in their development, eggs, oocysts and the like may exist in soil too, and for this reason any area from where plants are foraged, or animals caught, needs to be assessed in relation to what pathogens may be in the soil.

SOME OTHER WATER-BORNE PATHOGENS

BACTERIA

Escherichia coli	Gastroenteritis
Campylobacter jejuni / C. coli	Gastroenteritis
Helicobacter pylori	Ulcers – Stomach and duodenal
Legionella pneumophila	Pneumonia
Vibrio parahaemolyticus	Cholera
Vibrio vulnificus	Wound infections, otitis and lethal
Vibrio alginolyticus	septicaemia, gastroenteritis, respiratory dysfunctions, allergic reactions
Toxic cyanobacteria	
Cylindrospermopsis raciborskii	Liver damage, acute skin reactions hepato-enteritis, vomiting, constipation, kidney malfunction, diarrhoea

VIRUSES

Norovirus GGI & II	Gastroenteritis
Sapovirus	Gastroenteritis
HAV	Hepatitis
Rotavirus	Gastroenteritis
Enterovirus	Gastroenteritis
Adenovirus	Respiratory and intestinal influenza

PROTOZOA

Balantidium coli	Diarrhoea, abdominal pain, colonic perforation
Baylisascaris procyonis	Fatal or severe neurological disease, nausea, tiredness, liver enlargement, blindness, coma
Blastocystis hominis	Long-term diarrhoea, abdominal pain
Capillaria hepatica =*Calodium hepaticum*	Hepatitis, anaemia, fever, hyper-eosinophilia, even death
Cryptosporidium spp. (ie. *C. parvum*)	Gastroenteritis
Cyclospora cayetanensis	Watery diarrhoea, appetite and weight loss, cramp, bloating, nausea, fatigue, sometimes vomiting and low-grade fever
Fasciola hepatica [Liver fluke]	Nausea, vomiting, abdominal pain / tenderness. Fever, rash, breathing difficulty may occur
Giardia intestinalis =*G. lamblia* =*G. duodenalis*	Gastroenteritis, malabsorption, dehydration (loss of fluids), gas, greasy stools, stomach / abdominal cramps, stomach upset, nausea / vomiting
Naegleria fowlerii	Amoebic meningoencephalitis. Severe frontal headache, fever, nausea, vomiting. Later, stiff neck, seizures, altered mental status, hallucinations, coma
Acanthamoeba spp.	Eye infection leading to blindness
Toxoplasma gondii	Lymphadenopathy, flu-like fever symptoms, congenital infections

OTHER ZOONOSES

Ascaris lumbricoides	Abdominal discomfort, intestinal blockage
Ehrlichia chaffeensis	
Leptospira interrogans, L. canicola, L. hebdomadis, L. icterohaemorrhagiae	Weil disease. Febrile illness, pulmonary hemorrhagic syndrome
Spirometra mansonoides	
Toxocara canis, T. cati	Fever, coughing, enlarged liver or

	pneumonia, ocular toxocariasis
Trichuris trichuria	Stools contain mucus, water, blood
Cylindrospermopsis raciborskii	Liver damage, acute skin reactions hepato-enteritis, vomiting, constipation, kidney malfunction, diarrhoea
Ancylostoma duodenale [Hookworm]	Intestinal obstruction; cough, fever, and chest discomfort in pulmonary cases; anaemia through blood loss
Necator americanus [Hookworm]	Abdominal pain, diarrhoea, cramps, weight loss resulting in anorexia

DISEASE-CAUSING MICROSPORIDIA *

Brachiola vesicularum, B. algerae, B. connori

Enterocytozoon bieneusi, E. intestinalis, cuniculi, hellem

Microsporidium africanus

Nosema ocularum

Pleistophora sp.

Trachipleistophora hominis, T. anthropothera

Vittaforma cornea

* Single-celled microsporidia, which go through a spore stage, are often identified as protozoa, but recent molecular studies suggest they are more akin to fungi.

Although the list above includes a few exotics which appear in warmer climates it does not cover tropical water-borne diseases. And as the world climate warms up there is always the possibility that the pathogens of warmer climes, as well as their vectors, could begin to find new homes in parts of the world where they did not exist before.

In a post-disaster world I think any raw water source needs to be treated with the highest suspicion, requiring boiling before use. And if there is the slightest doubt about whether an edible plant has been sitting in, or splashed by, contaminated water it should not be eaten as a salad but instead cooked. Personally, when foraging wild greens, I have a rule of thumb (for me, you can do as you wish), that if I cannot establish whether an animal (human, domestic pet, or farm animal) is perhaps active around the area I am harvesting, then the greens are cooked. Never eaten raw. And in uncontrolled aquatic areas I follow a similar philosophy in that no plants, ever, are eaten raw, but always cooked.

BOTULISM

Botulism can be deadly. Although not a water-borne disease, the bug that causes the ailment and the toxin itself can be present in untreated water, and soil too, but the following information is placed here since it is relevant to the next sections on food, in particular to *preserving* food. For your own peace of mind it would be worth reading up more about the role of botulin in the food chain, since I am not a qualified medic and what follows is my personal understanding of botulism.

Botulism is the condition resulting from ingestion or inhalation of the nervine, muscle-paralysing, toxins produced by the anaerobic (lives in environments devoid of oxygen) bacterium *Clostridium botulinum*. More generally it is the foodborne toxin that is consumed via foodstuffs contaminated with the bacteria, so proper food processing and standards in preserving food are essential. Botulin toxin is one of the most toxic substances known to man and we have no natural immunity from it, so in everyday life the illness is considered potentially fatal (mortality is about 10%); in a post-disaster world without any forms of available medical help the problem will be compounded.

In itself *C. botulinum* is not harmful, and its spores can exist in the soil for many years, unable to do harm in our oxygen-rich, aerobic, world. However, where the bacterium itself is ingested then there is potential for it to reproduce in the anaerobic environment of the gut and produce highly poisonous toxins as a by-product of that process (the process does produce 5 or 6 toxic substances though only some of them are deadly). Any *C. botulinum* bacterium present in the atmosphere or soil may also get into wounds, and in the absence of air again cause poisoning.

At the onset of botulin poisoning (which generally manifests itself some 8 to 36 hours after eating a contaminated food), the symptoms may include sickness, nausea and stomach pain, vomiting, and diarrhoea often followed by constipation. There may also be double vision. The significant trait of the poisoning, however, is paralysis with a weakened condition. This creeping paralysis starts from the top down and may result in difficult swallowing, speech and, if left untreated, paralysis of the lungs resulting in death. One other key symptom pointer is that since we are dealing with a nervine *toxin* here, there is *no* fever associated with the infection.

So, how does *Clostridium botulinum* feature in the food chain? Well the bacterium and its spores are likely to be on any foodstuff that you may encounter, but the main concern is their presence during preservation and bottling of foods where they can live, and in the absence of air, produce those deadly toxins. Indeed, many of the cases of botulism are the result of consuming improperly preserved foods.

The technical keys to *safe* bottled or canned wet food preservation are heat, acidity, salinity, sugar, absence of air, or some combination of these. Where botulism can emerge is when these key factors fail to be at their optimum: the heat insufficient for cooking or sterilizing, acid or salt solutions too weak, sugar levels deficient, or seals insecure. One of the main culprits in domestic home-preserved botulin poisoning comes from canned vegetables, such as beans, where there is natural low-acidity. In other preserved items, like jams and pickle, recipes tend to provide more than enough sugar and vinegar content to produce an environment that inhibits bacterial growth.

Unfortunately, *C. botulinum* and its spores are not killed by merely by boiling in water. It requires a temperature of 121°c plus, which is the level commercial canners process at, or thereabouts, while some home pressure-canning cookers and pressure-cookers may also achieve the above boiling point temperatures required.

Conversely, the main deadly toxin itself is easily destroyed, at a temperature of 85°c held for 5 minutes, and the recommendation is that small amounts of home bottled food should be boiled for 10 minutes before use just to ensure any toxin present is neutered, while bulk food should be boiled for 20 minutes, giving time for the internal temperature to attain the critical 85°c for 5 minutes threshold.

If any home-preserved item that you have made exhibits gassy bubbles or froth, or a bad smell, then botulin may be present. And any bloated commercially prepared tins of food should be binned, as is best for cans with damaged and creased walls which may have microscopic fissures allowing ingress of air – in which *C. botulinum* can thrive.

PRESERVING FOODS

It is all very well procuring food day by day, but during the winter months most edible wild greenery will have disappeared, leaving you with the prospect of starving during winter, and indeed, when you look back at recipe books from the 16th to late 19th centuries it is noticeable how many recipes there are for pickling, and preserving meat. In the centuries before canning, freezing and freeze-drying it was food supplies laid up during the summer months that kept families alive during winter. However, botulism was probably a re-occurring event in the past, where foods were not properly preserved or stored; but then they did not understand the bacterial mechanisms working behind the scenes as we do today. Indeed, when using preserved foodstuffs you need to keep your wits about you; any signs of bloated lids or tins, unexpected bubbles in the food, and bad smelling foodstuffs, should act as warning signs for the possible presence of botulinum toxins.

In a true, long-term, survival situation you could well face the same challenges as folks in the past, so in this section I want to run through some of the simpler food preserving options available. In a true survival scenario you would probably need to start preparing salt reserves by evaporating sea water since domestic types would eventually be scarce and run out (see section on salt production towards the end of the book).

Quite deliberately I have drawn on many food preservation techniques that come from the distant past since that was the time in human history when folks depended on basic preserving techniques to keep their food through the winter. In reality, the discomfort of domestic life for the poorer classes was probably little different to a survival situation for us today. By today's health and hygiene standards some of these techniques would probably be regarded as heresy, but in time of survival when you're fighting for your very existence then it is your ability to preserve food resources that matters. None of the methods covered below give indefinite preservation of food, they merely extend usability by a matter of weeks or months.

Key to good food preservation is the removal or denial of moisture or air which allows the possibility of decomposition through moulds, bacteria, and yeasts. Oils and fats prevent air getting to food immersed in these substances while concentrated sugars, acids (as in vinegar), and salt produce environments where microbes find it hard to thrive. Drying food similarly denies the conditions for bug growth. Indeed, the water content of most food must be above 20% before bacteria can thrive, so by removing at least 80% (even higher in some foodstuffs) of the water in food it can be preserved in some way, while most bacteria (but NOT all) may be killed by heating food for 30 minutes at 65-71°c; a temperature that any decent campfire would generate in the near vicinity.

BOTTLING

Let us begin with 'bottling' of foods which should still be possible in all but the most difficult survival situations. Before we go into the bottling 'processes' a few pointers:

If you have managed to reclaim old jam jars and the like, then make sure any lacquered or laminated lids are pristine, and show no signs of the metal beneath (as this can react with preservative agents being used).

All jars will need to be sterilized by boiling in water (bringing the water to the boil, not dropping the jars in!), or by placing them near a fire where they can be heated sufficiently to kill bugs and bacteria. Alternatively, steam the inside using a kettle spout – making sure to hold the jars with a cloth or tongs.

In the absence of screw-lids seals can be made with waxed greaseproof paper, mutton fat, olive / vegetable oil, paraffin wax, or corks and sealant wax.

Where using home-made seals for items like jams one of the most common is grease-proof paper, and also waxed paper. Three layers are required, sandwiched together with a *'glue'* made of corn starch, flour, milk, egg white or some other type of gum, then cut into squares that will give 2 or 3 cm overhang over the jar mouth. At the point of sealing a jar the bottom surface of the seal is coated with the *'glue'* used, put smartly over the neck of the jar, then tightly tied down leaving no wrinkles or spaces around the top where air can creep in. Waxing the paper over the top would give added protection. To test a seal is good wait till the jar has cooled down and tap the cover. If the sound is drum-like then the vacuum is intact, while a dull thud would indicate the seal is possibly compromised.

Where hard animal fat is being used as the sealant (not soft pork lard) then it should be heated to melting point, the inner top of the jar wiped to remove any moisture or 'product' and then the fat poured in to a depth of 1 to 2 cm. Leave the jars to cool right down and the fat to solidify. If you find traces of juice have crept around the edge wipe this away and add another small layer of fat. You can also add a grease-proof paper lid as an addition.

For sealant oils, warm the oil and then pour a 1 to 2 cm layer over the processed cooked food, and finally cover with a tied-down paper lid to prevent anything getting into the oil layer. When it comes to using the preserved food then the oil can either be skimmed or siphoned off, or the jar held over a basin and given a sharp flick to remove the oil (a process somewhat like that used for bottles of wine where little bits of the cork remain after corking).

If you can procure large corks for bottling then these can be used too. They should be sterilized first in boiling water, then dried off, dipped in molten paraffin wax and stuffed into the mouth of the preserving jar, and finally painted over with more molten wax. Calico, cotton and muslin-type fabrics dipped in molten paraffin wax can also act as seals, but must be absolutely airtight. Where using paraffin wax to seal *fermented* vegetables it is important that all fermentation has stopped before the wax seal is poured as any gases forming below the wax seal can crack it an allow ingress of air.

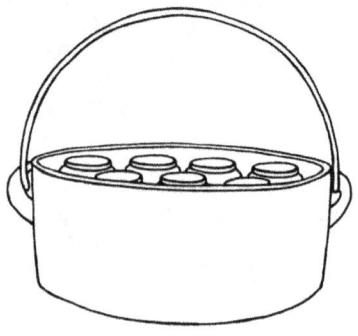

You will also need a 'sterilizer' (with a lid is best lid) for heating the bottled food. This could simply be a metal bucket, deep saucepan, or even the bottom end of an oil drum. All you are looking for is a vessel deep enough to allow the preserving jars to be fully immersed in water over your fire, plus an additional space for a false bottom (which could be a metal rack or even thick chicken wire supported by small stones). This false bottom is required to prevent the glass jars shattering or cracking when in contact with the bottom of the metal sterilizer.

Before you begin work ensure that any fruit or vegetables for preserving are not bruised or blemished, and free from ANY grit or dirt. Some fruits like blackberry or raspberry will not take vigorous washing and the best way of dealing with them is to pack them into the preserving jar then flood with water three or four times – up-ending the jar each time, with your fingers lightly blocking the mouth of the jar to allow the washing water to escape.

Generally 'the fresher the better' is another key to decent preserved food. The old rule of thumb for vegetables was 'two hours from garden to can'. In the case of fruits pick them just before they are fully ripe (preserving techniques can soften them so their shape is lost), while under-ripe fruit tends not to have developed a full flavour.

In a survival situation where life has almost returned to the Stone-Age then an oven is unlikely to be a feature of your life. Still, food bottling is still possible, using the water-bath method (which is where that *sterilizer* comes in).

For fruits (we'll deal with veggies shortly) your jars should be packed with fruit to just below the shoulder, and then or syrup (25 to 35 gm sugar to ½-litre water) added up to the shoulder level. Stand the jars in your sterilizer and carefully fill with cold water, again to the shoulder of the jars, and lightly cap to prevent water getting in. Gradually apply heat so the water comes to a rolling boil then simmer for an hour, then remove the jars *individually* and fully seal without delay. This is not a foolproof method of preventing botulinum developing as the heat of boiling water is less than that required to kill the bug.

Vegetables may similarly be 'bottled', however they present a more tricky preserving regime since, unlike fruit, they generally do not contain acids which help in the preserving process. So, not only must vegetables to be 'bottled' be boiled, they will also require an additional preserving solution either in the form of salt or vinegar. For vegetables the youngest and most tender items are the best; they should be picked as carefully as possible, and every particle of soil or grit removed since soil bacteria mostly require extended periods of heating to destroy them.

Using the same water-bath preserving regime, first blanch the veggies in boiling water (1 to 10 minutes depending on type of veggie) which will kill off some external bacteria and also shrinks the material and makes it easier to pack in your preserving jars. The packing should be done when the veggies are cold – closely packed but not too tight, to allow the preserving solution to circulate – and in scrupulously clean jars (ie. sterilized). Once the jars are filled add the preserving solution made with 70 gm salt and 140 ml of lemon juice (or other fruit acid) to 4½ litres of boiled water. Allow the solution to cool and then fill your preserving jars right to the top and cap them. For screw caps, tighten fully then release half a turn to allow expanding air to escape. Place the jars in your false-bottomed sterilizer and then fill with cold water so that it covers the jars above their contents line. Apply heat and continue heating gradually until the boiling point is reached and continue boiling 1½ hours. If the contents of the jars settle during cooking, then they can be topped up with more preserving solution (boiling) and then put back in the water bath for another 15 minutes. When done, the jars are removed individually and the lids secured. Place on a wooden or other similar surface to prevent the jars cracking as they cool.

DRYING VEGETABLES
Preserving food by drying in the sun is one of the oldest methods used by man. However, in northern temperate climates this is unlikely to be possible so artificially assisted drying will most likely be the method.

You can, of course, place the fruit, vegetable or meat to be dried, close to your fire; using constant heat to drive out moisture without cooking the food itself. One drawback with this is that acrid smokey fires will taint the preserved food with 'smoke', particularly if you are using a 'birdcage' drier suspended above the heat.

If you can construct yourself some sort of tin oven then you have a very much better chance of producing higher quality dried food for later use. The fire source needs to produce a temperature of around 60°c, in other words almost a 'cool' oven in domestic terms. Veggie greens or fruits should be spread out on trays evenly and preferably not touching. If you can construct a stacking shelf system in your tin oven then rotate the trays of drying food at regular intervals so that drying is even.

The drying wisdom of the past suggested that if the starting temperature was too low then the end product would have a sour taste. Better was to start with a moderate heat then increase the temperature in the middle stages of drying, and then reduce the heat in the final stages since most of the water content will have gone by that stage and excessive heat could scorch the greens.

Smaller fruits and vegetables will take about 3 to 15 hours to dry, and larger fruits 4 to 24 hours. Fruits, such as apple slices, should have a texture somewhat like leather – supple and bendy – not so brittle as to snap. Veggies on the other hand should be dried to a point where they are crisp and brittle, and when cut into show no trace of moisture. If in doubt, return the veggies to the drier for a little longer. Where large items are being dried then separate out any pieces which still show signs of moisture and return these to the drying process until completely dry.

Once prepared, dried foodstuffs can be stored in virtually any type of container that prevents ingress of moisture and air. Store in a cool, dark, place. To reconstitute dried veggies soak in cold water for 1 to 24 hours.

On an entirely practical side dried foods also take up smaller storage spaces, and also make transportation easier, lightening the burden of travel on foot.

SALTING VEGETABLES
The salting of vegetables can be either *dry* or *wet*. Where the greens can be compressed in the jar then the dry method is used, while the wet version is for awkward shaped veggies where dry salt may not penetrate (viz. cauliflower or broccoli-type shapes). The problem with brined (solution) vegetables is that the salt can take longer to wash out of the preserved veggie before use.

For dry salting wide-necked containers are required. The ratio of salt to vegetables used is 450 gm salt to 1.8 kilos of vegetable greens (some folks recommend a 1:3 ratio); the vessel filled with 1 cm layers of greens sprinkled with salt, and repeated till the vessel is filled up – the last layer being salt. Next, an inert (non-reactive) plate or similar is placed on top of the mass, weighted down, and left for 48 hours. During this time the salt will draw out liquid from the greens and which may cover them as a natural brine. You may also see a little bubbling from fermentation. Cap or seal the vessel – in the absence of proper sealable jars and old preferred method was to use molten paraffin wax poured to a depth of 2.5 cm. The greens should not be filled too near the vessel mouth. Grease-proof paper is not really an option for veggies, but a thick layer of wax may be an option. Store in a cool place.

The figures above are for small volumes of salted veggies (such as might be done in those thick, old, earthenware jars you seen in antique shops). If you were doing this on an industrial scale – as in 20 litre barrel size volumes – then the fermentation period may take 7 to 10 days in warm weather, and up to 4 weeks in cool periods.

Brining of vegetables is the *wet* method of preserving. After the vegetables are packed in the vessel, the concentrated salt solution is added and after a time fermentation will take place. As mentioned above, brined veggies can taste very 'salty'. If the preserved veggies will be used in a month or two (ie. short-term) then a better option that also provides a better flavour is to begin by using a 5% salt solution (very approximately 30 gm salt to ½-litre water), then increase the concentration to 15% through the addition of extra salt.

Pack the veggies and pour over the 5% brine, then put a non-reactive plate or similar on top of the greens, and weigh down to keep the greens below the brine surface. Another way of achieving this (right) is to cover the salted contents with thick plastic sheet and then weigh this down so the vegetable material is forced below the solution.

Bubbles will appear as fermentation takes place. Once fermentation has stopped (1-10 days) add more salt to the vessel in the ratio of twice the amount contained in the original solution. So if you had used 1 litre of brine containing 60 gm of salt, then you need to add 120 to 125 gm more salt to increase the brine up to around 15%. All that remains to do is seal the vessel with a non-reactive seal (molten paraffin wax, for example).

Before use, straight salted leaf greens are best soaked to remove the saltiness and then boiled with meat, while those that have gone through a full fermentation process can be cooked straight off and served with meats like bacon or pork.

SALTING MEATS
When salting meat it is essential that after the animal has been killed and skinned the carcass is allowed to cool completely down, otherwise the meat may become tainted, and salting cannot remedy tainted or stale meat. 'Fresh' meat is the key, with processing done before the meat begins to decay, and in frosty weather never with frozen meat since the salt cannot penetrate the meat fully, leading to uneven curing. For a really large animal such as a cow then it may take more than a day for the carcass to fully cool down. It is a good idea to do your salting in a cool and dark environment such as a cellar, which could also help to keep flies away from your meat. That said, salting meat in the cooler autumn-winter months is a good time simply because the air is cooler.

Begin by weighing out salt – 450 gm salt for every 4.5 kilos meat – and place a 2 cm layer in the bottom of a barrel (dark plastic or wooden). Cut the meat into approximately <u>even</u> size pieces about 12 to 15cm square, then closely pack the first layer of meat on the salt. Add a 1 cm layer of salt and repeat this process till the barrel is full, but reserving enough salt to form a thick final layer. Cover the top of the barrel to keep flies and insects away and allow the meat and salt to stand overnight before continuing.

In the old days the next stage was to add a solution of sugar, baking soda and saltpetre (in a ratio of 1.8 kilos sugar, 57 gm soda and 115 gm saltpetre to every 45 kilos of meat) but these are unlikely to be readily available in the brave new world. Finally, prepare a wooden (or other inert material) cover, place it on top of the packed meat and weigh down with an inert stone or brick to keep the meat below the level of the brine. The brining process will take some 30 to 40 days to complete.

While spoilage of the brine will be pretty unlikely during the cool winter months it is essential to keep a close eye on it during the warm summer period. If the brine starts to become somewhat thick (it should drip freely from the back of spoon or finger dipped into the solution) then the brine needs tipping away and a new batch made. The meat is kept in the brine until needed for use. If you can find a little sugar to add to the brine then this helps balance the astringent effect of the salt which tends to dry and harden the meat.

An old method of wet salting pork had layers of tightly packed pork and coarse salt in a barrel, and then a strong, cold, brine added. The concentration of latter was simply as much salt as could be dissolved in 9 litres of water, the mass brought to the boil and skimmed of any impurities, and then allowed to completely cool. As long as the meat was kept covered by the brine then it was claimed it would keep.

Where meat is to be kept for a matter of a few days then a light coat of fine salt rubbed on the surface may be sufficient to preserve the meat providing it is kept in a dark and cool place.

SALTING BEEF & OTHER MEAT
The following method was thought suitable for salting thin cuts of every kind of meat... 2.7 kilos of salt, 340 gm of sugar, and 170 gm of saltpetre (plus optional herbs and spices) were mixed together. This was then rubbed on the pieces of meat for a few minutes each day for six days, after which the meat was merely turned over in the brine once a day for six more days.

Another old trick for preserving meat (particularly pork) was to slice the meat, fry it until half cooked through, then closely pack the pieces in a number of small stone jars (rather than one large vessel) and cover the contents with molten lard or fat. As the meat was required for use it was removed from the jar and cooked, with more hot lard poured over the remaining exposed meat if that was not going to be used immediately. The advice was to keep the jars in a cool, dark, cellar.

A similar old process involved heating fat in a vat to 115-120°c then plunging meat joints into this and cooking for a few minutes to drive off surface and excess moisture from the meat (and also kill some of the bugs). The cooked joints were immediately packed into barrels and more fat (at 93°c) added to fill up the barrel. When preserving joints of meat it is important to remove bones where possible, and certainly jointed bones or knuckles which contain fluids.

POTTING SHRIMPS
A similar process to the above was involved in potting shrimps for long-term storage (not the short term potted shrimps that you tend to find for sale on the promenades of holiday resorts).

Boil the shrimps, pick through them to remove the shells and other debris, then spread them out evenly on a tray and place in a warm environment (such as an oven or smoking tray) to drive off the moisture – to a point where the shrimps do not stick together. Season to taste then pack into clean, dry, small pots / jars and again place in an oven to dry further, but not to a point where they are browned (remember you are looking to remove at least 80% of the moisture in a foodstuff to prevent bacterial decay). Remove the shrimps from the heat and allow to cool. Meanwhile, clarify some butter, then fill the jars with this and seal the jars with greaseproof paper or other covering.

DRYING MEAT
In a hot climate where salt is scarce meat can be dried by a process called 'jerking'; theoretically a quite simple operation consisting of cutting meat into thin slices, then either hanging it upon the branches of trees, or spreading it out upon the rock and allowing the sun and dry air to dessicate the meat (which may take 2 to 3 days).

For temperate climates where the sun cannot be guaranteed, let alone get hot enough to dry meat, meat can be jerked using the heat of a small fire. Near to the fire construct a framework upon which the meat strips can be hung – close enough to be dried by the heat source, but not so close as to cook, broil, or burn the meat strips. Remember, it's that less than 80% moisture level were aiming at here. Some salt rubbed on the meat strips as they were hung out to dry would draw out moisture from the meat and provide an additional level of preservation. Indeed, some methods of jerking involve piling layers of salt and meat strips, leaving these for 12 hours, then turning and resalting before hanging up to dry. When jerking meat make sure to remove all traces of fat since this can turn rancid, and if rain threatens cover the drying meat or take indoors. Where the *salted* jerk is being produced then soak the meat well in water before use, then cut small and cook till the meat is tender.

SMOKING

Red meat that has been pickled (in saltpetre) or cured / brined can be further processed by smoking, which adds another degree of preservation to your food, though thinly sliced meat can also be cured without pre-salting. In this process, where the meat is preserved in the pyroligneous compounds of smoke, finely sliced meat pieces are threaded through with thin cordage, or long bark-stripped twigs of a non-toxic species, then suspended over a cool smoke source in a 'smoke chamber'.

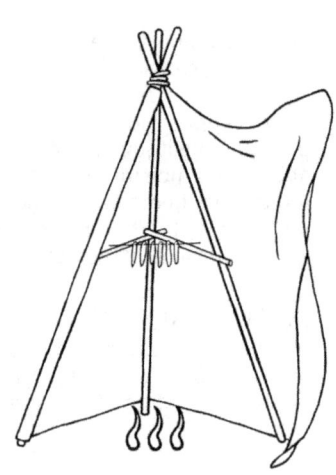

The smoke chamber can be anything from an old barrel (below and opposite) to a wooden tripod (right) wrapped round with a tarp or other non-flammable outer layer, then flooded with a constant stream of smoke.

Any tarp used in this type of design needs sufficient integrity to be able to resist heat, although the temperatures involved are not great. An alternative to tarp in the tripod design shown is to affix a lattice of dense branches of foliage on all sides – leaving holes (also covered over when not in use) for placing the meat, and constructing the fire. A gap also needs to be left for the smoke to escape around the top of the tripod, since the smoke must flow <u>over</u> the meat to do its job properly.

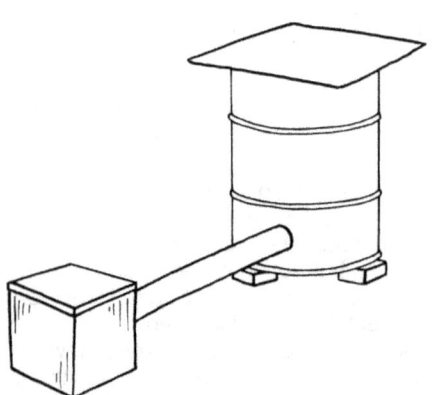

The smoke produced should be COOL, not hot; the aim being preservation, not cooking, of the meat pieces. In another type of design (left) the smoke source and chamber are separated; a slightly tilting pipe delivering cool smoke from smouldering sawdust or wood chips. Smoke flow is controlled by the 'lid' placed over the barrel top, having just enough of a gap to allow the smoke to drift away and draw in new smoke.

In some situations you may find a sub-level construction is required; either through lack of construction materials or for environmental or aesthetic reasons (opposite, left). One disadvantage of this design is that there is not always sufficient air available to allow continuous smoke generation, requiring constant attention. The simplest form of smoker, if you have access to cutting tools, is to cut a hole in the bottom of a barrel (opposite, right) to allow the smoke source

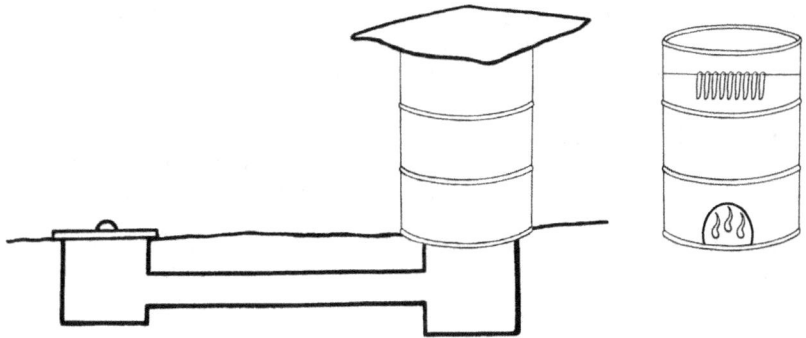

to be lit and maintained (add a few extra holes in the bottom for air too), and then creating an internal system for suspending the meat (fish fillets too) to be dried. Again, a lid is placed over the top to control smoke flow over the meat pieces.

The key to any of these smokers is cool and sustained flow of smoke. Non-toxic wood should be used, such as oak or apple, and not laurel or yew. The sliced meat needs to be cut thinly and <u>across</u> the grain, while the process shown is only suitable for red meats – beef, venison, bison, lamb – although goose meat is smoked too, but I am unsure how long the preservation period is.

SHORT TERM PRESERVATION OF BIRDS
Should you have some small game birds that you are not be able to use for a couple of days and might go off, then an old short-term method could provide a solution...

Pluck, draw and crop each bird, wash them well in two or three changes of water, and then rub them with salt. Meanwhile, bring a pan of water to the boil, then plunge each individual bird into the boiling water and, holding the legs pull the carcass back and forth through the water (ie. the water passes back and forth through the body cavity) for 5 or 6 minutes. Once done, hang the birds up in a cool place and when drained season very liberally with pepper and salt inside well. This should allow the birds a few days extra keeping time in your survival larder. Before roasting the birds, wash them well to remove the salt.

SNOW CHILLING
Snow and the cold may be an unwelcome guest in time of survival but from a food point of view snow can provide a means of temporarily preserving food, particularly meat. The meat (wrapped) may actually be buried in the snow but it may also be chilled in tubs or similar.

Cover the bottom of your container with 7 to 10 cm of clean snow, then lay down pieces of fresh meat (fowl should be filled inside their cavity with snow before adding to the box). Cover each meat layer with another 5 to 7 cm of snow, making sure to fill every gap between the pieces of meat with snow, and extending it to the edges of the container. The last layer must be snow, pressed down tightly then covered and kept in a cold place out of sun glare.

PICKLING WITH VINEGAR

Mostly when the term 'pickling' is used one thinks of vegetables in vinegar, though the brine and saltpetre mixtures covered earlier are actually sometimes referred to as 'pickle'. A number of recipes for making vinegars of different types are covered in the later food section but here are a few useful pointers in making vinegar for use...

SUGAR VINEGAR

This is how they conjured up vinegar in the old days... Add 900 gm sugar to 4.5 litres of clean water, then boil the mixture (removing any scum or impurities forming on the water surface). Transfer the liquid to a clean tub and when lukewarm add a slice of bread soaked in fresh yeast and leave it to 'work'. After a week place the fermenting liquid in a barrel (with NO bung, just a piece of thin material to cover the bung hole) and set it in the sun during summer, or by your fire in winter, for six months.

INCREASING VINEGAR STRENGTH

Vinegar for pickling needs to be strong (minimum 5%) so if the vinegar you have made seems a little on the weak side then put the containing vessel out in the frost overnight. The water in the vinegar will freeze – and the ice can be removed next day – so increasing the acid concentration. Repeat as necessary to further concentrate.

PICKLING MACKEREL

By all accounts mackerel could be kept for several months using the following process: Clean and gut, top and tail, your mackerel, then cut them into four or five pieces. Mix some spices (optional) with a handful of salt and rub the pieces of fish with this mixture. Next, fry the mackerel in oil until brown, then remove from the pan and allow to cool. Place the fish into a jar and fill it up with vinegar. As an added preservation measure oil could be poured on top of the vinegar as a seal.

EVAPORATIVE COOLING

Although not a means of 'preserving' food in the strictest sense, water can be used to keep your food cool by constructing a cooling box which utilizes the fact that *evaporating water* draws heat from the objects surrounding it. If a good flow of air is available then the temperature can be lowered by several degrees which is handy for preservation during the warmer summer months.

The two diagrams opposite illustrate the evaporative principle. On the left is a hessian type bag filled with moistened sand in which a food container in embedded. On the right a cloth in contact with the side of the cooling container wicks water from a reservoir below. Such examples work well in tropical climes but could also do so when there are hot spells of weather in temperate zones.

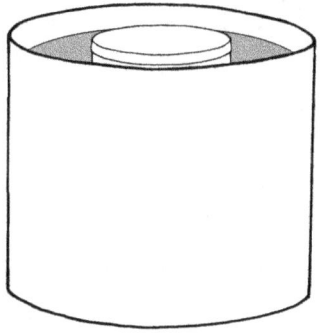 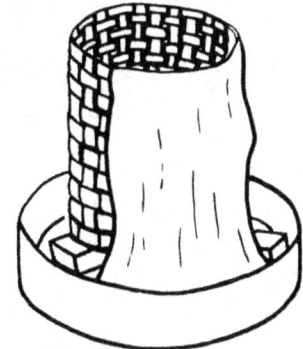

In urban survival mode your cooler box might be made by converting a redundant microwave oven (stripping out the internal gubbins so that just the outer carcass and door remain) and then covering it in a water-absorbant wicking material. Another alternative could be a small wooden drawer or wooden box with a solid bottom which is inverted and used to cover your food.

In <u>all</u> these cases the physical outer shell needs to be covered with an absorbant type of cloth (ie. cotton rather than man-made). In the case of the wooden items the cloth could be tacked to the structure to ensure good contact, while the microwave example may require string or other cordage type to bind the cloth to the metal structure (devise your layout so that the door can be opened and closed while also being cloth covered). The covering material is then saturated with water, and through evaporation will cool anything within the structure. If you can devise an automatic water drip system then your cooler can be used constantly. Of course potable water may well be at a premium in a survival situation so you would not want to sacrifice that for cooling food. However, low grade water (such as residual distillate from distilling water for purification purposes, or rainwater, or seawater) could all be used.

A really good food-cooling source is the water coming directly out of the ground from a spring. Unlike stream water, which may be warmed by the sun's rays as it passes over rock beds and through shallow areas, true spring water should be really cool. All you need to do is place containers of food in this source, or perhaps devise a local water capture 'pool' where the foods can be fully immersed in the cool water.

FATS AND OILS

Meat fat comes in various forms: rendered out through the cooking process, raw suet cut from fresh meat, and fat that remains on cooked meat joints or is cut away when butchering. There is also *topfat* (which forms on meat soup or broth when it has cooled down, or from boiling game). Turkey and chicken fat were reckoned to be a good substitute for butter in cream-based gravies. All of this fat can be saved for cooking with (as shortening or for frying), and there are slightly different approaches to preparing and saving it, although the processes are all quite similar.

As an aside, regarding tests for how hot fat is for cooking with: When a piece of bread thrown into fat browns in 60 seconds then it is at the right temperature for frying fritters. To re-heat and brown food apply a 40 second rule. Where food is cold and moist, or for frying potatoes, or needs to be re-cooked, particularly in bulky masses which reduces fat temperature, then apply a 20 second bread browning test. Generally, pre-cooked food needs hotter fat than food which is uncooked.

CLARIFYING FAT
An old-fashioned method of clarifying fat from physical *cooked* meats (but also uncooked fat), so that it may be used in the kitchen, is to cut off the cold fat and add it to a liberal quantity of cold water, then heat slowly and allow to simmer for an hour or more with the lid off. When cold, the cake of fat is removed and the underside, which may contain impurities of small meat particles etc., should be scraped away and the white, clean fat saved. If the flavour or colour, or both, are not satisfactory the process may be repeated several times until white fat is obtained – but the you need to consider your fuel resources in relation to this.

CLARIFYING DRIPPING
Beef fat dripping is removed from the dripping tray (placed below a roasting joint in front of a fire) before it has been overheated by the fire, and is poured straight into boiling water, to which some salt has been added. Debris and cinders sink to the bottom of the pan while the pure fat collects in a cake on the water surface once cooled. The fat cake is then broken up and placed into a jar or container and heated in a boiling water bath to solidify as one whole mass ready for further use.

Another, simpler, method was to put solidified dripping in large basin, and then pour over boiling water to melt the fat, and then let it stand till cold. Then the solid fat was removed, water thrown away, and impurities scraped off.

Mutton fat was regarded as much too tallow-like for use in cooking but could be transformed into candles (see elsewhere). That's not to say that mutton fat cannot be used, it just wasn't regarded as having a high enough quality. Lamb fat was used to fry fish and making pastry for pies.

RENDERING SUET
Both beef and mutton suet, and unrendered pig's leaf lard, require cooking in order to loosen the fat from the tougher membrane that holds it, and also separating out the blood veins that run through it. For this purpose the fat is cut into small pieces, covered with water and allowed to soak for a day to try and remove some of the blood matter, with the water changed once.

Then drain the suet, weigh, and place in a heavy (best) cooking pot, adding ½ cup of water for every 450 gm of fat. Cook the fat gently until no water remains and the animal 'bits' in the fat have lightly browned, then remove from the heat, allow to cool slightly then strain off the top fat into storage jars. I read somewhere that in the past German cooks would use skimmed milk rather than water as the cooking liquid. However, that may not be available to your doomsday kitchen, and I have the nagging suspicion that the incorporation of milk products into the rendered fat might reduce its storage life.

PURIFYING RANCID BUTTER
Poor quality butter can be used for frying and baking, but if butter has gone rancid then the bad taste tends to be amplified through cooking. There are several old tricks from the past which were used to 'bring back' tainted butter. The first involved placing a well toasted piece of bread for a few minutes into a pan in which butter was melted, as if for clarifying it. Another way was to drop the butter in a pan of boiling water, stir thoroughly, and when melted skim the melted butter off. The third option was to melt the butter in a pan then pour into cold water and skim off when hardened, repeating the exercise until the butter tasted decent again.

KEEPING BUTTER
Because of water products and whey in butter it is going to 'go off' sooner than rendered fats or, indeed, clarified butter, particularly in hot weather. A method of keeping butter in the absence of electrical refrigeration is to store it in a watertight container then sink this into a river or stream, or to bury it in the ground. Another old trick was to store lumps of butter in salt brine, weighing it down so that it remained below the brine surface.

Clarified butter often keeps for a couple of weeks in warm summer weather, but much longer if kept cool, while in the cold winter months that keeping time is extended considerably.

Clarified butter used for potting meat can be re-purposed for basting roast meats or for making pastry, though you might want to go through a fat clarifying process with boiling water if there is any suggestion of the butter being tainted, or has the 'taste' of the food item that it was previously helping to preserve.

CLARIFYING BUTTER

Butter goes rancid because the milk and whey products still bound within the fat 'go off', yet the actual butter fat can last for ages. To prepare butter that will keep for a long time it needs to be clarified in a somewhat similar manner to the other fats above. Melt the butter in a pan and bring up to a quite high temperature but without it smoking. The milk impurities will settle out in the bottom of the pan as white flecks. Pour off the top clear liquid butter into a suitable storage container/s; if using glass jars preheat them to prevent shattering. Seal the containers and store in a cool place. Use the last bit of fat and and 'bits' in the bottom of the pan for frying something.

PRESERVING BUTTER FOR WINTER USE

In times of plenty during the summer months, when cow's milk is more abundant, then that is the time to preserve butter for the winter months. It is essential that the butter is free from buttermilk and whey products before being preserved. One way to achieve that is to work the butter over with paddles while submerged in a bowl of very cold water, which will help draw out these impurities which can go rancid. The butter then needs to be further squeezed with wooden paddles to press out residual water itself from the butter mass.

The preservation side involves layering salt and butter (in a ratio of 28 gm salt to 450 gm of butter) in storage jars; a layer of salt first, then butter, and so on, with the final layer being one of salt. Each butter layer is pressed down hard over the underlying salt layer, while the top salt layer will need to be topped up with more salt as it turns to brine. The jars need to be sealed and then stored in a cool place. If the butter is a little too salty when it comes to using it, then spoonfuls can again be mashed in cold water to dissolve out the excess salt.

CLARIFIED GOOSE FAT

Goose is a very fatty meat (much more so than duck), and while that may sound like a dreadful waste of food, goose fat is an excellent and tasty commodity to have around your doomsday kitchen and also keeps well if kept in a cool place. If you have ever had potatoes roasted in goose fat then you will appreciate its value in adding a savoury touch.

When the goose is gutted, keep aside any internal fat (though you will need to keep it cool and covered – better still, render that fat immediately). Then, when the goose has been roasted pour off the fat, allow to set so that the fat can be separated from any dripping, and add this to the reserved internal fat. Simmer both fats, removing any scum that forms, then strain into a storage jar/s, seal down and store in a cool place.

POPPY OIL

The garden poppy (*Papaver somniferum*), also the opium poppy, is a source of a cooking oil, which would be worthwhile extracting if a sufficient patch of waste ground could be turned over to growing the plant. Quite simply, remove the seeds from the cases (discard), paste the seeds, then boil and simmer in water, finally skimming off the oil that rises to the surface. If you are lucky then 1.3 to 1.8 kilos of seeds will produce about one half litre of oil. In the normal production of poppy seed oil physical expression of the seeds is used, but that facility is unlikely to be available to most folks in a doomsday world.

At any time you are handling or processing hot fat or oil, be extremely careful as serious burns in a medically deficient post-disaster world could be life threatening.

THE ARMAGEDDON MENU

The recipe collection that follows is more about providing the doomsday chef with *alternative* ways of using some common and wild foods for the armageddon menu. There are also unusual cuts of meat and offal that you will encounter once you begin slaughtering animals for yourself (what to do with brains, lungs and animal feet, for example, rather than traditional cuts encountered in normal times). Not included are various ways of cooking up wild plants, since many of these can be simply cooked as 'greens', plus some simpler forms of cooking that you may have to resort to in your doomsday kitchen. Where quantities become more important to the outcome of the end result I have largely resorted to the rule of thumb in my previous written work: quantities that can be *visualised* in your mind. As long as you are *consistent* in your visualization of ingredient quantities (handful, pinch, etc.) then things should turn out fine. When it comes to baking, however, proper measurement is usually critical to a good outcome. For weights of ingredients you will need to devise your own strategy based on the weight of water (see top of page 209).

A few recipes are slightly above 'basic' level, but the thought process behind this collection of recipes is that overall they are mainly things which could be achieved through cooking over a fire, or an improvised wood/coal-fired oven (though in cases of bread-making you will have to construct your own design), and in the absence of many 'luxury' ingredients that we have come to expect.

In returning to what may feel like the Stone Age, as a result of some world-changing catastrophe, foodstuffs such as full-blown cereal grain will be hard to find (certainly flour will become non-existent for a period), and it is likely that you would need to resort to raising meagre patches of cereals, or be opportunistic and glean grains from former agricultural field systems. And there are a few recipes which are designed to utilize such directly acquired grains which will need de-husking before use (see page 343).

Although some recipes include sweeteners it is imagined that in a post-disaster world sugar would soon disappear until some enterprising souls begin to make sugar from beet again, or sugar cane production were revived in warmer climes. Honey might be an option though it is also likely to be a rarity, so the brave new world is not going to welcome the sweet-toothed with open arms.

Finally, and this ties in with many other parts of the substance of this book, cooking is the final factor in the *Cost of Acquisition* of a foodstuff. Can your cooking skills transform what you have caught, trapped or picked, or walked miles to acquire, into something that is palatable and makes you feel that you want to live another day in the new Stone Age?

NOTE: When processing <u>intestines</u> from livestock it will be advisable to wear protective gloves as a protection against the various worm-like pathogens that lurk in the animals and the eggs of which might be inadvertently spread under finger nails and so on to food.

SOUPS AND BROTHS

Lots of the better wild greens mentioned in the earlier part of this book can make good ingredients for soups and need little in the way of recipes to describe their use, just a little culinary imagination on your part. As a general rule, if you are boiling meat or vegetables then keep the cooking water for the basis of stock or soup rather than discarding it. Food waste is not an option in your doomsday kitchen. *Nothing* should go to waste – food, fuel or water!

So, at their very simplest level a soup or broth-type item may be made by adding oatmeal and herbs to the broth, or liquid, in which meat was boiled. *Left-over* bones, or portions of meat not used up in a main meal, can be stewed with peas or other vegetables and wild greens, seasoned, and other herbs added. *Bits* of lean raw meat can be stewed slowly then thickened with crushed barley, oatmeal, or even mashed peas and beans, or flavoured with turnips and carrots, and herbs if these can be obtained. In a doomsday scenario it is important to get some nutritive (preferably hot) food inside you; the niceties of *haute cuisine* are immaterial, while food which tastes good helps give you a better outlook on life for sure. But in the doomsday kitchen you must make do with what you have to hand, and apply a little bit of flexibility in your thinking.

BLOOD & GUTS SOUP

Fear not! This tasty soup is made with blood and intestines from a duck or goose, but other poultry / game fowl and common quadrupeds can also be used with the cooking time and method varied accordingly. If the thought of using the guts of an animal terrifies you then cook up the parts until tender, shred or mince, and then add the blood ingredient (which needs to be collected at the time of slaughter). In the case of quadrupeds their bone marrow is also added.

The stomach and intestines need to be thoroughly cleansed of their contents, being gently squeezed and washed out as often as necessary until clean. Slice the intestines into pieces and then drop into boiling salted water for 10 to 15 minutes. Remove from water, and drain, then place in a pan with stock or water (about ½-litre water to ½ cup of guts), along with bone marrow (removed from bone) if using. Place over the fire and simmer for 30 minutes.

Meanwhile, mix 1 cup of blood with 1 cup of water. Remove the pan from the heat and whisk in the blood-water mixture to prevent curdling. Add pepper (or other seasonings) to taste, and then place back over the fire. Cook gently for another 30 to 40 minutes, stirring regularly to prevent the blood sticking to the base of the pan. The blood will naturally thicken the soup, but an even thicker sauce-like soup can be made by adding a little flour during cooking.

BEEF & NOODLE SOUP

Boil some large beef bones (though other large animal bones can substitute) in a large vessel for a couple of hours. If you want a really thick soup then saw the bones in half so the cooking water can reach the fatty bone-marrow inside. Cook until you have 1.5 to 2 litres of broth remaining. Meanwhile, break a couple of eggs into a good cup of flour and kneed into a stiff dough. Roll this out into several very thin sheets and allow these to dry out for 30 to 40 minutes. Next, layer the sheets one on top of another and carefully roll them up like a Swiss / Arctic roll, then with a very sharp knife slice the rolled dough into strips about 5 mm thick, unravelling each batch of noodles as you cut them. Strain off the soup liquid into another pan over the heat, add the noodles bit by bit, then bring to the boil. Cook for about ten minutes, adding any seasoning that you may have. Being a beef based soup in more normal times one might add some tomatoes for flavouring, or shredded carrots.

OLD CHICKEN BROTH

Cut up the chicken into pieces and put it into a heavy-bottomed pot with 1.5 to 2 litres of water, an onion quartered, a handful of oatmeal, and some seasoning. Boil gently for a couple of hours, removing any scum on the liquid surface, then ladle off the liquid to serve up, shredding off any bits of flesh on the bones into the soup.

PIGEON & NETTLE SOUP

For one person take a couple of pigeons, disjointing one of them into the carcass, liver, gizzard, heart, neck, and so on. Boil these gently in a ½-litre of water until all the goodness has been extracted. Then strain the liquid into another cooking pot (small) and add the breast meat stripped from the carcass and shredded, plus some seasoning. Add ½-litre of water more plus the second pigeon, and a little bit of finely sliced onion, then bring to the boil for a few minutes before simmering gently with the pan covered.

Meanwhile, place several handfuls of tender young nettle tops with a small splash of water in a pan, and cook until wilted. Remove, spread on a board, and when cool enough to handle roughly chop. Add to the simmering pigeon pan with any small amount of residual cooking water. Next, melt a little fat in a pan and fry a handful or two of breadcrumbs until nicely browned, and add to the cooking pot. When the meat starts to separate from the bones, serve up.

PIGEON SOUP

Gently boil the livers and pigeon gizzards in stock or gravy for 30 minutes, then remove the gizzards but mash the liver with a fork. Mix a teaspoon of fat with a little flour, add to the pot and cook till the liquid has thickened. Set to one side but keep warm. Season the inside of the bird/s then truss – tying the legs together with string – then dust with a little flour before frying the pigeon/s in fat until browned on the outside, then add to the soup pan. Allow to boil gently for 30 to 40 minutes.

RABBIT SOUP

Joint one or two rabbits and lay the pieces in cold water for an hour, then dry the pieces and fry them till nicely browned, along with some thickly sliced onion. Transfer everything to a large pan that will hold 2 or 2.5 litres of cold water which is then added, along with seasoning. Allow to come to the boil then simmer gently over the fire for 4 or 5 hours. About 3 hours into cooking add several handfuls of shelled peas, plus their pods (with tough bits removed). Some shredded celery leaves would also be a nice tasty addition.

RABBIT SOUP #2
This is one for an old rabbit which would otherwise be tough eating. Parts of the offal may also be incorporated if you wish, or don't have other plans for that ingredient.

After gutting, cut the rabbit into pieces and place in a small-ish cooking pot with 1 litre of water. Bring to the boil, cover, and then simmer over the fire until the bones and meat separate easily (about 2 hours). Strain off the liquor into another cooking pot, and remove the flesh from the bones. Pulverize the cooked meat (and any offal) to a paste, then add this to the liquid along with seasoning. Cook for a further 5 minutes then serve. If you have a splodge of cream available, then stir in and make this richer.

EASY RABBIT STEW SOUP
Joint the rabbit as above and place the pieces in a pan with ham bones (preferably), or beef bones, some herbs and a bay leaf if available, plus onion for flavouring, then season with pepper if also available. Bring to a boil over the fire and then move the pan away from the direct heat to simmer until the meat is tender. Then cut the meat off the bones and return the meat to the pan, and let it simmer till the meat is disintegrating and flakey. Then strain the soup / stew liquid, strain off a cup and add a piece of flour and butter (or fat) previously mixed together. Stir in a ½-litre, or so, of seasoned stock, then adjust seasoning as required, and let everything simmer till thoroughly warmed through.

HARE SOUP
Skin, gut and wipe clean, a freshly caught hare, reserving as much blood as possible. Then joint the hare, cutting the saddle into a couple of pieces, and place in a pan with enough water to cover the meat (keep extra hot water available to top up as required). Also add any blood that you may have been able to keep, some seasoning, and a tablespoon of flour mixed with cold water. Bring to the boil, stirring all the time, and then allow to simmer gently for 1½ hours, from time to time removing any scum that forms on the liquid surface. If you can add a piece of celery or a carrot to the pot it will improve the final product.

Next, remove all the pieces of meat from the pot, and keep a choice piece or two to one side. Strip all the meat from the remaining bones, then either mince very small or mash / pulp as finely as possible. Keep to one side while you strain the liquid into another pan, and put this back over the fire. Add the pulped meat to the pan, check seasoning, then simmer for another 30 minutes. Serve with the selected choice pieces of meat alongside the soup.

POTATO DAY SOUP
You have managed to find or acquire some potatoes (in fact if you gleaned these out of an old field where they were grown as a crop you might be able to start up a new resource by growing-on some of the ones you find). Scrub them clean, remove any eyes or bad parts, and if large cut them into smaller pieces. If of 'new potato' size then use them as they are, or halve them. Meanwhile, put the bones, skin, and all the rough scraps and residue from a meat joint, into a saucepan, with 1½ litres of water and put on the fire to boil. While this is heating up, roughly chop a large onion and fry till browned, then add to the pan along with a carrot sliced up. Allow to come to the boil then simmer at a gentle boil for 2 hours, before adding the potato pieces, seasoning, and a little mustard if you have some. Cook for another hour, then remove the bones and skin, and mash everything else through a sieve to serve up as a thick soup.

BAKED BEAN SOUP
In the same way that you might chance upon potatoes in the post-disaster world, what would you do with a can of baked beans if you acquired one? They can obviously be used as they are, but one tin could be 'extended' by turning it into soup. And, of course, you might want to keep the tin for other uses too.

1 can baked beans
2 cups water or milk
1-2 tsp. fat
1-2 tsp. flour (also oat or barley flour)
Salt and pepper

Mash the bean contents of the tin and place in a pan with 2 cans of water or milk. Bring to the boil, then simmer. Meanwhile, mash together the fat and flour and add to the pan. Cook through until the soup thickens, add seasoning if required, and serve.

BONE SOUP
1 onion
2 tbsp. dripping / fat
3 tbsp. flour
1 litre water – warm
Bones
Carrot / turnip
Salt and pepper

Slice an onion then fry in melted dripping. Sprinkle over the flour, stir in thoroughly, and continue cooking until browned. Next, add warm water, bones, and season. Bring to the boil for a few minutes (removing any scum that forms on the liquid surface), then simmer for 2 hours over hot embers. Meanwhile, dice the carrot (or other root vegetables) and add these 30-40 minutes before completion of cooking.

TWO-SHOT MEAT SOUP
This refers to the dual outcome of the cooking process, and not that it took the hunter-gatherer two shots to acquire the main ingredient. Boil a joint of meat for which you intend to use the meat for a pie or hash-type dish. When tender, remove the meat for your pie, but take out the bones and put these back in the pot to cook for another couple of hours. Remove from the heat, strain, and leave to stand till the following day. Then remove the congealed surface fat (keeping this for further use), re-heat the soup, adding seasoning, finely chopped or shredded onion, and a few handfuls of oatmeal. Bring to the boil and then cook for a further 30 minutes. In the absence of oatmeal crushed de-husked barley or wheat grains soaked for an hour in water could be added, and the final cooking time extended until these grains are cooked through.

BASIC BROTH
Clarified dripping / fat / butter
1 onion – sliced
1 carrot – sliced thinly
1-1½ litres water / stock
1 cup peas
Bones (from a roast)
Oatmeal (optional)

This is a way of using up the scraps from a roast meat dinner. Indeed, any remaining vegetables from a meal could be added too, with a slight alteration to the cooking method. If very young peas are used then the pea shells may also be tender enough to add as a vegetable component, having first removed any stringy bits.

Fry the onion and carrots in a good knob of fat until quite well browned. Then add water (stock will give more taste), peas, bone remains and any scraps of meat from the roast. Bring to the boil briefly then simmer till the peas are soft. Remove from the heat, take out the bones, but scrape off any meat and return this to the pan. Add some seasoning plus a couple of tablespoons of oatmeal moistened in water (used as a thickener), then cook for a further 10 minutes so the oatmeal is cooked through.

OX / CALF / SHEEP / GOAT'S HEAD SOUP
This is a recipe designed to feed a large number of people (as you might find clustered round a communal campfire in a post-disaster world), while the vegetable content could vary. It is also cooked overnight, or throughout a whole day if started in the morning. If using smaller sheep and goat's heads then you would need a sufficient number to make up an equivalent volume to the ox head or alter the water volume. The head should be skinned, and the nostrils and oral cavity very thoroughly cleaned out. In the case of the goat and sheep you might like to add the eyeballs to the soup as lucky treats for someone. Essentially this is tasty refugee camp cooking.

Having cleaned the head, break it up and cut the meat off in pieces, and slice the brain. Put these in a cauldron large enough to hold 20 to 25 litres of water, plus the vegetables and meat.

Then add 4 to 5 kilos of peeled potatoes (halved, or smaller, if large), 2 to 3 kilos of turnips (perhaps replace with swedes, though I have not tried this myself), 2 to 3 kilos of sliced onions, and 1 kilo of peeled carrots sliced up, and sprinkle over 900 gm of oatmeal (as a thickener). Also add some general kitchen herbs, and seasoning. Pour in 20 litres of water, bring the contents to the boil (skimming off any scum that forms on the liquid surface), then cover the pot tightly and simmer very gently overnight. Next morning add water to make up the volume cooked off during the night. Allow to further cook until that water has heated up (unless you added boiling water), and then serve. Initially you will need to frequently stir the contents of the pot to prevent sticking / burning, then just occasionally once the main cooking period gets underway.

KIDNEY SOUP
1 cup kidneys
1 cup lean meat
1 small onion
Dripping / fat
1 litre water
Flour
Salt and pepper

Kidneys are not to everyone's liking, but if you have them left over as part of slaughtering an animal, it is a terrible waste not to use them. If you find the texture of the whole cooked organ not to your palate, try this alternative way of utilizing kidneys.

Mince the kidney and meat, then slice an onion. Melt some fat in the pan you intend to cook the soup in and fry the meat and onion for 5 minutes. Add water, a little flour as a thickener, and seasoning. Allow to come to the boil before reducing the heat and simmer gently for about 3 hours. Then, take the soup off the heat, pour through a sieve into another pan, and then press as much of the bulk ingredients caught in the sieve through the mesh with the back of a spoon. Re-heat and serve. In the decadent old world you might have served this with fried bread croutons.

GIZZARD & NECK SOUP
Geese, chickens and many other fowl species have a different method of processing food, since they don't have teeth to chew. Instead, they employ an organ called the *gizzard* – found between the stomach and intestine – which macerates the food along with the help of grit and ridged muscles. This somewhat makes the gizzard sound like inhospitable food, however it may be used as an ingredient (goose and turkey are best because of their physical size).

To prepare gizzard remove it as a whole section, then slit open on one side. Remove whatever gunk and gritty matter you find among the ridges of muscle tissue, and then peel away the membrane that lines the gizzard starting at the cut edge. Wash thoroughly then cut into slices.

Assuming the goose neck has been plucked and singed cut it into three or four pieces, then put them in a pan with the gizzards and 1 litre of broth or water, some finely chopped onion, whatever herbs you like (or can find), plus seasoning. Allow the water to come to the boil, then keep on simmering until the giblets are tender. Skim off any scum that forms on the liquid surface.

CHICKEN (OR GOOSE) GIBLET, HEAD & BONE SOUP
This recipe uses virtually everything that is not generally wanted on a fowl – liver, gizzard, heart, wing pinions and neck skin cut into pieces (both scalded to remove feathery bits). Even the feet could be added as an extra ingredient. Remember, as the good doomsday cook you must waste absolutely nothing.

Take the giblets from two or more birds (they must be absolutely fresh), scald them briefly in boiling water then trim them and place in a pan. Next, take the heads of the birds, cut the beaks off, split the heads in half and add to the pan. Take the leg bones, break them in half, and also place in the pan. Add enough cold water to cover the pieces, bring to the boil, and then simmer over hot embers for about 1½ to 2 hours – or until the giblets are tender – removing any scum that forms on the liquid surface. Once done, strain the solids from the pan though a sieve, picking out the giblets and any bits of meat, but leaving behind any bones. Cut the giblets up into fork-size pieces and keep warm, but return the liquid to the pan.

Then, melt a good knob of fat or butter in a separate pan and stir in enough plain flour to make a basic roux. Spoon in, bit by bit, some of the hot soup liquor – stirring constantly to avoid lumps. Allow to cook through and then add this to the main soup pan. Bring everything to a boil and allow to cook through for a few minutes, before returning the fork-size giblet pieces to the pan to warm through again.

OATMEAL / BARLEY & NETTLE SOUP
For one person, fry a handful of oatmeal lightly in fat. Add cold or tepid water and stir to a smooth consistency. Bring to the boil, then add a handful of nettle tops (chopped or whole as preferred), and season with salt. Simmer for 15 to 20 minutes. If you were in the real world you might like to spice this up with a little nutmeg and a slug of cream or milk.

OATMEAL SOUP #2
This can be made from left-over cooked oatmeal previously cooked up as porridge – nothing goes to waste, right? Put equal quantities of cooked oatmeal and boiling water in a pan and simmer gently until about a third of the liquid volume is gone, and the mixture almost jelly-like. If you have a sieve then strain

through that, then add about half the volume of milk gradually over heat, along with several knobs of butter (or dripping), a little puréed onion, plus seasoning (use something hotter than normal pepper if you wish). Add nettles for greens.

OX-TAIL SOUP
So simple this... providing cattle are available. Take a couple of skinned ox-tails, segment them into pieces and place in a pan with an onion (if available), plus seasoning. If you can get you hands on spicy items like cloves or allspice then add a pinch of either. Bring everything to a boil over the fire then move away from the direct heat and allow to simmer for a couple of hours or more, or until the meat begins to fall away from the bones. Then strain the liquid from the solids, pick off any meat from the bones and return this to the strained liquid. Put these back in a pan with a little flour added as a thickener and cook until the flour has cooked through. Adjust seasoning to preference.

STOMACH (TRIPE) SOUP
Made from the bowels / belly of beef cattle, or veal, the prepared stomach (see end of meat section on tripe) is washed then boiled in salted water for 30 minutes, then removed from the pot, refreshed with cold water, and washed again. Then cut the stomach into fork-size pieces and place in a pot with veggies such as onion and carrot to provide flavour, plus seasoning. Place the pot over a hot fire and simmer until the meat is really tender, then serve up with the veggies as a soup.

PIG LUNG SOUP
Wash the lungs thoroughly, filling with water 3 or 4 times and squishing round to remove slime and blood. Then cut into slices and boil for 10 minutes in salted water. Drain off the water, and add sliced mushrooms and a handful of well-crushed barley grains (ideally pearl barley preferred in real life) to the pan. Fill with hot water and seasoning, and simmer for an hour over the fire – adding extra water as required. Virtually any lung material can be used for this.

TERMINATOR STEW / SOUP
This recipe is for small mangled animals, possibly the rodents and small birds covered in earlier sections of this book, and those with small bone structures that are fine and sharp. Precise technique will depend on whether you have avians or quadrupeds for your main ingredients (but it could be both).

Skin, pluck or otherwise remove all the fur from the animal including that covering the head, then gut (keeping aside organs such as heart, liver and kidney). Sever the head from the main carcass, but keep the limbs attached, then drop into boiling water along with the head and offal. Cook at a gently rolling boil (15 to 20 minutes for a small animal, much longer for larger quantities or larger sized small animals), then remove from the heat, take out the pieces of meat and when cool enough to handle strip any available meat off the bones and set aside. Crack open the skull and winkle out the brain. Also set the offal pieces to one side. Next, break all the bones (but not too small to fragment them into sharp shards), and crush large bones, then return them to the cooking liquor and simmer for another 30 minutes.

Meanwhile, mash the brain and offal, and shred or flake the retrieved meat. Then strain the liquid through a <u>fine</u> sieve (to keep any shard-like bones at bay) into another pot and add the mashed offal and meat, plus whatever seasoning is available to you. Cook for a few more minutes to heat the meat through, or longer if you want the soup to have a thick texture (or use a thickener, or reduce the liquid before returning the meat to the pot). You never know but something like this might become an armageddon menu favourite. For an added twist, why not add some of the intestines, cleaned up, shredded, then fried till golden brown.

EEL SOUP

How you approach this recipe can be somewhat down to personal preferences. I prefer to skin eels before using, other folks deal with the skin post-cooking. Just so you know!

Right... Begin by skinning and gutting the eels, then cut them into pieces. Melt a bit of fat (or butter) in the bottom of a pan and add the eel pieces with a sliced onion (if available). Braise the eel pieces for a few minutes until they have browned. Next, cover them with some boiling water and bring the pan to the boil removing any scum that forms. Add seasoning, plus suitable herbs and parsley. Move the pan away from the direct heat and stew very slowly over embers for a couple of hours. Then strain the liquor from the eel pieces, setting the latter aside in a warm place. Thicken the remaining liquor with flour and butter / fat (plus a little cream if at all available to your doomsday kitchen) and serve up with the eel. Works great with slices of toasted bread, or crusts of bread which can be dunked. Also, the addition of light veggies such as peas, leek and cauliflower, can improve this recipe. For a further twist (if you have the resources available) add some fish of crab dumplings (see below).

CRAB (or FISH) DUMPLINGS

This is the sort of additional item that could be added to a fish soup, or even a crab meat soup, or a very thin chowder-like dish. The proportions are 1 cup each of crab meat and fresh breadcrumbs, to 2 small, beaten eggs, plus seasoning. Add beaten egg a bit at a time so the mixture does not become too soft, then form into round balls about the size of a cherry tomato and then add to the soup pot when it is at a boil. The dumplings should take about 5 minutes to cook. The same sort of thing can be done with cooked, flaked, fish.

SORREL SOUP

Sorrel is a quite common edible wild green weed and can be exploited for its acid-tasting leaves. The following recipe is a bit of a luxury since it assumes some other veggies that may not be available to you. Take a couple of handfuls of sorrel, a large carrot, and some sliced onion, and stew them in stock or thinned gravy. When tender, pulp the vegetables then mix in the yolks of two or three eggs, and cook further before serving. Great stuff!

PEAPOD SOUP

Pea pods are edible as well as the peas themselves. Use early season pods (having extracted the baby peas for use), trim off any bits of stalk and discard discoloured or unhealthy looking pods. Place in a pan with enough cold water to cover them, add a pinch or two of salt, and bring to the boil. Continue cooking (30 minutes per 450 gm weight), then strain off the liquid and put back on the fire. Add some milk and a little flour to thicken, and seasoning, and allow to cook for several minutes till the soup thickens. If the quality of the pods is good, and the taste is liked, then these could also be mashed up and added to the soup to provide a thicker end product.

THISTLE ROOT SOUP

Thistle roots
Potato [optional]
Meat liquor / gravy
Dripping or fat
Onion – chopped
Salt and pepper
Spices [optional]
Meat scraps – cooked [optional]

Thistles are ones of those ever-present weed species that can provide you with something useful to eat. For this recipe, however, I personally think that only the lateral spring runners of the Field / Creeping Thistle [*Cirsium arvense/is*] are usable. The taproots of the other main species listed in this book are often too woody to become a 'vegetable' except if they are 'slow cooked' for a long time.

Thistle roots are bland, but they offer you *bulk*. To be quite truthful the more additional flavours you can get your hands on for this recipe, the better; a swirl of cream to add richness, or paprika, cayenne or pepper for spice. In your doomsday kitchen such things will probably be absent, but you could well have the liquor left over from boiling meat, dripping from any fat skimmed off that boil-up and, of course, thistle roots. At least those three items provide you with a starting point.

So begin by cleaning up the whippy lateral roots of the field thistle, roughly chop, then place in a pan with the meat liquor and stew gently over a fire for 30 to 40 minutes (avoid rapid boiling as this can toughen up the root). Meanwhile, chop some onion and fry in fat till soft. If you have potato available, then dice and fry with the onion. Set these aside until the thistle roots are tender.

Remove the roots from the cooking liquor and place on a chopping board. Transfer the fried onion / potato to the meat liquor and allow them to simmer away while you deal with the roots. When they are cool enough to handle chop them finely, mash them to a pulp and return to the cooking pot (though remove any stringy interior root fibres). Add seasoning (spices if available), any left-over cooked meat scraps, and simmer for another half hour. Your doomsday kitchen has now produced thistle root soup.

GRASS SOUP
This armageddon menu recipe comes with a health warning, as in that I do not know whether there may be risks involved in the way that I have been using sprouted grass. Normally grass cannot be eaten by humans, and contains too much cellulose to be digested. What I have done for experimentation is collect the seeds of wild grasses (not the stuff from garden centres which is usually treated with toxic fungicides), sprout on moist tissue paper, then harvest when no more than 2 cm long, mostly 1 cm. About a handful of these are chopped and mashed up and then cooked with stock and thickened with oatmeal, or pearl barley added, or plain wheat flour used for thickening. Although untried, it should be possible to use sprouted grass seeds in other ways although, as mentioned, grass is not a recommended human foodstuff and I would personally not eat mature grass, or the sprouted seeds too often or in large quantities.

COUCH-GRASS SOUP
Two options here: either beat and bash young roots and boil in water, or cook roots in water till softened, and then beat and bash. The reason for this is that couch-grass roots are quite stringy, and in my view the fibres need to be removed before consuming. Add whatever stock, flavouring or meat to the cooked liquor. In my view I would not eat couch-grass too often or in large quantities as it has herbal properties (mainly diuretic).

CARROT LEAF SOUP
Very young carrot leaves may be eaten cooked in sensible moderate quantities, given that they are potentially allergenic to some folks, and contain alkaloids. They also contain large amounts of vitamin K. Throw away any green stalk material and just use a little of the frothy green, young, foliage (old ones are tough and bitter) along with some potatoes for a soup. A word of caution, however: collecting leaves that look like those of carrot can be a hazardous matter since there are poisonous look-alikes in the wild. However, if you sprouted some new greens from the tops chopped off carrot roots, then clearly there is no case of misidentification.

BASIC STOCK
A stock that can form the basis of soup, gravy, or for cooking other items in (provided the flavours do not clash), can be made from the cooking liquor of boiled meats, scraps of fresh meat or poultry left over from trimming up slaughtered animals, shank-bones, roast-beef bones, fowl bones, or any other pieces that your doomsday larder may provide. Also any vegetables, vegetable remainders, and vegetable peelings, and spices / seasoning if these exist in your larder can make a stock. Essentially, whatever combination of bits you can gather together can be simmered gently for several hours to extract the flavours. Skim off any unpleasant looking scum that floats on the stock surface as these may contain impurities in the cooking mass, strain off, and set the liquid aside for future use.

MEAT

Face it, prime meat cuts are going to be a thing of the past in the doomsday world, and you may have to physically source your own. If you are not using meat on the day of the kill, then obviously safe storage is essential, though the 'hanging' of some meats will improve their texture and flavour. However, *heat* is a key enemy of meat, particularly in the hot summer months, though the natural coldness of the winter months can work to your advantage in keeping meat fresh – particularly if there is snow available with which to chill meat.

The table below gives a very rough idea of the keeping times for game and poultry, and even then the meat needs to be in as cold as place as possible during the summer months if a fridge is not available. Be sure to use your nose to smell meat which has been hanging.

Another option that you might like to consider is the construction of a *meat safe* (page 148) which is essentially a cupboard with a tight-fitting door in which meat can be stored away from flies; the walls of the meat safe being made of fine metal mesh, which allows cool air to circulate around the meat but is fine enough to prevent ingress of even the tiniest flies. Metal gauze should be used in preference to cotton muslin or similar as the metalwork can be scrubbed down to clean it. On the other hand, if you could devise a meat safe with cotton walls that could be removed and washed (boiled) from time to time then that would be fine. The key in either case is to prevent flies and bugs getting at the hanging meat, as well as storing in a cool or cold environment. During rainy periods, or where the air is moist, keeping times will be much shorter.

	Summer (days)	Winter (days)
Rabbit	2	4
Hare	3	6
Young Pigeons	2	4
Pheasant	4	10
Duck, Goose, Turkey	2	6
Partridge	2	6 to 8
Chickens	2	4

If you are not a veterinarian, or knowledgeable about animal growth, there's a good chance that you will not be able to tell the age of the animals you acquire in the wild for food. They may well be old, and old meat can be dreadfully tough! One way round this is to *slow-cook* the meat, particularly by stewing gently for many hours. There are also certain cuts of meat, such as the lower leg, neck, and shoulder, which can benefit from the *slow-cook / stewing* regime.

Meat may also be boiled, and although this sounds like a simple task, the method has pitfalls. Don't boil meat furiously, as that will make it tough; although it will do wonders in extracting the gelatine from the bones. Instead, use a regime that gently boils the meat – that *slow-cooking* regime again – starting by placing the meat in cold water and bringing it slowly to the boil, then moving the pot to where the heat of the fire is gentler but can maintain a gentle boil. For fresh lamb work with a boiling time of 15 minutes per 450 gm. Salted meats require at least 20 minutes pound, frequently longer. Never throw away the water in which *fresh* meat has been boiled as it can form the basis of soup or broth, or be used to boil up the next lot of meat. Scoop out any scum that forms on the surface of the cooking liquid.

If you have no oven available then fresh meat, game and poultry may be baked in a heavy iron pot with a lid to cover – those Dutch ovens, as I call them, are great. In such cases begin by searing the surfaces of the meat in a hot frying pan or griddle till the meat has a little colour. The idea here is to retain the meat's natural moisture behind the sealed surface, rather than let it escape and evaporate as the meat is heated in the cooking pot. That is a scenario for a very dry and tough piece of meat. After searing place the meat into the pot with some fat and a little boiling water. Cover with the lid and cook over a moderate heat, frequently removing the lid to baste with the cooking juices in the bottom of the pot.

Broiling and barbecuing is perhaps one of the less successful cooking methods when the age and freshness of an animal is not known. Tough, old, meat frequently gets tougher when cooked in this manner, and would be better stewed as mentioned before, or braised.

If you want to barbecue over a griddle or coals then the coals need to be glowing hot and and producing clear flames. Most fresh meat steaks and chops, cut about and 2 cm thick, take a matter of minutes to cook in such a regime (about 5 to 8 minutes per side). Also, thin cuts of meat are not really suited to this method of cooking as they will dry out quickly.

DONKEY... and HORSE

Horse meat is well known as food in France and Italy, but never let it be said that the humble donkey doesn't get a look-in as a foodstuff too. Around the world you will find donkey burger, donkey stew, and donkey salami for sale. Essentially donkey meat can be used in recipes that call for horse meat, mutton, beef and venison, and benefits from slow-cooking. As with traditional sausage-making with pork gut / intestines, donkey sausages are possible too (see other related intestine recipes that follow), made from cuts of meat you would generally use to make any sausage.

In Italy you might expect to be offered Stracotto d'Asino, donkey stew; cubed donkey meat typically slow-cooked with bay, juniper, tomato and, of course, garlic. Sometimes the meat is marinaded in these overnight. Where the meat is from an older donkey, then long braising with red wine and onions is an option. I am aware that such additional ingredients are unlikely to be available to your doomsday kitchen but the thing is to show you that donkey (and horse) are invaluable food resources for your doomsday kitchen.

Also in Italy, particularly in the Piedmont region, you might be offered Salame D'Asino, donkey salami (in fact for the last few decades they have run an annual donkey salami festival). Formulations vary, but you may well find 50:50 mixtures of donkey and pork meat, while others have 100% donkey meat with some fatty bacon or pork added, plus the inevitable garlic and herbs.

In China donkey burgers are popular, while slow-cooked spiced donkey (8 to 24 hours – so ideal for day-long cooking over the embers of a fire) is served shredded or sliced and popped inside wheat buns as street food, or it can be served with noodles or congee. There's also a dish comprised of donkey kidneys, testicles and penis known as Donkey's Three Treasures. Although I have been unable to track down a recipe for this I am sure that it follows along similar lines to other offal recipes covered in this book, albeit with Chinese flavourings.

I cannot say that I have personally tried donkey, though I have used the meat of its cousin – horse – in France. In my view that tended to be better braised; having first attempted to broil a horse steak as one would do with a beef steak, and found it to be awfully tough. But then I might have been doing something wrong. Incidentally, in Kazakh and Mongolian cultures horse meat is a major food item, along with horse meat sausages.

So now you know, a donkey is not just for kiddies rides along the beach during holidays! It has another purpose in life, your armageddon menu.

GOAT STEW
The structure of bone and muscle positions on a goat carcass is somewhat akin to that of a lamb / sheep, however there is a lot less fat on the animal while goat meat has a different flavour. The absence of large amounts of fat and sub-cutaneous fat to keep the meat moist means that cooking methods for goat meat tend to favour slow-cooking on a low heat, or with plenty of moisture, or retained moisture (in that respect goat meat parallels pheasant), hence *stewed* goat. If the meat is rather gamey then marinate in vinegar and salt prior to use.

Ingredients for this can be very flexible, but as a starting point I suggest that for 2 cups volume of cubed meat, you use one small onion, and two or three tomatoes (assuming they are available), plus ½ clove of garlic if you have some.

Over the fire brown the meat in some fat in a heavy-bottomed pot or Dutch oven. As the meat begins to brown, add the onion and garlic. Stir continuously, and when the onion starts to soften add the tomatoes (quartered or sliced), 2 cups of water or stock, and seasoning. Cover the pan and simmer gently over hot coals for 1½ hours (top up with water as required).

FULL MONTY STEW
I have called this my *full-monty* stew since it contains many of the internal organs of a four-legged animal (goat, donkey, horse, pig, cow), while individual parts are covered in many of the recipes that follow. Check these items for more insight into the preparation of the key animal parts, particularly intestines. However, the key ingredient here is the animal's BLOOD which forms a main component of the sauce.

On the meat side you will need for this: animal intestines, heart, liver, spleen, kidney, tongue, belly meat, and, of course, blood collected at the time of slaughter while there is still blood pressure in the veins. Brain and ears could also be optional additions. Other non-meat items required are water (or stock), fat, onion, mushrooms (optional), and seasoning. You might also like to add oatmeal, pearl barley or even potatoes to thicken the stew and provide carbohydrates, but I suggest in your initial trial of this recipe that these are omitted, since the end result of should have a somewhat thick sauce that you get with squid cooked in their own ink – coating the food rather than running off like a thin gravy.

Begin by taking cleaned intestines and boiling them for 10 to 15 minutes in a small pan of salted water, then remove, drain, and cut into 5 to 7 cm pieces when cool enough to handle, and set aside. Discard the cooking water. Then fry some sliced onion in the pan until it softens. Set aside.

Meanwhile, in a second pan of boiling water, throw in all the other animal parts you are going to use and boil for 10 minutes in just enough water to cover them, removing any scum that forms on the liquid surface. Take off the heat, and remove (1) 2 cups of the cooking liquor which must be allowed to cool, (2) the meat, and (3) half of the remaining cooking water for future use in soups etc., and also to top up the stew as required (remembering that the gravy wants to be thick).

Next, cut all of the meat into fork-sized pieces, and put back into the pot with, the onion, mushrooms (sliced or halved, if using), seasoning, and prepared intestine. Return the pot to your fire. Mix 2 cups of blood with the cooled, reserved, cooking liquor and stir this into the pot [this prevents the blood coagulating into lumps as happens when the blood hits boiling liquor]. Allow to simmer very gently for 1½ to 2 hours, topping up with a little reserved cooking liquor from time to time if the sauce becomes too thick for personal liking.

If you want the stew more brown coloured, then the diced meat can be quickly stir-fried at the beginning until it has some colour, and then used.

MEAT CUTLETS
2 tbsp. dripping / fat
3 tbsp. flour
½ cup meat liquor / stock
1 cup cold cooked meat – finely chopped
1 shallot or small onion – finely chopped
Salt and pepper
1 egg – beaten
Breadcrumbs
Fat / butter for frying

Melt the fat in a pan, then add flour and stir together to ensure a smooth paste. Add hot gravy, stirring into the flour-fat mixture, and boil till the flour is cooked.

Remove the pan from the heat. Next, add the chopped meat and onion, plus some seasoning, and mix well. Turn out the mixture onto a plate and allow it to go cold. Form the mixture into patties, brush each with a little beaten egg, dust with breadcrumbs and then fry in hot fat.

SHEEP OR COW'S BLOOD PUDDING
** To be used as food the blood needs to be drained as soon as the animal is slaughtered, otherwise it tends to congeal and pool in the veins and arteries once the blood pressure drops.

Take the blood of the slaughtered animal, mix with some milk, then add seasoning, suet chopped small, and oatmeal. Mix well, then pour into the prepared intestines of the animal (tie off lengths at both ends according to the size of the puddings you want). Bring a pan of water to the boil, but just before throwing in the raw puddings add a little cold water to the pan (takes the edge of the fierce heat which may split the skins). After a few minutes boiling and the contents of the skins have begun to solidify, prick each of the skins to allow any expanded air to escape.

BLOOD PANCAKES
For these you want equal quantities of blood, milk and flour (wheat, barley or rye), eggs, some onion and seasoning, and fat to fry the pancakes in. [Refer to ** on Blood Pudding recipe above]

    Begin by mixing up a batter of the blood, flour, milk, and beaten egg yolk, then cover and allow it to rest for an hour. Meanwhile, chop some onion very finely and fry till softened. When cool add to the batter, add seasoning, and mix thoroughly. To cook the batter, melt fat in a frying pan and pour in a cupful of the batter at a time, and cook until the pancakes are browned on either side.

SCRAMBLED BLOOD
The background to this is cooking blood a little bit like scrambled egg, except that the blood is not beaten into submission but rather forms what appear to be like soft curds rather than yellow snow.

    This recipe is for pig and lamb's liver, but could be extended to other animals. In a heavy-bottomed pan fry finely minced onion in some fat over fire embers. When totally softened, stir in seasoning and then a ½ to 1 cup of blood (per person), and cook over a moderate-low heat. Rather than stirring rapidly, simply wait for the blood at the edges of the pan to become firm and then push into the centre of the pan with a spatula or wooden spoon. As the firmed up blood is pushed away, uncooked blood will take its place for the process to be repeated until all the blood is cooked. The end result should look more omelette-like than 'bitty'. Serve spoonfuls on unhealthy fried bread. [Refer to ** on Blood Pudding recipe above].

BLOOD FRY-UP
A variation on the above, but using up stale bread offcuts, starts with the same fried minced onion part in the above recipe. Meanwhile, stale bread is soaked in a little milk and beaten egg and then mashed up. Pour the blood into the pan and start to cook as above, then drop spoonfuls of the bread-egg mixture into the cooking blood, a little like dumplings. [Refer to ** on Blood Pudding recipe on the previous page].

BLOOD CAKE
I have inserted this recipe here since we are on a blood *roll*, as it were, though it can equally be made with duck and chicken blood if you have sufficient quantities of that after dispatching a large number, but pig or lamb's blood is fine too. [Refer to ** on Blood Pudding recipe on previous page]. The method for producing this is pretty straightforward...

The blood is allowed to cool down a little so that it begins to thicken up (having added seasoning, and any other flavourings you want), then boiling water is added in the approximate ratio of 1 part blood, to 2 parts boiling water. Once the blood begins to coagulate pour off the water and put the blood into a mould to form a solid (but soft) shape. To prepare the blood cake cut it into cubes and either steam these, or place on skewers, smear with a little fat, and grill over embers.

LIVER CAKES
Essentially this recipe can be used for the livers of any large animal, rather than the small livers of rabbit-size creatures. Calves liver is good, while pig's livers may need to be boiled first if you find their taste too strong.

Chop the liver very finely, along with a couple of slices of fatty, streaky, bacon. Season with pepper and sprinkle over several handfuls of breadcrumbs. Mix everything thoroughly, then stir in a little milk – just enough to moisten the mixture and enable it to be formed into flat (not too thick) patties. Dust the patties in flour and fry in hot fat until browned on each side.

LIVER SAUCE
Trim, wash, and then boil the livers of rabbits or fowls. Remove livers from the pan, reserving the liquid for soup. Chop the livers very finely, almost to a minced paste (with a little parsley wilted in the cooking liquor if you like), and season. Then melt some dripping or butter, and when it boils stir in the liver to make the sauce.

LIVER PUDDING
Grate boiled liver and put in a mixing bowl, along with breadcrumbs, finely chopped bacon, and 2 egg yolks. Mix everything well, then transfer the mixture to a large greased cup, cover with paper, then steam for 30 minutes.

LIVER LOAF
2 cups beef liver
1 cup minced meat
2-3 tbsp. onions - finely chopped
1-2 eggs - beaten
2-3 tbsp. fat (bacon/ham best)
Salt and pepper

Lamb and pig liver can also be used for this. Start by trimming up the liver, slicing into chunks, and then gently boiling in water (the addition of onion and carrot will improve the flavour). When cooked, remove from the pan, drain, and when cool enough to handle chop very finely.

Place the chopped liver (almost minced is better) in a mixing bowl with the minced meat, chopped onion and seasoning. Mix everything well, than add beaten egg a bit at a time until the mixture is moistened with egg (as a binder), but not runny or fluid.

You then have two ways of cooking this:

(1) Grease aluminum foil liberally with fat then make a large sausage of the mixture in the centre of the foil, and then wrap the foil around. Place near hot embers of the fire and cook for 30-40 minutes, turning from time to time to ensure even cooking. Allow to cool a little before removing the foil.

(2) Make into small loaf-like shapes on a baking tray or in an ovenproof dish, brush with the melted fat, and then bake in a hot oven for about 30 minutes, basting from time to time. You can also fry burger-like patties of the mixture.

GAME LIVER / KIDNEY TOASTS
The livers or kidneys from any game or poultry should not be discarded and they can be mashed and added to soup or gravy. But then you might prefer them whole as here... Cut some bacon rashers into strips big enough to wrap each piece of sliced offal (if large - especially kidneys - cut down in size). Add a sprinkling of pepper or cayenne before wrapping up. Broil, barbeque or griddle each bundle for about 5 minutes on each side then serve them on fried toast.

BROILED KIDNEYS
A straightforward way to barbie kidneys over the fire. Cut each kidney length-ways, then skewer them to prevent them curling during cooking. Score the surface with a knife and sprinkle with seasoning before broiling them over a hot clean fire for about 10 to 12 minutes, or until done. Turn them frequently so that they are evenly cooked.

As an alternative, fry them in some fat in a pan. When done, set aside and keep the kidneys warm. Stir a teaspoon or two of flour into the residual pan juices, then add a little warm water to the flour-fat mixture and stir rapidly to make a gravy to serve with the kidneys.

KIDNEY-STUFFED ONIONS
Large onion/s
Minced kidney
Salt and pepper
Gravy

Peel as many onions as required and place in boiling, lightly-salted, water. Reduce the heat to a gentle rolling boil, cover, and parboil for about an hour. Then remove each of the onions with a slotted spoon, take out their centres and stuff with the minced kidney. Place in another pan with some gravy (about 1 cup) and seasoning, cover, and stew slowly for about another hour or until the meat is cooked through and the onions are tender (test with a skewer).

Keep the removed onion centres and cooking juice from parboiling as they can offer other cooking options.... such as a mutton broth incorporating crushed wheat, barley, or oat grains. Or a stuffing when combined with breadcrumbs, sage and seasoning for stuffing duck or goose, or serving alongside pork.

CREAMED KIDNEYS
Lamb kidneys
Onion
Fat / dripping
Barley flour
Milk
Salt and pepper

Having washed the kidneys thoroughly put them into a small pan with just enough water to cover, place over the fire and parboil for 8 to 10 minutes. Meanwhile, mince a little bit of onion, and set aside.

Remove kidneys, blanch in cold water and then trim off any stray bits, slit open to remove the hard centre, and cut into slices. Next, heat some fat in a frying pan and brown the minced onion. Remove the pan from the fire, stir in ½ to 1 tablespoon of barley flour thoroughly so the mixture is quite smooth. Return to the heat, and add milk, a bit at a time, stirring continuously or whisking with a fork so that a smooth sauce develops. Add seasoning, then the sliced kidneys, and simmer gently for 15 to 20 minutes.

STEWED LAMB / DEER TONGUE
Put the tongues in a pan with water and boil for 1½ hours. Then remove the tongues and place in cold water, before removing the skins. Next, fry off a sliced onion (and any other vegetable that you want to use, like sliced carrot or turnip). Sprinkle in a dusting of flour (to provide thickening properties), mix in and cook for a few minutes. Add hot stock to the mixture, stir thoroughly, then add the peeled tongues (sliced if you want) to the pan when boiling, along with seasoning. Cover, and simmer gently for another hour over hot embers.

BARBIED SHEEP'S TONGUES
As in the previous recipe start by parboiling the tongues in a little stock for about 30 to 40 minutes, then skin each tongue. Next, melt some fat (salty bacon fat is best) in a frying pan and fry the tongues gently for a few minutes after adding seasoning, and sprinkling liberally with breadcrumbs on both sides. Finally, broil slowly on a griddle until thoroughly cooked through.

SHEEP'S TONGUES – ROASTED
Parboil lamb's / sheep's tongues as mentioned in the recipe above, then wrap them in fatty bacon slices (or even caul), and further wrap inside aluminium foil, then roast in front of a moderate fire (ie. not blistering hot), making sure to turn them to ensure even cooking. After about 20 minutes, carefully remove the wrapper so as to retain the fat and cooking juices. Baste the tongues with the juice and continue to roast for another 20 to 30 minutes, or until nicely browned.

LAMB'S / SHEEP'S HEART
The concept behind this recipe can be transferred to the hearts of many animals (beef, oxe, calf, deer) though the cooking time will need to be varied according to size of the heart and animal species. Although it is designed for cooking in an oven, a Dutch oven slung over the embers of a fire will also do the job.

Wash the heart/s thoroughly, trim off any pipes or valve flaps, then soak in salted water for 30 minutes. Meanwhile, make a stuffing mixture of breadcrumbs and chopped onion, to which a little seasoning and mixed herbs have been added, and then a splash of milk. Mix everything well together. Dry the hearts then fill the cavities with this stuffing.

If you can lay your hands on some greaseproof paper, tie a piece around the hearts to keep the stuffing in place, or sew or skewer the openings. Melt some fat in a baking dish then bake the hearts, covered, in a slow oven for 1½ hours basting every 20 minutes.

A variation, used for cooking calves' hearts, is to stuff the hearts, brown them in dripping in a heavy-bottomed pan along with carrots and onions, then a little water is added, the pan covered, and everything cooked gently for an hour (checking every now and then that there's enough liquid in the pan, and things are not burning). Simple braised lamb's hearts, suitably seasoned, taste great too!

SHEEP'S / LAMB'S TROTTERS
Calves feet and goat's feet can also be cooked in the following way. Thoroughly scrub, scald and wash the trotters in hot water; removing and wool and all traces of dirt.

Fry some sliced onions and carrots in a deep pan in dripping or suet. When the onions are softened add seasoning. Meanwhile, mix a couple of spoons of flour with the same volume of water and work into a paste (will act as a thickener). Place the trotters in the pan along with just enough water (or stock) to cover them. Bring to the boil, rapidly stir in the flour-water mixture and cook for a few minutes. Cover the pan then move it to a position where it can simmer gently on the fire for 3-plus hours.

When boiling cow-heels as a dish in their own right they should be boiled for five or six hours, or until the bones will slip out. They are then served.

STUFFED SHEEP'S TROTTERS
There are two variations under this heading, but both follow the same principle of stuffing the trotters.

Essentially, boil the trotters in stock until the bones slip easily out. Meanwhile, make a stuffing of minced chicken or other fowl livers, and similar, with a few breadcrumbs. When the trotters are cool enough to handle, remove the bones and fill with the stuffing, dip in melted fat, sprinkle with breadcrumbs, and then cook over the fire in a Dutch oven (or wrap in aluminium foil) and bake gently over the embers.

The other alternative is to boil the trotters to a similar state as above, then fill up the space with fried bread and a few chopped herbs, bake as above, and then serve with a sauce.

BULLOCK / CALF / DEER HEART
Soak the heart in well salted water for an hour. Stuff the hearts (toasted breadcrumbs, suet, minced onion, seasoning, egg yolk), sew up the openings, and then roast them in front of a good fire, regularly basting with dripping or fat. Reckon on 15+ minutes per pound cooking time, but it may take 1½ to 2 hours for a large bullock heart. The hearts should be roasted with the pointed end facing downwards, and cooked till well done. Bullock's heart may also stuffed and then *baked* in a covered dish for 2 to 3 hours, if you have an oven. Left-overs produced by either cooking method can be thinly sliced, and then warmed up with a little gravy and served as another doomsday meal.

VEAL / LAMB LUNG, LIVER AND HEART
Wash all the parts and wipe dry. Stuff the heart (see above) then roast. Meanwhile, parboil the thoroughly washed lungs (save the cooking liquor), then mince them finely with some of the liver. Place in a pan with seasoning, a little bit of minced onion, and some of the lung cooking liquor and then stew for 30 minutes or until the sauce will coat the back of a spoon. Slice the remainder of the liver and fry the pieces (with some bacon if you can obtain). Serve the heart sliced alongside the fried liver, with the lung and liver gravy poured over.

Another way of preparing these body parts is to parboil the heart and lung, mince them, and then stew in a similar manner as above, then serve with the fried liver slices.

LUNG SOUP
Calve's, pig, sheep or a deer lung can be used. Begin by cleaning the lung very well, thoroughly washing out the interior, and cutting away any main bronchial tube remaining, and similar. Dice the lung, then place the pieces in a deep pan along with some sliced carrots and turnips, and enough water to cover everything. Bring to the boil, add some seasoning, then cook at a gently rolling boil for about an hour, from time to time skimming off any scum that forms.

CALVES / LAMB'S LUNGS
Trim the lungs as mentioned above. Dice the lungs, then wash the pieces repeatedly in several changes of water to thoroughly remove any blood. Place in a pan of cold water and bring to the boil and cook for 15 to 20 minutes, then strain and refresh the pieces in cold water. Then place the pieces in a pan with some fat, and heat. Sprinkle in some flour and mix thoroughly, before stirring in hot beef stock or gravy. Stir constantly till the liquid thickens then add seasoning and herbs (garlic, bay, parsley, for example) to taste. Add thinly sliced onion and simmer for half an hour over embers.

LUNG STEW
Lung has a weird feel to it, like a close-grain sponge material. Thoroughly clean out the lung/s then boil in salted water for 25 to 30 minutes. Remove from the pan (keeping the cooking liquor), and when cool enough to handle dice the lung into pieces about the size of small sugar lumps.

Meanwhile, in a deep pan fry off some sliced onion till softened, and also dice a potato or two. Add the diced lung and potato to the pan, add seasoning (and whatever other spices you have available), and add enough of the reserved cooking liquid to cover the ingredients. Place over the fire and simmer until the potatoes are cooked through.

ANOTHER VARIATION
Similar to the above... Boil lung and liver, and then slice up. Add to seasoned vegetables (and whatever other flavourings you can rustle up – chilli is great) which have been partly cooked. Add cooking liquor to the pot, and then some flour mixed with a little water as a thickener. Simmer for about 30 minutes until the vegetables are done, and the sauce thickened.

VARIATION #3
Clean up the lung, cut into slices, then season with salt and pepper. In a heavy-bottomed pot fry the lung pieces in fat till nicely browned, then drench them in flour, and cook for another 2 or 3 minutes. Meanwhile, fry off some chopped onion and bacon, and slice a few mushrooms. Add just enough stock to cover the frying lung pieces, then add the bacon, onion and mushroom. Cover and simmer over the fire for 1 to 1½ hours. For a thicker sauce, remove the cover about two-thirds through cooking.

BRAIN CAKES / RISSOLES
You have probably never thought about eating the brains of animals, but in your doomsday kitchen life is about to 'get real'. Brains are edible food so how can you possibly deny them from your daily food intake? Serious survival existence depends on your ability to put personal squeamish notions aside and get through to the next day, and beyond.

Having removed the brains from the animal's head soak the brains in salted cold water, with a couple of teaspoons of vinegar added, for an hour. Then carefully remove the outer skin membrane and trim off any stray brain stem and nerves, and wash thoroughly. Drop into boiling, salted, water for a few minutes, then remove from the pan and mash the brains up in a bowl along with some seasoning (if you have any other spices available add these now). Next, beat the yolk of an egg then mix this thoroughly into the brain mash. Heat some fat or butter in a frying pan and spoon in the mixture, forming little patties which should be fried on both sides until lightly browned.

BRAIN CAKES – ANOTHER WAY
Having skinned and trimmed up the brain of any stray brain stem (as above), chop it very finely (almost mince). Place in a bowl and add seasoning, a little beaten egg and enough flour to make the mixture begin to stick together. Spoon dollops of the mixture into hot fat and cook as above.

EGGED BRAINS
Brains
1 tbsp. flour
2 eggs
2 tbsp. milk
Fat
Salt and pepper

Similar to the two recipes above, blanch the brains in hot water, remove skin etc., then dice. Next, in a bowl beat the eggs, flour and milk thoroughly then stir in the diced brain pieces. Grease a pan or loaf tin with fat, then pour in the brain batter mixture, and bake for 25 to 30 minutes.

FRIED BRAINS
Calf, sheep, or pig brains can be used. Wash and soak the brains as in the first brain recipe above then cook the brains in boiling water for about 15 minutes and they are firm enough to keep their shape. Then carefully remove the skin and any fibres and nerves that are visible. Then slice the brain into pieces, dip in a light batter and fry.

FRIED BRAINS #2
Somewhat similar to the above. Dust the sliced, cooked, brain with a little flour, then dip each piece into beaten egg, cover with breadcrumbs, and fry till lightly browned on both sides. Serve with a gravy.

BAKED RABBIT / SQUIRREL BRAINS
A method for rabbit and squirrel brains, though no doubt it could be turned to good use in cooking goose and turkey brains too, and to a much lesser extent (because of their small size) chickens, pheasant and duck. All the latter heads can be skinned and boiled in the skull for food.

Remove the skin from the head if not done so during skinning and gutting, then wash out the oral cavity just in case there are some nasty bits of putrefying gunk lurking between the teeth. Open the jaw and push the end of a long, non-toxic, wooden stick inside, and then out through the neck opening. Wedging the stick over very hot embers spit cook the head for 25 to 30 minutes. Allow to cool until hot enough to handle, then break open the soft skull and eat the brain contents. A teaspoon is a handy implement for this.

LAMBS INTESTINES [See NOTE on page 242]
Essentially what we are talking about here are animal parts that would be one of the natural casings used for making sausages in real life. The intestines need to be very thoroughly washed in salted water (having had any contents squeezed out) until they look almost transparent. If you have a water source with pressure behind it (ie. working mains tap) one of the best ways of cleaning out intestines is to pass running water from a hose through the guts.

For this recipe you will need to save the fatty cawl (the fatty membrane that surrounds the guts), as well as have some of the animal's liver. Other stuffing ingredients such as breadcrumbs, hard-boiled egg, and finely minced or pulped onion (to add flavour), will also be an advantage. If you don't use cawl fat, then consider adding pure fat to the stuffing.

Spread out the cawl fat on a flat surface, layer finely sliced liver on this, then smear over a little minced onion, and season. Add any other stuffing ingredients you wish at this stage. Roll up the cawl and stuffing into a thin sausage-like length, cut into pieces about 25 cm long and stuff into the intestine; pushing and squeezing down the tube. If you want to be neat, tie off the ends of the intestine, then wrap each sausage round a stick, and rub a little fat on the intestine exteriors to stop them drying out too much (though internally the cawl will melt to produce a lot of fat). Grill over embers for around 15 to 20 minutes, or until cooked through.

ANOTHER WAY
Since the intestines are many metres long then they can be wound around and between two 15 cm sticks (from non-poisonous varieties of trees!), so that the end result almost looks like a ball of rubber bands. This can then be marinaded

in something flavourful for a few hours, and then the intestine ball either deep-fried or roasted in an oven for an hour or until nicely browned. Where roasting, smear some fat on the intestines. Serve up sliced.

Also consider wrapping lamb's or pig heart, liver and other offal in the intestines and then roasting or baking over the fire. This works really well.

GOAT INTESTINES – STEWED [See NOTE on page 242]
If the thought of green entrails sounds unappealing then perhaps this recipe might not be for you. In fact the green comes from sorrel leaves added to the mixture, and even then they don't really make things day-glow green, but rather look like a herby addition!

Begin by thoroughly washing the small intestines (use a water hose where available), place in a pan and then boil for 10 to 15 minutes. Drain, and when cool enough to handle cut into slices, then set aside. Stir-fry a little garlic, chopped onion, and chopped chilli (assuming available) for 3 or 4 minutes over the fire, then add the sliced intestine, and enough water to submerge the contents of the pan. Simmer for 50 to 60 minutes (adding any extra water as required). Meanwhile, finely chop 2 or 3 handfuls of common sorrel leaves and add to the pan after 30 minutes of cooking time has elapsed. Stir in well.

PIG'S BITS – CAWL ROASTED
Somewhat resembling the lamb's intestines roasting recipe opposite, but not stuffed inside the animal's intestines – which you can hold over to provide your doomsday kitchen with sausage casings. [See NOTE on page 242]

Prepare some pig's liver and sweetbreads and cut up roughly, along with some fat, plus some lean pork meat pieces beaten thinly. Place everything in a bowl and add seasoning and a little minced onion. Mix everything well then wrap sausage-like lengths of the mixture in cawl, fastening each 'sausage' with non-flammable cordage, then slowly roast in front of the fire.

PIG TROTTERS & 'BITS' MINCE
You will need three pans for this, otherwise do it in stages. In one pan boil pig's trotters, with just enough water to cover them, until tender, along with a thick slice of bacon or ham if you wish. The addition of a few peppercorns would improve the flavour if they are available.

In a second pan boil the pig's heart, liver, and lungs (scrupulously cleaned out), until tender. Then remove the parts from the pan and chop them very finely, and place in a third pan with some of the cooking water to make the minced mixture a little fluid, though not soup-like. Add the trotters to this pan when they are tender, and the bacon or ham chopped up. Mix a spoon of fat with the same volume of flour (as a thickener), and add to the pan, along with seasoning. Simmer everything over hot embers for 10 minutes or so, stirring thoroughly so that the thickener is both cooked through and well distributed. Serve up with whatever greens you have, and fried bread.

All the cooking water used in the first stages of this recipe can be reserved for soup, sauces, or gravies, or used to boil up another meat joint.

CALVES HEAD
Wash, and then soak the head in pre-boiled water for an hour. Rub with salt to help remove blood. Once the brains have been removed wash these well and place in a pan of cold water for cooking later. Place the head in a pan of water and allow to come to the boil, before letting it simmer gently for 2 to 3 hours depending on size and if the skin is on (2 hours for skinless, 3 when with the skin). From time to time skim off any scum that forms.

To prepare the brains, scald them with boiling water, and when cool enough to handle remove the skin. Then boil the brains along with a few mixed herbs for about 20 minutes or so, then remove from the pan, chop finely and place in another pan in with a little melted dripping. Add seasoning, stir thoroughly, set aside and keep warm.

When the head is cooked, remove whatever meat possible, and place in a dish. Remove the tongue, skin it, and also place in the dish (cut in pieces if required). Finally, add the chopped brain to the dish, and if necessary give everything a final warm-up before serving with a gravy.

LAMB'S HEAD
Split, skin and wash the head well, particularly the oral cavity. Remove the tongue and wash also. Put the head and tongue in a pan and cover with water. Bring to the boil then simmer for 1½ hours, removing any scum that forms. Root vegetables can also be added during the main cooking phase. Peel the skin off the tongue before serving.

LAMB'S HEAD & NECK / LUNGS / LIVER / HEART
Skin a lamb's head (neck attached if the cauldron is large enough), split up the forehead, then remove the brains and set aside. Remove the eyes (these could be kept and added to the stew 'as a treat'), then clean out the nose / nostrils very thoroughly, rubbing well with salt. Place the cleaned head, plus the heart and lungs on the boil and cook for 60 to 80 minutes.

Remove the head and neck from the pot (reserve the cooking liquor) and dry off before coating with beaten egg, sprinkling breadcrumbs over thickly, and seasoning. Place this in a suitable baking pan in front of the fire to brown nicely, turning it to get an even colouring.

Meanwhile, mince up the heart, lungs and liver, with some seasoning, and a spoon or two of flour as a thickener, and place in a pan with some of the hot cooking liquor. Stir the mixture well then place over the fire and simmer for around 30 minutes to form a thick-ish gravy.

As for the brains, mash these well with a couple of beaten eggs, one or two tablespoons of flour, seasoning, plus a slug of milk to make a batter which is then fried in a similar manner to the *brain cake* and brain fritter recipes previous (see page 265).

SHEEP'S HEART & LUNG MINCE
As a variation on the heart / lung section above... Clean the heart and lung (see pigs lungs details elsewhere) thoroughly, boil them for 30 minutes (reserve the cooking liquor), then mince finely when cool enough to handle. Meanwhile, mix a knob of fat with some flour, throw into a pan with a cup of the cooking liquor. Add in the meats along with some minced or puréed onion and seasoning. Cover the pan and stew gently for 30 minutes over the fire. Add a little more liquor if you want the mince more fluid.

DEER (OR GOAT) HEAD HANGI
Actually, this isn't a hangi in the truest sense of the word, though the method is somewhat akin. Dig a hole a bit larger than the deer head, then light a fire in the pit adding lots of fuel to build up a mass of glowing coals in the hole. Having cleaned the head thoroughly, place it neck end down among the coals (keep half the coals back), then cover with green grass, the reserved coals, then earth. Pat down the earth and then build a fire right on top of the deer-hangi pit, and keep it going for about 6 hours. If you were *organized* time-wise then this ground level fire could be your camp fire for the evening / night so that next morning the head is dug up already cooked.

GOAT HEAD & FEET
Scald the head and feet (ie. trotters) and remove the hairs, scrub the feet well, then place everything in a pot large enough to hold them. Bring to a boil and cook for 10 minutes skimming off any scum that forms, then remove from the pot and discard the cooking water.

Cut the tongue off, and when cool enough to handle remove the skin, and set aside. Remove and discard the teeth from the jaw. Place the meat pieces back in the pan along with a chopped onion. Add enough boiling water to cover the contents of the pan, then bring to a gently simmering boil, cover, and cook for a couple of hours (top up the water as required). Meanwhile, chop four or five large handfuls of sorrel leaves, and set aside.

Next, remove the goat pieces, and strain off the cooking liquor into another container (what you don't use for this recipe can be used later for soup / broth). Discard all the debris in the pan, and place it back over the fire. In a little fat, fry some chopped garlic and onion for a few minutes (and also add any spices / chilli that you like – if you have any available – at this stage).

Then return the goat pieces to the pan and stir-fry for a few minutes, before adding about 2 cups of the cooking liquor, and the chopped sorrel. Bring to the boil, cover, and then simmer for 25 to 30 minutes, or until the meat separates easily from the bones, and then season. Add more of the reserved cooking as required – in my view this is better with a sauce that coats the back of a spoon than a thin gravy.

AWFUL OFFAL OATMEAL PUDDING
Oatmeal
Left-over cooked offal (heart, liver, spleen preferred)
Blood
Milk
Suet – chopped
Onion – finely minced
Sugar or honey (optional)
Salt and pepper

This is to use up parts and cooked left-overs of animals like lamb, goat, pig and oxe, but there's no earthly reason why venison could not be used. I must admit to liking this made with the minced-up remainders of lamb's or ox-heart. In fact this sort of sausage combination hides a multitude of animal parts that many folks would normally balk at, but disguised behind a familiar sausage shape it seems less threatening. The addition of a tiny amount of sweetener can make the final outcome slightly less strong. Remove the spleen membrane before use.

Mix some blood collected during slaughter with a little milk and set to one side. The onion should be almost purée-like in consistence. Prepare and clean sausage skins as mentioned elsewhere among these recipes. Meanwhile, put two or three handfuls of oatmeal in a bowl, and about a handful of chopped suet (it wants to be solid suet as rendered pork fat makes for a sausage filling that is too soft – in my view). Add some seasoning and the minced onion, and then evenly distribute the ingredients with a fork. Next, add the blood-milk mixture a bit at a time until a dough forms that has the consistency of sausage meat (thin or thicken as required with extra blood-milk mixture or oatmeal).

Fill the sausage skin with the mixture and, depending on whether you want small individual sausages, or a long continuous coiled one, tie off the sausage skin as preferred. Drop the blood pudding/s into boiling water and cook for five minutes. Then carefully remove from the cooking pot, place on a work surface and prick with the tines of a fork (allows air to escape during cooking). Return to the pot and continue boiling for half an hour, then remove from the water and hang up to cool – or eat some immediately.

To use cooled sausages re-heat in boiling water for 10 to 15 minutes, or slice and fry, or grill them.

SHEEP'S TONGUE – PRESSED
Take several sheep's or lamb's tongues and remove the root from each. Place in a pan and boil gently for 2 hours. Then remove from the pan, skin the tongues when cool enough to handle, cut into pieces, and place in a suitably-sized bowl along with seasoning. The pieces should fill the bowl slightly proud of its rim.

Add a little of the cooking liquor, then put a plate over the bowl and press down with weights until cool and set.

BEEF / OXE / DEER TONGUE
Soak the tongue in water for a day. Place in a pot over the fire, bring to the boil, and then simmer or boil slowly over embers for 3 to 4 hours. Remove the skin and then slice and fry, or serve with gravy. Batter and breadcrumb them too.

PICKLING TONGUE
Thoroughly wash and scrape the tongue (almost rasp with a stiff brush) then slit the root end of it. Rub thoroughly with heaps of salt, ensuring some penetrates the slit root. Place in a covered dish overnight, and keep in a cool place. Drain off the tongue the next day, and then rub with a powder pickle made of 55 gm each of salt, saltpetre and sugar. Rub absolutely thoroughly, place the tongue back in the emptied dish and sprinkle over any residual pickle powder. Keep in a cool place. As the tongue is not immersed in pickle, it is essential to spoon the liquid pickle that forms over the tongue each day. You might actually want to add a little more salt. In 3 to 4 weeks the tongue can be used.

SMOKED TONGUES
Cut out the roots of the tongues then soak the remaining part in cold water for 3 hours, before scraping (almost rasping) the surface well. Next, rub the tongues well with a mixture of salt and saltpetre, then put them in a non-reactive container which can be sealed, finally sprinkling a handful of the pickle on the tongue before covering. Sprinkle over spices if you have some. After 8 days remove the tongues, attach them to a pole by the tongue tips, and place them up a chimney to dry in the smoke. When you want to use them, wash the tongues, scrape them again, and then cook in stock.

CALVES EARS – STUFFED
Clean, singe, and cook the ears in stock, then allow to cool and stuff – either with a meat or non-meat stuffing. Dip the ears into beaten eggs and roll in breadcrumbs. Repeat this one more time. When ready fry the ears lightly till nicely browned. If the sight of whole ear offends, slice and batter them.

LAMBS EARS AND SORREL
Clean up and singe the ears, then stew them gently till tender. In another pan, place a large handful of sorrel leaves, some fat, a good slug of hot broth or light gravy, and seasoning. Cook for gently for 5 to 10 minutes then serve the sorrel broth with the ears when cooked through.

SHEEP / MUTTON TAILS
Skin, wash, and disgorge the tails of excess blood in warm water. Then fry them off quickly in some fat or dripping, before braising them till tender. Then joint the tails and serve with veggie greens or nettles – a sorrel purée is also good.

ALTERNATIVE #1
Clean the tails as above (joint if you wish), then braise with diced bacon, and sliced carrots, turnips, onion.

ALTERNATIVE #2
Braise tails then let them cool. Dip into beaten egg and then breadcrumbs (or a light flour batter). Repeat once more, then fry till nicely browned.

PIGS TAILS
First singe off all the hair, then braise them with onions, and serve with a pea purée.

SWEETBREADS
Soak the sweetbreads (the pancreas) for an hour in cold, salted, water. Rinse off then parboil for 10 minutes, then refresh in a bowl of cold water, trim off any straggly bits of pipework, and slice. Melt some dripping in a small pan and when hot add the sweetbread. Cover the pan and cook gently for 20 minutes.

FRIED LAMB'S BITS
Take lamb's kidneys (skinned, then split and the white core cut out), sweetbreads (pancreas) and liver. Dredge well with flour, then fry them in hot lard, dripping or fat until lightly browned, then allow to drain before serving.

OX PIZZLE
For pizzle, read penis. One assumes that donkey, sheep and deer pizzles could also be used as alternatives. Perhaps sale of pizzle is outlawed by some EU directive, since it is something that I have not tried myself, nor have I ever seen it for sale in a butcher's giving one the option of trying it. So what follows are a few notes gleaned from reading round the subject, particularly in the world of far eastern culinary delights.

Three key culinary points appear with this ingredient: first, the long white urethral tube <u>must</u> be removed: second, cooking time appears critical – too long and the result is soft and slimy, while rapid boiling and consuming hot makes the texture very chewy; third, that the meat is pretty tasteless and needs lots of flavours added.

There also appear to be three schools of thought in the pre-cooking part of pizzle preparation. One method simply has the washed pizzle placed in a bowl and then boiling water poured over. After a minute or so the pizzle is removed, allowed to cool until hot enough to handle, cut along its length to remove the urethra, and then the inside washed thoroughly.

In a second method the pizzle is skinned first, sliced lengthways to remove the urethral tube, thoroughly washed before the whole thing is soaked in cold water for half an hour, then cooked.

The third method puts scalded pizzle (no mention of urethral removal) in a pan of cold water, brings to the boil, skimming the water as required, then reduces to a simmer and cooks for 3+ hours. In this last case the pizzle is then cut into fork-size pieces and then essentially stir-fried with flavourings.

In option two the pizzle was cut into fork-size pieces, then briefly boiled before being added to a skillet with fried onions and a slug of white wine then braised for two or more hours until done. The first method slow-cooked pizzle pieces for 8 to 10 hours with spices.

COW'S UDDER
Again, this is an ingredient that I have never had the opportunity to explore, but in parts of Europe cow's udder is a traditional dish, either fried or served in a flavoured white sauce.

Gleaning from several sources, it appears the udders are soaked in tepid water for a couple of hours to cleanse them, then boiled in new water until the skin can be removed. They are then further boiled in salted water until they become tender, after which the udders are sliced into long strips, and then either egged, dipped in breadcrumbs (sometimes cheese is added) and fried, or they are stewed.

MY ALL-DAY STEW
Place in a large stewing pan several pounds of beef shin, a calf's foot, and a pig's liver. Add enough water to three-quarters fill the pot and place over a good strong fire. Cover, and bring to the boil (from time to time removing any scum the forms), and add root vegetables of choice – cut into pieces if very large. Boil gently for 3 hours, adding seasoning after 2 hours, then allow to gently simmer for another 3 hours while you do other doomsday kitchen chores.

STEWED TENDON BROTH
A much overlooked item of food are the cartilaginous tendons, the slow braising of which suits cooking over the embers of a fire. Beef or pig's tendon can be used, but perhaps also lamb and deer tendon, though I have no experience of those two. My way of cooking tendon (which are about finger thickness size) is more of a method than a precise recipe.

Wash the tendons, drop into boiling water for a few minutes, then remove. Place in a deep pan with an equal amount of other bits of uncooked beef and meat scraps. Add seasoning, sliced onion, bring to the boil for a few minutes, then reduce to a very gentle simmer, cover, and braise for 4 to 8 or 9 hours. Keep skimming off any scum that forms, and also top up with a little extra hot water from time to time if the liquid starts to reduce in volume too much. Once cooked, remove the tendon pieces, allow to cool until hot enough to handle, cut into 2 to 3 cm pieces, and then return to the pot to warm through again. This stew / broth can take all sorts of flavourings, from traditional mushroom, to spicy Thai, to Chinese soy and anise, and so on. You can also serve it with some shredded boiled cabbage, and a few spuds.

ONE WEEK GRAVY
For this use the large meat scraps of whatever animal has been slaughtered (cattle for a beefy flavoured gravy). Place the pieces in the boiler and cover with water. Boil at a gently rolling boil for an hour or so, then lift out the largest meat chunks, break them up and then cut into smaller pieces to help release the juices. Place everything back in the pan (add an onion and herbs if you have these) and then stew gently over the fire for another couple of hours or until the liquid looks like a nice rich brown gravy. Strain into a holding container and allow to cool. You can scrape off the hardened fat that forms immediately, or leave it in place as a seal for the gravy beneath. If kept in a cool place the gravy will keep a week, much less if the weather is hot.

POTTED HAM
Cut the remains of a boiled ham into small pieces, then pound it to a paste bit by bit, adding a little clarified butter to help keep the paste smooth. Add seasoning to taste. Pot the mixture in small jars or bowls, pressing the mixture down to avoid leaving any pockets of air, then cover the surface with more clarified butter. Sealed tightly and stored away in a cool place this should keep for a few weeks.

CALF'S-FOOT JELLY
Put two calves feet into a large pot with 2½ to 3 litres of water, bring to the boil over the fire, then move the pan to a position where it can simmer for 3 or 4 hours. Keep skimming off any scum that forms. When cooked, filter the liquor through a fine sieve or filter into a bowl, and let it go cold and solidify. Then remove all the solid fat on the top (though you might like to keep the surface fat in place if you don't want to use the jelly immediately). This jelly can be used for making sweet dessert jellies, or savoury recipes in a similar manner to aspic.

DEER / OX MARROW BONE
Any large-boned animal such as a deer, sheep, goat, horse, pig or general farm livestock has the potential for large-scale extraction and use of the bone marrow. Smaller animals (rabbits) and birds also have marrow in their bones but in small quantities that are really only extracted once the bones have been crushed and then the fat cooked out in boiling water.

Generally speaking the most easily processed bones of the quadrupeds mentioned are the leg bones, which should be cut into 5 to 7 cm lengths for simplicity if you want to extract the marrow, otherwise you will need to dig out the bone marrow with a long spoon or other similar implement. Another option is to simply throw the sawn bone pieces into a stew, soup or broth and cook till the marrow has melted out.

There are two options for preparing the marrow as food – cooked in the bone, or extracted first. If cooking in the bone, stand the bone pieces on one end in a Dutch oven (put the wider end of the bone down so they don't tip over), cover and then bake over the fire for 15 to 20 minutes, or until there is no pink or redness left. The bone pieces may also be cooked on their side, but the contents will ooze out. In the old days cooks would seal up both ends of the bone pieces with a thin layer of pastry and then bake them. Serve the baked marrow on toasted bread.

The second method of preparing the marrow is to soak the pieces in cold water for an hour or so to remove blood impurities then to push the marrow out with a finger or other implement. Actually, soaking them in warm water makes the extraction slightly easier. The marrow may then be baked as before, but for a shorter time since there's no bone material involved. The fats, however, will ooze everywhere in your cooking pot. The extracted marrow may also be poached in water.

ROAST RABBIT
Gut (keep the liver and kidneys), skin, and prepare your rabbit. Take the liver and kidneys and parboil with a little bacon or ham, then chop these up finely, add a handful or two of breadcrumbs, some seasoning, and a little finely chopped onion. Mix well, stuff the rabbit with the mixture, then sew the cavity up with natural cordage or string. Rub the rabbit with fat or dripping, then roast on a spit in front of your fire for 1 to 1½ hours. Have a roasting tray with a small amount of water and a knob of dripping set beneath the roast, and baste frequently. A hare can be treated in exactly the same way, though you may like to save the blood to add to the gravy, or bake small blood patties with ingredients similar to those used in making black pudding.

BOILING RABBIT TIP
The secret to an edible boiled rabbit is long cooking; cooking for a couple of hours till the meat comes away easily from the bones. Although a single boiled carcass will be cooked through within an hour it has the body elasticity and tenderness of a rubber duck. Cook longer till the meat separates from the bones.

SALTING BEEF
For a 4½ kilo piece of lean meat you will need salt, plus a preserving mixture of ½ cup sugar, ½ cup salt and 14 gm of saltpetre for the brining part.

Put the meat on a tray, sprinkle all over with salt, and leave it for 24 hours (place a cover over it to protect against flies, but make sure the cover doesn't touch the meat). Then hang the meat up to drain. Rub the previously prepared preserving mixture into meat, massaging it into any folds, creases or gaps in the surface of the meat. Tip out any liquid contents of the tray and lay the meat in it, again cover and place in a fly-free zone. Rub the preserving mixture into the flesh each day. It will be ready for use in about 10 days (but can be kept longer), at which point boil the meat very slowly, and when cooked allow to remain standing in the cooking pot to relax for 30 minutes.

If the piece of meat has bones in it then these are best removed prior to salting, particularly any bone joint or knuckle. These contain watery synovial fluids which can break down and decay and so contaminate the rest of the salted meat. Where a bone has been removed, make sure to salt the cavity well.

COW'S (& OTHER QUADRUPED) STOMACH / TRIPE

Imagine, if you will, one of those shaggy cotton bathmats that has been doused in a dark green dye, clammy and damp, and smelling like a drain. Well that is what the stomach of a cow, or most other ruminating herbivores, looks like before it is transmuted into *tripe*. Raw stomach is dark grass green on the inside and after thorough washing for several hours still doesn't look too great. The next stage is to boil the stomach gently for a couple of hours, or even longer, which gets rid of more green and the end product has a beige colour with a hint of green. Commercial operators then bleach the stomachs to look bright white, which is what you may see for sale in butchers. Personally I am not a great fan of plain tripe in its white, gelatinous, form, but when fried or strong flavours are added then it's a perfectly okay foodstuff. There are two or three main grades of tripe, depending upon which part of the stomach they come from, the most prized being honeycomb tripe.

The stomach of virtually any ruminant quadruped should be equally usable as tripe – goat, donkey, lamb, for example. Indeed, lamb tripe gently simmered with herbs and flavourings I think is much more delicate than bovine tripe.

BAKED TRIPE

Cut the tripe into squares 7 to 10 cm across. Next, make a batter of breadcrumbs, seasoning, and a couple of egg yolks. Spread some of the mixture on one side of each piece of tripe, then roll up like a Swiss roll, and either secure from unravelling either with small sticks pushed through, or natural cordage. Smother with melted fat and then bake for 60 to 90 minutes – they want to be nicely cooked through while getting a good 'eat-me' brown colour. From time to time baste the pieces with more fat.

DEEP-FRIED TRIPE

This is one of my preferred ways of eating tripe, since the crisp batter adds texture to counter-point the naturally squidgy texture of the tripe, while there is the opportunity to add flavourings (Thai-style in peacetime, for example). Depending on your preferences, either cut the tripe into fork-size pieces, or slice into 7 to 10 cm lengths, and about 1 cm wide. Meanwhile, beat an egg, and prepare breadcrumbs. Simply egg the pieces, dip into breadcrumbs, repeat a second time, then drop the pieces into hot fat and fry till golden brown.

ROASTED TRIPE
A very similar recipe to the one above. Spread an oblong piece of tripe with a stuffing made of breadcrumbs bound together with beaten egg and seasoned. Roll up the tripe and fix with natural cordage. Roast or bake for 60 to 90 minutes and serve sliced in pieces with gravy. One thing that I still have on my 'to do' test list is stuffing tripe with chopped liver, which I think would give the tripe a flavour lift.

TRIPE FRITTERS
On the pretext that many unpleasant things fried golden brown can appear inviting, try this with your tripe...

Chop the tripe small, and place in a bowl with some seasoning. Then make up a thick flour, egg and milk frying batter and stir into the chopped tripe a bit at a time. The consistency of the mixture wants to be an oozy flow, rather than fluid or stiff. Fry off spoonfuls of the mixture until nicely browned, then serve.

DUFFLE-BAG SPLEEN
What on earth can this be all about you must be wondering? Well to begin with remove the membrane from the spleen – unless you decide that it is to your advantage to keep it in place to maintain the integrity of the meat shape. The problem is that the cooked membrane gets pretty tough, hence its removal. Place the spleen flat on a work surface and cut off the pointy part, but keep it. Next, make an incision in the meat which looks like an inverted 'T'; cutting straight down half way through the spleen and then making lateral cuts on either side of the first cut... just like an inverted T and then fill the cavity with a stuffing of choice (a bit like opening and filling a duffle bag). If a bit over-stuffed suture with natural cordage. Smear with oil of fat and bake covered for 25 to 45 minutes depending on spleen size.

Pork and goat spleen work well the Indian spices (if available to you), while my own feeling with lamb spleen is that it is perhaps better with more sauce-like and onion flavourings, as well as being stuffed with spiced minced meat. For the narrow pointy bit of spongy spleen that you cut off mash it up and make an alternative pâté with it.

ACORN MEATLOAF
Mix 1 cup of almost dry acorn mush with ½ cup of minced meat, 1 or 2 handfuls of breadcrumbs, a beaten egg, 1 tablespoon of puréed onion, some seasoning, and a spot of mustard (optional). Turn the mixture in a loaf tin, or form a thick sausage shape and wrap in aluminium foil, then bake in a preheated oven or Dutch oven for 45 to 50 minutes.

REMEMBER – the key to preserving food is to deny bacteria a moist and oxygen-rich environment where they can thrive, using either SALT, VINEGAR, & SUGAR / HONEY as the preservative to deny those conditions. Regarding preserved foods, read the section on BOTULISM on page 224.

FISH

To a certain extent I think the simple cooking of fish (fried, broiled, or boiled) is really within the grasp of most folks so the number or recipes in this section is much reduced; merely providing information on a couple of items plus some alternative ways of using fish.

In a fish that is fresh the gills should be red, the eyes bright and plump, and the whole fish stiff. Pale gills, sunken eyes, and flabbiness indicate a fish in bad condition. Also, a finger pressed against the flesh of a fresh fish will leave little or no permanent impression.

Fish should be cleaned properly before being prepared for the recipe, and the cavity well flushed out with water post-gutting.

Where the fish is to be boiled then it should be placed into the cooking pot with cold or tepid water. And although a fish should be cooked well it needs to be done gently at first, otherwise the outside is likely to break before the inside is cooked through. A little salt, plus a spot of vinegar (if available) to provide firmness to the flesh, should be added to the cooking water. Once cooked (the meat should flake off the bones easily), the fish should be removed from the water as soon as it is done, otherwise the quality tends to deteriorate.

In the absence of a fish slice, or a cooking vessel with a removable fish plate for lifting the fish as in domestic-goddess cooking, you could improvise by constructing a fish-lifter out of some wire netting and then lay your fish on this to be cooked in the pot. Another alternative to stop the fish breaking up as it is lifted is to lay the fish to be cooked on a piece of cotton, or other non-synthetic, material.

Freshwater fish with a muddy taste can be soaked after being cleaned up with lots of salt and water. The very smallest fish, such as whitebait, minnows, or sticklebacks, can be deep-fried in plenty of fat without gutting (having previously dusted them with flour), or egged and dusted with breadcrumbs then fried. Where a larger fish is to be fried (or broiled) wipe it dry and season before placing in a heavy-bottomed frying pan containing hot fat or dripping, and fry briskly. It's a good idea to keep the fat used for cooking fish separate from that used for frying other foodstuffs, to prevent everything getting a *fishy* taste.

PLANKED FISH
This is a very simple way of cooking a fish beside an open fire. After gutting the fish thoroughly, remove the head and tail, then split it down the back and flatten out on a plank with the *skin side down*. Fasten the fish to the plank with cordage, or improvised pegs, sprinkle with salt and pepper and rub with some melted fat (butter preferred). Stand the plank almost vertically upright close to the fire and simply let the fish cook until done.

FRIED EELS
Wash the eels, remove head, tail and skin (don't throw away as they can be used to make a stock for a soup). Cut the eel into pieces about 5 to 7 cm long, open the pieces out (almost like spatchcocking), then sprinkle salt on both sides. Leave the pieces for 30 minutes, then dry off, flour lightly, and fry in hot fat.

STEWED EELS
Prepare the eel pieces as above and place them in hot salted water for 30 minutes. Meanwhile, prepare the sauce that the eels will be cooked in by putting the head and tail trimmings and a sliced onion in a small pan with enough water to cover them. Bring to the boil, simmer for at least 30 minutes, then strain and keep the liquor warm.

Next, melt a large knob of butter in a saucepan and add about the same amount of flour. Stir to provide a smooth mixture, then pour the warm strained liquid over this mixture, whisk in, and bring to the boil. Remove the eel pieces from the salted water, drain them, and add to the pan. Stew the pieces gently for about an hour. When tender add a good slug of milk, season with a little pepper, and add more salt if required.

SORREL-STEWED EELS
Take a small skinned and cleaned eel, cut into lengths 7 to 10 cm long. Meanwhile, shred a large handful of sorrel and place in the bottom of a cooking pot. Add the pieces of eel, a bit of minced or very finely chopped onion if you can, and then 1 cup of water. Cover the pan and simmer on embers for 30 to 40 minutes. Giving the pan a shake from time to time, and checking there is still some water in the pan.

The sorrel here helps counteract the somewhat oily nature of eel meat. Another way of tackling that is to gently boil pieces of eel to release some of the oils, and then eat the meat.

FISH PUDDING
1 cup cooked fish
3 tbsp. breadcrumbs
2 tbsp. fat (butter preferred)
1 egg
½-1 cup milk
Salt and pepper

Choose a mould or pudding basin to suit the size of your fish, and then grease it. Next, flake the fish and mix with breadcrumbs in a bowl and add seasoning. Put the milk in a pan, place over a medium heat, and add the butter to melt. Pour this butter-milk mixture over the fish-bread mixture in your bowl and combine thoroughly. Allow to cool a little, then beat the egg and add to the bowl. Mix thoroughly, and then turn out into the greased mould. Cover with greased paper then steam until the pudding is firm to the touch.

FISH MOULD
This is similar in principle to the above, but another alternative. To a cup of finely chopped (boneless) fish leftovers, add one beaten egg white and ½ cup of thick white sauce. Mix and place in a greased mould or cup and boil in a pan of hot water for 25-ish minutes or until firm.

FISH CUSTARD
This is also somewhat similar in outcome to the two recipes above, and again could be used to take care of any fish scraps. Flaked fish is put into a mixing bowl, and then the custard mixture (1 dessertspoon flour, 1 tsp. melted butter, a beaten egg, and half a cup of milk) added. Transfer to a dish or cooking pot of suitable size and cook in a Dutch oven for about 30 minutes, or steam in a similar manner as the fish pudding recipe previous.

FLATFISH CUSTARD ON TOAST
Boil the fish, skin, and then separate the flesh from the bones. Next, melt a knob or two of fat and stir in an equivalent volume of plain flour, then whisk in warm milk bit by bit until a cream-like consistency is reached. Add the flaked fish to this sauce, season to taste, and put back over the fire until it the mixture just boils, then set the pan to one side but keep warm. Meanwhile, fry some thinly sliced bread until nicely browned, then spread the fish mixture over this and serve. A slight variation on this is to slightly under-fry the bread to a light brown, cover with the fish sauce, sprinkle liberally with breadcrumbs, and then bake the slices in a Dutch oven (obviously a large one is required for a group of people, so that method might not be practical).

FISH CAKES
Flake the meat of a cooked fish from the bones (make sure to remove any residual bones too). Place the pieces in a bowl with cold mashed potato. Add a little minced onion (almost to a purée), seasoning, and mix thoroughly. Beat an egg and stir into the mixture – adding breadcrumbs if required to stiffen the mixture, or a little milk if it is too stiff. Form into patties or balls and fry in fat or dripping.

FISH-POTATO CHOWDER
Potato – cubed
Onion – minced
Fish
Fat / dripping
Water / milk
Flour
Salt and pepper

Chowder is more traditionally made with sweet corn, but it is doubtful that exports of that would be available in a post-disaster world. A sort of equivalent stew is possible using spuds, varying the ingredient mix to taste.

Begin by softening a little onion in some fat. Clean the potatoes and cut into 1 cm cubes then add these to the onion, along with fish cut into fork-sized pieces. Using 50:50 milk and water, add enough liquid to cover the ingredients in the pan, and some seasoning. Place over the fire and simmer for 15 to 20 minutes or until the potato is almost tender. Mix a little flour with some milk to a batter-like consistency then add this to the pot. Cook till the liquid has thickened up. A little parsley might be a luxury addition to complement the fish.

STEAMED FISH
Steamed fish can be particularly full of flavour and nutrition if a suitable cooking vessel is used that can retain the cooking juices. Clean the fish well and sprinkle it inside with some minced sorrel leaves (shredded or chopped is fine too). Place on a buttered / greased dish, cover with buttered or greased paper (to prevent pan condensate from dripping on it) and place in a suitably sized pan or steamer. Allow to cook until the flesh readily flakes away from the bone. The liquor found in the dish can either be added to an accompanying sauce, or reduced further and served alongside the fish in its own right.

STUFFED MACKEREL
This is really a variation on the above. Gut the mackerel but leave the head and tail on, then fill the cavity with finely chopped mussel, oyster or scallop meat that has been previously cooked, plus a handful (or two) of shredded sorrel. Sew or bind up the cavity and then bake or grill over the fire until done, making sure that the fish is placed at an angle so that the yummy cooking juices in the cavity do not run out.

KIPPERED SALMON
Place the fish on its side, make a small incision with the tip of a knife at the tail end, making sure not to puncture the belly by inserting the knife too far. Unzip the fish and remove every piece of gut and visible blood, then remove the head, cutting it off behind the gills. Wash the fish thoroughly, roughly pat dry, lay flat on a board, then sprinkle a handful of sugar in the cavity followed by a bigger handful, or two, of salt. Cover with a cloth and let it pickle in a cool, dry, place for thirty-six hours. If the weather is sunny expose the kipper to the sun and dry air for a couple of hours to accelerate the curing process. After 36 hours the kipper should be drying out, but it will keep a considerable time.

DRIED SALMON
Gut the fish thoroughly, scald it with boiling water, then rub the whole fish well with salt, and hang up for 24-hours to drain. Meanwhile, mix 85 to 100 gm of powdered saltpetre with 55 gm each of salt and sugar. Rub this mixture well into the salmon, then place the fish on a dish for 2 days. Rub it again with more salt, and leave for another 24 hours, after which it will be ready to dry. Drain the fish, wipe off excess salt and liquid, butterfly with a couple of previously scalded (ie. sterilized) sticks to keep it spread open, then hang in the chimney of a wood fire to smoke. To cook, broil the dried fish.

SALMON 'LOAF'
You want about two cups of cooked, flaked, salmon to 2 cups volume of mashed potatoes for this. With its' 30-ish minute cooking time this could be cooked alongside something else in your doomsday kitchen oven, but not with bread loaves since those need an uninterrupted heat of a much longer duration.

Grease a basin or loaf tin then coat the sides with toasted (or browned by lightly frying) breadcrumbs – or use plain biscuit crumbs, holding some crumbs back. Next, line the sides and bottom with mashed potato, also holding some back. Season the flaked fish, then fill the mould, add more crumbs and potato to the top, and then place in a moderately-hot oven to bake for about 30 minutes. In a civilised world you might have turned this out on a plate to serve, accompanied by a sauce.

PRESERVING MACKEREL
When (or perhaps IF) you find yourself with a glut of mackerel on your hands, then consider preserving some for later use. Select the best fresh fish, gut and clean thoroughly. Then either briefly place them in boiling water (very much like blanching spinach) or lightly fry. Next, remove the head, tail, and skin, then divide and remove the bones and backbone. Rub the flesh thickly all over with salt seasoned with a little pepper. Layer the fish pieces into a non-reactive container, then cover with a strong vinegar and seal. For long-term storage top with a layer of melted clarified fat or butter. The fish should keep several weeks, maybe months.

ANOTHER WAY
Fillet the mackerel, dry the fillets off then rub salt well into the flesh. Fry the fillets in clarified fat, then allow to drain on something absorbant. When cold put them into a container, cover with vinegar, and then pour on a layer of oil to seal. This will keep some time.

STEWED OYSTERS
If you don't like the experience of eating raw oysters then you can lightly cook them. When you open them preserve the liquor and strain it; wash the grit from the oysters, and simmer very gently in their liquor. In a non-doomsday world serve with pepper, cream and butter sauce, with crackers or bits of bread. If the oyster is cooked enough it plumps up slightly and the edges begin to curl.

PAN-FRIED OYSTERS
Having shucked the oysters, feel each one over to ensure there are no shell particles sticking to them. Melt some fat in a pan, pop the oysters in and then gently stir-fry until the edges begin to curl. Nice when served with toast. Another avenue open to you if you are dealing with squeamish eaters would be to batter and fry the oysters, or try the next recipe.

OYSTER SAUSAGES
Where you have folks who find the visual look of oysters rather unappealing then transform the shellfish into a sausage shape. Wash and clean 2 cups of shelled oysters then quickly stir-fry in a tiny amount of fat till they firm up. Take the oysters out of the pan and chop them finely and place in a bowl. To every 2 cups of oysters add 2 cups of breadcrumbs, two eggs, and some seasoning. Mix together thoroughly and leave to firm up for 2 or 3 hours, then form into individual sausage shapes, flour them, and then fry in fat until nicely browned.

SHELL-BAKED OYSTERS
This is something of a variation on the above, again for folks who find oysters visually offputting. Physically prepare some oysters as described above then mash with breadcrumbs, add some seasoning, and then beaten egg white in the proportion of 1 white to 1 cup of whole oysters used. Fold the egg white in, then spoon into the oyster shells, and bake in an oven until nearly brown.

ROASTED OYSTERS
Clean the oysters then cook them in the shells over the hot embers of your fire. They will take about 6 to 8 minutes.

BAKED FISH WITHOUT AN OVEN
Seasoned outdoors' folks will be familiar with the principles behind clambakes and hangis, and I don't want to go through that since the subject is covered extensively in survival books and on the internet. However, I saw this little variation on that theme while out on exercise participating in SERE instructor training. It is designed for baking *small* fish when you have no pan available. One might suggest that you could simply grill fish over that very same fire and avoid the labour of making the 'mini hangi', as I term it. That, however, might not be practicable for whatever reason, and this process allows you the flexibility to leave the cooking food unattended for hours without any fear of it burning, while you forage for water or fuel, or do whatever else is necessary to secure creature comforts around your doomsday kitchen.

Dig a hole in the ground about 30 cm deep and large enough to contain the fish without them touching the walls of the hole, while keeping whole the first earth sod that you cut from the ground. Line the bottom of the hole with a layer of stout dry twigs to act as bottom insulation. Prepare also: (1) 4 or 5 stout twigs from a non-toxic shrub or tree (the number will depend on fish length) and (2), a piece of hessian or cotton-type material soaked in water and slightly larger than the area of the dug hole.

Meanwhile, have some igneous (not sedimentary) type stones heating up in a really hot fire. When heated to virtually glowing (water sprinkled on them should sizzle and form beads) *very carefully* transfer these rocks to your hole in the ground placing them on the raft of twigs. Cover the stones with a shallow bed of non-toxic foliage (grass or dock leaves, for example), and then place your gutted fish wrapped in more leaves on top of this. A few centimetres above the fish create a shelf that spans the hole with your 4 or 5 selected twigs in step 1. Cover this with the wet hessian from step 2 (green grass will also do), and then carefully insert the sod of earth over this and gently tamp down. With some of the soil dug from the ground seal any gaps around the edge of the sod so that no heat escapes. Simply leave the fish to cook while you go and do your other chores. The fish cannot burn since the heat inside the cooker diminishes over time, but is hot enough to cook the fish flesh.

COOKING BIVALVES
Most bivalves (razor clams, clams, gapers, mussels and so on) can be cooked along similar basic principles, amending cooking time depending on the size of the individual bivalves and the bulk of shellfish to be cooked. In the world or *real* cuisine chefs obviously add all sort of flavourings and buttery sauces that will not be available to the doomsday cook.

To begin with wash the shellfish to remove as much sand and grit as possible. Then place in a cooking pot with a little water and place on the fire till the water just boils and the shells open (discard unopened ones). Once cooked, remove the fish from the shells in readiness for the next stage – in which the fish may be fried (sometimes breadcrumbed), cooked in a flavoured sauce, or put in a soup or pottage. A general problem with cooking bivalves in my view is that it if they are rapid-boiled then they tend to take on the consistency of rubber grommets, and then the only feasible way of making them half edible is a long slow cook, as in a soup, or stewed with seasoning, or use them as grommets.

Cockles are excellent with bacon or ham, or fried with oatmeal and chives, or just in oatmeal alone.

BIVALVE FRITTERS
Let's say your efforts at steaming bivalves have turned out rubber grommet-like, and are chewy. You may be able to save the day with the following further cooking method:

Mince or finely chop the cooked shellfish, and set aside. Then make up a flour and milk batter, adding a separated beaten yolk or two to the mixture (depending on the amount of shellfish). Next, beat the egg whites and set aside. Stir the chopped fish into the batter, and then fold in the egg white. Have some hot fat in a frying pan and drop spoonfuls of the mixture into the fat. Cook until nicely browned.

PICKLING FISH
To pickle any freshly caught fish, start by cleaning, gutting (also removing the bloodline) and scaling them, before washing thoroughly and then wiping dry. Slice each fish into pieces 2 to 5 cm thick, place these in glass jars with salt (1 tbsp. per jar), and then fill with hot strong vinegar. Additional pickling spices or flavours such as horseradish, pepper or allspice will add extra to the flavour.

Then cover the jars loosely with their lids, and place in a warm oven for a few hours, or place close to a fire. After the jars have warmed up tighten the seals, remove from the heat, and store away when cool. The pickled fish should keep for a week or two if stored in a cool place.

VARIATION
Having prepared, dried off, and sliced white fish into pieces, layer the fish with salt in a sealed, non-reactive, container, and allow to remain for a week. Then prepare a strong brine, drain the fish from the accumulated brine in the container, and then pour in the new brine and reseal. The fish should keep for several months. To use the fish, soak in water to extract the salt prior to cooking.

FISH FLOUR
Once a widely used soup ingredient for indigenous Arctic peoples fish flour is something that I have neither made nor had the opportunity to try, but for the doomsday cook it would make sense to attempt this if there were a glut of fish caught. Industrially, fish meal (as used for feeding livestock) is made by cooking, pressing, drying and then grinding fish guts and remnants. Almost certainly such a complex method would not have been used by Arctic peoples who, presumably, simply dried filleted fish in the cold Arctic air on sunny days, and then ground it into a powder. The industrial product will keep for up to six months, but how long a home-made fish flour would keep without spoiling will be dependent on how dry it can be made. One also presumes that oily fish such as salmon or mackerel would not have been used in the 'old' process since the oils would almost certainly have retarded the drying process and potentially gone rancid with keeping.

SHARK LIVER
If you happen to catch a small-ish shark while fishing or trapping in shallows then this presents another culinary opportunity for the doomsday chef. Shark steaks, cut across the body in the same way as salmon, and about 2 cm thick, make a lovely meaty meal when baked with oil drizzled over (or fat) and seasoned with pepper.

However, do not neglect the brains and cook those, and also the intestines cleaned and deep-fried – in essence a fish tripe, exactly the same as fried cod tripe. And then there's the liver... these will not be colossal on a small shark, but when gently fried (with a bit of seasoning if you have some) make a brilliant alternative to the livers from farm livestock.

> **If any home-preserved item exhibits gassy bubbles or froth, or a bad smell, then botulin may be present and the item should be discarded. So, use your eyes and nose to check any preserved foods before using them. Regarding preserved foods, read the section on BOTULISM on page 224.**

POULTRY AND GAME FOWL

BEAN CAN PIGEON
The idea of this recipe is to be able to cook up a pigeon if (a) you don't fancy the effort of boiling or roasting the bird over the fire, or (b) you don't trust the water quality enough to have the food cooked in that water.

Skin and gut the pigeon, but keep the liver. Have a small pot of water on the boil and drop the liver into this to cook for a couple of minutes (alternatively, lightly fry). Fish the liver out, place in a bowl and mash into a paste with a fork. Add seasoning, a hard-boiled egg mashed up, a good handful of breadcrumbs, and a little fat. Mix these together with a little raw beaten egg then stuff the inside of the pigeon, and close up. Season the pigeon, then push inside the bean can, and place in a pan of cold water over the fire. Cover the can with a flat stone or brick to prevent water getting in, and weigh the can down. Boil for 1 to 2 hours or until done. When done, take pigeon out of the can, throw in a little fat and flour mixed together to make a thickened gravy from the juices in the bottom of the can, and serve with the pigeon.

STEWED PIGEON
1 pigeon
1 cup stock
1 small onion
1 rasher of bacon
Salt and pepper
2 tbsp. fat or dripping
2 tbsp. flour

Pluck and gut the pigeon and put in a pan with the stock, sliced onion and carrot, bacon and seasoning. Cover the pan and simmer slowly over embers or a gentle fire for about one hour. About ten minutes before serving mix the dripping and flour together with a little water to a cream-like consistency then stir into the pan. Bring to the boil up for about five minutes to cook the flour through.

ROAST PIGEON
Pluck and gut the bird, then truss the legs. Make a stuffing of the liver chopped up and mixed with breadcrumbs, seasoning, a little fat and fill the cavity with this. Skewer and roast the birds for 30 to 40 minutes, basting them often with fat.

ROASTING GOOSE
Take a dressed and prepared goose and fill the cavity with a stuffing made of onion (parboiled prior to chopping finely), breadcrumbs, seasoning, and sage leaves if available to you. Get the fire burning clean and bright, place the goose on a spit about 45 cm from the fire (see section on cooking with open fires – page 183) with a drip-tray beneath containing a little water and knob of fat. Pin a couple of large dock leaves over the breast bone (thick paper or foil would

be used in the real world). Move the bird towards the fire as it roasts, removing the dock leaves for the last part of cooking. Make sure to baste the goose often using the liquid in the drip-tray.

FRIED GOOSE / DUCK GIZZARD & LIVER
This recipe can also be done with chicken too!

Prepare the gizzards as per page GIZZARD & NECK SOUP on page 248, then cut into four or five pieces, and place in a bowl to marinade (for example, with onion and mushrooms, or spring onion and ginger, or sugar and vinegar for a sweet and sour flavour combination) for 15 to 20 minutes.

Meanwhile, parboil the goose liver, having made sure to remove the gall bladder without breaking it. Don't overcook the liver; it should still be slightly soft to the touch, not firm. Remove from the pan, drain, and then slice and keep warm.

Melt some fat (duck or goose if available) until it starts to smoke, then stir-fry the gizzard and liver for 2 to 3 minutes, adding a slug of the marinade.

ALTERNATIVE
Lay the livers in milk for an hour or so then dry, slice, dip in beaten egg and then breadcrumbs, and then fry for a few minutes.

GOOSE SAUSAGE
This can be prepared either by casing the chopped meat in the goose guts as you would do for a traditional sausage, or it can be cooked in the tough outer skin of the goose's neck, once it has been plucked and singed, the windpipe removed, and then the filling tied inside with cordage. If using the gut then this needs to have been properly cleaned as you would do when preparing the intestines from any other animal. Although I have not tried the 'neck option' with other birds like duck and chicken, that ought to be a possibility too.

Make a mince that is made from a third each in quantity of goose meat, lean pork, and fatty bacon, plus seasoning. Stuff the intestine or neck (in the latter case sew the ends up post-filling) and roast or bake.

GIBLET SAUCE
Don't throw away livers, lungs, gizzards, and hearts of fowl and gamefowl. Use them. Place all of these cleaned parts in a small pan and boil them gently until very tender, then chop finely. Reduce down the liquor in which they were boiled, then return the chopped pieces to the pan along with a little clarified butter and some seasoning. Stir the mixture well and serve with the roasted fowl. For a thicker sauce add in the yolk of an egg or two along with the clarified butter, then cook through until the sauce thickens.

Just for your information, across Europe there are many traditional flavour combinations for cooking giblets: apples and red currants, or mixed with steamed fruits such as plums, cherries and pears, and even with potatoes and sprouts. Hope that gives you a bit of inspiration.

GIBLET PIE
This recipe rather assumes that you have the option of using an oven, but the cooking method could be altered quite easily to turn it into a *boiled* suet pudding type of dish.

You will need the giblets of a goose or two ducks (more if you like), a ½ kilo of cubed steak meat, an onion or two (sliced), seasoning and suet pastry.

Wash the giblets and place them with the steak in a heavy-bottomed pan with enough cold water to just cover them. As the water begins to simmer add the onion, plus seasoning / herbs. Cook gently for 1½ to 2 hours, then remove any woody herbs used, and let the meat and giblets get cold. Meanwhile, line a pie dish with suet pastry and then fill with the meat mixture, add more seasoning if required, then add the gravy from cooking the meats (reduce if too thin and watery). Cover the pie with a pastry top (see Bread, Biscuit & Baking section) and then bake in an oven for about an hour, or until the crust is browned.

BOILED DUCK
If you want to boil a duck because you don't have the means of roasting one then salt the dressed bird for a couple of days, wrap in a natural fibre cloth, place in a pan of water, and then boil gently over the fire until done. You don't have to use a cloth but it will hold the bird together in one piece as it cooks. Good served with an onion-based sauce. If the cooking water has reduced a lot, then you may be able to use if for onward use in a broth or soup, while allowing it to cool down may allow the harvesting of some *topfat* that forms on the surface of the cooled liquid, duck being quite a fatty bird.

ROOK PIE
I cannot say that I have tried the following cooking method, but it is a process that was used for cooking rooks hundreds of years ago. The rooks were plucked and gutted, heads and feet removed, and the backbones cut out and discarded. The carcasses were then steeped in salted cold water for several hours to remove any rank flavour. After seasoning the birds were placed in a dish on a layer of meat, had melted butter poured over, and then were covered in pastry and baked for 45 minutes.

CHICKEN FEET
Chicken feet are essentially bone, cartilage and skin, rather than a source of meat. Still, suitably treated and flavoured then the skin will give you something to chew on, and provide a little sustenance. You have two options in cooking them; either boil the feet first and then fry, or fry then cook in sauce. You eat

them by chewing / sucking off the skin. Here are a couple of preparation methods:

#1. First, clip, cut or chop the nails off the feet and discard, then thoroughly wash the feet in hot water, rub with salt, and leave for 10 or 15 minutes. Rinse off the salt, drop into boiling water and simmer for about 1½ hours. When tender, drain the feet and fry with some salt and spices until they are lightly browned and almost dry.

#2. Toenail clipped feet are fried until golden brown, then seasoning and spices added, plus enough water to cover them. Bring to the boil then simmer until tender (again 1½+ hours), but this time there will be sauce to accompany the cooked feet.

CHICKEN / DUCK FEET GRAVY
If the thought of eating chicken feet is really too off-putting then use them to make a simple gravy to go with your meal, or perhaps a thin soup (untried, but just a further passing thought). Wash the feet well, and place in a small pot with the chicken neck (plucked and singed), liver and gizzard, plus a handful of toasted breadcrumbs. Add 1 cup of water, place over the fire and simmer until half the liquid has gone. Strain off the liquor into another pan, and discard the animal bits with the exception of the liver. Mince or paste this and add to the liquor. Then add a knob of fat rubbed together with a little flour to the pan. Return the pan to the fire and continue cooking till the gravy has thickened up, stirring all the time to prevent lumps forming.

TURKEY WINGS
No doubt you have encountered fried chicken wings as nibbles at parties, and wondered exactly why anyone bothers preparing the wings given the small amount of meat available on them. Turkey wings (also goose) are a different matter, given the much larger size of the birds.

In a doomsday kitchen turkey wings should not be wasted. Scald them with hot water, pluck the feathers, and then singe the wings to eliminate any remaining feathery bits... with the exception of the last end segment which is essentially worthless and not worth spending time on plucking. Chop this end section off so that you only have the two major wing limbs. Bend the joint between the two backwards till it 'gives'. Place the pieces in a cooking pot with a little minced onion, some sliced mushrooms and a spoon or two of fat. Stir-fry the ingredients over a hot fire till the wing pieces start to become a little browned, then add enough stock or old gravy to cover the contents of the pan and simmer gently for 25 to 30 minutes (longer for more wings) then season to taste. To thicken the sauce you have two options: the usual fat and flour mixed, or beaten egg yolks. On the other hand you could just let the contents simmer until the sauce thickens to the consistency that you want, although the meat might be falling off the wing bones.

SMALL BIRDS
If, in the post-disaster world, you need to resort to scavenging and eating the small birds that we enjoy as part of our appreciation of nature, then this is how you can cook them. It's based on examples of cooking Ortolans, Thrush, Wimbrel, Larks, Starlings, and many other small bird species that have been used as food in the past. However, if millions of people end up hunting small birds for food then there's going to be not much birdlife left. Pluck and dress the birds, split the carcass down the back, open out flat like a butterfly, and clean well. Smear the birds with fat, season, and then broil gently over a hot, smokeless, fire.

To broil a pigeon so that it doesn't get too dry, put a knob of fat inside the dressed bird, along with seasoning and a tiny splash of water. Truss up, and tie the ends down to seal in the inner contents, then egg and breadcrumb the birds and broil near hot embers.

PHEASANT IN CLAY
For those moments when you are stuck for a cooking method for a pheasant (or duck too), then this method may find a use. Draw and gut the bird, and also remove the head and most of the neck, but leave the feathers intact. Season inside the cavity, then rub soft and sticky clay all over the feathers working it a little into the plumage before fully encasing the carcass with the clay. Make a small pencil-sized hole in one of the cavities to allow any expanding air inside to escape without cracking the clay casing. Then place the clayed bird among hot coals and heap some over as well, and bake for 40 minutes. Then remove the bird from the fire and peel off the feathers and skin. You will need to ensure that there is a constant supply of new coals available during the baking process.

OLD CHICKENS / GUINEA FOWL
Tough old chickens or fowls do not generally make the greatest of eating and are usually destined for the stockpot. They may, however, be put through a slow-cooking process that tenderizes the meat to provide you with a morsel of solid food. Should the process fail, then you still have a base for soup or stock.

Place the plucked, dressed, bird in a covered pan or cooking pot with enough water just to submerge it. Place the pot over a part of the fire where it can simmer gently for 3 or 4 hours. Rapid boiling of the bird will cause the meat to be tough.

CHICKEN GUT GRILL
We are talking here about the large intestines of a chicken. These are better if they can be marinated in some spicy or favourite flavours prior to grilling, but then that option might not be open to you. One thing that I have not tried with chicken guts is stuffing them, as with a pork sausage. I am sure they would taste infinitely better with a stuffing of breadcrumbs and chopped liver, but in the absence of a chicken-gut filling gadget this remains untried. If the thought of eating poultry guts doesn't appeal, batter and fry them to hide from sight.

Thoroughly wash, gently squeeze out, and wash, and repeat as necessary, until no gut waste remains in the intestines (or use a hose, or unzip with scissors and then wash out). Drop the intestines into boiling salted water for 10 to 15 minutes (partly cooks, but also kills bacteria – thinking here of the propensity for salmonella to lurk around poultry). Remove from the boiling water, refresh in cold water, and then pat dry. Cut the intestine into 60 to 90 cm lengths (if a marinade is available then soak in that for 30 minutes), then loop onto individual wooden skewers (zig-zag them like a firecracker). Smear with some melted fat and then grill over embers, turning over every couple of minutes to avoid burning and also adding more fat basting.

GOOSE INTESTINES

These can be served in a number of ways, being either stewed, stir-fried, or crispy fried. The intestines need to be thoroughly washed in running water and any traces of stomach contents squeezed out, then rubbed with salt and washed off.

If you were in possession of aromatic spices / herbs you would then marinate the goose guts for 1 or 2 hours, having cut them into pieces to allow better penetration of the marinade. Next, drain the pieces about 2 cm or so long and blanch in boiling water for 30 seconds, then refresh the pieces in cold water, and drain for the next stage of cooking. If you want the guts to look like spaghetti cut them lengthways. It's really down to you appearance-wise.

If you were going to cook the gut pieces up with the goose heart and liver, then these need to be stir-fried first in a little fat for a few minutes (until there is no bloody pinkness in the liver), and then the goose guts added with a good slug of stock or other flavoursome liquid to provide a gravy, and stir-fried for 4 or 5 minutes. If you prefer them more crisp and dry then stir-fry without any liquid. For a more braised-like outcome, add more liquid and simmer gently for a longer period – 10 to 20 minutes.

BREADS, BISCUITS & BAKING

A very generalized ingredient guideline for making bread is 1 part of liquid to 4 or 5 parts of wheat flour, with the liquids to be mixed at a blood temperature warmth, and the yeast mixed with lukewarm water before being stirred into the flour. Keen bread-makers will possibly be horrified at this 'generalization' but it gives someone with no knowledge of bread-making a starting point to work from.

In my view there are two *key* points about bread-making; first, that at its basic level it is a much simpler process than is often imagined, and second, that ingredient quantities and certain timings are often critical – as in allowing the dough to rise properly and to be baked for the right length of time.

There's also a little old rule of thumb on batters and doughs that I came across in an ancient cookery book and which could be helpful: 1 cup of liquid to 1 cup of flour produces a batter that *pours*; 1 cup of liquid with 2 of flour makes batter that will *drop* from a spoon; 1 cup of liquid to 3 cups of flour makes a *soft dough* that may be handled; 1 plus 4 produces a dough that can be *rolled*.

In western society wheat flour is the most commonly used base for making bread, but there is absolutely no earthly reason why other grains are not more widely used for flour. What you do find with breads and cakes made with other grain flours (barley and oats for example) is that the doughs are not as elastic as those made from wheat (the gluten content of wheat dough stretching to accommodate the gas produced by the yeast) so these non-gluten grains tend to produce a more dense end product, with the loaves being smaller and not so light. Indeed, they are often deliberately made smaller for this reason (their greater density), or turned into griddle cakes and biscuits.

Baking time for non-wheat doughs generally tends to be longer than with wheat-based products, while a more careful eye over timing is usually required. And because these other grains are much lower in gluten than wheat flour the end results are often much more crumbly; this can certainly be the case where rice flour is a major ingredient (though it is unlikely rice will be available to your doomsday kitchen). Don't forget potato flour as an addition to bread or cake-type product, or add in cooked, riced (or mashed), potato to the mix. This makes for a much lighter product. Where mashed potato is used then the dough needs to be made much stiffer since the water content of the potato will soften the dough as it ferments. Where rolled oats are available these can be trans-formed to a flour if put through a meat grinder.

Rye is another grain for bread-making but although it contains gluten that gluten is not readily accessible (for technical reasons way beyond the scope of this book), and so rye flour is often mixed with wheat flour to provide the elasticity element. Interestingly, I was reading the journal of a mid-17th century farmer recently, and in that he says that the poor people were mixing pea and rye flour for their bread, and for his own family's the daily 'winter' bread was made of equal quantities of rye, barley and peas, with pure wheat bread only being produced for special occasions. Interestingly, the writer of this journal says that the miller mixed the pulse and grains prior to milling, rather than the individual flours being mixed together.

Baking times will depend very much on the type of oven that you have manufactured (see page 159), and its thermal efficiency, and the best recommendation is to trial bake a couple of small items before committing precious ingredients that might be made inedible. A wheat loaf might take an hour to bake though it might run up to two hours, while rolls need a hotter oven but a shorter baking time. As a general rule wheatless breads and similar products will need a little more baking powder or yeast added to them, and often less fat and salt.

Because an oven must not be opened during the baking of bread knowing the temperature of the oven was a pretty crucial matter in the days before thermostatically controlled temperatures. One old way of testing the temperature for baking bread in a kitchen range oven was to see how long it took to brown a teaspoon of flour, or piece of thick white paper. A browning time of 5 minutes was regarded as showing a suitable temperature.

Another point, your oven heat should not be too fierce at the start of baking since this results in the crust cooking before the loaf interior, and becoming dark and thick by the time the crumb is cooked through. Furthermore, if the outer crust hardens too fast then the gases produced in the baking process cannot escape and form a large pocket of gas, the pressure of which can separate the crust from the crumb.

NATURALLY LEAVENED BREAD

Although some of the recipes that follow contain mention of yeast and baking powder as raising agents these may not (and almost certainly won't immediately be) available in a post-disaster world. And since bread is regarded as a staple food one way round this lack of yeast products when making bread is to fall back on the production and use of natural yeasts that circulate in the air. All that is required is water, flour, and time.

The process described below probably goes back to the dawn of bread-making and depends on natural airborne yeasts to produce fermentation in a flour-water substrate, thereby releasing bubbles of carbon dioxide which can be harnessed to provide a bread-like consistency we are familiar with; although bread made with leaven generally has larger and more irregular holes than loaves made with commercial yeast.

Natural leavening has an advantage over yeast used on its own, in that the fermentation process can take place even in cold weather (if there are acclimatized natural yeasts circulating in the cold air at the time). Indeed, in the farthest northern climes of America in past centuries naturally leavened bread was the only type of bread available during the winter months because the climate was too cold for commercial bakers' yeasts to work. That said, *more leaven* is required to be added to a dough mixture during winter months than in summer-time because the natural yeast, like the commercial kind, develops less quickly in cold weather.

One drawback to natural leavening is that as a by-product of fermentation acid compounds are produced which can give the bread a slightly sour taste; carbon dioxide products dissolving into water within the dough. Indeed, if you ever come across an old recipe that uses *sour-dough* or *sourdough* then that refers to the item under discussion.

If the naturally produced leavening is used properly there should not be too much of a sour taste in the final bread product, and in fact it appears that an old trick (I am not too clear how common this was, but two early 19th century books make reference to it), was to 'correct' the acids formed in the dough with a *base* chemical such as powdered chalk – calcium carbonate. One of those two references I have says: *a 'small quantity of carbonate of lime, soda or magnesia'* would eliminate the acid. No quantities are specified, but the chemistry behind the corrective process makes absolute sense.

Two other points about going down this *natural route* of raising bread: first, that flours other than the wheat variety may be used – everything from rye to beans, as long as there is starch available for the natural yeasts to feed on; second, that making bread this way takes MUCH longer and this needs to be factored into the daily activity cycle of your doomsday kitchen. Indeed, because the leavening is composed of living organisms (the yeasts) it needs to be fed. Yes, really! So if you're not going to be making bread every couple of days, or will be away from base camp for days at a time, then sour-dough baking might not be so useful. It is, however, a way of making raised bread in the absence of bakers' yeast which is unlikely to be available to the doomsday cook.

So, to make the leavening... and I should point out that there were variations on the technique depending on individual bakers and the country where bread is being made, but the following will provide you with an outline of the process as a starting point.

Begin by thoroughly mixing a cup of plain flour with one cup of water in a bowl to produce a thick gooey batter. Leave this exposed to the air for a short while so that yeasts in the air have a chance to land on the surface, then cover up and leave in the warmth for several hours (around 21°c), or even overnight. By that time the volume of the mass should have doubled in size and bubbles of trapped carbon dioxide be visible. This is your *sour-dough* base. Rye flour is a good starter for the base (1 cup flour to ½ cup of water), and then intermixed with other flour for use, while the principle applies to bean and pea flour too.

The next stage of the process is for this *sour-dough* to be incorporated into a plain flour and water dough that has already been worked up thoroughly and allowed to rest a short while. Depending on the baking practitioner the volume of leaven to dough ranged from one-third to one-sixth. This, however, would almost certainly depend on the quality, purity, and gluten content of the flour used, and could well have varied from batch to batch of flour from the mill.

For the doomsday cook it is worthwhile doing a small test batch before committing valuable food resources.

Once the *sour-dough* has been fully worked into the *new dough* salt is added, then worked in until it has dissolved and no grains remain. The wisdom behind adding salt at this point is that salt added earlier in the process stops or retards the yeast fermentation process. As the natural yeasts in the sour-dough begin to work on the new dough, more CO_2 is released and the dough is allowed to *rise* for a couple of hours. Some bakers knead the dough and let it rise a second time, though older sources seem to suggest that where dough was allowed to rise for too long then the acid taste of dissolved CO_2 reappeared, while too short a time before baking in the oven produced heavy bread.

Before being formed into loaf shapes, part of the raised dough is kept aside to form the *mother* for the next sour-dough batch, and where this is not going to be used for a couple of days a little more water and flour batter needs to be stirred into the mixture to feed it and keep the natural yeasts alive.

A somewhat simpler sourdough for when there are only imprecise methods of measuring is to mix a teaspoon of salt with a cup of flour and then add to 1 cup of the fermented dough for making bread in a hot oven. With a stiffer mixture sourdough biscuits and cookies can be made, and when rolled thinly flapjacks can be produced. A little sugar added to the mixture gives the output a more welcoming colour. Anyway, there you have it. Bread without commercial yeast.

POTATO BREAD
A dough is made of boiled mashed potatoes (about 3 or 4 medium-sized) and kneaded with one or two cups of flour plus a little of the hot potato cooking water, and then allowed to ferment overnight in a warm place until the dough rises. Knead for a second time, let the dough rise a second time, then form into bun or loaf shapes and bake.

OLD BREAD
In your doomsday kitchen old bread should NOT be thrown away – unless absolutely rank and decrepit, and also assuming you have the facility to bake bread. There are carbohydrates to be had even in the crumbs gleaned from cutting slices of bread, plus useful culinary twists. Bread pudding (savoury or sweet), for example, may be made from old dried bread, or crumbs can be an addition to fishcakes, croquettes, and similar fried patties. Partially dried out bread can be made into croutons. Along with herbs and onion bread crumbs can be used to stuff poultry or meat, or they may be used to thicken sauces, as well as make a true bread sauce in its own right. In the absence of preservatives home-made bread may not keep as well during warm summer months, and develop mould after a few days; but obviously you can cut the mouldy patch off and continue using the remainder of the bread. If the bread is starting to harden, then it may be a good candidate for fully drying out and storing long-term. In which case, break the loaf into smallish pieces and put in a tin and place this

in an oven or close to the fire. The aim is not to brown the bread but simply drive off all the moisture content, after which you can keep the dried bread in a sealed container for later use. Crumbs containing lots of fat (as in biscuit crumbs) will not keep as well as plain bread crumbs.

If you don't want to convert bread that's drying out into crumbs then you can try to *recover* stale bread by dipping it just momentarily in cold water and then re-baking it in a cool oven. Another option is to steam slices of bread in a colander over boiling water in a covered pan.

DEAD BREAD FINGERS
Remembering that nothing should go to waste in your doomsday kitchen this is not really a recipe but a hint for attempting to use up bread that has turned out a disaster during baking, having reached 110% on the dreadful bread scale. It is an amalgam of egged bread and Melba toast in concept, and the notion that many things can taste better fried – like insects and bugs. Because eggs will, in themselves, be a valuable item in the doomsday kitchen I suggest that you test a sample before committing lots of precious egg. Also try frying a piece of the bread on its own too, and then either sprinkling with salt, or dipping into something sweet to render it tasty.

Cut the leaden bread very thinly (think of that thin-sliced industrial white bread provided by supermarkets, and then halve that thickness again; or visualize thin sliced rye bread), and then cut into strips about 2 cm wide. Beat an egg with a tiny slug of milk added, and soak the sliced bread overnight, or at least for many hours; turning occasionally to ensure every piece is properly soaked with egg. All that remains to do is fry the bread pieces. With luck your dead bread might just have a second life! It's not gourmet stuff, but it may feed you and save wastage.

BARLEY-OATMEAL DROP BISCUITS
2 cups barley flour
3 tsp. baking powder
1 tsp. salt
½ tbsp. clarified fat
1 cup milk

Add the baking powder to the flour (half the barley flour can be replaced by oat flour or meal). Melt the fat in a small pan then add warm milk, stir together then add to the dry ingredients and work together well. Grease a pan or metal tray and drop spoonfuls of the mixture onto it then bake in a hot oven for 15 to 20 minutes.

BARLEY BANNOCKS
Mix barley meal or flour with water, add a little salt, then, roll it out to a paste 1 cm thick, divide it into cakes of the form desired, and bake in front of the fire, or in the oven, to a light brown colour.

BARLEY BREAD
2 cups wholemeal flour
1 cup barley flour
1 cup warm water / milk
2 tsp. sugar
4 tsp. yeast
½ tsp. salt

Boil milk and / or water (or a mixture), place in a mixing bowl and allow to cool. Mix the sugar, salt and yeast with a little tepid water, then add to the bowl. Mix (preferably sifted) the two flours together, stir into the liquids, then knead to a soft dough (add more flour if a little too soft). Cover the bowl and let the dough rise to double its bulk, then knead for a second time. Divide the mixture into two and place in greased pans or loaf tins and allow to rise for a second time. Bake in a hot oven for 30 to 60 minutes depending upon loaf size.

BARLEY FLOUR COOKIES
1 cup sugar
½ cup clarified fat
3 cups barley flour
½ cup milk
1 egg
Salt
2 tsp. baking powder

Mix fat and sugar in a bowl, then all the remaining ingredients and quickly work into a dough (add savoury or sweet flavourings at this point if you wish to do so), adding a little more milk if the dough is too stiff. Roll out, cut into cookie sizes and then bake.

HARD BARLEY BISCUITS (Plain)
Warm 4 tbsp. of fat (butter preferred) in as much milk as will wet 4 cups of flour sufficiently to make a stiff pastry dough. Knead very well then roll out thinly and cut into biscuit shapes. Prick the biscuits with holes using a fork, then bake for about 6 minutes.

HARD BARLEY BISCUITS #2 (Fatless / Plain)
Very similar to the above recipe but with the addition of egg yolk, and dropping the fat content. To 4 cups of flour put the yolk of one large egg, and sufficient milk (water is okay too) to mix the ingredients into a stiff dough. Knead it well, then roll out thin, cut into shapes, prick with a fork, and bake in a slow oven.

SWEET BISCUIT VARIATION
To 4 cups of flour, add ½-cup of softened butter or clarified fat, 1½ cups sugar, five eggs and some spices (cloves and cinnamon, or caraway). Mix everything very well till thoroughly combined (add more egg or a little milk so the mixture is

'fluid' but without being a liquid) then spoon the mixture onto metal baking trays. Bake.

BACKSTONE CAKES
If you have some cream that has gone off, don't throw it away, try this: Mix a cup of flour with sufficient sour cream to form into a dough. Roll it into a single round cake (or cut into squares), and bake over the fire on a griddle or heavy-based frying pan. Cut open and serve very hot with butter or jam spread over.

OAT BISCUITS
Place 4 cups of oatmeal into a basin. Melt 1 tbsp. of fat or lard in 2 cups of boiling water, then pour this over the oatmeal. Stir rapidly into a dough. Turn out the mixture onto a board and roll thinly – to a point where it just holds together. Cut into whatever shapes you like then firm these up by placing them on a griddle over the fire for a short time. Afterwards they may be toasted on each side until they crispen up.

OAT CRACKERS
2 cups rolled oats
3 tbsp. clarified fat – melted
½ tsp. salt
Water

This is made very much along the same lines as the recipe above, but with a higher fat content. Pour the melted fat over the oats, and rub together with your fingers. Add boiling water to the mixture a bit at a time, and work into a very stiff dough. Roll out, dusting with whatever other flour you have to prevent sticking. Cut into shapes and then bake in a slow oven until crisp and nicely browned.

OAT MIXED BREAD
Mix 1 unit each of oatmeal and wheat flour with ½-unit of skinned and mashed boiled potatoes. Knead these into a dough with warm milk, salt, and a quantity of yeast proportionate to the amount of oatmeal, flour and potato ingredients. Form into loaves and bake for at least 2 hours. This bread should keep reasonably well for a week. Not tried, but another possibility to raise this bread would be the addition of proper sour-dough leavening.

OAT & PEA BISCUITS
Take 1 cup of pea flour and soak it in 2 or 3 changes of water over 2 days, then drain and mix the drained mush with 1 cup of oatmeal plus a large pinch of salt and knead into a dough with enough warm water to make a stiff dough (if a little on the sticky side I would add more oatmeal). Roll out to about 2 to 3 mm thick and then bake on a griddle over embers. For something different add chopped or diced cooked bacon to the mixture.

OATMEAL GRIDDLE CAKES
1 cup cooked oatmeal
1 tbsp. clarified fat
3 tbsp. starch (corn, *Arum*, *Typha*)
1 cup milk or water
2 eggs – beaten
½ cup barley flour
½ tsp. salt
2 tsp. baking powder

The source of the starch for this is really immaterial, and could be extracted from the roots of the reed-mace (*Typha*) or the <u>toxic</u> root of the *Arum maculatum* or *Italicum*. Do NOT attempt starch extraction from *Arum* unless you know EXACTLY what you are doing!

Melt the fat and add to the cooked oatmeal in a bowl and combine thoroughly. Then add the beaten eggs and milk, and work in. In a separate bowl mix the barley flour, starch, salt and baking powder and add to the liquid mixture. Beat everything together thoroughly then spoon out onto a hot griddle to cook.

ANOTHER – SIMPLER
Made without any fat, nothing could be more simple that this method. Place 2 or 3 handfuls of oatmeal in a bowl with a large pinch of salt, then mix in warm water a bit at a time until a stiff dough forms. Dust a board with more oatmeal and roll the dough out to wafer thickness, cut into shapes, and cook quickly on a griddle over embers till lightly browned on both sides.

OATMEAL PANCAKES
When wheat flour is running out then this recipe is good for extending it. Mix 3 parts of oatmeal with 1 part of wheat flour, add a pinch of salt, and stir in warm water to make a thin batter. Add baking powder, let it rise, and then pour ladles of the batter into a well-greased, hot, frying pan to cook individual pancakes.

BEAN & WHEAT BREAD
Soak a cup of dried bean flour (haricot or broad bean) in a bowl of water, changing the water every day for three days. Then drain through a fine sieve. Meanwhile, knead a cup of wheat flour with a pinch of salt and a little yeast or sour-dough starter, and allow to prove. Add the drained bean flour, knead in, and prove a second time. Divide into small buns and bake.

BEAN BREAD
This is not a true bread, but I wasn't quite sure how to describe the end product – perhaps vegetable patties? Take one or two cups of bean flour (haricot or broad bean types), mix with water and allow to soak for two days, changing the water 2 or 3 times. Then strain off, and place the soaked flour in a bowl with enough extra water to make a really thick batter, along with a large pinch of

salt. Grease a griddle or heavy-bottomed frying pan with bacon fat or salty butter and spoon enough bean batter to make small patties. Cook over embers till done, turning regularly so they do not burn, but being careful not to break up the patties.

BREADCRUMB MUFFINS / GRIDDLE CAKES
1½ cups dry breadcrumbs
1 cup milk
½ tsp. salt
1 tbsp. honey / sugar
1 egg – separated
1 tbsp. clarified fat – melted
½ cup any flour
3 tsp. baking powder

Heat the milk almost to boiling point in a pan then stir in the breadcrumbs (biscuit crumbs can also be used). Remove the pan from the heat and allow to soak for 20 minutes.

Meanwhile, mix the flour and baking powder (and sugar if using) and set aside. Also beat the egg yolk and, separately, the egg white. Then beat the breadcrumb mixture very well. Next, add the salt, egg yolk, melted fat, and honey, followed by the flour and baking powder. Mix well together then fold in the beaten egg white. Pour into suitable moulds and bake in a moderate oven for 20 minutes, or cook like griddle cakes.

BREADCRUMB DUMPLINGS
For every cup of dried breadcrumbs you will need 1 tbsp. of flour, 1 egg, and some water. Mix the crumbs and flour in a bowl, with a smidgin of seasoning, then beat the egg and add to the bowl, and mash everything together, dribbling in a little water or milk to make a stiff dough. Make small balls of the dough and add to soup while boiling. When the dumplings are cooked they float. The addition of a little chopped or minced cooked liver, or cooked and flaked fish, can transform the plain nature of these dumplings, but the volume of water added to the mixture will need to be reduced.

BREAD OMELETTE
½ cup stale breadcrumbs
½ cup milk
4 eggs – separated
Fat
Salt and pepper

Mix the breadcrumbs, a large pinch of salt, and the milk and allow to mingle for 15 minutes. Meanwhile, beat the egg yolks, and egg whites separately (actually this is not essential, but makes for a lighter omelette). Then, stir in the beaten yolks, and a pinch of pepper, into the crumb-milk mixture, then fold in the beaten whites and combine thoroughly. Pour into a frying-pan which has some melted fat in it, and cook slowly over the fire until the underneath firms up, then set the top in an oven for 5 to 10 minutes. In the absence of an oven flip the omelette over to cook the other side.

APPLE-BREADCRUMB BAKE
3 cups apples (chopped)
1 cup dry breadcrumbs
3-4 tbsp. honey
1 cup water

Assuming apples and bread are available, mix chopped apples with breadcrumbs, place in baking dish or pudding basin of suitable size, then drizzle over the honey and water which have been boiled together. Sprinkle a few more handfuls of crumbs over the top and then bake for 2 hours in a moderate oven.

APPLE BREAD
An unusual bread for the autumn months may be made by combining 1 part of apples to 2 parts flour (by weight) in the normal bread-making process. Very little water is required since the apples – unless of a rather dry kind – contain lots of moisture. Peel, core and chop the apples, then cook them so they may be pulped. Mix the flour, apple pulp, and the usual quantity of yeast that would be used to make the loaf, and work into a dough. Place the dough in loaf tins, allow to rise for 8 to 10 hours in a warm place then bake.

APPLE BISCUITS
Boil a dozen apples to a pulp, then sieve the pulp and add two pounds of sugar and mix thoroughly. Roll the mixture into bun-sized rounds about 1 cm thick, and dry them gently in very slow oven so as not to melt the sugar content.

QUICK CAKE
5 eggs
1⅓ cups sugar
¼ cup water – warm
1 cup flour

The ability to provide a cake with some sweetness could provide a morale-boosting lift in an otherwise thoroughly dispiriting situation, though the ability to source sugar may be an issue.

Separate out the whites of two eggs and set aside. Place the remainder of the eggs in a mixing vessel and beat together. Dissolve the sugar in the warm water, then add to the beaten eggs. When cold thoroughly mix in the flour, a bit at a time. Beat the two egg whites until stiff, then fold into the flour-egg-sugar mixture. Distribute thoroughly, turn into a cake mould or paper, and bake in a hot over for 40 to 45 minutes.

SIMPLE CAKE
I have included this vintage formulation for a 'pound cake' because it is designed for its simplicity, although it uses butter. A good clarified fat could substitute, but it will not have the richness of butter. Still, a bit of sweet cake over which you can smear crushed fruits might not go amiss in the doomsday menu. The ingredient proportions are 450 gm each of flour, sugar, and butter, and 8 eggs. The whole lot is beaten well and then baked for 45 minutes, or thereabouts.

PIE PASTRY
You will see that some of the recipes elsewhere call for pastry crusts or toppings. If that sort of thing is unfamiliar territory to you, don't worry – here is the solution to a very straightforward pastry mix. Of course, in an ideal world you would roll it out on a board with a rolling pin, but flattening the dough out with your hands or a bottle may be the only way in the doomsday kitchen.

Put 8 cups of flour in a bowl and rub into it 1½ cups of lard, wet with water, enough to work it up, add a sprinkling of salt, roll out and cover the pie.

PASTY PASTRY
Another very basic pastry for work on works on the proportions of 1.5 kilos of flour to 700 gm of fat (or butter) plus 1 egg, then with enough cold water to work into a dough.

OATMEAL CASING PASTRY
2 cups finely ground oatmeal
1 tsp. clarified fat.
1 cup boiling water.

Use the ratio between the ingredients above as the baseline, and make larger or smaller quantities as required. Put the oatmeal in a bowl with the fat, and then add the boiling water. Mix into a stiff dough, roll out thinly and line the pie dish, then bake in a hot oven before filling the pastry casing to firm the pastry up.

BARLEY OR RYE PASTRY
1 cup rye or barley flour
¼ cup fat
½ cup starch (corn, *Arum*, *Typha*)
½ tsp. salt
½ tsp. baking powder
Cold water

Read comments on *Arum* starch flour in the previous OATMEAL GRIDDLE CAKE recipe.

Mix the dry ingredients in a bowl then add the fat, cut into pieces. With cold hands work the ingredients together till you have a consistency of something like oatmeal. Next, work in cold water a bit at the time until the mixture just sticks together.

TURNIP BREAD
Peel and then boil young turnips until they are soft enough to mash. Mix with an equal quantity of wholemeal flour, plus yeast and salt in proportion to the two main ingredients. Mix into a dough, prove as per normal and bake – allowing a slightly longer baking time. Initially there is a slight turnip taste (not unpleasant) to the bread, but with a little keeping this diminishes.

ACORN BREAD
The following recipe I found on one of my many trawls of rare books in the British Library. It is from the very early 19th century and seems to produce acorn bread by a much simpler process than I would generally employ (see section on Nuts). But then I am keen to remove as much tannin as possible from the acorn mast substrate before I consider it safe as a general ingredient, and in the old days they probably did not realize the harm that could come from consuming tannin-laden acorn flour. I quote: *'Take a quantity of acorns, fully ripe, deprive them of their covers and beat them into a paste, let them lay in water for a night, and then press it from them, which deprives the acorns entirely of their astringency. Then dry and powder the mass for use. When wanted, knead it up into a dough, with water, and roll it out into thin cakes, which are to be baked over the embers.'* By the way, do not bother making acorn coffee. It is pretty dreadful stuff, and you would be better off making dandelion root coffee which is infinitely better.

ACORN DUMPLINGS
For acorn dumplings make up ½ cup of combined acorn flour and plain wheat flour (no more than 50% acorn flour, and preferably more like 25% of the mix, and re-hydrate with just enough water to plump it up before adding to the wheat flour). Add 1 heaped teaspoon of baking powder to the flours, one beaten egg, 1 tablespoon of oil or fat, salt, and just enough milk to transform the ingredients into a thick batter, almost a dough. Drop spoonfuls of the mixture into boiling salted water [or flavour with a stock cube or herbs]. Cover the pan and cook for about 10 to 12 minutes. Serve with a sauce of your choice, or in a stew. Also, when making white bread, if you have some leftover, risen, dough drop spoonfuls into boiling water, cook for 15 minutes, and serve with stew.

ACORNBURGER
Mix into a stiff dough ½ cup each of granular acorn mush (with most of the water, but not all, pressed out) and oatmeal, plus a bit of minced onion and some seasoning. Allow to stand for 15 to 20 minutes, then form the mixture into thing burger-like patties and fry. The amount of water in the mush determines how easily the stiff dough forms.

ACORN PASTRY
A quite pleasant acorn pastry that I have used for quiche-like items can be made with 110 gm of fine acorn mush almost squeezed dry, 55 gm plain flour, and 85 gm of fat, plus a pinch of salt added. Where this pastry is used to line a baking tin then it is best to blind bake it first since acorn pastry that has absorbed moisture is rather claggy.

A FINAL NOTE ON CEREAL GRAINS
If you are going to prepare your own barley or oat flour or meal then the tough outer husk must be removed before the grains can be worked with. More background to this can be found on page 343 under the heading of IMPROVISED GRINDING / POUNDING TOOLS.

CHEESE & DAIRY

COTTAGE CHEESE
Cottage cheese can be easily made from milk or cream that has just become sour. Here are three slightly different ways of producing it.

Measure the soured milk and place in a bowl. Add at least the same volume of boiling water and let it stand for a few minutes. Arrange a cheese-cloth, or other cotton-type strainer, pour the milk into the cloth, then hang up to drain overnight (or at least 5 or 6 hours), or place where the contents can freely drain.

The second method involves heating the soured milk VERY gently till lukewarm, and then maintaining this heat level until the curd forms, and then draining as above.

Recipe number three involves taking the raw, soured and curdling, milk and placing it in the cheesecloth to drain off the whey. After it has drained the contents of the strainer are washed under cold running water (removes any lingering sour-acid taste), and then hung up again for 20 or 30 minutes. There are parallels here to the first recipe, in that the more water used the less apparent the residual sour taste.

GOAT PANEER
Paneer is the curdled cheese that is used in Indian cooking, and pretty well-known these days to lovers of Indian cuisine. Unlike the naturally curdled cream cheese in the recipes above, this type is formed through artificial curdling with some form of acid – lemon juice, vinegar or, in one experiment of mine, the juice from common sorrel leaves which contains oxalic acid. Cow's milk is normally used but it can be made from goat's (and other) milk. The process is very simple, which is ideal for the doomsday kitchen cook, however it does require a lot of fresh milk to produce a volume of cheese, which may rule this dairy product as next to useless. On the other hand if you have an excess of milk, then this is another way to turn it into a valuable solid foodstuff.

The process is as follows: heat fresh milk (in a non-reactive vessel) until it is teetering on the edge of boiling, then take the pan off the fire, and add vinegar (or other acid) in the proportion of ¼ cup vinegar to 4.5 litres of milk. Stir in the vinegar thoroughly and allow to stand for 15 minutes to allow the curd to fully coagulate. Next, drain the curd from the whey in a cheesecloth as in the cottage cheese recipes above, and hang up for an hour to drain. An alternative is to place the laden cheesecloth on a flat board, spread evenly to about 1 cm thickness, place another flat board on top and weight it down. This provides you with a flat cake of paneer which can be cut into cubes for cooking.

PRESERVING CREAM (SWEET)

The following recipe makes the presumption that you have both cream and sugar available, which you might not in survival time. It is designed to keep cream for several weeks, although the use of this will probably be limited to making desserts or adding to coffee.

Dissolve 340 gm of sugar in a pan with just enough water to melt it over a fire. Bring the solution to the boil for a couple of minutes then add 340 ml of cream and mix thoroughly. Remove from the heat and allow to cool gradually, then pour into a sterile bottle and seal.

PRESERVING EGGS

The eggs must not be more than 24-hours old for this to work... Eggs may be preserved for several months by greasing brand new fresh laid ones all over with melted mutton suet, and packing them in egg boxes with the small ends downwards.

Another method to preserve eggs for some several weeks is to lower the fresh laid eggs for a minute into water that is almost on the boil.

VEGETABLES

The recipes which follow do not largely deal with the edible wild species covered earlier in the book since many of these plants may be boiled or stewed like most domestic vegetables, while more bitter items may be shredded and steeped in hot water to make them more palatable. Where recipes for preserving vegetables are shown it is important that you understand the potential problems with regards to botulism and vegetable preservation. Furthermore, in harvesting edible greens from the wild, or even domestic ones that may have been irrigated by sources of dubious water quality, then those greens should be cooked and NEVER used as a raw salad item. Waterborne diseases can be bad enough even when you are fit and healthy, but with your body's defences potentially immuno-compromised in a post-disaster world, then these diseases could get the better of you. Cook all veggies where possible, or unless you are absolutely certain of water purity.

HERB PUDDING
Bistort, young nettle tops, fat-hen, young dandelions, blackcurrant leaves, broccoli sprouts, chickweed, turnip tops, sorrel, and two or three onions are the base ingredients. Shred the chosen leaves (mixed, or not, as available), squeeze out as much sap as possible, then layer the leaves into a cotton pudding cloth, scattering in barley meal and a little oatmeal as successive layers are added. Tie the cloth up, place in a pan of hot water and then boil for two or more hours. Turn the mixture out into another pan, add seasoning, a good knob of softened butter, and a beaten egg. Mix everything well for a couple of minutes over embers then serve.

BEAN (OR PEA) LOAF
2 cups cooked beans
2 cups stale breadcrumbs
1 tbsp. onion – finely minced
1 egg – beaten
Frizzled fried bacon (optional)
Water / stock
Fat
Salt and pepper

This recipe sort of follows on from the preceding one although the beans are not pulped. A similar sort of product can be made using whole cooked peas, but they could also have been mashed up (as you might get from cooking mushy peas). You can use virtually any liquid you like for the liquid ingredient input. Beef stock is quite good. This is also a good way of using up stale bread from your doomsday kitchen.

Combine the first 5 ingredients then mix in stock a little at a time until the mixture holds together. Fill a greased loaf tin or similar with the mixture, then bake for 30 to 35 minutes, or until a knife inserted into the centre of the custard comes out clean when removed.

GREEN BEAN PUDDING
Beans (broad / runner) – cooked
Breadcrumbs – dry
1 egg – yolk
2 tbsp. butter

For this the quantity of beans to egg should be about a handful of cooked beans per egg. This is better served with a sauce of some description, though it will go well with salted bacon or ham.

Rub the cooked beans through a sieve if you have one available, otherwise mash them to a pulp but not to a purée-like consistence – unless you prefer that. Place the mash in a bowl, season (a pinch of nutmeg would be a wonderful addition if you could get some). Melt a large knob of butter or fat and add to mixture, plus the egg yolk beaten. Mix together well. Grease a pudding-basin or mould large enough to accommodate the amount of bean mush and then dust with the breadcrumbs. Fill with the bean mixture and bake in a moderate oven until firm to touch. Alternatively, boil for an hour in a basin.

BEAN CUSTARD
1 cup cooked bean pulp
1 cup milk
2 eggs – beaten
Fried bacon bits (optional)
Fat
Salt and pepper

On its own this tastes pretty bland, so the addition of some frizzled bacon / ham bits gives the bean paste a lift, or just highly season it with salt and pepper.

Mix the egg and milk, then stir in the bean pulp and seasoning and mix the ingredients thoroughly. Pour into a greased mould but do not fill to the top, and then place this in a hot water-bath or pan of hot water. The water should be at the same level as the mixture in the mould. Simmer gently for 25 to 30 minutes, or until a knife inserted into the centre of the custard comes out clean when removed.

POTTED BEANS
Take cooked haricot or broad beans and press them through a sieve into a bowl (if there's no sieve available simply mash with a fork). Add melted clarified butter and seasoning to the bowl, then put the mixture into shallow dishes for immediate use, or glass jars for storage. If for storage, then pour a layer of clarified butter over the mixture, seal, and store in a cool place.

PEAPOD SOUP
Put about the volume-equivalent of 1 litre of peapods into about 1 litre of boiling, salted, water and cook for 40 minutes. When soft and tender mash the pods through a sieve with the back of a spoon, back into the pan. Boil 2 cups of milk and add a good knob of butter. When the butter has melted add to the mashed peas with some seasoning, plus a sprig of mint chopped up if you can find any (corn mint [*Mentha arvensis*] or water mint [*M. aquatica*] would do at a push, but they are somewhat bitter). If feeling in a rather decadent mood, serve with croutons of fried bread.

CABBAGE (or KALE) MISH-MASH
Here's a way of using up a rather old or dejected-looking cabbage and bacon scraps, utilizing that tried and tested flavour combination of ham / bacon with cabbage.

Melt a little dripping in a pan and then throw in finely chopped scraps of bacon or ham (if adding the rinds then tie these together and remove later). Slice a medium-sized onion, add to the pan and cook till softened. Meanwhile shred the cabbage, then add it to the pan with seasoning and salt. Cover, and sweat / simmer slowly over embers until almost tender (but never allow the greens to fry). At which point add about ½-cup per person of boiling water, stir in and continue cooking for another 15 to 20 minutes, then season to taste.

If you would like a much thicker consistency to this mixture fry a little flour and fat in a separate pan until browned, then stir into the bacon and cabbage mixture, cooking until it has thickened.

CHESTNUT SOUP
This recipe may not be possible unless you can get access to celery, or another celery-like flavouring. It is, however, one way of using up those rather meagre windfall sweet chestnuts which never really ripen in the British Isles because of the lack of sunshine – a very different matter on Continental Europe.

Boil one cup of sliced celery stem, or a celery head, in 1 litre of milk. When the milk is flavoured stir in a handful or two of pulverized sweet chestnuts. Bring to the boil, then simmer some 20 minutes, stirring to ensure the chestnut does not stick to the bottom of your pan.

FRUMENTY (Savoury or Sweet)
Depending on how quickly people return to growing grain crops locally in the post-disaster world, then there may be the possibility that you are able to glean cereal grains from field boundaries that have not been harvested or, in a worse case scenario, scrabble among the stubble *gleaning* whatever fallen cereal grains are available on the ground. There may also be legacy cereal specimens in field systems from previous years' crops. Gleaned grains contain useful nutrition and should not be overlooked. Other cereals such as barley and oats could be utilized in a similar manner, but the recipe that follows is for *wheat*.

Take 2 or 3 cups of collected wheat grains and try to crush them so that the outer layers are cracked and will allow the ingress of moisture. Place these in a pan with slightly more water than covers them, cover with a lid, and boil very gently for 3 or 4 hours (in essence you are making a *wheat porridge*). Check the water from time to time and add a spot more should the contents of the pan look as if they are going to dry out. A variation on this which I tend to use more often is to crush the wheat, soak in water overnight, and then boil for 45 to 60 minutes – it saves on fuel.

The next stage allows you to make a *savoury* or *sweet* frumenty... Start by beating an egg and whisking it into 1 litre of milk. For the *sweet* frumenty add any combination of fruit, nuts, honey and spices to the egg-milk mixture. For the *savoury* kind add salty bacon or ham. Either way, stir the mixture well and add to the cooked wheat in the pan, and then cook for another 15 minutes, then serve. If you prefer the final result more liquid, then simply add more milk in the final cooking phase.

STEAMED POTATOES
This idea of steaming some potatoes might come in handy if you were steaming or boiling some other item in a large vessel; doubling-up on the cooking capacity to make best use of precious water resources and space. The potatoes will need to placed on a perforated base or in a chicken-wire nest and suspended in the pot of boiling water above the waterline. With the water boiling continuously the potatoes will need about 30 to 40 minutes steaming.

COOKED DANDELION
Dandelion leaves can be very bitter, particularly when old. However, with the correct treatment then they can be made more spinach-like as a vegetable, though there will be a trace of bitterness still present. Select young, pre-flowering, leaves, stack in a pile and shred them finely. Place in a bowl of tepid water for an hour, then drain, and drop the shredded leaves into boiling salted water for a couple of minutes. Drain and serve them seasoned along with some melted dripping, or place them back in the pan and cook with a cup of gravy and thicken with a knob of butter mashed with a little flour. The saltiness of some frizzled bacon sprinkled over is a good balance against residual bitterness in the leaves.

NETTLE-OFFAL STEW
Boil a small, chopped, onion in ½ to 1 litre of water. Meanwhile, parboil in as little water as possible young nettle tops – about 1 to 2 handfuls per person. After a couple of minutes remove these from the heat, drain, and press out excess water with a spoon. Next, mash about 1 tablespoon of fat in the same amount of flour, and add to the cooking onion. Stir and then whisk in till the liquid thickens. Add the parboiled nettle tops, distribute thoroughly, and allow the mixture to cook at a gently for about 15 to 20 minutes. Season to taste, then add shredded, pre-cooked, offal to the mixture and cook through for another 5 to 10 minutes.

NETTLE & DANDELION FRITTERS
Nettle and dandelion leaves
4 eggs – yolks / whites separated
$2/3$ - $3/4$ cup plain flour
1 cup water and milk
Salt
Fat / dripping (or butter) for frying

You want to use the freshest nettle greens or tops (generally found in the Spring), and young dandelion leaves which are not too bitter. Beat the egg whites and set aside (these will be used to give frothiness to the batter). Place milk / water and flour in a bowl and stir into a smooth paste, add a pinch of salt, then little by little the egg yolks, finally folding in the beaten egg white. Make bundles or packets of the greens, dip into the batter and then fry them.

TURNIP TOPS
Turnips are a biennial root crop, and the young greens which form in the first and second years can be used as a vegetable (preferably do not use the first year ones, or at least only a few, since the foliage is needed by the plant to grow its root). Turnip greens have a bit of a bitter edge, so the best way to cook them is to shred or chop the leaves, and then boil in plenty of boiling water for about 20 minutes (if they are young leaves). If you still feel there's a bit too much of a tang to them, then cook for a further 5 minutes in gravy. The best leaves are harvested around March-April (seasonal variations not factored in).

Other green 'tops' that may be cooked for food are those of salsify and scorzonera, although these need to be in the latter stages of year one (they are biennial plants again) or before the flower stalks emerge in year two which, in any case, would be the best time to harvest the roots for use. Parsnip tops too, can be boiled for use, although they have a bit of an unusual taste. If the crowns chopped off the roots are planted in soil, new young foliage should appear which can be cooked up.

CHICKWEED & WILD STRAWBERRY SALAD
I have included this item from my *Cooking With Weeds* eBook on Chickweed because I think that in a post-disaster world a little pleasant food will lift your spirits, while chickweed is also an annual weed that self-seeds several times a year and so is present for a reasonable time.

A small clutch of wild strawberries are crushed with a little oil and vinegar (that you may have made using other vinegar-making recipes in this book) and then drizzled over chickweed sprigs.

Note, however, where salad greens are harvested from areas of human or animal activity then I would recommend cooking the greenery and not use it as a salad item.

DANDELION AND BRAMBLE SALAD
Again, this is another quite straightforward idea that will *lift* the rather bitter-tasting leaves of dandelion and make them more palatable (remember, however, that you should not use unwashed raw foliage if you cannot determine animal movements around the picking area). Simply collect the smallest and most tender dandelion leaves that you can find during the blackberry (bramble) season. Collect a handful of the nicest tasting bramble berries, then crush these with a little oil and vinegar and use as a dressing for the dandelion leaves. In the absence of oil, melt a little fat in a pan along with vinegar and bramble juice and then drizzle this over the leaves. If you cannot find young dandelion leaves, shred older ones and place into tepid water to draw out some of the bitterness, repeat if necessary, then drain off the shredded leaves and dress as for the young leaves.

CHICKWEED AND POTATO FRITTATA
1 medium potato – cooked
Onion / shallot – minced and cooked
2 handfuls chickweed
1 medium egg – beaten
Fat
Salt and pepper

The onion component of this is not essential but the concept behind the recipe is designed to provide you with a mixture of animal protein (egg), vitamins from the greens, carbohydrates from the potato, and some fat. Other tender wild greens – such as spring nettle tops – can be substituted for the chickweed.

Dice the potato and place in a bowl, along with the chickweed torn into pieces, seasoning, and cooked onion (it needs to be pre-cooked as the frittata hardly takes any time to cook through and so does not have time to cook the raw onion). Stir in the beaten egg, then turn out the mixture into a pre-heated frying pan with some fat in it. Cook over a moderate fire for 4 or 5 minutes then flip over to cook the other side. Carry on cooking till both sides are nicely browned and the egg cooked through.

ELDER FRITTERS
Wash clusters of elder flowers or the smallest flower bud clusters, then dry off and dip in a light flour, milk and egg frying batter (tempura is better) and fry off.

WILD GARLIC BREAD PIZZA
This is really neither pizza nor bread, but gives you an idea of what the final outcome looks like – a flat unleavened bread pizza. There are two options in final the stages of processing the dough; either form the dough into two equal size balls and roll out into rounds, or roll into one large round and then fold over to form a 'D' shape. The wild garlics referred to in the title can be ramsons (*Allium ursinum*) or three-cornered leek (*Allium triquetrum*) which is found extensively in the Mediterranean region as well as the south of England.

In warmer parts of Europe and the Mediterranean basin the young foliage of *Allium vineale, roseum, pallens, moly* and *neopolitanum* could substitute. Ramsons will be found as far as western Russia. Both plant species have their garlicky aromatics driven off by the aggressive application of heat so you will potentially needs lots of greenery. This is more of a side-dish than pizza.

1 cup plain flour
½ cup water – warm
1 cup wild garlic (shredded just before use)
Salt and pepper
Fat – melted

Gradually mix the warm water into the flour in a bowl and work into a dough (have a little extra flour for dusting hands if the dough is too sticky). Then knead the dough on flour-dusted working surface until it is elastic, form into a ball, and cover with a plastic bag or whatever similar item you have in your doomsday kitchen. Let the dough sit for 30 or 40 minutes, then divide into 2 balls. Roll each of these out to a thickness of slightly less than 2 to 3 mm.

Thinly smear a little melted fat on the centre part of one side of each round only. Sprinkle the shredded wild garlic into the centre of one round, and add a tiny touch of seasoning. Top with the other round, greased side towards the garlic greens, then seal round the edges using a little water or beaten egg to help. Place a heavy-bottomed pan or frying pan over embers, melt some nice salty fat (or butter) and then fry the 'pizza' until nicely browned on both sides.

SPRING GARLIC & GREENS DUMPLINGS

For this the young leaves of ramsons (*Allium ursinum*), three-cornered leek (*A. triquetrum*), or any of the species mentioned above, and also a few additional spring nettle tops are used. Although the temptation is to parboil these greens to tenderize them, that will add too much moisture to the dough. Instead, chop the greenery small, and then soften in a little bit of melted fat or butter in a pan. Allow the greens to cool down, drain off any excess fat and liquid, then mix in fresh breadcrumbs in the ratio of 1 cup of crumbs to each ½ cup of greens, add seasoning, and then moisten bit by bit with beaten egg until a firm-ish dough forms. Form into cherry tomato-size balls and then, using a spoon, lower into soup just on the boil towards the end of the cooking time, and cook for a few minutes. This method is important since the texture of these dumplings is very fragile.

PEAS FOR WINTER USE

Cook freshly shelled peas for 5 or 6 minutes in boiling salted water. Drain, and then completely dry off on a cotton cloth. Then place the peas on something like a baking tray and place in a mild oven heat until they harden. Check drying progress from time to time, then remove the tray once the peas are absolutely dry, and store away for later use. There must be no moisture present otherwise they will spoil. To check they are fully dried out, crack open a couple of peas and see that the interior is hard.

ANOTHER WAY
Prepare the peas as in the first stages of the above method, then when dried off (but not dried out) put the peas into scalded, sterilized jars, pour over melted clarified fat, then close up or seal tightly and store away in a cool place. For use simply put jars (with seals removed) into boiling water and cook till done.

GENERAL PICKLING OF VEGETABLES
A general way of picking small vegetable items, or those shredded smaller (such as cabbage), is to soak them for 24 to 48 hours in strong brine, then drain them, roughly dry off with a cloth to remove excess salt, then place into jars and pour boiling vinegar over until the contents of the jar are fully submerged. Seal immediately and store in a cool, dark, place.

PRESERVING FRENCH BEANS
Prepare a brine of two thirds water to one third of vinegar, then add salt in a proportion of 450 gm to 1.7 litres of liquid. Heat the mixture (but don't boil) and stir to dissolve the salt.

Meanwhile, trim off the stalk material, then boil them for 15 minutes, before draining and refreshing in cold water. Then dry off the beans thoroughly with a cloth, and place in the sterile jars to be used for storage. Pour the hot brine over the beans until it rises almost to the rim of the jar. When cool pour over clarified butter or fat to seal from the air, and then cover or lid the jars properly.

PRESERVING POTATOES
A quite long-term method of storing potatoes – at least to stop them germinating – is to dip baskets of them into boiling water for 1 to 2 minutes (maximum), then partially dry with a cloth before placing in a warm oven to fully dry off. Place in sacking or paper bags and store in a dry, frost-free, environment until needed.

ANOTHER METHOD
Peel the potatoes then grate them raw. Place the pulp into coarse cloth then squeeze the water out by putting into an improvised press (this not only squeezes out the moisture but also forms the potato pulp into flat cakes). Dry the cakes in a moderate oven or near the fire – but not close enough to cook the potato. When completely dried out store away in a sealed container for further use.

Do not discard the water squeezed out from the potatoes as that could be the base liquid for a soup, or there may be enough residual starch grains that could be isolated and dried for later use.

MUSHROOM KETCHUP & DRIED MUSHROOM
In past centuries this ketchup was very popular and is a handy way of making a tasty flavouring source, particularly if you have a glut of mushrooms on your hands and do not wish to waste them. The method below allows you to produce both the ketchup and also a source of dried mushrooms for later use.

Take mushrooms that are beginning to sag and dry a little, wipe them clean with a cloth, before cutting into slices. Sprinkle some salt in the bottom of a non-reactive container then add layers of the sliced mushrooms, sprinkling salt quite thickly as each layer is added. Let the mushrooms stand for 3 or 4 hours then pound to a pulp as best possible. Cover, and allow the mixture to stand for a further 2 days, stirring a couple of times each day then re-covering.

Season the pulp with pepper and then transfer to a pan placed in a water bath that is brought to boiling temperature. Continue cooking the jars for 2½ hours, after which time strain off the resulting mush liquid into a separate pan. This is then simmered very gently over the fire for about another hour, reducing the water content of the liquid further. Allow to cool down somewhat before bottling the ketchup in heated sterile bottles, to be lightly capped at first then fully sealed tight. Store in a cool place.

The mushroom mash that remains can be pressed flat on a baking tray or similar then dried in an oven or near the fire. When absolutely bone-dry powder the mushrooms and store in bottles for later use.

MUSHROOM POWDER
Peel the mushrooms, and slice off the end of the stalk, which should also be separated from the mushroom 'cap'. Do not wash the pieces but instead put them on a plate and place in a warm oven or Dutch oven placed near to a fire. Make allowances for the moisture to escape. When the mushrooms are brittle and dry they can be powdered, then bottled and stored in a dry place.

POTTED MUSHROOMS
This is my take on an old method of keeping mushrooms for later use. Small mushrooms are wiped dry and then, in my case, *dry-fried* to drive off most of the moisture in the mushrooms. Old recipes stewed the mushrooms in butter and then drained them. In the dry-frying method, simply keep the mushrooms stirred around as they are cooked in the frying pan. For a while you get squeaky sounds as you stir, but as the mushrooms begin to sweat their water content, that sound goes. I keep on cooking till the liquid evaporates (remembering that water is a perfect medium for bacteria to grow) and then add a good dollop of clarified butter and continue cooking for another 5 to 10 minutes, then I drain them of the butter, which often does contain yet more watery content. Allow the mushrooms to cool then pack into jars and pour on hot clarified butter, cap, allow to cool, then store in a cool place. These will keep a good few weeks.

PICKLED TURNIP TOPS
Cut off any withered leaves or branches from the turnip tops, then boil the good greens remaining in salted boiling water until tender. Cool, pack them into storage jars and pour over a strong pickle of vinegar and salt. Young turnip leaves growing on winter-stored roots can be used in salads.

Incidentally, although young turnip roots make a good vegetable, older ones are generally bitter and stringy and, in my view, are only fit for leaving in the ground and the harvesting the seed for future use.

POTATO-STARCH

Starch is called for in a number of recipes in this book, and may also be used as a general thickening agent. However, in a post-disaster world the following starch extraction technique may not be regarded as a valuable way of using scarce food. That said, the cellular material left over could still be cooked up as food. At its core the process simply involves grating potato into water, which is a pretty straightforward operation though somewhat labour intensive as it is done by hand. The one thing you need to watch, however, is the drying process since starch in the presence of moisture and heat will break down and become gooey. So the starch must be dried very gently.

Half-fill a bucket or bowl with cold water. Wash and peel some potatoes, cutting out any bad looking or damaged parts. Rest the grater on the bottom of your bowl of water (you want to be using the coarse rasping face, or very finest toothed side), and grate the potatoes. From time to time stir the contents of the bowl with your hand, and then stir everything really well for several minutes once you have done grating potatoes.

Place a clean, coarse, cloth over a colander and strain the pulp into another bowl, squeezing the pulp almost dry. Allow the liquid to settle for a couple of hours, or until clear, then incline the bowl and pour off the water gently so as not to disturb the bottom sediment. Add another batch of water, stir up, let settle, and repeat the draining procedure. Repeat the process one more time. It is likely by the third draining that a layer of discoloured cellular material will have formed on the surface of the starch sediment. This must be very carefully removed to reveal the pure starch beneath.

All that remains to do is filter the starch through a fine cloth, and then spread out thinly on that cloth, dry gently (a breezy sunny day would be ideal), and then bottle the starch when fully dried.

HORSERADISH POWDER

Collect horseradish roots around November / December, or in Spring at the very first sign of the flower stem emerging. Wash and trim up the roots, then cross-slice into sections about 2 mm thick. Place the pieces in the bottom of a large Dutch oven or similar large area drying platform and dry *very* gently in a warm heat (excess heat will drive off the pungency). Once the pieces break with a snap then they can be powdered, or keep them whole and powder for use as required. The powder or pieces must be stored in an airtight container.

DRIED CHICKWEED

This is something that I learned from a lady who had lived in Kenya for most of her life, and who told me that this technique was used for preserving common chickweed for the winter months. Young sprigs of chickweed (not older ones since they are dreadfully tough) are dropped into salted boiling water for a couple of minutes then drained to allow most of the water to escape, before being spread on mats to be dried in the heat of the sun. In the absence of Kenya's blistering sunshine I have used the artificial heat of an oven on a low setting, and you do indeed get a preserved veggie green when reconstituted by boiling in water. Both the salt and absence of moisture are acting as preserving agents here, and stored in an airtight container the salted greens should last a fair length of time.

DANDELION SALAD GREENS

This is not a recipe as such but, rather, a description of a method for producing dandelion salad greens that was used on board ships around the divide of the 18th-19th centuries, possibly earlier, and could be adapted for the post-disaster world model to provide you with fresh salad greens.

Dandelion leaves are bitter, but not if they are light-blanched (denied light – as when an object is left on a grass lawn then removed weeks later to reveal a patch of pale yellowy vegetation). So the trick is to light blanch dandelions in *quantity*. The guys in the olden days would cut holes in the sides and top of wooden barrels, fill the barrel with earth and then place dandelion roots in each of the holes. Foliage would start to sprout and then the barrel would be placed below decks where it was dark. Voila, after a few weeks at sea they had fresh greens to eat on board ship. This concept could be adapted to growing the plants in thick plastic bags (since barrels or similar containers are likely to be wanted for water storage) and kept somewhere dark. Simple flower pots kept in the dark would make an alternative, while a door from the debris field could act as a light block for plants growing on flat ground. Every now and then the barrels need to be brought out into daylight and the dandelion foliage allowed to grow to full size since the root stocks need to be re-invigorated through photo-synthesis otherwise they will die off.

REMEMBER, where there is any suspicion of the water supply to growing plants, or the soil is actively used by animals, then your greens (like chickweed) should be cooked and not used as a salad.

Foliage of both domestic and edible wild plants that is abnormally discoloured and yellowing should not be eaten. In the Outdoors if a plant in its natural habitat has yellowing, unnaturally curling, or dying leaves it could indicate that poisons are at work; on the other hand the plant may have simply reached the end of its annual growing / foliage cycle.

SEAWEED

If you are close to coastal areas with access to fresh seaweed straight from, or growing in, the water then this is a valuable food resource – both fresh and when dried for longer-term storage. Use only small amounts of seaweed in your diet since the large ones are, in my opinion, somewhat indigestible in bulk (see the Seaweed notes on page 127). However, the larger species can be shredded finely for use, cut into small pieces, or slow-cooked.

SEA LETTUCE CHOWDER
1 medium potato – peeled and diced
1 small onion – finely chopped
Water
1 to 3 hand-size sea lettuce fronds – washed and shredded
Fish – cooked and flaked
Milk – splash (optional)

Put the potato and onion (if you can find some) in a pan with some water, bring to the boil over the fire and then simply let them simmer till almost tender. Drop shredded sea lettuce in and flaked fish. Allow to simmer another 20 or 30 minutes. The addition of a splash of milk, or the luxury of a knob of butter stirred in at the end improves things.

GUTWEED FISH CAKES
½ cup cooked white fish – flaked
½ cup mashed potato
1 tsp. minced onion (optional)
Gutweed – roughly chopped
Pepper – pinch
1 egg – beaten
Breadcrumbs
Fat

Wash the gutweed well as it always seems to hold lots of the finest sand among its wrinkled texture. The egg in this recipe is added in just enough quantity to moisten the other ingredients and bind them together when cooked, not to form a runny gloop.

Put the flaked fish, mashed potato (on the dry side preferably), onion, and gutweed (also dried off as best possible) into a bowl with a little beaten egg (add just as much as necessary). Fold everything together, rather than mash, and then form balls of the mixture about the size of a large tomato (not supersize). Flatten each ball into a patty, sprinkle with breadcrumbs (pressing them onto the patty surfaces), and then shallow-fry in fat for 4 or 5 minutes on each side, or until a nice golden brown colour.

The two seaweed species above are, in my view, the most easily cooked items. The kelps tend to be bulky and thick and require very long, slow, cooking. One of the things I normally do with them is shred the kelps thinly and then add to brown rice when it is cooking; which also salts and flavours the rice but has enough time to cook the seaweed. However, in a post-disaster world rice of any sort is unlikely to be readily available.

LAVER BREAD

Porphyra species are the seaweeds that are boiled down to make 'laver bread'. It's a straightforward process: gently boil the laver in lots of water until a whole gloopy, dark green-black, mass forms. This is then generally allowed to cool down before mixing with oatmeal and forming into patties which are then fried (traditionally in bacon fat).

LAVER SEA-MARMALADE

This item has been inserted because it offers a useful short-term method of preserving seaweed other than drying. However, the recipe rather assumes you have access to an oven, and also some beer.

Pick through the laver and remove and dead pieces and any animal life present, then wash in salt water and drain then shred it. Place in an ovenproof pot, sprinkle with pepper, several knobs of fat (preferably butter), and add enough beer to cover the laver. Bake until tender and until most of the liquid has evaporated (but do add a bit more beer if the laver starts to dry out before it is cooked through). You can either use it hot from the oven, as an accompaniment to roast and barbecued meat, or store it for later use. In which case, put portions of the cooked laver into small pots and press down, then pour clarified fat / suet over the top to seal.

KELP FRITTATA

Finely shred a piece of kelp about 10 cm square, place in a pan, bring to the boil then cook for 30 minutes. As the pot comes to the boil add a couple of small to medium-size potatoes, then remove these when just tender. Allow to cool then either dice the potatoes, or slice about 5 mm thick. Meanwhile, beat an egg and set aside. Also (optionally), take a slice of bread, cube, and then fry to make croutons. Drain the kelp and place in a bowl with the potato pieces. Add the croutons if using, and then stir in the beaten egg. Mix thoroughly then pour the mixture into a heavy-bottomed pan with a little fat and fry for 4 or 5 minutes on one side, then flip the frittata over and cook the second side until the mixture is firm. This can be done with gutweed and sea lettuce too.

SUGAR KELP & BEAN STEW

Cut tender young sugar kelp fronds into small pieces, about thumb size, then boil in water for 20 to 30 minutes; allowing a loose handful per person. Meanwhile, finely cut some onion, and fry until soft. Then add cooked haricot beans to the pan (about 1 cup per person). Normally I will add a bit of chilli and tomato to the mixture at this point, even a bit of garlic. Next, drain the seaweed and add to the pan. Stir everything well together, add a slug of stock (or a bit of reserved seaweed cooking water), and simmer for 5 minutes.

SEAWEED PICKLE

Take cleaned fresh sea lettuce or small gutweed, cut into small pieces then soak in vinegar for a couple of days, turning the mixture of each day. Then remove from the vinegar and add spices if you have any (ginger, chilli and mustard is a good combination), plus some oil (sesame in real life), and garlic (onion would be an alternative taste option). Mix the ingredients thoroughly then bottle for use.

OTHER SEAWEED OPTIONS

Seaweeds are an amazing foodstuff that in normal times offer a wide variety of culinary twists and options, but there's rather a limitation when there is a complete absence of flavouring options available (carrots, tomatoes, chilli, for example, will be but distant dreams in the doomsday kitchen). Some other things you might like to experiment with:

(1) Dry laver until bone dry (don't wash in fresh water), then powder the fronds to make a sort of savoury salt. Most other substantial seaweeds are too thick to powder easily, while sea lettuce is a rather tasteless option for this 'salt'.

(2) Regarding sea lettuce; shred the fronds and add to mashed potato.

(3) Another sea lettuce option, if your coastal location has common sorrel (*Rumex acetosa*) available, is to juice or purée sorrel leaves, then heat the purée with a little fat (butter or oil much preferred), and then use this as a dressing for the shredded seaweed.

(4) If you were to have access to spices then a curry can be made with sea lettuce. Serve with a flatbread. In peacetime try trialling a curry of sea lettuce (*Ulva* sp.), spices and coconut cream.

(5) Shred sections of thicker (but not too thick) kelps and deep-fry them as seaweed crisps. The gutweeds, too, can be deep-fried though do be careful of spitting fat.

FRUIT

Where recipes for preserving fruit are shown it is important that you understand the potential problems with regards to botulism and fruit preservation. In a world without refrigeration I would tend to use any opened preserved fruits within a week of opening, and boil them before eating.

WILD CHERRY SOUP
For this recipe use sour cherries that you come across in the wild. Some variations in ingredients are included although the cooking method is the same throughout, and the proportions given are for a small test batch to see whether the flavour combinations suit your palate.

Remove the stones from a handful of cherries and place in a suitable-sized cooking pot with just enough water to cover them and 1 tbsp. of sugar, bring to the boil then simmer for 15 minutes. Meanwhile, mix 1 tbsp. of plain flour (or 2 tsp. of starch or oatmeal) with a little water to thicken the soup. Ready, also, 1 beaten egg yolk, or 1 tbsp. of sour cream.

After the cherries have simmered, remove the pan from the heat and whisk in the flour or starch thickener for a minute then return the pot to the heat and cook till the soup thickens up. Lastly, take the pan off the heat and whisk in either the beaten egg yolk or sour cream, allow to heat through and then serve.

PLUM SOUP
Cook a handful of plums in just enough water to cover them, plus a handful of breadcrumbs. Cook until softened then mash with a fork (better to press through a sieve if available). Add seasoning, additional sweetener if required, and serve with fried bread.

FRUIT (OR SAVOURY) PUDDING
Although the base ingredients of this recipe (bread, milk and egg) are used to make a fruit pudding, it would be possible to transform it into a savoury item using pieces of cooked meats such as ham or bacon, or perhaps flaked smoked fish (untried).

Soak about 220 gm stale bread (roughly the amount that would fit in a ½-litre glass if torn into small pieces) in slightly more than 1 cup hot milk. When softened, beat or mash smooth and add a ½ cup of sugar or honey, plus 2 well-beaten eggs and soft fruit such as cherries or plums that have been stoned. Put the mixture into a greased pudding-basin or mould, cover with greaseproof paper or pudding cloth and steam till firm.

BAKED PEARS
If you can find good eating pears then in my view they are best eaten ripe. However, pears that are rather gritty and hard – not having had a lot of sun to develop them properly – can sometimes be redeemed by slow cooking.

So, peel the pears, cut each in half and remove the core part. Place them in a stew-pot (add a clove or two if you have these – otherwise straggly wood avens [*Geum urbanum*] roots), and sugar if you have some. Pour in sufficient water to cover the pears, cover with a lid, and set over a gentle fire or embers and stew for four or five hours.

BOTTLED FRUITS
This is a short-term preservation method for bottling gooseberries, plums, cherries and currants, and will take the best part of a day to complete. Pick over the fruit to remove any damaged and blemished ones, then wash them and place in wide-necked jars. Add scrupulously clean cold water, and place the jars in front of the fire (if the fire is very hot then to avoid thermal shock of the glass start the jars off a couple of feet away, and move them forwards as they heat up). Lightly cover the jar necks to prevent ingress of airborne bugs. Once an acceptable distance is established the fruit will start cook and soften on the fire-side so, wearing hand protection, you will need to turn the jars from time to time to ensure the cooking process is even (about 12 to 14 hours for the larger fruits, less for currants). When cooking is complete pour some clarified butter or fat into the neck of each jar and seal with waxed paper or screw-on lids, while still hot, and later store in a cool place. Before pouring on the fat or butter, make sure the jar is filled reasonably full since the fruit will settle as it cooks. You may need to sacrifice some of the contents of one jar to top up the remainder. Use a very clean spoon (preferably sterilized) in any transfer process.

As a processing alternative, put the jars in a pan of water up to their necks, and place over the fire. Allow the water to come to a gentle boil and simmer until the fruit is cooked, then seal. Screw-top jars are good for processing in water baths like this since the caps can be loosely placed on top to prevent water splashing into the fruit but allow expanding air to escape.

FRUIT JELLIES / CONSERVES
Fruits like plums, cherries, currants, and apples all make good jellies without the addition of a gelling agent provided the fruit is picked slightly on the under-ripe side (over-ripe fruit does not contain sufficient pectin to gel). Boil the fruit in lots of water then strain through muslin or a jelly bag into another pan, measuring the volume of liquid. Add sugar in the ratio of 450 gm to every ½-litre of juice. Place the pan over the fire and bring to a boil, then continue boiling quite rapidly. After 15 to 20 minutes, take a small spoonful of the liquid and drop it on a cold plate. If it gels (sets) then the jelly can be stored in sterile jars. Where the fruit juice fails to gel, continue testing every 5 minutes until the correct point is reached. When testing remove the pan from the heat each time so the liquid does not cook more than is required for the gel point to be reached.

If you have a disaster and the liquid fails to gel, then you could consider transforming the mixture into a fruit wine through fermentation.

APPLE JELLY
Peel, core and quarter cooking apples, then place them in a pan with just enough water to cover them. Boil rapidly and when the apples disintegrate add 2 cups more of water and boil for another 20 minutes. For a clear-ish jelly strain through cotton cloth, but if appearance is not of concern simply place the apple mush in a container/s to set.

APPLE PANCAKES
¾ cup flour
2 eggs
2 medium-size apples
Salt – pinch
1 tbsp. sugar
½-1 cup milk
Lard / clarified dripping (butter preferred) for frying

In a bowl mix the flour, beaten eggs, salt and a little sugar with the milk (add half to start with, and gradually more if the batter is too stiff) to produce a smooth batter. Peel the apples, slice very thinly, and add them to the mixture. Take large spoonfuls of the mixture and fry on a griddle or in a frying pan, until golden brown on both sides.

APPLE PUDDING
Take 3 or 4 cooking apples, drop them into boiling water for a few minutes, then when hand-hot remove the skin and pound them to a pulp. Mix in 2 or 3 handfuls of crushed biscuits (ginger biscuits are great, but an unlikely ingredient in your doomsday kitchen), 1 to 2 cups of cream (if you can obtain), sugar to taste, three whole eggs beaten, plus the beaten white of 2 or 3 more, which should be folded into the mixture at the end. Place into a mould and then bake until set.

For something really different try making a sorrel and apple crumble, if you have the ingredients available for the crumble component. In this case pre-cook sliced apple and then put it in a dish with fresh, raw, sorrel leaves, then layer over the crumble mixture. There's no need to pre-cook sorrel leaves here since they will wilt down like spinach during the cooking process, although you may prefer them chopped and mixed in the fruit mixture.

DRIED APPLES
The drying of apples would be highly useful in a post-disaster world since no sugar is required, nor is there any requirement for the upkeep of rubber jar seals, metal caps, and so on, associated with bottling fruits. On the vegetable side sweet corn, beans and peas would also be good candidates for drying.

If you are fortunate enough to be living in the shelter of a permanent dwelling or house after a disaster, and there is sufficient heat in the kitchen from the fire or stove, then the sliced apples are hung up to dry in the warmth. After peeling, coring, slicing and dipping briefly into boiling water to allay discoloration, the apple pieces are threaded through with inert cordage (methinks fishing line would also make a good candidate too) and hung up to dry. When absolutely dry, store the pieces in an airtight container.

Dried apple is reconstituted by steeping the pieces in hot water until re-hydrated, and the stewing gently until tender. The leftover water may either be consumed as a beverage or used as part of the apple pudding.

DRIED DAMSONS
This process will allow damsons to be kept for many weeks but requires a sustained slow heat, which may not be possible with a general campfire. Gather ripe damsons that have no damage or infestation. Place them on a cotton cloth and place in a slow oven or by the gentle warmth of a fire for 2 to 3 days. With clean hands turn them from time to time to allow even drying. Continue drying in the warmth until prune-like, then store in sealed jars. I suspect if one was to make a syrup and then further process the dried damsons in that, and then store, the final product may keep for months since lots of moisture will have been removed during drying while the sugar would act as a further preservative.

DRIED BOILED CURRANTS / BILBERRIES
Boil either fruit for 30 to 40 minutes then spread the pulp in thin layers upon non-reactive trays. Place the trays in a warm oven (or out of doors if the weather is sunny and fine – though cover the trays with breathable fabric material to allow air circulation while preventing flies walking over the fruit). Once the fruit layer starts to harden off on the top surface, cut into squares and flip the pieces over to dry from the other side. If necessary, flip once again to extract more moisture from the other side. Sprinkle the pieces with fine sugar then pack into an airtight container; first sprinkling more sugar on the bottom, and then packing tightly into the container. A little extra sugar between each layer will not go amiss. Reconstituted in hot water the fruit pieces can be used as a fruit pulp, or if in a very liquid form used as a drink.

BLACKBERRY DESSERT
Take cooking apples (peeled, cored and sliced) and blackberries and place in a pan with some sweetening. Stew very gently over embers until they soften – you may wish to start the process off by adding a splash of water, but don't add so much that the fruit actually boils in water.

Meanwhile, take a couple of handfuls of breadcrumbs and stir-fry till golden brown in some fat along with a sweetener. Allow to cool. Serve the fruit with the fried breadcrumbs sprinkled over.

PRESERVED SORREL
This recipe is for short-term preservation of sorrel. Pick, wash clean, and then drain the sorrel. Drop for just a minute or so into boiling water till it softens slightly (it will disintegrate if overcooked). Drain th eleaves, place them in a non-reactive bowl, cover, and leave for a couple of hours. Then chop the leaves finely and place in a pan (again, non-reactive) with a sprinkling of salt, and cook over embers gently until it becomes like a thick paste, stirring the mass with a non-reactive spoon to prevent burning or sticking to the pan bottom. Remove from the heat and while the greens cool down a little, scald some jars and then fill these almost to the brim with the warm sorrel. Put in a cool place with a cloth draped over the jar tops, then when cooled off seal the surface with clarified butter or fat, and then the next day put the lids on, or tie greaseproof or waxed paper over, and finally store in a cool, dry, place.

GOOSEBERRY VINEGAR
This is an alternative source of vinegar for use in your doomsday kitchen. Whether it can reach the minimum 5% strength suitable for pickling without being deliberately concentrated I am uncertain. That said, the instructions for one old recipe talks simply about doubling the fruit and sugar content to achieve pickling strength gooseberry vinegar though how realistic that suggestion is remains to be explored.

Boil some water (3.5 litres to every 4.5 litres of fruit) and allow to go cold. Meanwhile, bruise ripe gooseberries and place them in a suitable-sized vessel. Add the water to the fruit, stir thoroughly, and allow to stand for 3 days, giving the mixture a stir every few hours, then strain the liquor through a sieve into another vessel. To each 4.5 litres of liquid add 450 gm of sugar, then stir to dissolve the sugar as best possible. Transfer to a large, closed, fermentation vessel and slip in a finger of toast spread with yeast. Cover the bung-hole over, but don't seal it up, and then place in a spot where the sun can warm the brew and finally allow it to sour a few months later.

SUGAR VINEGAR
The following simple recipe is based on something from the past, but is one of the most straightforward ways of making vinegar – assuming sugar is available, of course.

In 4.5 litres of water hot water dissolve 900 gm of sugar and when cooled down add yeast and stir in. Cover, but do not seal the fermentation vessel, then place it in a warm spot for 3 months or so, by which time the liquid should have turned vinegary.

HONEY VINEGAR
There is not a natural home for this recipe within the other parts of the book so it seemed like a good idea to tuck it alongside the other home-made vinegars. Honey, itself, is virtually indestructible in terms of long-term preservation, and given whatever circumstances you find yourself in you might want to evaluate

whether it is really worth transforming this naturally sweet resource into vinegar which can also be put to food preservation uses.

To make the vinegar dissolve 450 gm of honey in 1.2 litres of warm water, then place the mixture into a fermenting vessel which has the bung-hole lightly covered with coarse cloth – allowing air to enter but keeping insects out. Place in a warm environment and let it ferment for 5 or 6 weeks by which time it should start to become acid through exposure to air. By exposing to freezing temperatures some of the water can be removed from the mixture and the vinegar strength concentrated.

CIDER VINEGAR

Not quite as 'passive' a form of vinegar-making like the sugar or honey vinegar recipes above, but a way of making your own cider vinegar. Though you are likely to need a cider press to achieve things.

Simply, transform the crushed apple juice into cider, and then allow the air to get at it for about six months.

Another cider vinegar can be made by adding sugar to the liquid in which dried apple slices have been re-hydrated, then encouraging this to ferment in the presence of air to produce acid vinegar.

REMEMBER: For *safe* pickling vinegar needs to have an acetic acid concentration of at least 5%. Also, use non-reactive cookware and utensils when processing the pickles.

DESSERTS

There are other recipes dotted round elsewhere in the recipe texts which theoretically are 'desserts' or could be used for that. The main problem in this area of food is that many of the sweet and spicy ingredients that could be used for puddings simply will not be available to the doomsday cook for quite some time post-disaster. So what I have listed below are a few recipes that may prompt your experimentation with substitute ingredients or cooking processes.

LAYERED HONEY CAKE DESSERT
2 large eggs
½ cup runny honey
½ cup potato flour
½ tsp. baking powder
½ tsp. salt
Fruit – cooked and mashed

This recipe will give you an opportunity to experiment with potato flour as a cake or baking ingredient in substitution for wheat flour. Pre-cook the fruit as a purée, although fresh ripe fruit such as raspberries or strawberries could also be used in the cake sandwich for immediate use.

Mix the potato flour and baking powder (sift together if at all possible), and set aside. Then separate the egg yolks from the whites, and beat the yolks with the honey really, really, well. Sprinkle over the salt and briskly stir in. Beat the egg whites until stiff then fold into the honey-yolk mixture, then stir in dry ingredients. Pour the mixture into two cake tins or trays of suitable size and bake for about 20 minutes (moderate oven). When cool make up a fruit sandwich cake.

BILBERRY FRIES
Check the bilberries over, wash them, then place in a pan with some sugar. Squash the contents of the pan with a fork and heat over the fire until the mixture just boils. Stir to make sure the sugar has dissolved (or use honey). Meanwhile, fry some pieces of bread in fat until golden brown. Spread the cooked fruit on the toast to serve. This works well with blackberries too.

MUFFIN or BREAD-PRESERVE PUDDING
In preparation, lightly grease a pudding basin. Then cut bread (white preferably) in thin slices, or muffins in half, and spread fruit preserve or jam on each piece. Next, line the basin the with the first slices / halves, and then build the layers up until the entire basin is almost filled with the bread / muffins – but not packed down tightly.

Mix ½-litre of warm milk with four beaten eggs (sweeten if you like), then pour this evenly around the contents of the basin. Cover with greaseproof paper tied down with cordage. Place in a pan of boiling water and cook for 20 minutes, then serve. A quite simple, but spirit-lifting, treat from the doomsday kitchen for those feeling cold and gloomy.

HONEY CUSTARD
2 cups milk
3 eggs
Ground cinnamon – large pinch
¼ cup runny honey
Salt – large pinch

We are all probably familiar with baked custard tarts and crème brulée-type desserts. This basic custard recipe uses honey as the sweetener, and could possibly be bulked out with some breadcrumbs or, more obviously, cake or biscuit crumbs that are already inherently sweetened.

Heat the milk in a pan, almost to boiling, then set aside but keep warm. Beat the eggs then stir in the honey, salt, and spice (if available). Finally, stir in the milk and whisk together thoroughly with a fork. Pour into cup-size moulds then either boil in a water-bath as in the previous BREAD-PRESERVE PUDDING recipe overleaf, or bake gently near the fire until set.

SOURDOUGH PANCAKES
Leftover or excess sourdough can be used to make pancake batter, though the dough perhaps makes better savoury ones than sweet. Thin the dough with milk as necessary before cooking.

DAMSON PUDDING
Make a batter of 1 cup milk, 2 beaten eggs, 2 tablespoons each of flour and sugar. Stone 1 cup damsons, cook them until just softened, then mix into the batter. Fill a greased basin with the mixture. Cover with paper or foil and boil for 30 minutes. If you have the energy peel the skin of ripe damsons and use them uncooked in the mixture which will make the pudding less tart. Domestic plums could also be used for this recipe, but they would not need to be pre-cooked if they are ripe and of a really sweet variety.

BEVERAGES, WINES AND BEERS

SIMPLE SLOE / DAMSON WINE
4.5 kilos ripe damsons / sloes
4.5 litres cold water
1.4 kilos sugar

The damsons or sloes used for this must have developed their blue-ish bloom on the skins for this recipe to work. Essentially that 'bloom' is the wild yeast which interacts with the sugar.

Put the lightly crushed damsons / sloes in a vessel suitable for fermenting, and pour the cold water over and allow to stand for a week. Then strain and add the sugar, mixing in well to dissolve most of it. Cover the vessel (not too tightly as the fermenta-tion gases must be allowed to escape) and ferment for 6 or 7 weeks then bottle when there is no more activity in the liquid. If you can let the liquor ferment in a vessel with an air-lock attached so much the better.

BLACKBERRY WINE
Blackberries – enough to provide 4.5 litres juice
1 litre water
1.4 kilos sugar

Mix the ingredients together in a fermentation vessel, then cover and leave till fermentation ceases – though stir the mixture occasionally. Bottle when finished fermenting. As with the damson / sloe wine, allow a means for fermentation gases to escape, while a vessel with an air-lock would provide better protection from air and microbes tainting the brew.

BLACKBERRY WINE
The fruit needs to be collected on a dry day so that there are yeasts present on the fruit surface (preferable there would have been no rain for a week or so). Mash the fruit with a fork to extract the juice, measure the volume, then place in your vessel. Boil water and when cooled off a little pour over the fruit in the proportion of ½-litre water to ½ kilo of fruit. Stir well and allow to stand 4 days undisturbed. During this time a yeasty crust will hopefully have formed. Siphon off the liquid gently, to avoid disturbing any sediment, into a suitably sized pan where it can be warmed very gently, and sugar dissolved at rate of 450 gm sugar to 4.5 litres of juice. Turn into a fermentation cask, with the opening air-locked and leave in a warm-ish place until fermentation has ceased. Then close cask tightly and bottle 6 months later.

RHUBARB WINE
Chop 2.3 kilos of young rhubarb stalks, then roughly pulverize them, and place in a tub with a gallon of water, and allow to stand for 3 days, stirring regularly. On day four strain the liquid into a wide-mouthed fermentation vessel (like a bucket) and add 1.4 kilos of sugar, and mix well to dissolve the sugar. Leave the

brew to ferment for 4 or 5 days, by which time a crust should have formed. This should be removed – carefully to avoid breaking it up into the liquid.

Pour the liquid into a suitable-sized cask or polypin, making sure the vessel is full, and lightly stop the bung-hole but don't fully seal down. Two weeks later fully stopper and leave the brew to rest for 8 or 9 months. Then draw off the liquor, add a little more sugar to rebalance sweetness if required (if it starts to ferment again then allow to rest, and then draw off once again). In 4 to 6 weeks bottle the brew in readiness to drink around June-July.

Of course, the residual rhubarb 'mash' could be cooked up and eaten.

PEAPOD BEER
Place peapod shells into a large pan with enough water to slightly more than submerge them. Bring to a boil then remove to a part of the fire where they can simmer gently for 3 hours to extract the sweetness. Strain, allow to cool to blood temperature then add yeast, allow to ferment, then bottle or drink. To make the beer more bitter boil some hops or wood-sage (*Teucrium scorodonia*) and mix the decoction with the cooling peapod wort.

NETTLE BEER
Boil 2 litres of young nettle sprouts in 4.5 litres of water, strain the wort, add 230 gm of sugar (plus a teaspoon of ginger if you have the luxury of that). When at blood temperature add yeast and allow to ferment, bottling when coming near to the end of fermentation. Can be consumed a few days later.

GENERAL WINE-MAKING
Lots of fruits, with the addition of sugar and yeast can produce a wine, with a very generalized mixture being 1.4 to 1.8 kilos of fruit, 1.6 kilos of sugar, 4.5 litres of water and about 14 gm of yeast. The following is a breakdown of many country wines and their relative ingredient proportions and should give you a starting point to work from.

	Fruit (k)	Sugar (k)	Water (l)	Yeast (gm)
Apple *	1.6	1.4	6.8	
Beetroot	1.4	1.4	6.8	14
Blackcurrant *	1.8	1.8	4.5	
Cherry	2.3	1.6	4.5	7
Elderberry	2.3	1.4	4.5	14
Plum	1.6	1.8	4.5	7
Rosehip *	1.6	1.6	4.5	
Mulberry *	1.8	1.6	4.5	
Pear	2.3	1.4	4.5	14
Sloe *	1.6	1.6	4.5	

* Surface yeasts can provide the active principle for fermentation.

BREWING & DISTILLING

Party-Time? Anyone familiar with brewing their own beers and wines may wish to skip this section since it is designed as an overview of the brewing process, rather than present the 'craft' of brewing / wine-making. For brewing novices the information might inspire you to explore the subject a little further to become familiar with the processes, and experiment at home for a bit of fun. In that respect there are numerous books available on home-brewing and wine-making.

So why the emphasis on brewing in a post-disaster world? Well it's severalfold... Centuries ago, when water purity was dreadful, one of the few relatively bug-free drinks available was beer (it was actually termed *'small beer'* since it contained lower quantities of alcohol – less than 2% – than the strong beers consumed for partying). The safety key to this 'small beer' was that the water to make it had been BOILED, whereas the water drawn from local rivers, streams, or other groundwater sources was likely to be contaminated with faeces – human as well as animal – and a variety of other nasty parasites which might variously give you a fatal dose of cholera, dysentery or typhus. Just think for a moment of the health and hygiene chaos that follows flooding or tsunami-like disasters, where access to safe, potable, drinking water becomes a major concern.

So brewing of 'small beer' has an element of hygiene about it, and when you read in old books that several hundred years ago we would consume a few pints of ale with EVERY meal that does not mean our ancestors were a bunch of piss-heads, simply that they were drinking liquids that were safe to consume. Yes, there was an alcoholic content to be sure, while the other brewing ingredients would provide flavour that made the beer more palatable than plain water (which would probably have been murky looking in any case, even if it contained no parasites whatever), but at least most of the bugs would have been dead. Well hopefully.

Beer (or other country brews) also provides access to two very useful substances in nature's chemistry set – *alcohol* in its raw state, and *acetic acid* (vinegar). The concentration of alcohol in small beer is not going to be sufficiently high to make it useful as a pure alcohol source, but if the alcohol levels can be increased upwards to 10 or 15% then that alcohol can be distilled off, and provide the source of a flammable fuel or be useful for first aid. The vinegar route is achieved by allowing the beer brew to go sour by exposing it to air (in the old days this sour liquid was known as *alegar*), though the concentra-tion of acid in solution is not sufficient to use the liquid for pickling food.

Naturally formed vinegars from cider or wine are similarly unsuitable because of their small acid content, since pickling vinegar needs to be a minimum of 5% to provide proper protection from bacterial decay. There is, however, an easy way of concentrating the acid, though it is a winter-time occupation... Simply leave casks or containers of low-grade vinegar exposed to frost overnight and remove the ice that has formed the following day. There will be some acid mixed in with the ice and so is lost in the process, but the liquid which remains in the cask will be much more acidic.

So, onwards to beer-making. The chemistry behind the process is pretty straightforward: take a sugary, flavoured, solution, add yeast, and wait. What happens is that the yeast, which is a live organism, feeds on the sugars in solution and so is able to reproduce. In so doing, alcohol is produced as a by-product of reproduction. Voila! You have your beer, wine or cider depending on the brew at hand.

There is, however, a snag in the post-disaster world. Where do you get your sugar from, since the consumer-age sugar-bag tree will no longer be sprouting forth? The answer lies in two sources, either from malt or from honey. In the past honey itself was fermented to produce a drink called *metheglin*, and also *mead*. For traditional brewing however it was *malt* that provided the sugar source from cereal grain, and if you want to make beer then you are going to have to turn your hand to becoming a maltster. These rosy thoughts preclude the possible problem of finding a source of common cereals, or beehives or bee nests for honey, while the brewing process itself will require a source of precious fuel, and water which may not be readily available in quantity.

The physical process behind the malting process is again quite straightforward, although the organic chemistry behind the scenes is complex at the micro level. Take barley (the traditional source for beer-making malt) or wheat, germinate the grains in quantity, then mill or crush them, and finally steep in hot water to extract the sugars (*maltose* or *dextrose*) which have formed during germination. This, then, is the source of the sugary malt which the yeast will feed on to produce alcohol.

Without the germination process the cereal grains cannot be transformed into beer since their starch content remains exactly that, as starch. If you boiled unmalted grains you would simply be extracting the flavour from the husks, and indeed barley and wheat wines can be made through such a process once sugar is added to the boiled liquor so that fermentation can proceed in the presence of added yeast.

MAKING THE STUFF
In overview, the process of making beer-like alcoholic beverages is – with occasional variations – boiling the *wort* (water containing herbs like hops with sugar or malt), fermentation, racking and resting, fining, and bottling (or putting in barrels).

For brewing aficionados the quality of the local water (hard or soft, or shades in between) can affect the taste and palatability of the final product. In extreme hard and soft water cases then you may want to adjust the water chemically. However, in a post-disaster world getting your hands on the requisite alterant substances may not be possible, so the best route is possibly to test-run small batches of brews to see how the water quality influences the final outcome. To check for hard water in the field, boil some water for twenty minutes or so, to evaporate part of it, and then look to see if there are any chalk-like deposits on the sides of the pan. Another alternative is to look for telltale calcine 'fur' in nearby domestic (or farmyard) pipes, taps or kettles. Obviously rusty water which has been standing in iron or metal containers will be unsuitable, though collected rainwater (very soft) will probably be the cleanest source – assuming there are no contaminating airborne particulates around.

Having selected herbs that will provide the taste of your brew (normally hops, but dandelion and burdock too, for example), these need to be boiled in water; not only to extract the flavours, but also sterilize the water and any pathogens that may be attached to the herbage. Boiling will also allow any stray proteins in the water to floc as scum.

The water must reach boiling point for at least one minute (at sea level, longer at higher altitudes) and then continue for a minimum of 30 minutes at a gently rolling boil. If using raw malted grains rather than sugar you may need to boil for much longer to extract all the sugars.

The next step is to add the yeast to the wort, which has been strained of the herbs and allowed to cool down. Cooling is important – remembering that yeast is a live organism – because if the liquor is hot then the yeast can be killed off before it can get to work. In the old days yeast used to be added when the wort was at 'blood temperature'.

The type of yeast used is also important – certainly if one was being a purist about the beer produced. Brewing, or brewer's, yeast (mainly *Saccharomyces cerevisiae*) is not likely to be readily available in the post-disaster world. However.... this yeast strain is also used in baking, so there is hope perhaps.

Indeed, in the old days it would appear that some households simply used the same yeast mixture that was employed for making their bread. There are actually differences in the make-up of various brewing and baking yeasts – one key factor for the brewer being that some baking yeast tends to sink to the bottom of the wort as it ferments, and is therefore not so efficient. Note, however, that yeasts used for making lagers are actually bottom dwellers, if one can put it like that. Another factor is that baking yeasts tend to be more 'active' in their CO_2 production, whereas proper brewer's yeasts can be gentler.

In the old days the trick to circumvent yeast dropping to the bottom of the fermentation vessel was to spread the yeast over the surface of a slice of toast which was then floated on the top of the cooled wort; so providing a large active area of the yeast buds to do their work.

FERMENTATION
The bubbly bit of the process... Once the yeast is added (being well stirred-in, the fermentation vessel loosely, not tightly covered, and placed in a warm-ish environment of 15-21°c) it begins to 'work' on the sugars held in solution, forming a frothy layer of suspended carbon dioxide bubbles on the liquid surface. The initial layer of foam is usually skimmed off, allowing the yeast to form a crust on the surface as it reproduces itself.

If the type of yeast you have is a 'top fermenter', as opposed to a bottom-dwelling type, then from time to time you will occasionally need to agitate the floating yeast crust that forms, then replace the cover. The reason for this is that if the wort is not allowed to have a bit of air to breathe, because the crust smothers the entire liquid surface, then the brew can also become sour – although the liquid does need to be kept away from full-on exposure to air. Bottom fermenting yeasts don't cause this problem and the fermentation vessel can be tightly secured (with an airlock) at the start of fermentation.

After about one to two weeks the yeast should have completed its work, and the next step is to siphon off the liquor into a spotlessly clean large bottle (a carboy, for example) or narrow-necked container which can be made air-tight. In siphoning off the liquid, try not to disturb the sediment at the bottom of the fermenting vessel, though inevitably this means you will loose a small amount of your brew.

At this point in serious brewing the liquid will have 'finings' added, which help clear impurities in the brew by allowing them to settle. Often the substance used is isinglass (derived from the swim bladders of fish, and unlikely to be readily available in a post-disaster world) though gelatine can be used... and perhaps is more likely to be available to the doomsday kitchen if you can render down animal bones for their gelatine. One other item which has been used for fining is the seaweed Irish Moss (*Chondrus crispus*), sometimes added during wort boiling from what I understand. However, in the absence of ANY fining substance whatever, don't worry, the brew can still be consumed without clearing, although it may appear somewhat cloudy. But then doesn't some scrumpy cider?

All that remains to do now is allow the brew to *rest* for a week – enabling any residual CO_2 to escape through an air-lock (more below) and any remaining yeast in solution to finally settle out – and then bottle if storing for longer term use. As always with brewing every container or implement used in the making of the brew needs to be scrupulously clean, if not sterilized, or else the brew is likely to go off through bacterial contamination.

AIR-LOCKS & OTHER USEFUL SNIPPETS
Home-brewers and wine-makers use commercially available glass or plastic airlocks which conveniently slip into pre-holed bungs or corks. These airlocks simply allow the release of any fermentation gases to escape by being bubbled through a water seal, while preventing ingress of air which will foul and sour

the brew. In the field you can rustle-up an equivalent device using a piece of siphon tube; one end pushed through a bung which seals the settling container, while the other end is placed in a water-filled milk bottle, jar, or small container allowing the CO_2 to bubble through the liquid.

If you were in need of distilling alcohol for whatever reason then the traditional method of achieving this is to use a still where the vapour is condensed in tubes passing through coolant water. But what if you have no tubing, or a boiling container? Well, the answer may rest in the design below. It is a cross section of a still formerly used in China.

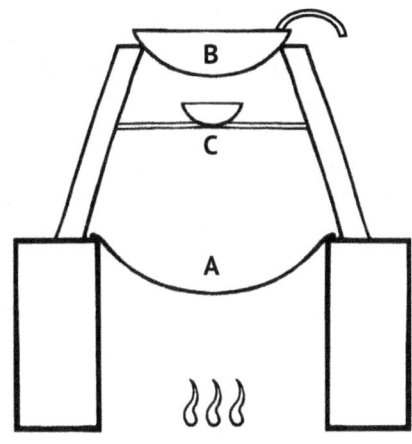

The pan [A] with the fermented wort or mash is placed over a fire contained by brickwork; the edges of the pan tightly fitting recesses in the blockwork. Above and around this is an enclosable structure that surrounds the distilling work area. [B] is a metal vessel filled with cold water that is changed from time to time during distillation, while [C] is the collection vessel, placed on a shelf of metal rods or wooden dowels.

As the liquid in [A] heats up, alcoholic vapour is released which condenses on the cold underside surface of [B] and drips down into [C]. A small pipe connected to the coolant vessel allows warmed water to be released before new coolant water is added.

In a doomsday world this design could be utilized to distil clean water from contaminated sources, although the supply of fuel will need to be considered.

Obviously in a post-disaster world you would need to assess precious fuel and water resources which may be needed for other things, or at a later time in the year, rather than converting them into alcoholic drinks.

ROOT CROP & FRUIT STORAGE

The place that you store root crops needs three key attributes: dryness, good ventilation, and a cool temperature (varies between species) averaging something between 0° and 4°c. Some thick-skinned apples can be stored at, or marginally below, freezing, then thawed out slowly. Cellars can provide a good place for storage IF they match the criteria above. In normal times, where domestic heating is available, then any boiler / heating pipes would need to be lagged, and perhaps the boiler boxed in too.

The second, and critical, essential of successful storage is the *quality* of the physical item to be stored. No vegetable or fruit item that is imperfect – cut, bruised, soft, or with suspected viral lesions – should be stored, as just the one bad one in a batch can spoil all the others, wasting your time *and* valuable food.

Potatoes are a good root crop to store in a *dark* cellar or shed. Spread them out on wooden trays (which can be stacked on top of each other if the trays are vented at the base and sides) so that no tuber touches its neighbour, the tray being raised a couple of brick lengths above the floor. In the case of rather crowded trays, as the potatoes get used up then more space becomes available to thin out the remainder.

Beets, carrots, parsnips and turnips too can be stored in a cool, dry, cellar. Select only *perfect* ones, pack them carefully in boxes of sand making sure that individual roots do not touch, and layering sand and carrots till the box is full. Any young sprouting greenery from stored turnip roots can be eaten as a salad.

Keep the winter's stock of cabbages and turnips stored in the garden rather than a cellar. Select your storage box then place 15 cm of DRY earth in the bottom, and then sink the box to half its depth in a trench in a DRY part of the garden. Fill the box with the vegetables – perfect cabbage heads, carefully handled to prevent the outer leaves being bruised, and perfect turnips with no external blemishes or surface breaks. Place the vegetables HEAD DOWN then lightly cover them with another 20 to 25 cm of dry soil. When, or if, severe frosts and weather occur then a thick layer of straw will need to be added on top of this, and perhaps some other rain-resistant plastic sheet material for added protection.

If you don't have storage boxes then do not despair, they can be dispensed with by devising a deep trench system. Dig a trench 1 metre deep in a dry soil area of the garden, place your carefully selected cabbages head down as before, close up the hole with a pile of dry earth, cover with a heap of straw, and then this with the rain-resistant material. Lack of soil moisture is a key element of successful storage of root crops.

In the outdoors potatoes can be stored in trenches during the frosty winter period. Select a dry spot with a porous soil, or at least one that will not hold water so that it saturates if it rains. Dig a trench 45 cm deep (and as long as required to accommodate the number of potatoes you have). Line the bottom of the trench with 5 to 8 cm of dry straw. Being careful not to bruise the potatoes, or use damaged ones, stack layers of the tubers so that the layers narrow with height until the top row has just a single line of potatoes (viz. the apex of a roof). Pack the remaining space in the trench with more straw, and then another 15 cm on top of that. When flush with the trench top cover the trench with bales of hay, then place a tarp over these and weigh or tie down, but do not hermetically seal the hay with the tarp.

Pears may be kept for a good number of weeks providing they have been handled right. They should be picked when firm but still be in an unripe state. Each one should be wiped clean and wrapped individually in waxed paper, then stored away in a cool, dry, dark place.

Apples, too, can be kept for a long time. If you are lucky, then for up to a year… but nothing is guaranteed. They need to be picked on a dry day (I think in preference I would have a couple of dry days so that there is as little moisture around on the apple surfaces as possible). They can then be stored in a couple of different ways: they are placed on a dry floor for 3 weeks before being carefully wiped, and then stored between layers of straw without touching each other, and with a final layer of straw added to prevent frost damage should the storage area be prone to really low temperatures.

The second storage method is similar in that apples are placed in a storage container in which a layer of dried sand is placed at the bottom, then the apples layered in between more dry sand without any apples touching. The container is sealed and then stored in a cool, dry, frost-free place.

CEREAL GRAINS AND MILLING

There may be a point in a long-term, post-disaster, world where you need to utilize actual grain; either as a handout (because there are no working mills to produce flour), or grains that you glean from redundant field systems. There may also be a need to propagate those seed grains over several years to start grain production again. So this section briefly covers the main cereal grain types, while also providing brief notes on grinding cereal grains for use.

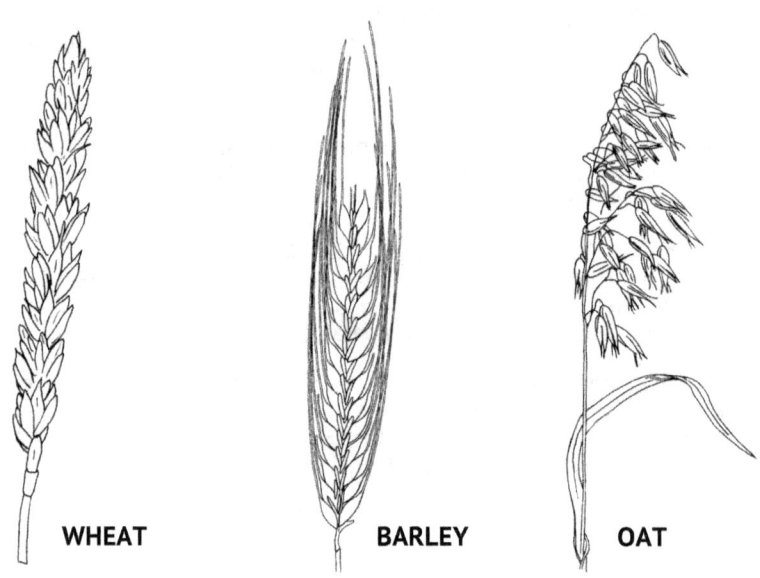

WHEAT   **BARLEY**   **OAT**

WHEAT (*Triticum*)
There are many varieties of wheat, some which have spiky 'beards' while others do not, and are classified as soft or hard types, and also by their grain colour which can range from white to those with a reddish tinge. Varieties with very large kernels do not always produce the biggest yield; larger grains on a smaller head being outperformed by varieties with many smaller kernels on a long head.

As well as being classified as hard or soft types, wheat is divided into winter and spring varieties, depending on when they are sown. In 'hard' varieties of wheat the grains have a higher content of protein and gluten than in the 'soft' grain wheats which are more often used to produce baked items that are lighter. Flour made from soft grain wheat types will sometimes have a proportion of hard grain added to boost the protein levels. One of the hardest grained wheats is durum which is generally used for pasta, and is sometimes mixed with soft wheat.

OAT (*Avena*)
Oats like a cool, moist, climate best, with a moist clay-loam soil preferred, though poor soils are tolerated. The grains are ready to harvest when they have passed through their 'milk stage' (a grain pressed between the fingers will produce a milky juice) and matured, and some leaves of the plants are already showing signs of yellowing. If allowed to ripen much beyond this stage then the grains are prone to *shattering* – where the grains fall away from the head when it is touched.

BARLEY (*Hordeum*)
Barley has a central role in beer brewing, yet it makes a nutritious flour that can be used for making bread, and in this respect is good for anyone who is gluten-intolerant. Barley can be grown under a wide variety of climatic conditions, even in quite northerly latitudes, while it requires less water for growth than other cereal grains yet can tolerate abundant water conditions. Barley root systems are not as vigorous as those of wheat and oats, and it tends to have a problem with adapting to soil types, yet copes with a wide climatic range. The best yields come from rich, fertile, well-drained sandy loam soils, but also well-drained loams and clay soils being tolerated. When threshed the grain hull is not removed.

RYE (*Secale*)
Another hardy grain crop that is widely grown across the central temperate European climes is rye, since it is able to thrive in cool climates where wheat and other cereals cannot flourish. However, rye can be grown in warmer climate areas, and it favours soils of a light, sandy loam type, and is pretty drought tolerant (it requires less water than wheat to grow because of its highly developed root system). Indeed, rye is able to tolerate soils which are poor in humus, though on very depleted soils the yield / quality will not be great. For grain production rye seeds are sown in the autumn for harvesting the following summer.

WILD GRAINS
Although there are some wild grasses and sedges that have edible seeds the drawback with these in my view is that the energy expended in harvesting the small seeds and de-husking may not be rewarded by sufficient nutritional return. If you want undertake a bit of research then I would concentrate on the following species variously found in temperate Europe and North America: *Avena fatua, Cladium mariscus, Dactylis glomerata, Digitaria sanguinalis, Echinocloa crus-galli, Glyceria fluitans, Hordeum jubatum, Milium effusum, Phragmites communis, Schoenoplectus lacustris* and *tabernamontani, Setaria viridis, Sorghum halapense*.

	SPRING	WINTER
WHEAT	Ashby, Belvoir[H], Granary, Mulika, Paragon, Tybalt.	Alchemy[S], Batallion, Beluga[S], Claire, Conqueror[H], Consort, Cordiale, Crusoe, Denman[S], Duxford[H], Gallant, Grafton[H], Gravitas[S], Hereward[H], Horatio[S], Humber[H], Invicta, Panorama, Relay[H], Scout, Solstice, Tuxedo, Viscount[S].
BARLEY	Belgravia, Chronicle, Moonshine, Odyssey, Overture, Shuffle.	Archer, Flagon, Florentine, Pearl, Retriever, Saffron, Talisman, Winsome.
OAT	Ascot, Atego, Canyon, Firth, Husky, Rozmar.	Balado (dwarf), Fusion (dwarf), Grafton, Tardis.

[S] Soft wheats which are not very good for biscuits

[H] Hard wheat

If you were ever to encounter stored wheat then the names of some of the hundreds of wheat cultivars grown across Europe include:
Agami, Altigo, Apache, Aristotle, Asketis, Barok, Bermude, Biscay, Boregar, Bussard, Camp Remy, Caphorn, Carenius, Celebration, Centenaire, Centennial, Cézanne, Colbert, Compliment, Contender, Corvus, Cubus, Dekan, Edgar, Ephoros, Expert, Falstaff, Fatima 2, Florian, Folio, Fortis, Fortore, Foxtrott, GK-Othalom, Hekto, Henrik, Homeros, Hyland, Hymat, Inspiration, Interest, Intro, Isengrain, Istabraq, Julius, Kaspart, Ketchum, Koch, Lear, Legat, Levis, Limes, Linus, Lion, Ludwig, Madrigal, Matrix, Maverick, Meister, Meunier, Mulan, Norba, Nucleo, Ordéal, Orpheus, Orvantis, Patrel, Profilus, Raspail, Razzano, Rochfort, Rockystart, Runal, Sahara, Santana, Scor, Soissons, Sophytra, Sponsor, Tabasco, Tamaro, Tirone, Tobak, Tommi, Tourmalin, Unicum, Zappa. If you find grain stores or sacks bearing these names then at least you will understand what is being referred to.

MILLING GRAIN
Milling of cereal grains by hand is a thankless and tiring task, and it is perhaps unsurprising that at the first opportunity humans had to pass this chore to someone else to do they did so, and for the last century or so the drudgery has been banished to large industrial machinery. With cereals like oat and barley the tough hulls need removing even before they can be processed for flour. In a post-disaster world it may be necessary to re-learn old skills, and the brief notes that follow outline some of the principle ways of grinding cereals.

The very first method used by man to get at the goodness of cereal grains was with a stone crusher and a hollow stone; simply beating the grains into submission by repeated pummelling. Then the saddlestone method seems to have developed (below left) where a stone muller was worked backwards and forwards to 'grind' the grains. Many museums are littered with examples of these saddle-stones which became hollowed with time and wear. A pre-threshing machine technique for quickly getting at the cereal grains was to take bundles of the dried cereal on the stalk, and then set fire to the ears, beating the end with a stick to dislodge the grains.

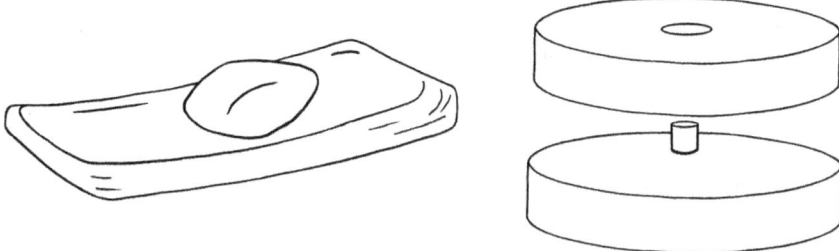

Then there developed the first stone querns where the grain was milled between a revolving top-stone and fixed bed-stone (pictured above right). In the centre of the lower bed-stone a wooden (and eventually metal) pin projected upwards, and fitted into a socket in the top-stone which was fitted with a wooden or metal bridge (technically known as the *rynd*). This bridge helped centre the spindle but also had channels that allowed grain to be poured in. A short stick was embedded in a hole in the top-stone which allowed the operator to turn the stone and so mill the grains between the stone surface.

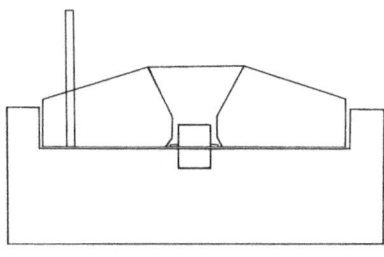

With time more sophisticated querns appeared, with the central top spindle hole bored out to form a hopper-like structure, called the *feed eye* or *swallow*. The querns sometimes became table or bench mounted, while the surface of the grindstones also started to be grooved for greater efficiency. Another development saw the short wooden turning stick replaced by a long pole which extended upwards towards a hole in the ceiling of the dwelling, allowing two people to simultaneously move the bar which turned the top-stone.

341

As watermills and windmills semi-industrialized the milling process millstone technology became much more sophisticated, with all sorts of furrow designs experimented with to improve efficiency. The furrow design pictured right is one example of many; the long cuts being the 'master' furrows, the two behind the 'secondary' furrows. These furrows helped distribute the grains and meal over the grinding surface; the ridged areas partly reducing the grain, while the hollows allowed a meagre supply air which helped keep the grinding surfaces cooler than they would otherwise be, but also allowed the transit of meal towards the rim of the millstones.

On closer inspection there is a lot more sophistication to the griding process than merely rubbing two stones together – at least in industrial milling, as the diagram below shows. In fact it is only the stone surfaces towards the edges that actually do the grinding; the first, inner, sections of the millstones being curved and then flattening in the grinding zone. The feed eye, which catches the grain, by degrees unifies and pushes it outwards, reducing it to meal, and then finally flour which is ejected at the edges. If you were going to make your own grinding stones in a post-disaster world, then it might be worth considering incorporating this concept. Personally, I think it should be possible to construct a rudimentary quern from dense slabs of pavement concrete, although there might be considerable wear. That said, many domestic querns of old were made of sandstone which cannot have been much more wear resistant.

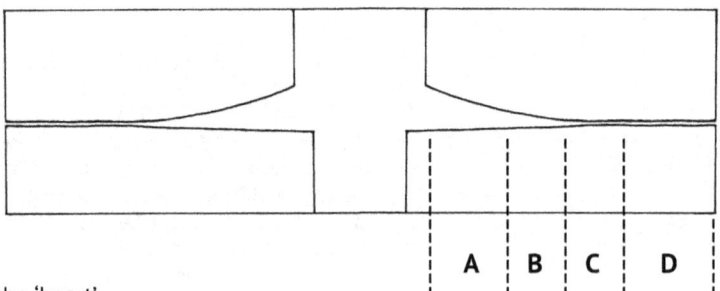

A – the 'heart'
B – intermediate zone
C – reducing zone
D – grinding zone

IMPROVISED GRINDING / POUNDING TOOLS

An alternative to grinding grains between bricks, stones or concrete in a post-disaster world is to construct an equivalent of the heavy wooden pestles used for pounding grain in the developing world. Think of any videos or pictures that you may have seen of places like Africa where villagers pound sorghum, millet and maize in large wooden mortars and you should get the idea.

There are, in fact, two stages to the grinding / milling process; particularly important in the case of preparing barley and oat grains which have a tightly clasping outer husk that must be removed to get at the useful part which can be milled. The husk around wheat grains is not so problematic to remove. So you will need to develop a couple of processing tools – one for dehulling and another for crushing and primitive milling, as it were.

For dehulling barley and oat grains you need to find yourself a heavy wooden pole, though not too heavy – remembering *economy of effort*. Ideally you want to be able to raise the pole 30 to 40 cm above the grain without too much effort, but for it to have sufficient mass to slam back down into the grain mass without too much additional personal effort expended. To prepare the grains for dehulling add just sufficient water to moisten the outer husk layer and leave for an hour or two until the husk has softened somewhat. The moistened grains should not appear wet. Place the grains in a container (essentially a mortar) and then pound the grains with your improvised pestle. Gradually the husks will separate with the pounding action, at which point the grains need to be sieved or winnowed to isolate the cereal grains proper. Now you can start to crush the grains, either with bricks or stone or the following improvised crusher.

For your grinding or milling pestle you need to securely tape (or otherwise fix) together three steel tubes that have several millimetres of thickness to the wall, are about 2 to 3 cm wide, and about one metre long. Scaffolding poles are, in my view, a little bit too heavy and also a bit too wide though sections of poles could be used if there is nothing else available.

To grind your de-hulled grains place them in a flat bottomed metal can or container that is placed on a good solid floor, preferably concrete or brick, and then begin to pound the grains. From time to time sieve the mass to remove the finer flour part, returning the coarser material for further processing. If your cooking requires perfectly dry flour then you may need to dry the hulled grains before you pound them.

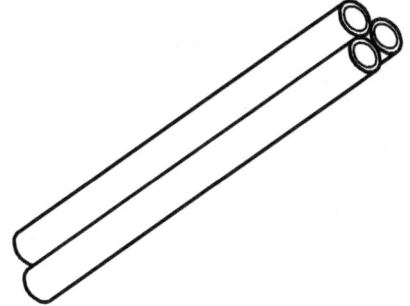

SALT, SALTPETRE & SOAP

Previous sections have covered the making of vinegar which is a vital food preservative in the doomsday kitchen as is salt, and here I wanted to provide some ideas of where to find two of the other key chemicals used in cookery, and which have been mentioned among the recipes – salt and saltpetre – while the soap-making activity is doomsday-kitchen chemistry which can make use of leftover kitchen by-products.

Saltpetre will be a hard commodity to find in a post-disaster world (it is hard enough to come across it in domestic life today), yet it is one of the old stand-by food preservatives. It tends to harden meat, which is maybe where its preservative properties operate.

Although a readily available and common substance true salt is likely to disappear from doomsday kitchens of a post-disaster world, until someone gets the salt production chain back into full swing. If you live near to a coast then you could manufacture salt for yourself, though it is a long procedure, and potentially expensive in terms of fuel consumption where heat is used to evaporate salt pans. Indeed, I personally would not view evaporation of raw salt water by fire an option. Too much wood needs to be consumed to achieve a small return. However, as you will see in the process outlined below, the application of fire at the end of the process does make sense.

SALT

Making salt by forced evaporation of raw seawater will NOT be a viable proposition for the doomsday chef, particularly in the more northern temperate climes of Europe. Far too much fuel will be expended in boiling off the water content to extract salt, when those fuel resources could probably be better used to cook food or keep you warm. I suppose one possible alternative would be to boil vegetables and meat in salt water drawn from the sea, if you happen to be located near to a shoreline.

The only places where natural evaporation of seawater is likely to be a realistic proposition are coastal regions around the north and south Mediterranean. But that could change in temperate areas if there to be sustained hot weather during the summer months. During the 18th century 'bay salt' was extracted from coastal areas in Hampshire; but only during the drier summers and on a somewhat *ad hoc* basis. What could possibly be achieved in cooler areas is for seawater to be partially concentrated through natural evaporation, with the final stages done mechanically with the application of fuel-based heating.

The schematic below is of an 18th century design from France where sea salt was harvested in the Brittany region. Seawater is let into the first reservoir [A], which is 50 cm in depth and where the saltwater is allowed to partly concentrate, before being allowed through a gated sluice (S) into [B]. Here, more sluiced

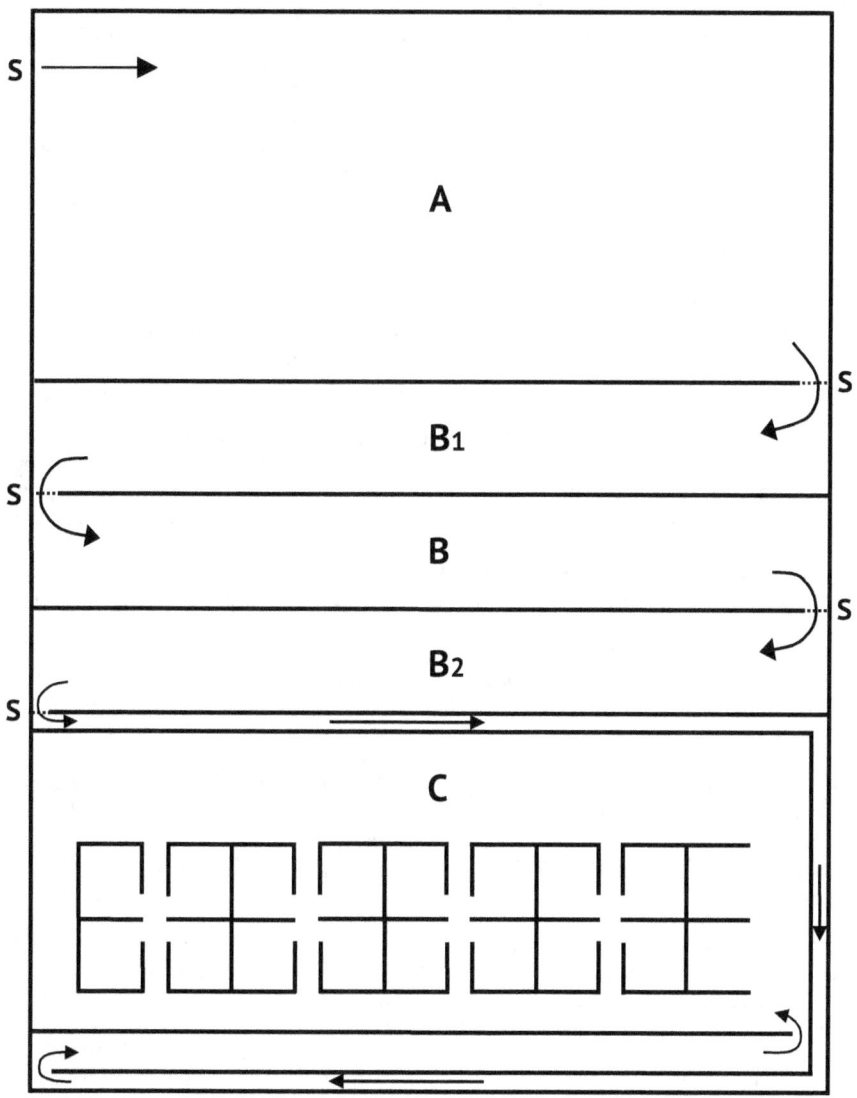

zones, some 25 cm deep, allow the salt concentration to be increased before the brine is channelled into the salt pit area [C]. Here the depth of the brine is only 2 to 3 cm deep, with the salt allowed to crystallize in the pits, being raked off every couple of days.

The site of any natural salt processing endeavour needs to be quite carefully chosen; allowing the natural rhythm of the tides to bring in saltwater, and also allow the salt pits to be drained at low tide. So a low piece of ground close to the sea is required, and one which is free from any freshwater sources (such as springs), or liable to freshwater flooding. The area needs natural banks or rising ground as barriers to the sea, or such barriers can be manmade, and the area needs to be on a bed of clay or other non-percolating soil.

SALTPETRE

Saltpetre, or potassium nitrate (KNO_3), is a chemical perhaps better known for its use in the production of gunpowder, and also candle wicks, but was a key to food preservation for many centuries. Just to confuse matters, the sodium nitrate product extracted from bird guano in south America, and also used in food preservation, was known as 'Chile saltpetre'.

The key to potassium saltpetre production is the oxidation of ammonia (NH_3) components in the presence of potassium ions, and partly aided by bacteria. And where do you find lots of ammonia? Yes, in dung heaps, cess pits, cow byres, sheep pens, and the like. How jolly. These days the industrial production of potassium nitrate is made through a variety of means that mingle and mangle chemical salts to produce the highly purified chemical. One of the main industrial chemical routes is the reaction of potassium chloride with sodium nitrate [$KCl + NaNO_3 = NaCl + KNO_3$], and there are numerous other patented chemical processes. However, in a post-disaster world it may be necessary to re-create the old processes for extracting saltpetre in the absence of an industrial infrastructure. Time to get dirty.

To begin with it should be said that the production of saltpetre through *natural* means takes about 18 months to 3 years when started from scratch, hence it is not going to be an immediately available product (unless you already have a cow byre or sheep pen with a nitrate-rich earth floor), but if there is no other source of saltpetre then the old way is perhaps the route to go.

The formula for this is dung, frequent sprinklings of urine, lime (not a readily available commodity even as you read this) and / or plant material in the form of wood or plant ashes, or plain vegetation that can rot down, time, and protection from the rain – which would leach out the chemicals. If there is heat available, as in clement weather, then the decay process happens more quickly. Vice versa, in cold the process is slower and virtually stops in the dead of a cold winter. Over a year or so a white film of impure saltpetre would form on the surface of the mixture. This was scraped off, mixed with water and saltpetre crystallized out, though it appears the final product was never very pure when compared to the modern industrial chemical manufacture of potassium nitrate.

In the old days it was common for cow byres to be dug out every so often as part of farm life, so there was no need for the artificial construction of the 'nitre plantations' used in the 18th and 19th centuries for the industrial production of saltpetre. Another method of old was to set up lath and plaster-type hurdle structures which contained the dung and urine mixture and over a period of a year or so the saltpetre effloresced through the plaster into crystalline deposits that partly contained nitre (saltpetre). These 'saltpetre brushes' as they were sometimes called, could then be scraped off and processed. Just a thought, but if one was to construct a saltpetre 'plant' from scratch, then cinder blocks might perhaps replace lath and plaster of old, although something present in the chemistry of modern building blocks could possibly effect the purity of the crystals efflorescing.

SOAP

The inclusion of SOAP in this book may seem a little weird, but there is a point. In my view you do need to keep up standards of hygiene as best possible when it comes to being around food, even in stressful situations. In fact it is probably more the case since your immune system may be compromised due to the stressful conditions. At the same time your doomsday kitchen should provide two of the building blocks for making soap – animal fats and lye (in the form of wood ashes from your doomsday kitchen fire). The only other ingredient needed is water, while the process is pretty straightforward although there are certain hazards that you need to be aware of: (1) strong liquid lye can chemically burn your skin, and (2), you will be handling large quantities of boiling water and liquid fat / edible oil which again can burn. So the soap-making process requires care.

The caustic lye, fundamental in the production of making soap, can be made simply of the wood ashes from the fire hearth – not the remains of huge burnt logs, but smaller burnt branches and twigs of 'live' wood and also burnt leaf and stalk material from both trees and some other plants. If you think about it logically the leaves and outer layers of a tree are where the *active* biological processes take place, rather than the old hardwood of the trunk. The main active chemical present in this 'wood lye' is potassium carbonate; not to be confused with the even harsher caustic, sodium hydroxide, which is also used in soap-making and, confusingly, also called 'lye'. Potassium lye makes a soft soap while the sodium type makes hard soap, and the chemistry required to make caustic sodium lye is likely to be beyond the technical resources available to you in a post-disaster world.

When making wood lye, never use ashes from any of the conifers since these contain resinous compounds unsuitable for soap-making, and it would probably be unwise to use something like yew (*Taxus baccatus*) given its highly toxic nature. Hardwoods such as oak, beech, sycamore / maple, apple, for example, all make good candidates for lye production. Funnily enough, bean stalks contain lots of the same chemicals required, as do corn husks, although those are perhaps unlikely to be readily found in a post-disaster world.

To start making your soap you need to collect ashes from the campfire over a period of time in a waterproof, preferably airtight, container; the ashes from any single day's cooking is not going to progress your lye production very far. The reason for keeping the ashes out of reach from the air is that the 'active' chemicals you want to extract from the ashes react with the air and reduce their potency. At the same time you need to collect grease or old oil, and store.

For making the raw liquid wood lye you need to obtain a non-reactive leaching container since the caustic nature of the lye will corrode metals such as aluminium and iron, and may also affect some plastics. If you are going to use a plastic container such as a garden water butt, dustbin, or kitchen pedal-bin, it is probably wise to conduct a test with a small amount of lye (made in a glass jam jar) on a small corner of the plastic container to check its suitability.

IF you can find a large plastic container compatible with caustic substances and so labelled with chemical warning signs, then that would obviously save a lot of heart-ache. Other alternatives for the leaching container are old wooden beer or wine barrels, and also hollowed out logs (non-coniferous). In the latter case burn and then chop out the log centre (as if you were making a stubby dugout canoe). Whatever the container you adopt it should then have three or four 1 to 1.5 cm holes bored in the bottom for lye collection.

Over these holes place a layer of something non-reactive that can act as a filter – straw, small stones or pieces of brick with a sand covering, or perhaps some sort of rock wool substance. Then set the barrel on sturdy supports that will allow a collecting vessel (again non-reactive) to be placed under the drainage holes.

Next, fill the leaching barrel with your saved wood ashes, ramming them down as you add them. When you get near to the top of the barrel make a hollow in the top of the ashes, and pour in enough *boiling* water to fill the hollow, and then keep topping up as the water soaks downwards. With the ashes compacted it will take several hours, even a day or so, before the first drops of lye appear. Keep the hollow continually topped up, though once lye drips begin to appear the use of boiling water is not absolutely necessary. Soft water, or rainwater, is best. The ashes may well settle as they become wetted with the water, in which case add more ashes to the container if you have any left, and add more hot water to activate the leaching process in the new ashes.

Let the lye solution stand 24 hours or until the solids have settled, then pour off the liquor. For the lye to be the correct strength for making soap it should just float a fresh egg (a little bit of the egg just protruding above the liquid). If it doesn't then you have the option of concentrating the liquid through: (1) forced evaporation by fire, or (2), letting excess water naturally evaporate over several days. The colour of the solution is irrelevant to solution strength (indeed the sodium and potassium compounds that you are essentially trying to get at, are white crystalline substances in normal life). If the egg floats higher in the liquid, rather than just have a little dimple showing, then the lye is too strong and needs water adding.

If you have not already done so then you need to prepare some clean tallow or fat (refer to clariyfing fats in the Fats and Oils section elsewhere) – which you can be doing while the lye settles. The cleaner and more pure the fat is, the better looking the soap.

To make soap – the following process is for a soft, almost liquid, soap – prepare three pots or suitable-sized vessels which can be heated over the fire. It can be done with two, but there is more control over the process with three. Those that are in contact with the lye will need to be non-reactive. Also prepare a stick made of deadwood (not greenwood) as a stirrer, as this also needs to be non-reactive. To be perfectly honest I have had very mixed results using this process, often finding it hard to achieve proper saponification, but then it is not an everyday activity or me, unlike the food side.

Melt the fat in one pot, and keep it hot and fluid. In a second pot bring the lye up to a gently rolling boil. Place the third pot over the fire and add a couple of ladles of fat then one of lye, boil and stir with the stick while the mixture begins to take on a consistency like cream. Continue adding and stirring equal amounts of the ingredients until the pot is about half full (more for safety than anything else). To check that the proportions of lye / fat are roughly correct, drop a little of the mixture onto a plate and allow to cool. If there's an excess of water droplets then more fat needs to be added, and vice versa. Refine the mixture and test further. With further boiling the mixture becomes thick and does not adhere to your stirrer.

To make a hard soap it is said that adding salt (a source of sodium) to the mixture above will help it separate and be able to form blocks, however it has not worked for me. Perhaps I don't do enough soap cooking to get it right. For real hard soap you need to use proper caustic soda (Sodium hydroxide, NaOH) which is a really nasty chemical if not handled with care. However, where sodium hydroxide is used for soap making the thick gloopy mixture can be poured into wooden or other non-reactive moulds (explanation in a moment), and allowed to cool and solidify after a few days. Then, depending on the size of your moulds, cut into useful size bars and store for 3 or 4 weeks to 'cure' and harden. This is necessary because there are still some chemical processes going on in the soap with the caustic lye and fats which means that it can react with aluminium – hence the need for those non-reactive moulds. Until 'cured' the soap should also be handled with protective gloves.

A safety note regarding the use of wood ash lye. In its purest form lye (Potassium carbonate, but also Sodium carbonate) is a strong alkaline chemical reagent that can damage skin in a concentrated form, but is nowhere near as dangerous as NaOH or KOH which cause real chemical burns. When making your soap it will be advisable to wear eye protection, rubber gloves (the longer the better), and if at all possible some sort of apron. Keep, also, a bottle of vinegar handy as the acid can help neutralize the lye. Have the lid of the vinegar bottle unscrewed but still in place – this will save on delays in undoing the lid if there is a spill. My suggestion is that you keep everyone not involved in the soap-making process far away from the work area in case of spills, and on NO account be tempted to working round the campfire in bare feet when soap-making. Protect yourself!

When working with lye, add the lye to oil or fat, and not the other way round. Similarly, if you decide to work with lye in crystalline form (either commercially produced, or any that you have evaporated down to crystalline form) it is imperative that lye is added to water gradually, and not water to the crystals, as it produces heat that significantly raises the temperature of the liquid solution.

There may be scope for increasing the alkalinity of the mild potassium carbonate to stronger potassium hydroxide. The process would be somewhat involved and require a source of chalk or limestone [Calcium carbonate, $CaCO_3$]. If the carbonate is heated strongly [about 900°c plus] it produces calcium oxide [Quicklime, CaO] with CO_2 evolved as a gas. Quicklime moistened with water produces a crumbly calcium hydroxide powder [$Ca(OH)_2$] which, when combined with the mild K_2CO_3 produces potassium hydroxide [KOH] and calcium carbonate (mostly in a solid form which may be filtered out).

Sodium cabonate obtained from burning plants from the seashore such as various *Chenopods*, *Salicornia*, *Salsola kali*, as well as some seaweeds, produces an ash that may be used in soap-making and when treated with quicklime produces caustic NaOH which is better for making harder soaps.

However, in a post-disaster world accessing seaweed or chalk is going to be out of the reach of most folks, so you may have to get used to a life of simply being glad to wash with plain old rainwater.

CANDLEMAKING

Should you not use all the fat from your doomsday kitchen for cooking purposes, or making soap, then the excess can be transformed into candles for lighting your way or warming your hands. To be perfectly honest, it is unlikely in any post-disaster world there will be domestic electrical lighting available, and you will need to *actively manage fat resources*; allocating portions for cooking, lighting and, potentially, fuel. There could be times where any of these requirements may, individually, take prime consideration.

Behind every good candle 'burn' there are a few principles that need to be considered. If you have never perused the principles of how a candle functions, here's it is: a central wick is surrounded by a mass of fuel (fat, or wax), and when lit the radiated heat of the flame melts the fat immediately nearby, which is then drawn up by the wick material through capillary action to be vaporized in the flame, burnt, and so on.

Wicks are made of a variety of substances; most are usually braided cotton filaments, but thin paper wrapped around fine wire core is another type. Synthetic fibres are not suitable for wicks. One thing I have never tried, but it might be worth investigating, is whether nettle cordage would make a viable wick material. Ideally, the wick and wax should burn off at the same relative rate, otherwise wicks can either drown in molten fat or burn too rapidly and burn away before enough liquid fuel is available to combust.

Where the fuel source is potentially sticky or tacky, as with animal fats, then wicks need to be quite thick, as they also do when a thick candle is being produced. However, a thick wick can produce a large flame that melts more fat than can be burnt, so the excess floods or drips over edges of the candle. The fat used for candle-making needs to be a hard fat like sheep tallow or made from beef suet, rather than pork lard which, on its own, is too soft.

When it comes to candle production and melting the fat care needs to be taken as you are dealing with hot liquids that burn! Yes, it is an obvious fact, but in a post-disaster world you need to extra careful because there won't be hospitals or medics available to mend you. The fat should only be heated to a point where it melts, not raised to a super-high temperature where smoke is produced or where the fat reaches a flash point and the fumes produced spontaneously ignite and cause personal injury or a fire risk. For that reason when melting the fat avoid using a fire where swirling flames are present, using, rather, a bed of hot coals or embers. Best practice would see the fat melted in a water-bath or double-boiler, but that may not be practicable. Also, keep *water* away from your melted fat, whether it's from a shower of rain or any other source. Hot fats and water make nasty bedfellows (just think of how things spit in a frying pan if a little moisture is present, and you are going to be dealing with hot fat in bulk!). The only exception to this is bucket or container of cold water placed relatively nearby in case you get hot fat on your skin. If that does happen then immerse the area in the cold water immediately, like lighting, rather than try to brush off the hot fat which simply spreads the burn area.

Make sure that all the working surfaces, melting pots and moulds are stable and sound. Again, just be methodical and careful given the circumstances; do not leave any melting fats unattended, wear suitable protective clothing, and keep children away from your candle-making operations. Personally, I would keep *anyone* not required for the candle-making session away from the area because, should an accident happen, then the more bodies in the area the harder it is to scramble out of the way of harm.

Aluminium, steel and iron cooking pots or containers are best for melting the fat. However, consider the size of the melting vessel, because if a bulk of hot fat drops or spills then there is real potential for a bad accident or fire. And rather than pour from the bulk melt container itself, use a ladle or smaller vessel (with a spout if possible) for pouring the molten fat to where it is required. Lastly, do the pouring *away* from the fire or heat source so any spills do not ignite. Think safety first!

With a suitable volume of melted fat available you then have three methods of producing candles: DIPPING, CASTING and POURING.

DIPPING

This is the most straightforward method of making a candle, but it can be a slow process. All you need to do is repeatedly dip a wick into a pot of molten fat and each time allow the new layer to cool for a few minutes, and continue dipping until the required candle thickness is achieved. To speed things up, you could possibly build a jig that allows several, or even more, wicks to be dipped at the same time.

With this method, and all the other candle production methods, it is a good idea to 'prime' the wick at the start. All this simply means is that the wick is initially allowed to soak in the hot fat for a couple of minutes to fully absorb the hydrocarbons into its structure, and makes for better burning.

One point to be aware of when dipping candles; keep the molten fat as far as possible at a constant temperature. Should the fat temperature rise, then fat will be melted off the dipped wick rather than a new layer added to it. Wicks only need to be dipped for a few seconds each time, allowed to harden over a few minutes, then re-dipped.

CASTING

Cast candles are the fastest to produce in the sense that once they have been poured then you can walk away and get on with some other chore while the fat hardens. The downside of this method is that there are some fiddly preparatory and post-production activities required.

To begin with you will need to acquire, or make, some sort of mould. This could be as straightforward as a small sardine or tobacco tin (which becomes the candle holding container in its own right), to fizzy drinks cans suitably de-topped and de-bottomed. Personally I think the smaller 'mixer' size drink cans are the most suitable. If there is a plastic lining to these drink cans it will need to be burned off prior to use, and any burrs from cutting off the can bottom smoothed down. What you should end up with is a smooth metal tube to hold the cooling fat. Plastics are unsuitable for casting candles because they may melt.

For each tube you need to fashion a snug-fitting, removable, baseplate that contains the hot fat and holds the wick at the bottom of the tube. This plate can be a section of thin plywood, or even the lid off another type of tin. In either case a small hole for the wick needs to be punctured into the centre of the base plate. Another item that you need to procure are twigs of about pencil thickness to hold the wick in place at the top of the mould.

To cast the candles: take some primed wick, pass it through the baseplate hole where it should be held in place with a small knot, piece of tape or smear of clay (to prevent the fat running out). Next, pass the wick through the metal tube and tie the other end to a twig at the top. Centre the wick (prevents uneven burning), rolling it round the twig to give it good tension. Lastly, seal round the outside of the tin where it meets with the baseplate with clay. If clay is not available then another method of blocking off the bottom of the mould is to dribble in spoonfuls of fat, swirl around the seam, and repeat this until about 1 cm layer of fat has formed in the mould like a plug. All that remains to do is ladle in the main bulk of fat and allow it to cool.

The main pour should be done gradually so that pockets of air don't form as the fat cools. As the fat cools it may also sink and form a hollow at the top. Simply top this up with additional hot fat. When solidified, release the wick wrapped round the twig, and pull the base plate gently. Should the candle not wish to budge, find a stick or branch that is nearly the diameter of the metal tube and forcibly push the candle out.

POURING
Poured candles are not, in my view, a very productive method of candle production as only one candle can be made at a time. The only advantage of this method is that it gets round situations where only small quantities of molten fat may be heated at a time, or no suitable depth container is available for dipping the wicks.

Quite simply, a primed wick is held over a container to catch excess fat, and then ladles of hot fat poured down the wick; each layer allowed to cool for a few minutes before the next pour. As with dipped candles the temperature of the fat needs to be constant, otherwise overheated fat will remove previous layers rather than add a new one.

Finally, a number of other pointers regarding lighting / making candles with fat. First, that the fat needs to be as clean and pure as possible (follow the processes mentioned in the Fats and Oils section for clarifying fat). Second, if you do not have enough fat to make long candles, simply melt some fat in a tin, add a twisted piece of cotton rag, and light it. Third, where you do have sufficient quantities of fat available make up batches of candles ahead of time. Tallow candles also seem to burn better and longer if they have been through a sort of curing process – resting for some time after they are made. Fourth, protect your candles from vermin (they are made of a tasty foodstuff for a rodent).

A related means of lighting is to soak pieces of the porous, dry, end of season cat's-tail (*Typha* sp.) stems in fat and burn these. For soft pork fat, fill a shallow sardine tin and submerge a couple of wicks into the grease.

RUSH LIGHT
True 'rush light' or 'rushlights' were made from juncus rush (*Juncus effusus*), or similar, which contain a porous pith into which fat can be absorbed as a fuel. The traditional method of preparing these was to cut rushes in their green state, and as long in length as they could be harvested, and then have the pointed flowering end squared off. Next, the green skin was peeled away in strips all the way round from top to bottom, with the exception of one piece – about 20 to 25 percent of the rush circumference – left in place. This allowed the soft and fragile inner pith to retain some structural integrity. The stripped rushes were then dipped in hot melted fat, where they remained until fully impregnated with fat and then removed to a flat surface where they could firm up. To burn your rushlights the rushes were placed in holders which had wire pincers that grasped the rush but allowed it to be advanced as it burnt down.

ICE-HOUSES

No electricity or gas, no ice, right? Wrong! Well possibly. Casting my mind back to references about iced food recipes in Victorian cookery books (even early 19th century works), I started to do some research into how they procured ice in times before electricity and the mechanical production of ice. In the 19th century ice-houses became the 'must have' fixture for every large country house with pretensions of being one of the trend-setters and Society fashionistas. The stored ice, as far as I can read between the lines, was not actually used *in* drinks a we do with ice cubes today, but rather to chill foods for the table, to preserve food for longer periods, and to provide the coolant for making ice-cream. In a post-disaster world, the prospect of being able to keep ice as an additional resource could be extremely useful – especially for the evening G&T.

Personally, I do not have the room to develop a fully functioning ice-house in the garden, and the information that follows is summarized or quoted from a variety of old sources. I hope it will inspire you to perhaps do some more research of your own, and perhaps experiment to see what potential may exist for storing ice for your doomsday kitchen.

Let's begin with some fundamental principles. Old writers repeatedly emphasize that the two KEY points to successfully keeping ice are *insulation*, and the *drainage* of melt-water from the stacked ice. As one of them puts it: '*...wherever there is moisture, the ice will be liable to dissolve.*'

Two forms of construction or design were used: a sub-level form built into the ground, with the other type being a ground-constructed, insulated, building with hollow walls filled with insulating material. Situating a sub-level ice-house on a slope or hillside was deemed good design practice for handling melt-water drainage, while chalk strata, stoney earth, or gravelly soil were regarded as essential for drainage and keeping that nasty stuff water away from the stored ice.

Double sets of doors were generally a feature of most sub-level designs, particularly large ones. The kitchen hand sent to fetch ice entered through a first set of external doors which were then closed behind before entering the 'ice chamber' through the second door. In some instances there were recommendations that the inner doors were covered over with additional straw insulation in between ice collection visits. According to one old reference – and it is just one – a fully packed, sub-level, ice-house could store ice for 2 to 3 years. That is a quite staggering length of time given the technology in use. It should be noted, however, that the volumes of ice could be enormous, but more of that shortly.

The simplest ground-surface ice-preserves (one could not call them ice-houses) were simple stacks of ice covered with insulation. The following description is taken verbatim and relates to my re-drawn figure of the design principle:

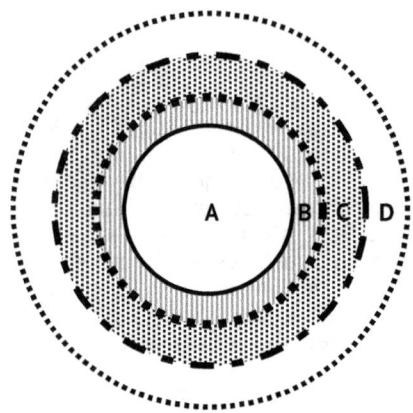

'*To keep ice in sacks* or *heaps in the open air*, an elevated circular platform (a) is raised of earth; on this the ice is piled up in a conic form during a severe frost, and the addition of water enables the builder to form the cone very steep. On this cone wheat-straw is laid a foot in thickness (b), over this a stratum of faggot-wood or spray (c), and finally another thick stratum of thatch or long litter of any sort (d). In this way ice will keep a year, care being taken to expose it to the air as short time as possible in taking out supplies.'

The big country houses and stately homes had both the manpower to construct massive ice-houses, but also to maintain the stack, as well as having lackeys to fetch the ice for the kitchen. The diagram below is a composite put together from several old sources which shows the typical cone-shaped 'ice well' design that was used in the British Isles. Whether this feature is common to old ice-houses elsewhere in other parts of the world I have not yet researched.

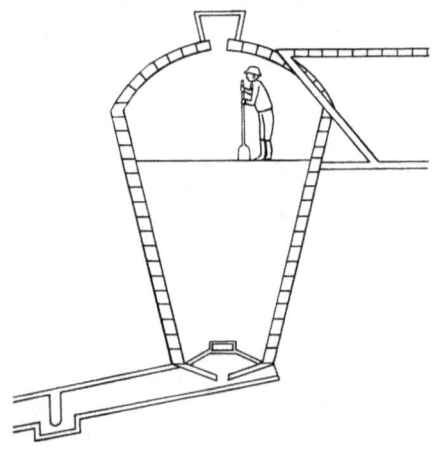

In the coned 'ice well' the structure is built into a hillside, so as to be a walk-in structure with two sets of doors provided. At the base was an old cart wheel set over a melt-water drainage channel. Ice was dropped in through a sealable chute at the top since that minimized ingress of warm air, while some unfortunate lackey was tasked with the duty of ramming the mass solid. Small amounts of water were occasionally sprinkled onto each layer of ice as it was packed down to help it weld together. Once the structure was full it was often, but not always, covered over with wooden shuttering upon which layers of straw were added for extra insulation. When it came to the walls of these 'ice well' structures – which could be 50 cm thick – there does not appear to have been consensus. Some texts refer to unmortared bricks being best, since this allowed melt-water to slip away more easily into the surrounding dry soil, but other designers do not mention any specifics. Frequently there would be an ornate folly-like, cavity walled, hut built over the top of the structure. This added a further thermal trap, particularly if a series of double doors was included, and also hid the structure from sight.

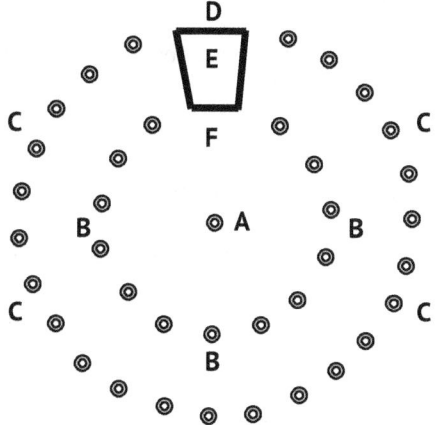

The design (left) is a schematic of a description of an ice-house outlined by William Cobbett in the early 19th century, which appeared in various publications for many decades.

To précis that description:
'A is the centre of a circle, the diameter of which is 10 feet, and at this centre a post should be set up, to stand fifteen feet above the level of the ground, which post ought to be about nine inches wide at the bottom, and not a great deal smaller at the top. Great care must be taken that this post is perfectly perpendicular, otherwise the whole building will be awry. B, represents twenty-eight posts, nine feet high, and six inches wide at the bottom, without much tapering towards the top. These posts stand about two feet apart from centre to centre... C, are thirty-eight posts, five feet high, and five inches wide at the bottom, without much tapering towards the top.... The space between these two rows of posts, is four feet in width, and.... is to contain a wall of straw; E, is a passage through the wall; D, is the outside door of the passage; F, is the inside door. A in the centre, is the place in which the ice is to be deposited. The walls should be formed between the posts of clean wheat or rye straw, and closely and smoothly. Plates of wood are to be laid on the top of the two rows of posts for receiving the rafters of the roof. The roof should not be at a lower angle than forty-five degrees, and should be covered with strong laths, to which the roof thatch (of wheat or rye straw, and four feet thick) is to be secured. The bed upon which the ice is to be laid, should be formed by laying round logs, about eight inches in diameter, across the area, leaving spaces between them of about a foot. Over these, poles, about half the size of the last, are to be laid across in an opposite direction; and six inches apart over these, a third course, two inches in diameter, and three inches apart; upon these again, a course of still smaller rods, one inch apart; and, finally, upon these two inches of dry twigs and branches, or strong heather, free from moss or grass; upon this bed the ice is put, broken and pummelled, and beaten down together in the usual manner; when the house is filled it should be shut closely up.'

The source of ice varied, but always appeared during the winter months. Some enterprising individuals would await the winter frosts then cut sections from frozen lake and pond ice, while others would place containers full of water outside to freeze over, and add this to the ice-well stocks. In the cities ice became a commodity traded like any other kitchen ingredient though, as you can tell from the method of harvesting, this product was by no means pure.

To see how these 'ancient' designs translated into early 20th century models – used especially in rural areas where mains electricity had not yet reached – seek out the following four sources for some interesting designs for ice houses using materials that we would be more familiar with today:

The Use of Ice on the Farm, Ruddick, J.A.; Bulletin No.20, Dairy & Cold Storage Commissioner's Series. Department Of Agriculture, Ottawa, Canada. July 1907.

Ice Cold Storage on the Farm, Graham, R.R.; Bulletin 207. Ontario Department of Agriculture. December, 1912.

The harvesting and storing of ice on the farm, Farmers Bulletin (No. 1078). US Dept. of Agriculture. January 1920.

The Ice Well for the Dairy Farm, Circular No. 155. Jan. 1931, Revised November 1938. USDA, Washington, DC.

On a general note: where ground level ice-houses were constructed it was recommended that the structure would be surrounded by a trench to carry away rainwater, certainly if the soil was not of a freely percolating type. Where sawdust or wood chippings are used to create insulative walls then these materials need to be at least 30 cm thick and separated from the ice by a moisture-resistant membrane, otherwise moisture will start the sawdust rotting, the process of which is likely to raise the temperature of the insulation and melt your ice.

HERBAL MEDICINE PROPERTIES

Herbal medicines are an area of botany that I do not get involved with since I believe talking about such things should be left to those who are best qualified to speak about such matters. However, in the absence of blister-packs with instructions then I think I would be heading for the nearest hedgerow or garden to see if there was something usefully available. Just like any modern OTC or doctor prescribed drug, herbal medicines can cause side-effects so it is important that a tolerance test is done before administering plant medicines. Indeed, if you look back at old medical books from hundreds of years ago, when herbal medicine was at its fore, the writers always (well frequently enough anyway) advised that plant medicines should be chosen and administered according to the physical state and tolerance of the individual patient.

These are some of the plants that I might consider using, and I suggest that you do a bit more research work to see how they were made up into medicines since that is beyond the scope of this book.

Bilberry (*Vaccinium myrtyllus*) – diarrhoea
Blackcurrant (*Ribes nigrum*) – sore throats / colds / diarrhoea
Blackthorn (*Prunus spinosa*) – styptic
Bramble (*Rubus fruticosus*) – diarrhoea / mouth-throat infections
Chamomile (*Chamaemelum nobile*) – anti-spasmodic / carminative
Chickweed (*Stellaria media*) – wounds
Coltsfoot (*Tussilago farfara*) – coughs
Comfrey (*Symphytum officinale*) – sprains / bruises
Dandelion (*Taraxacum officinale*) – appetite / digestion
Elecampane (*Inula helenium*) – expectorant / coughs
Fennel (*Foeniculum vulgare*) – coughs / digestion
Feverfew (*Tanacetum parthenium*) – tonic / digestive bitter / headache
Fir (*Abies*) – scurvy
Ground Ivy (*Glechoma hederacea*) – coughs
Horseradish (*Armoracia rusticana*) – expectorant / rheumatism
Lime (*Tilia* sp.) – throat infection
Meadowsweet (*Filipendula ulmaria*) – headache / fever
Mints (*Mentha* sp.) – digestion / nausea
Mugwort (*Artemisia vulgaris*) – appetite / digestion
Oak (*Quercus*) – external wounds
Ribwort (*Plantago lanceolata*) – catarrh / mouth-throat inflammation
Shepherd's Purse (*Capsella bursa-pastoris*) – styptic
Stinging Nettle (*Urtica dioica*) – rheumatism / diuretic
Willow (*Salix alba, caprea, fragilis* etc.) – headache / fever
Yarrow (*Achillea millefoilum*) – external wounds / styptic

OTHER RESOURCES

A number of traditional paper as well as digital wild food resources are available through the Wild Food School website:

The Essential Hedgerow & Wayside Cookbook (Paper or Digital)
[ISBN 0 9544158 2 5]

The Essential Acorn, Hazelnut, Chestnut &c Cookbook (Paper or Digital)
[ISBN 0 9544158 7 6]

The Essential Rabbit, Venison & Pheasant Cookbook (Paper or Digital)
[ISBN 0 9544158 6 8]

The Essential Backpacker's Wild Food Cookbook (Paper or Digital)
[ISBN 0 9544158 3 3]

The Essential Nettle, Dandelion, Chickweed & Thistle Cookbook (Paper or Digital)
[ISBN 0 9544158 1 7]

WFS *Edible Bugs Guide* (Digital format)

WFS Occasional Papers: *Indigenous Cooking Solutions* and *Cutting Your Food Bills* (which looks at cultivating certain wild plants in small spaces).

Under the banner of Wild Food Wisdom (wildfoodwisdom.co.uk) there are available a range of digital eBooks for tablets, laptops and organizers, under the series name *Cooking With Weeds*.

RECIPE INDEX

ACORN BREAD, 303
ACORN DUMPLINGS, 303
ACORN MEATLOAF, 277
ACORN PASTRY, 304
ACORNBURGER, 303
ACORNS – Processing & Preparing, 140
APPLE BISCUITS, 301
APPLE BREAD, 301
APPLE JELLY, 323
APPLE PANCAKES, 323
APPLE PEEL TEA, 136
APPLE PUDDING, 323
APPLEADE, 136
APPLE-BREADCRUMB BAKE, 301
AWFUL OFFAL OATMEAL PUDDING, 270

BACKSTONE CAKES, 298
BAKED BEAN SOUP, 246
BAKED FISH WITHOUT AN OVEN, 283
BAKED PEARS, 322
BAKED RABBIT / SQUIRREL BRAINS, 266
BAKED TRIPE, 276
BARBIED SHEEP'S TONGUES, 262
BARLEY BANNOCKS, 296
BARLEY BREAD, 297
BARLEY FLOUR COOKIES, 297
BARLEY OR RYE PASTRY, 302
BARLEY-OATMEAL DROP BISCUITS, 296
BASIC BROTH, 247
BARLEY PREPARATION, 343
BASIC STOCK, 253
BEAN & WHEAT BREAD, 299

BEAN (or PEA) LOAF, 307
BEAN BREAD, 299
BEAN CAN PIGEON, 286
BEAN CUSTARD, 308
BEEF & NOODLE SOUP, 243
BEEF / OXE / DEER TONGUE, 271
BEVERAGE PLANTS, 134
BILBERRY FRIES, 327
BIVALVE FRITTERS, 284
BLACKBERRY DESSERT, 324
BLACKBERRY WINE, 329
BLOOD & GUTS SOUP, 243
BLOOD CAKE, 259
BLOOD FRY-UP, 259
BLOOD PANCAKES, 258
BOILED DUCK, 288
BOILING RABBIT TIP, 275
BONE SOUP, 246
BOTTLED FRUITS, 322
BRAIN CAKES / RISSOLES, 265
BREAD OMELETTE, 300
BREADCRUMB DUMPLINGS, 300
BREADCRUMB MUFFINS / GRIDDLE CAKES, 300
BROILED KIDNEYS, 260
BULLOCK / CALF / DEER HEART, 263

CABBAGE (or KALE) MISH-MASH, 309
CALF'S-FOOT JELLY, 274
CALVES / LAMB'S LUNGS, 264
CALVES EARS – STUFFED, 271
CALVES HEAD, 268
CARROT LEAF SOUP, 253
CHESTNUT SOUP, 309

CHICKEN (OR GOOSE) GIBLET, HEAD & BONE SOUP, 249
CHICKEN / DUCK FEET GRAVY, 289
CHICKEN FEET, 288
CHICKEN GUT GRILL, 290
CHICKWEED & WILD STRAWBERRY SALAD, 311
CHICKWEED AND POTATO FRITTATA, 312
CIDER VINEGAR, 326
CLARIFIED GOOSE FAT, 240
CLARIFYING BUTTER, 240
CLARIFYING DRIPPING, 238
CLARIFYING FAT, 238
COOKED DANDELION, 310
COOKING BIVALVES, 284
COTTAGE CHEESE, 305
COUCH-GRASS SOUP, 253
COW'S STOMACH / TRIPE, 276
COW'S UDDER, 273
CRABS, KILLING AND COOKING, 89
CRAB (or FISH) DUMPLINGS, 251
CREAMED KIDNEYS, 261

DAMSON PUDDING, 328
DANDELION AND BRAMBLE SALAD, 312
DANDELION SALAD GREENS, 312
DEAD BREAD FINGERS, 296
DEEP-FRIED TRIPE, 276
DEER (OR GOAT) HEAD HANGI, 269
DEER / OX MARROW BONE, 274
DRIED APPLES, 323

DRIED BOILED CURRANTS / BILBERRIES, 324
DRIED CHICKWEED, 317
DRIED DAMSONS, 324
DRIED SALMON, 281
DUFFLE-BAG SPLEEN, 277

EASY RABBIT STEW SOUP, 245
EEL SOUP, 251
EGGED BRAINS, 265
ELDER FRITTERS, 312

FIR (SPRUCE) TEA, 136
FISH CAKES, 280
FISH CUSTARD, 280
FISH FLOUR, 285
FISH MOULD, 280
FISH PUDDING, 279
FISH-POTATO CHOWDER, 280
FLATFISH CUSTARD ON TOAST, 280
FRIED BRAINS, 265
FRIED EELS, 279
FRIED GOOSE / DUCK GIZZARD & LIVER, 287
FRIED LAMB'S BITS, 272
FRUIT (OR SAVOURY) PUDDING, 321
FRUIT JELLIES / CONSERVES, 322
FRUMENTY (Savoury or Sweet), 309
FULL MONTY STEW, 256

GAME LIVER / KIDNEY TOASTS, 260
GENERAL PICKLING OF VEGETABLES, 314
GENERAL WINE-MAKING, 330
GIBLET PIE, 288

GIBLET SAUCE, 287
GIZZARD & NECK SOUP, 248
GOAT HEAD & FEET, 269
GOAT INTESTINES – STEWED, 267
GOAT PANEER, 305
GOAT STEW, 256
GOOSE INTESTINES, 291
GOOSE SAUSAGE, 287
GOOSEBERRY VINEGAR, 325
GRASS SOUP, 253
GREEN BEAN PUDDING, 308
GUTWEED FISH CAKES, 318

HARD BARLEY BISCUITS, 297
HARE SOUP, 245
HERB PUDDING, 307
HONEY CUSTARD, 328
HONEY VINEGAR, 325
HORSERADISH POWDER, 316

KEEPING BUTTER, 239
KELP FRITTATA, 319
KIDNEY SOUP, 248
KIDNEY-STUFFED ONIONS, 261
KIPPERED SALMON, 281

LAMB'S HEAD, 268
LAMB'S HEAD & NECK / LUNGS / LIVER / HEART, 268
LAMBS EARS AND SORREL, 271
LAMBS INTESTINES, 266
LAVER BREAD, 319
LAVER SEA-MARMALADE, 319
LAYERED HONEY CAKE DESSERT, 327
LIME BLOSSOM TEA, 136
LIMPET SOUP, 77
LIVER CAKES, 259
LIVER LOAF, 260

LIVER PUDDING, 259
LIVER SAUCE, 259
LUNG SOUP, 264
LUNG STEW, 264
MEAT CUTLETS, 257
MUFFIN or BREAD-PRESERVE PUDDING, 327
MUSHROOM KETCHUP & DRIED MUSHROOM, 314
MUSHROOM POWDER, 315
MY ALL-DAY STEW, 273

NATURALLY LEAVENED BREAD, 293
NETTLE & DANDELION FRITTERS, 311
NETTLE BEER, 330
NETTLE-OFFAL STEW, 310

OAT & PEA BISCUITS, 298
OAT BISCUITS, 298
OAT CRACKERS, 298
OAT MIXED BREAD, 298
OAT PREPARATION, 343
OATMEAL / BARLEY & NETTLE SOUP, 249
OATMEAL CASING PASTRY, 302
OATMEAL GRIDDLE CAKES, 299
OATMEAL PANCAKES, 299
OATMEAL SOUP #2, 249
OLD BREAD, 295
OLD CHICKEN BROTH, 244
OLD CHICKENS / GUINEA FOWL, 290
ONE WEEK GRAVY, 274
OX / CALF / SHEEP / GOAT'S HEAD SOUP, 247
OX PIZZLE, 272
OX-TAIL SOUP, 250
OYSTER SAUSAGES, 283
PAN-FRIED OYSTERS, 282

PASTY PASTRY, 302
PEAPOD BEER, 330
PEAPOD SOUP, 252 & 309
PEAS FOR WINTER USE, 313
PEPPERMINT & BLACKBERRY LEAF TEA, 136
PHEASANT & PIGEON, 51
PHEASANT IN CLAY, 290
PICKLED TURNIP TOPS, 315
PICKLING FISH, 284
PICKLING TONGUE, 271
PIE PASTRY, 302
PIG LUNG SOUP, 250
PIG TROTTERS & 'BITS' MINCE, 267
PIGEON & NETTLE SOUP, 244
PIGEON SOUP, 244
PIG'S BITS – CAWL ROASTED, 267
PIGS TAILS, 272
PLANKED FISH, 278
PLUM SOUP, 321
POPPY OIL, 240
POTATO BREAD, 295
POTATO DAY SOUP, 246
POTATOES STEAMED, 310
POTATO-STARCH, 316
POTTED BEANS, 308
POTTED HAM, 274
POTTED MUSHROOMS, 315
PRESERVED SORREL, 325
PRESERVING CREAM (SWEET), 306
PRESERVING EGGS, 306
PRESERVING FRENCH BEANS, 314
PRESERVING MACKEREL, 282
PRESERVING POTATOES, 314
PURIFYING RANCID BUTTER, 239

QUICK CAKE, 301

RABBIT SOUP, 244
RABBIT SOUP #2, 245
RAZOR CLAMS, 80
RENDERING SUET, 239
RHUBARB WINE, 329
ROAD-KILL, 18
ROAST PIGEON, 286
ROAST RABBIT, 275
ROASTED OYSTERS, 283
ROASTED TRIPE, 277
ROASTING GOOSE, 286
ROOK PIE, 288
ROSE HIP TEA, 136

SALMON 'LOAF', 282
SALTING BEEF, 275
SCRAMBLED BLOOD, 258
SEA LETTUCE CHOWDER, 318
SEAWEED PICKLE, 320
SHARK LIVER, 285
SHEEP / MUTTON TAILS, 271
SHEEP OR COW'S BLOOD PUDDING, 258
SHEEP'S / LAMB'S TROTTERS, 262
SHEEP'S HEART, 262
SHEEP'S TONGUE – PRESSED, 270
SHEEP'S HEART & LUNG MINCE, 269
SHEEP'S TONGUES – ROASTED, 262
SHELL-BAKED OYSTERS, 283
SIMPLE CAKE, 302
SIMPLE SLOE / DAMSON WINE, 329
SMALL BIRDS, 290
SMOKED TONGUES, 271
SNAIL PREPARATION, 28

SORREL SOUP, 251
SORREL-STEWED EELS, 279
SOURDOUGH PANCAKES, 328
SPRING GARLIC & GREENS DUMPLINGS, 313
STEAMED FISH, 281
STEWED EELS, 279
STEWED LAMB / DEER TONGUE, 261
STEWED OYSTERS, 282
STEWED PIGEON, 286
STEWED TENDON BROTH, 273
STOMACH SOUP, 250
STUFFED MACKEREL, 281
STUFFED SHEEP'S TROTTERS, 263
SUGAR KELP & BEAN STEW, 319
SUGAR VINEGAR, 325
SWEETBREADS, 272
SWEET CICELY TEA, 136

TERMINATOR STEW / SOUP, 250
THISTLE ROOT SOUP, 252
TRIPE FRITTERS, 277
TURKEY WINGS, 289
TURNIP BREAD, 303
TURNIP TOPS, 311
TWO-SHOT MEAT SOUP, 247

VEAL / LAMB LUNG, LIVER AND HEART, 263

WEIGHING, 209
WHELKS, BOILED, 78
WILD CHERRY SOUP, 321
WILD GARLIC BREAD PIZZA, 312

www.ingramcontent.com/pod-product-compliance
Lightning Source LLC
Chambersburg PA
CBHW071952220426
43662CB00009B/1104